MILES CITY SADDLERY CO.
MILES CITY, MONT.
MAKERS
ORIGINAL COGGSHALL SADDLES

Saddleries of Montana

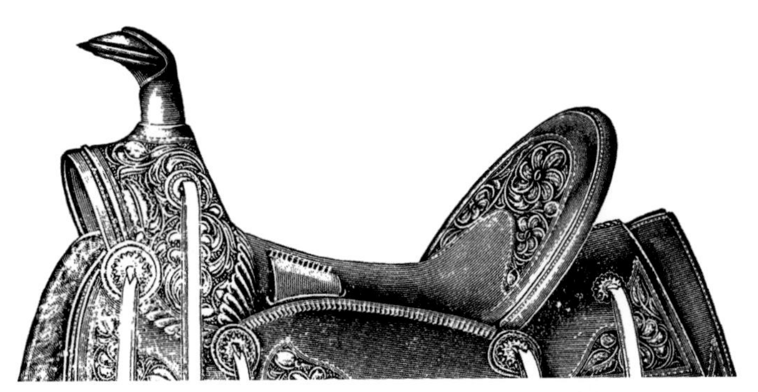

Saddleries of Montana

Montana's Makers from Territorial Times to 1940

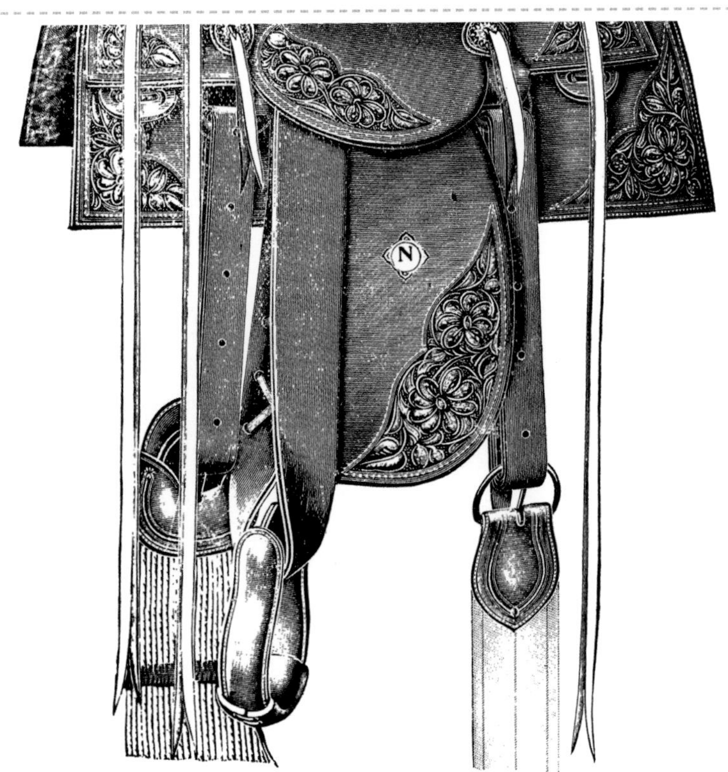

Jay C. Lyndes
Bobby R. Reynolds
E. Helene Sage

4880 Lower Valley Road • Atglen, PA 19310

Other Schiffer Books by the Author:

Native American Horse Gear: A Golden Age of Equine-Inspired Art of the Nineteenth Century, E. Helene Sage, ISBN 978-0-7643-4210-3

Eddy Hulbert, Silversmith: Artistry in Dryhead Country, Montana, E. Helene Sage, ISBN 978-0-7643-4726-9

Bridle Rosettes: Two Centuries of Equine Adornment, E. Helene Sage, ISBN 978-0-7643-3859-5

Other Schiffer Books on Related Subjects:

Painted Sky: 106 Artists of the Rocky Mountain West, E. Ashley Rooney, Foreword by Rose Fredrick, ISBN 978-0-7643-4961-4

The West That Was, John Eggen, ISBN 978-0-88740-330-9

Cowboy Collectibles and Western Memorabilia, Bob Ball & Edward Vebell, ISBN 978-0-88740-505-1

Library of Congress Control Number: 2016957803

Designed by RoS
Cover design by Molly Shields
All photographs are by Bobby R. Reynolds unless otherwise noted.

Type set in EngravrsRoman BT/Perpetua

ISBN: 978-0-7643-5274-4
Printed in the United States of America

Published by Schiffer Publishing, Ltd.
4880 Lower Valley Road
Atglen, PA 19310
Phone: (610) 593-1777; Fax: (610) 593-2002
E-mail: Info@schifferbooks.com
Web: www.schifferbooks.com

To the ranchers and cowboys of Montana, past and present,
and to the makers, collectors, and scholars
of the Western American tradition
epitomized by the Territory and State
of Montana

Acknowledgments

The authors thank Schiffer Publishing, Ltd., for their contributions to the preservation of our national heritage through the books that they publish. A special acknowledgment is due to our editor, Sandra M. Korinchak, and to Eileen Neligan, for her processing of the manuscript.

We thank Glenn VerBeck (Miles City, Montana) for his unselfish contribution of knowledge and for his research on the saddleries of Miles City. The Frontier Museum (Glendive, Montana) performed research for us on early saddleries in Eastern Montana. Nancy Watts (Lewistown Public Library, Lewistown, Montana) contributed valuable data on saddlers of Fergus County, and Steve Allison of the *Miles City Star* allowed us to use his photograph of Glenn VerBeck.

Ken Hamlin (Bozeman, Montana) provided many of the scans depicting letterheads, letters, and envelopes of early Montana saddlery establishments. Rick M. Bachman (Florence, Montana) also generously shared his collection of paper ephemera. We are grateful to Brian Lebel (Santa Fe, New Mexico) for his consistent support of our literary efforts. Tim Leland (Sidney, Montana) contributed information on eastern Montana saddle makers. We thank them all.

Contents

Figure 1.1.
Early photopostcard (mailed Feb. 27, 1910) of harness horses standing outside the *AL. FURSTNOW'S SADDLERY*. The caption states: *RANCHER BEING OUTFITTED, FOR 24 HORSES, THE WAY WE DO BUSINESS IN MILES CITY, MONT.* Made by Olson Photograph Co., Plattsmouth, Nebr." c. 1890s–1910.

1

Montana: A New Land

Saddleries in the early Western United States and its Territories designed, imported, manufactured, and sold a myriad of products for cowboys, ranchers, farmers, miners, loggers, and every settler that ventured west of the Mississippi River during the century spanning the mid-1800s to the mid-1900s. In a sense, a western saddlery was a sort of "horse hardware store," and often offered farming implements, building materials, and clothing to its customers. Examples of horse-related equipment included saddles, bridles, bits, spurs, chaps, hats, cuffs, boots, quirts, horse blankets and grooming tools, trunks, sleighs, and buggies/wagons. A saddlery formed a nucleus of a growing town or city and was an important source of its livelihood. Figure 1.1 illustrates a day of business in Miles City, a major outfitting town.

Saddleries of Montana presents a history of these enterprises that contributed to the progress of the Territory and State of Montana. They are organized by date and area, and the time span covered (from approximately the third quarter of the nineteenth century to the 1940s) reflects the territorial status of the region that eventually became Montana, continuing through statehood (1889) and the development of ranches, mines, farms, and towns, and in the twentieth century, the endurance of two world wars and the Great Depression.

Yet not only the times but also the geography of Montana determined the location, number, and output of the saddleries in this time period. The name "Montana" was indeed well chosen, as the western third of the state is extremely mountainous, with additional smaller mountain ranges throughout the rest of the state (today, there are 77 named ranges in Montana, all part of the Rocky Mountains). Montana Territory (M.T.) (1864–1889) was derived from portions of a large area originally comprising the Territories of Oregon, Washington, Idaho, and Dakota. It achieved statehood on November 8, 1889, as the forty-first state admitted to the Union. Aspects of its geography were important influences on the styles of its ranching (cattle, horses, and sheep) and other endeavors that required harness teams, wagons, plows, and freighting vehicles. Montana is the largest landlocked state, bordering on three Canadian provinces (British Columbia, Alberta, and Saskatchewan), North and South Dakota (Dakota Territory) on the east, Wyoming (Territory) on the south, and Idaho on the west and southwest. It received input from its neighboring states/provinces and from individuals with varying ideas on the settlement of a new land, especially those inclined to the ranching and farming opportunities offered by this immense and essentially unspoiled Territory. Over sixty percent of the land was prairie, comprising the northern section of the Great Plains, and numerous river valleys lay between the mountain ranges. Unlike many of the other western states in which cattle ranching was prevalent, the Montana valleys were well-watered by major rivers (forming parts of three major watersheds) coursing over its surface. For cattle ranching, Montana was irresistible.

It is also important, however, to acknowledge the climate of Montana, which was as varied as its geography. Frequent heavy snowfalls and sub-zero temperatures took their toll on humans and animals and were instrumental in determining not only the equipment needed for ranching in these areas, but also the success of the saddleries selling that equipment. If ranches failed due to the death of herds, the saddlery businesses generally failed too. The major "die-up" of 1886–1887 is an example of the symbiosis between cattlemen and saddleries. This unprecedented weather condition across Montana Territory was the demise of many ranches and their supply houses (see chapter 2, Miles City).

Figure 1.2 is a map of modern-day Montana's counties, with eight different geographical areas highlighted. Each area's number corresponds to the chapter in which its saddleries are described. For example, Eastern Montana (Miles City, Glendive, Forsyth, etc.), Area 2, is covered in chapter 2 and features Moran Brothers, Robbins and Lenoir, Al Furstnow, Miles City Saddlery, and J. S. Collins, among many others. The areas reflect the state's geographical features and, consequently, the enterprises and their suppliers. For example, Fort Benton (in Area 5) was an early fur-trading post established in 1847 and later became a military post; Virginia City (in Area 8) revealed large gold placer diggings, and Butte (in Area 7) was the center for silver and copper mining. In contrast, Miles City/Custer County and surrounding counties (in Area 2) were prominent in cattle ranching, and Fergus County (in Area 4) was the site of a major cattle operation (Stuart, Hauser, and Davis) that was started in 1879. Therefore, one would expect to find numerous and high-quality saddleries in Areas 2, 3, and 4 that provisioned ranch hands, cowboys, and cattlemen. Areas specializing in mining, on the other hand, required different kinds of equipment and their saddleries devoted a significant portion of their output to harness and heavy rigging for transport and freighting. This predicted relationship between region and saddleries is generally correct, although, as will be seen in the succeeding chapters, interesting exceptions and distributions of saddlery/harness equipment existed in both Montana Territory and State.

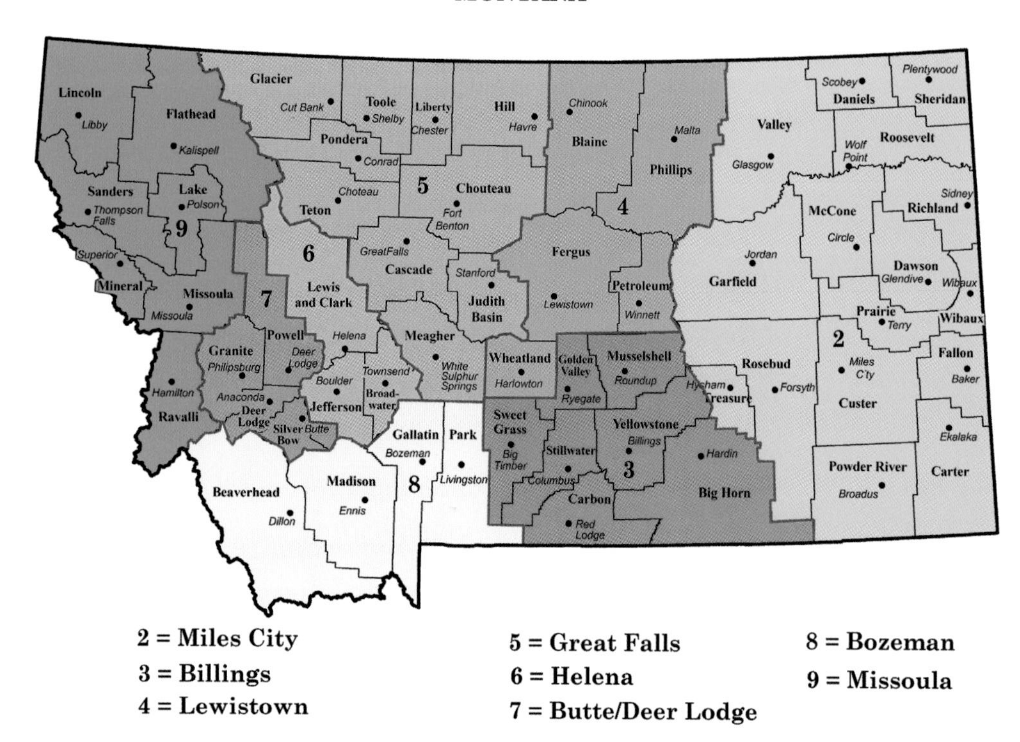

Figure 1.2.
Modern-day map of Montana showing counties, major towns, and cities. Areas highlighted in different colors refer to the areas featured in the next chapters, e.g., Area 2 in light green depicts Miles City, Glendive, Wibaux, and Forsyth, the saddleries of which are discussed in chapter 2.

Table 1.1 lists many (if not most) of the saddleries of Montana and M.T., with the chapter/area numbers corresponding to each of them. In each of the next chapters there is a table containing a subset of the saddleries from table 1.1. These area-specific saddleries include additional data indicating the particular town or city in which the saddlery was established, as well as the dates of its operation. It is important to point out that many of these dates are incomplete or imprecise, as there is a dearth of information available, especially with respect to the Territorial businesses and the smaller towns. In some cases all that we were able to find was a letterhead, invoice, or envelope with a given date; in these cases the date provided for the saddlery is shown in the tables in parentheses.

Because we have chosen to focus largely on equipment associated with cattle ranching, and the saddleries both rare and prominent in their production of working and collector-quality items, many of the photographs pertain to saddles, chaps, and related paraphernalia. Figure 1.3 shows an early saddle with identified parts that are referred to in the various captions throughout the book. An important emphasis has been placed on the marks imprinted on the leather by each saddler—these identifiers are unique and serve not only to define the maker, but also as a reference guide for collectors, who are often faced with decisions regarding the authenticity of given pieces. In many cases throughout the book, these "maker marks" have been enlarged to reveal critical details.

Much of the information on individual saddlers and items is contained in the captions to each figure, whereas the general text provides background on the history, geography, and economic importance of each area.

We regard this book, the first attempt to summarize the saddleries of Montana Territory and State (approximately 1860s–1940), as a work in progress. As additional saddleries, their products, and new information appear in the marketplace, in museums, and in library archives, our comprehension and appreciation of this remarkable enterprise, in the context of Montana history, will continue to grow.

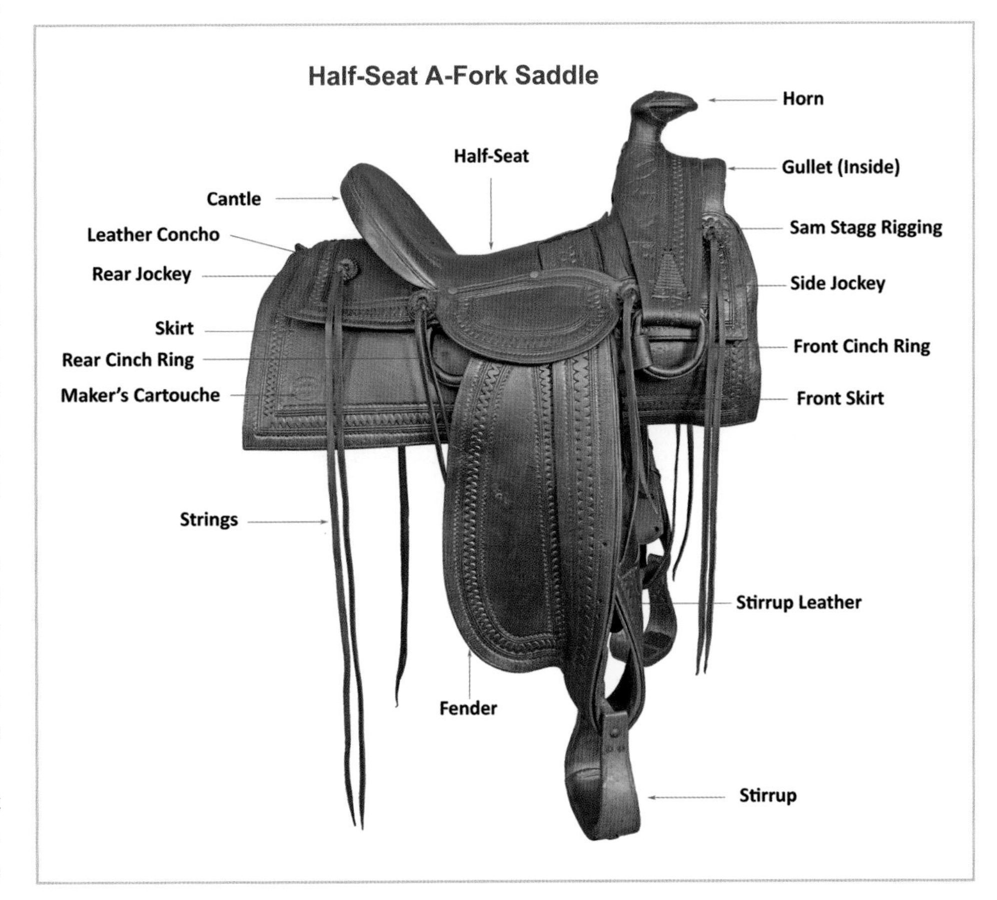

Figure 1.3. An early half-seat A-fork saddle with parts identified. (It is marked on the rear skirt J. F. LONG/MAKER/LIVINGSTON, M.T.) These parts are referred to throughout the book.

Table 1.1. Saddleries of Montana[1]

MAKER	CHAPTER[2]
Ario, Victor	5
Art Benjamine & Co.	4
Auerbach & Brothers	6
Barret & Jacky	7
Barret & Jacky & Kramer	7
Beardsley	7
Becker & Huff	2
Beckman, August	6
Bennett Brothers	7
Bogwers, M. S.	2
Bourret, Joseph & Co.	8
Bozeman Implement, Carriage & Harness Co.	8
Bricker, D. G.	7
Browning Saddlery Co.	5
Butte Saddlery Co. (E. H. Irish & T. H. Wilson)	7
Butte Saddlery Co. (T. H. Wilson & E. Zimmerman)	7
Carson, Alex C.	6
Chapman, F. B.	3
Cheyenne Saddler Shop (B. R. Roberts & W. Glassman)	6
Cockrell Implement Co.	7
C. E. Coggshall Saddlery	2
Collins, J. S. & Co.	2
Connolly Brothers: Jack, Patrick, & Andrew	7
Connolly Bros. Saddlery: Jack & Pat	3
Jack Connolly Saddlery	8
Pat Connolly Saddlery	3
Crockett, Samuel H.	8
Cut Bank Saddlery Co.	5
Davidson, A. J. & Moffit, John	5
Davidson, A. J.	6
Davidson, A. J. & Co.	6 & 7
DeKalb Harness Co.	4
Demers, Alexander L.	9
Demers & Waters	9
DeVore's Saddlery	6
Dillon Implement Co.	8
Donovan & Spear	3
Duke, A. B.	3
Duke, W. H.	8
Duke, W. H. & Work, John	8
Engelfried & Esler	8
Engelfried, Ferdinand	8
Esler, Frank	8
Ettinger, Harry	4
Fernald, W. H.	4
Fisher, Theo	5
Fitzhugh, Harley	7
Fletcher, Harry H.	2
Forsyth Hardware & Saddlery Co.	2
Forsyth Harness & Saddlery (C. A. Potter)	2
Frakes, Geo. M.	7
Furstnow, Al. & Coggshall, Charles	2
Furstnow, Al.	2
Furstnow, Al. Saddlery	2
Gerhart, J. R.	2
Gibbons, J.	5
Gibbons & Maher	5
Gilroy, Edward	8
Glassman, William	5
Glassman, William & Roberts, B. R.	6
Goettlich, Charles	5
Goettlich, Ernest (Pioneer Harness Shop)	8
Goettlich, Ernest & DeBord, William	2
Goettlich, Ernest L.	2 & 8
Great Falls Harness Store (J. J. Gibbons)	5
Great Falls Saddlery	5
Grisette, Arthur	4
Griffin, Frank	8
Guth, H. F.	4
Haines, S. J.	8
Halvorson Harness & Saddlery	7
Hanauer, Joseph	2
Harlem Saddlery (Cowan, W. S. & Corbett, Robert)	4
Hatfield, I. H.	8
Heavener, F.	6
Helena Saddlery & Tent Co.— Ernest Goettlich	6
Hoellecker, G. D.	2
Holtcamp & Bailey	2
Holtcamp, H. C.	2
Hudson, H. B.	2
Huff, E. M.	2
Irish, E. H.	7
Jacky	7
Jacky, Christian	9
Jacky, Valentine	6
Jeffrey, Christopher C.	4
Jeffrey, G. L.	3
Jelinek, Frank J.	2
Johns & Hallinan	2
Johns Brothers	2
Johns, George	2
Jubinville, N.	7
Jubinville, Noel & Nance, John	7
Jubinville & Irish	7
Judith Hardware Co.	4
Koke, B. H.	4

Ketcham, William S.	8
Knapp & Buck	6
Kohn, Herman	8
Kraemer, Frederick	8
Leland, John	8
Lewistown Saddlery	4
Lobenstein, W. C.	6
Locke & Work	8
Long, J. F.	8
Macdonald, James	5
Mann, W. M.	6
Markham, Charles	6
Marotz, G.	9
McDonald, J. D.	7
McRae-Strasburger Harness Co.	7
C. L. Metz	7
C. L. Metz Saddlery	7
Miles, Arthur W.	8
Miles City Saddlery ("Coggshall" Saddlery) Co.	2
Moran & Co. (Hugh, John & Frank)	2
Moran Brothers: John, Frank & Hugh	2
Moran, Collins & Co.	2
Moran, H. & Zimmerman, William	2
Moreland & Ario	5
Neill, R. W.	6
Nevills, J. N. & Co.	7
New Harness Shop	7
Nissen, John	8
Nye, Fred J.	6
Owenhouse, E. J.	8
Parks, Neil A.	8
Potter, R.	5
Power, T. C. & Bro.	5
Pioneer Harness Shop (K. Schmid)	2
Pioneer Saddlery & Harness Shop (McDonald, Ed)	2
Racek Bros.	3
Racek, C.	3
Regan, Matt	4
Reinhard, J. P.	9
Richards, Frank E.	7
Richardson, W. H.	4 & 8
Ritschel, G. J.	5
Roberts, B. R. & Best, William	5
Roberts, B. R. & Co.	6
Robbins, George E.	2
Robbins, George & Lenoir, Charles	2
Rockwell, Thomas D. & Tovey	3
Ronan Harness & Saddlery Co. (Lawrence, F. H.)	9
Rosencrans, L. H.	5
Sampo, Selestin	2
Schneider, Wm.	3
Secord, George	8
Secord, George & Jacobs, Edward C.	6
Secord & Faucette	8
Sentinel Butte Saddlery Co.	3
S. J. Haines & Co.	8
Smith, C. E.	3
Smith & Hodgman	7
Solberg, J. S.	3
Spencer, Loyal W. & Nye, Fred J.	6
Spicker Harness Co.	4
Spratte & Thomann	4
Stafford, George M.	4
Steffen, J. B.	5
Stephens & Jeffrey	4
Stipek & Lyon	2
Stipek, Frank J.	2
Stipek, J. J. (Glendive Saddlery, Bee Hive Store)	2
Stippek Bros.	2
Sullivan & Goss	7
Sullivan, Joseph	5
Talmage, W. A.	3
Ten Eyck, W. B.	3
Three Forks Saddlery	8
Two Dot Hardware Co.	4
VerBeck, Glenn	2
Peter VerBeck's Saddle Shop	2
Waters, W. W.	5
Waters & Wales	5
Webster, A.	4
Wellman, William	5
Wynn Brothers	2
Yegen Brothers	3
Young, Andrew	4
Zimmerman, M. V.	2
Zimmerman, W. J.	2

1. Products made or sold by these saddleries included harness, saddles, bits, spurs, whips, boots, bridles, accessories (horse blankets, grooming tools, trunks, bags, and/or robes), vehicles (sleighs, buggies, wagons, carts), and Indian-made goods (e.g., saddle blankets).

2. Numbers refer to the area of Montana, as shown in figure 1.2.

Lincoln
Libby
Flathead
Kalispell
Glacier
Cut Bank
Toole
Shelby
Liberty
Chester
Hill
Havre
Chinook
Blaine
Malta
Phillips
Valley
Glasgow
Scobey
Daniels
Plentywood
Sheridan
Roosevelt
Wolf Point
Pondera
Conrad
Sanders
Thompson Falls
Lake
Polson
9
Teton
Choteau
5
Chouteau
Fort Benton
4
McCone
Circle
Richland
Sidney
6
GreatFalls
Cascade
Superior
Mineral
Missoula
7
Lewis and Clark
Stanford
Judith Basin
Fergus
Lewistown
Petroleum
Winnett
Jordan
Garfield
Dawson
Glendive
Wibaux
Prairie
Terry
Wibaux
Missoula
Granite
Philipsburg
Powell
Deer Lodge
Helena
Meagher
White Sulphur Springs
Wheatland
Harlowton
Golden Valley
Ryegate
Musselshell
Roundup
Hysham
Treasure
Rosebud
Forsyth
2
Miles C'ty
Custer
Fallon
Baker
Hamilton
Ravalli
Anaconda
Deer Lodge
Silver Bow
Butte
Boulder
Jefferson
Townsend
Broad-water
Gallatin
Bozeman
Park
Livingston
Sweet Grass
Big Timber
Stillwater
Columbus
Yellowstone
Billings
3
Hardin
Big Horn
Ekalaka
Powder River
Broadus
Carter
Beaverhead
Dillon
Madison
Ennis
8
Carbon
Red Lodge

2

Eastern Montana

Miles City

Glendive

Wibaux

Forsyth

Eastern Montana, defined here as Area 2, was clearly the most significant producer of horse- and ranching-related equipment in both the territory and state. The sheer number of high-end saddleries, coupled with their size and longevity, resulted in a reputation, centered on Miles City, for quality and innovative merchandise throughout the West (spanning especially the last quarter of the nineteenth and first quarter of the twentieth centuries). "The saddle that made Miles City famous" (Furstnow); "the birthplace of that three-quarter rig" (Terrett)—statements like these are a fitting introduction to the saddle makers of this exciting area of eastern M.T. and the State of Montana.

Miles City, now the seat of Custer County, was essentially founded by Army sutlers in 1877, near the Tongue River Cantonment, established in 1876 after the Battle of the Little Bighorn. A permanent fort, Fort Keogh, was subsequently built and Miles City was relocated to its present site. The town was alive with speculators in livestock (both cattle and sheep) in the 1880s, as there remained open range, along with a railroad line by which cattle could be shipped to Chicago for slaughter. There was abundant free grass in this part of M.T., and cattlemen from as far away as Texas drove large herds to Miles City for fattening and eventual shipment. In the following chapters, it will become clear that the cowboys from Texas, Colorado, and the Northwest exerted some influence on the development of a saddle type ideally suited to the ranching practices of not only eastern but also other areas of Montana.

A "golden era" of saddle and tack production occurred in Miles City between approximately 1885 and 1945, when at least two major saddleries and several smaller ones were in business, in direct competition with one another. VerBeck (1998) cites 15 to 35 men working in this trade during this era, with a population in Miles City ranging from only 5,000 to 9,500.

There must have been a considerable amount of competition as well as cross-fertilization among these firms, as the leather workers, including those with the highly developed skills of floral carving and stamping, tended to drift among employers (depending on the wages and the availability of work) and thus influenced styles and production designs. This dissemination of new designs and decorative styles was typical, especially in the earlier stages of the craft, and was not unique to saddlery work; it also occurred in other early handcrafting and manufacturing, for example, the hitched horsehair bridles produced by inmates in the western prisons, and the decorative carousel figures seen on machines produced in the northeastern United States.

What was special and distinctive about the "Montana rig"? There was clearly a basic model in the California and Texas/Mexican saddles, and most of the saddle makers who had established themselves in the Miles City area were from the East, Midwest, or Europe and were thus familiar with English and military tack. In 1871 alone, approximately 500,000 cattle were driven north to Montana Territory, mostly from Texas and the southern Great Plains. Saddles were needed that were lighter in weight than the Mexican style, and the open plains precluded the need for the cumbersome leather tapaderos that covered the stirrups and protected the rider's feet from the brush and mesquite of Texas. Importantly, only one cinch was necessary (single-rigging), as opposed to the double-rigging used by the Texas cowboys, because the amount and style of roping were different on the northern ranges. The so-called three-quarter rig, with a single cinch and lighter construction, thus evolved, which was easier on the horse, comfortable for the rider, allowed a dally-style of roping in which the rope was wound ("dallied") around the horn as opposed to its being tied fast to the horn, and even lent itself to decorative embellishment of the leather. In contrast to the so-called center-fire rigging that the Oregon-based cowboys exposed to the northern ranges, the three-quarter design moved the cinch ring roughly in line with the front of the seat. This style gradually received acceptance throughout the West. It did not entirely supplant the alternate styles, however, and many Montana saddle makers continued to produce double-rigged, heavier saddles, a few even with the option of tapaderos.

The advent of the mail-order catalog was highly influential in the spreading of new ideas and designs, and as will be seen in succeeding chapters, the saddleries that adopted this outreach plan were better able to survive difficult economic times, and their various products became known throughout the United States and many foreign countries.

This chapter is divided into specific sections that feature individual saddleries or saddle makers, most of whom were located in Miles City, with outliers in Glendive, Forsyth, and Wibaux. We have avoided where possible distribution houses and general merchandisers, and have focused on the actual makers and owners of the prominent saddleries. Glenn VerBeck of Miles City has contributed a carefully researched compilation of saddle, harness, and leather workers active in Miles City, information that has been included in this chapter. In approximate chronological order, these establishments are described below.

Table 2.1 is a list of Area 2 saddleries, about many of which there is regrettably little information. There are discrepancies in the literature concerning the exact dates during which a given saddlery was in business. We have taken a conservative approach to this problem and, wherever possible, have included a range of dates for some of the firms and, from newspapers, invoices, or letters, an exact date on which business was conducted; the latter has been cited in parentheses in table 2.1 and in the tables that appear in succeeding chapters.

Table 2.1. Saddleries of Montana[1]

MAKER	LOCATION	DATES[2]
Becker & Huff	Forsyth	
Bogwers, M. S.	Miles City	1900
C. E. Coggshall Saddlery	Miles City	1899–1909
Collins, J. S. & Co.	Glendive/Miles City	(1885), 1885–1887
Conway, J. F.	Miles City	
Fletcher, Harry H.	Forsyth	(1901)
Forsyth Hardware & Saddlery Co.	Forsyth	(1905)
Forsyth Harness & Saddlery (C. A. Potter)	Forsyth	(1901–1903)
Furstnow, Al. & Coggshall, Charles	Miles City	1894–1899
Furstnow, Al.	Miles City	1894–1894 (5 mos.)
Furstnow, Al. Saddlery	Miles City	1899–1982
Gerhart, J. R.	Miles City	1894–1894 (5 mos.)
Goettlich, Ernest	Miles City	1881–1885
Goettlich, Ernest & DeBord, William	Miles City	1880–1881
Hanauer, Joseph	Glendive	1886–1887
Hoellecker, G. D.	Glendive	1901
Holtcamp & Bailey	Forsyth	1905
Holtcamp, H. C.	Forsyth	(1905)
Hudson, H. B.	Sidney	(1909)
Huff, E. M.	Forsyth	1900 Directory
Jelinek, Frank J.	Forsyth	1890s
Johns & Hallinan	Glendive	(1909)
Johns, George	Glendive	1909–1912
Johns Brothers, George & Charles	Glendive	1908–1909
Miles City Saddlery ("Coggshall" Saddlery Co.)	Miles City	1909–1961
Moran & Co. (Hugh, John, & Frank)	Miles City	1887–1895
Moran Brothers (John, Frank, & Hugh)	Miles City	1884–1887
Moran, Collins & Co.	Miles City	1887–1887 (7 mos.)
Moran, Hugh & Zimmerman, William	Miles City	1896–1896 (10 mos.)
Pioneer Harness Shop (K. Schmid)	Miles City	1880–1885
Pioneer Saddlery & Harness Shop (McDonald, Ed)	Miles City	? –1879
Robbins, George E.	Miles City	1895–1902
Robbins, George & Lenoir, Charles	Miles City	1891–1894
Sampo, Selestin	Glendive	
Stipek, Frank J.	Wibaux	1898– ?
Stipek, J. J. (Glendive Saddlery, Bee Hive Cash Store)	Glendive	1900 Directory; (1906), (1910); 1908–1937
Stipek & Lyon	Glendive	
Stipek Bros.	Wibaux	
Pete VerBeck's Saddle Shop	Miles City	1946–1976
VerBeck, Glenn	Miles City	1944– late 1950s
Wynn Brothers	Wibaux	1898–1903
Zimmerman, William J.	Miles City	1895–1896

1. Products made or sold by these saddleries included harness, saddles, bits, spurs, whips, boots, bridles, accessories (horse blankets, grooming tools, trunks, bags, and/or robes), vehicles (sleighs, buggies, wagons, carts), and Indian-made goods (e.g., saddle blankets).

2. Dates in parentheses are specified on the company letterhead or in a newspaper/journal advertisement. Inclusive dates for the tenure of the company have been provided where data are available and reliable.

I. Hugh Moran and Moran Brothers

A territorial maker highly sought after by today's collectors is the firm of Moran Bros. John and Frank Moran left the J. H. and J. S. Collins Saddlery in Cheyenne, Wyoming, and opened their firm in Miles City in 1884. They immediately became known for their quality workmanship (Furstnow and Zimmerman were employees; see below). Hugh Moran joined his brothers in 1885 as business manager. The *Daily Yellowstone Journal* (November 6, 1885) states that Moran Bros., "newly located in their new and commodious business house in the Leighton & Jordan block . . . make a specialty of using H. Messing & Son's bits and spurs." It is clear that much of the saddle skirting, other leather, and certain bits, spurs, and hardware were imported from California by the better, larger saddleries in Montana (see below for other examples). Possibly because of the "Great Die-up" during the winter of 1887–1888, when business was surely meager, the Moran brothers merged with J. S. Collins & Co. in Miles City to form Moran, Collins, & Co. However, this partnership was dissolved seven months later; Collins returned to Cheyenne and the Miles City firm became Moran & Co. (M.B.A. Moran, H.M. Moran, and Mary Moran, co-partners) (*Weekly Yellowstone*, Sept. 23, 1893). For approximately the next decade, Moran & Co. developed a widespread reputation for their excellent work, and they employed additional saddle makers who contributed to this fame (Gerhart, Huff, and Geo. Robbins, to name a few). By 1894, Hugh Moran was sole proprietor of Moran & Co. and purchased the saddlery of J. R. Gerhart, but by 1895 Moran & Co. was purchased by Wm. Zimmerman, with whom Hugh Moran formed a partnership that lasted ten months (1896), after which the firm declared a state of bankruptcy, with their stock purchased in a sheriff's sale by Furstnow & Coggshall (see below). It is possible that Hugh's involvement in politics and other local functions diverted his interest from the saddlery business and contributed to its failure (VerBeck, 1998). In addition, there was substantial competition from other Miles City saddleries.

Miles City, Montana, Sept 13 1886

Mr. Joseph [illegible]

To MORAN BROTHERS, Dr.,

Wholesale and Retail Dealers in

Harness, Saddles, Bridles, Bits, Spurs, Etc.

STOCK SADDLES TO ORDER A SPECIALTY.

Sept 13	To 1 Saddle	55 00	
	" 1 Bit	5	
	" 1 Bridle	3	
			63 00
			38 00

Paid

Figure 2.1.
Invoice from ***Moran Bros.***, of Miles City, M.T. The cost of a saddle, bridle, and bit was $63.00.

Invoices and catalog cards from the firm of Moran Bros. are shown in figures 2.1 through 2.4, respectively. The square-skirted, loop-seat saddles with Sam Stagg rigging shown in these figures were a trademark item. A rare and beautiful example of a Moran Bros. saddle is shown in figures 2.5 and 2.6 (see captions for complete description). The tooling on the saddle leather, the angora pockets, and the tapaderos, coupled with the rare territorial mark, render this piece one of the most outstanding items in this book. A drawing of this rig and its accompanying bridle, silverwork, and spurs was done by the Montana artist Charles M. Russell in 1886 (figure 2.7). Moran Bros. also "have just received a fine line of side saddles" (*Daily Yellowstone Journal*, March 11, 1886).

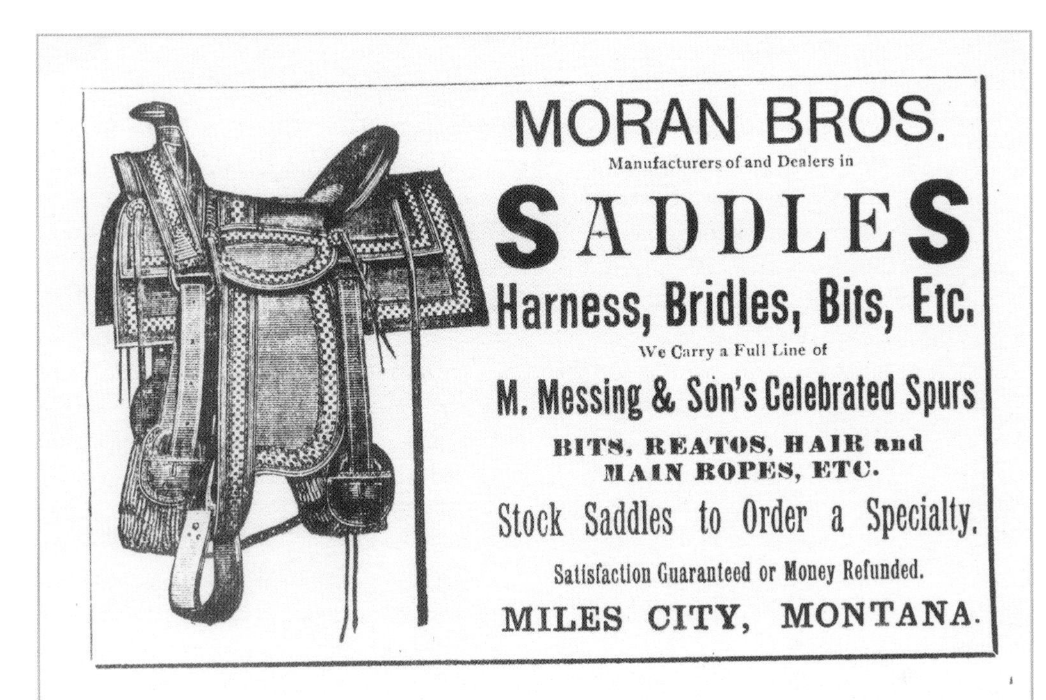

Figure 2.2.
Advertisement for **Moran Bros.** saddles, et al., Miles City, Montana. Note the representation of "M. Messing & Son's Celebrated Spurs."

Figure 2.3.
Moran Bros. cabinet card (front), Miles City, M.T., showing saddle No. 12, at $40.00.

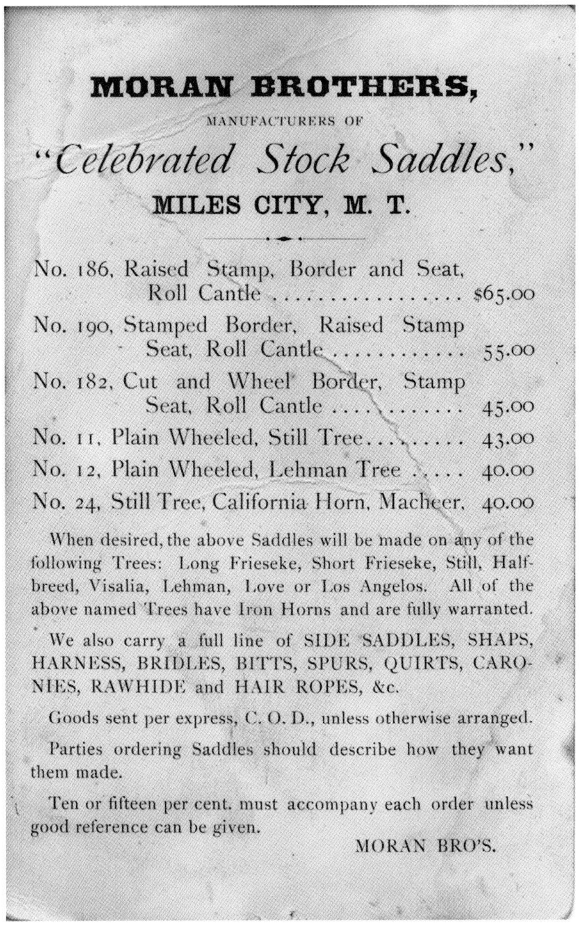

MORAN BROTHERS,

MANUFACTURERS OF

"Celebrated Stock Saddles,"

MILES CITY, M. T.

No. 186, Raised Stamp, Border and Seat, Roll Cantle $65.00
No. 190, Stamped Border, Raised Stamp Seat, Roll Cantle 55.00
No. 182, Cut and Wheel Border, Stamp Seat, Roll Cantle 45.00
No. 11, Plain Wheeled, Still Tree 43.00
No. 12, Plain Wheeled, Lehman Tree 40.00
No. 24, Still Tree, California Horn, Macheer, 40.00

When desired, the above Saddles will be made on any of the following Trees: Long Frieseke, Short Frieseke, Still, Half-breed, Visalia, Lehman, Love or Los Angelos. All of the above named Trees have Iron Horns and are fully warranted.

We also carry a full line of SIDE SADDLES, SHAPS, HARNESS, BRIDLES, BITTS, SPURS, QUIRTS, CARO-NIES, RAWHIDE and HAIR ROPES, &c.

Goods sent per express, C. O. D., unless otherwise arranged.

Parties ordering Saddles should describe how they want them made.

Ten or fifteen per cent. must accompany each order unless good reference can be given.

MORAN BRO'S.

Figure 2.4.
Moran Bros., cabinet card (back), describing different options available for their saddles, including the types of saddle tree and leather decorations. Note that they also carried side saddles, ropes, harness, shaps [*sic*], bits, and spurs.

Figure 2.5.
This ***Moran Bros.*** saddle is probably one of the earliest silver-mounted saddles that exist in cowboy collections. The silver concho on the skirt at the rear of the seat is engraved by Atanasio Larios and matches the conchos on the ornate bit marked "A. Larios" and dated "1886." The conchos on the bridle and spurs also match. Moran Bros. advertised their use of Messing Bros. and other fine silver from California. The saddle has the original angora serapes and is in near-mint original condition. It has the finest tooling money could buy at the time and is a true work of art. The style is reminiscent of the contemporaneous Main and Winchester offerings but is clearly marked "Moran Bros., Miles City M.T." on the seat.

Figure 2.6.
The seat mark on the silver mounted (concho) saddle dated to 1886 (figure 2.5).

Figure 2.7.
C. M. Russell went to Miles City in 1886 with a trail herd to be shipped to Chicago. He must have seen the "outfit" the horse and cowboy are wearing in the drawing he made while there or soon thereafter. Several drawings were done in that time period and were sent to Russell's friend "Pony Bill." The drawing almost exactly matches the ***Moran Bros.*** saddle made in 1886 (the Larios bit in the bridle is marked 1886 along with Larios's name). It is highly possible that the saddle outfit in figure 2.3 is the model for the Russell drawing. It is unlikely that there were two extremely ornate outfits in Miles City at the same time that Russell was there that prompted him to feature the whole outfit in his artwork.

Additional items produced by Moran Bros. and shown here are a gun rig and cuffs (figures 2.8 and 2.9), a wide-loop Montana-style holster (figures 2.10 and 2.11), saddle pockets (figures 2.12 and 2.13), and a wide pistol belt with a Bridgeport bracket (figure 2.14 and 2.15). Each of these pieces bears the rare Moran Bros. M.T. mark. This section ends with a photo by R. C. Morrison of the Moran Bros. Saddlery sign in Miles City (foreground) (figure 2.16).

Figure 2.8.
This entire "rig" (belt, holster) is exactly what the collector seeks. This one was owned by Oscar Broadus, who came up the Texas Trail three times pushing longhorn cattle and finally remained in Montana. The town of Broadus, Montana was named for him because it was built on his land.

Figure 2.9.
A nice crisp ***Moran Bros.*** territorial mark on an equally crisp holster. Marked Moran gun leather is rare and is highly sought after by collectors (figure 2.8).

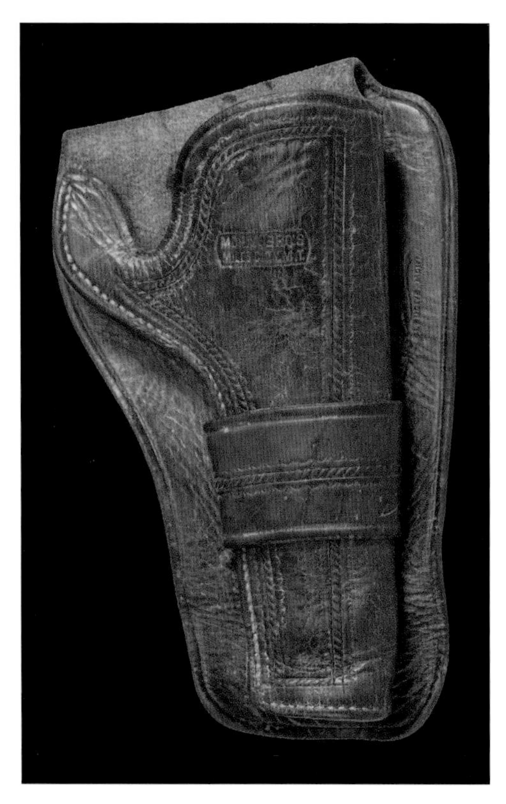

Figure 2.10.
Moran Brothers, Miles City, M.T., made this single wide-loop, Montana-style holster. It was probably made for a Colt Lightning and is a fine example of the standard saddlery holster they offered before they ceased business in 1887. "A.S. Foss / Glendive, Mont." Is also stamped on the holster: Foss was an early photographer (c. 1885) in Glendive who photographed the famous Sioux Chief Red Cloud.

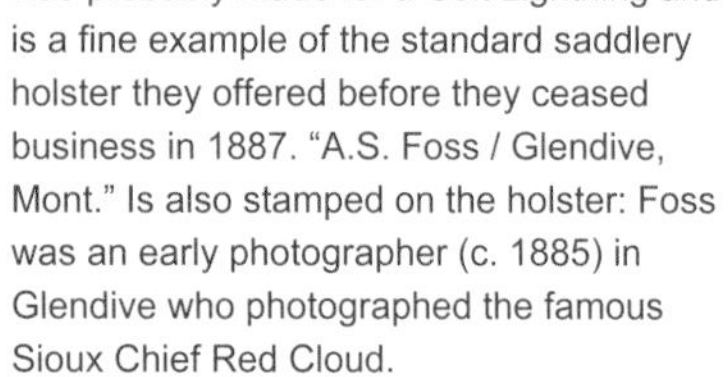

Figure 2.11.
This mark is the standard ***Moran Brothers*** mark used on smaller items throughout the time they were in business and is absolutely authentic (figure 2.10). For a collector this mark is as good as it gets for items that have that great "cowboy" look.

Figure 2.12.
Saddles and saddle pockets of the early 1880s were generally smaller and made of a lighter grade of leather. This pocket is one-half of a pair, the other side of which is lost to history. Made by ***Moran Brothers***, it is marked with one of the smaller marks used by the saddlery.

Figure 2.13.
A clear example of the small ***Moran Brothers Miles City M.T.*** mark. It was used primarily on items such as the saddle pockets (figure 2.12), bridles, and spur straps.

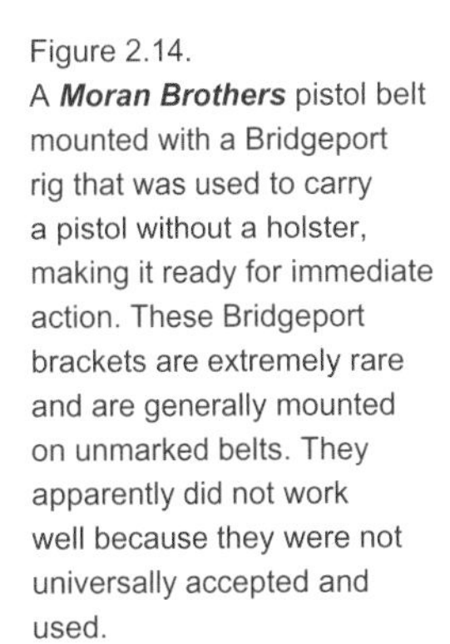

Figure 2.14.
A ***Moran Brothers*** pistol belt mounted with a Bridgeport rig that was used to carry a pistol without a holster, making it ready for immediate action. These Bridgeport brackets are extremely rare and are generally mounted on unmarked belts. They apparently did not work well because they were not universally accepted and used.

Figure 2.15.
The larger double line-bordered ***Moran Brothers*** mark (figure 2.14). All Moran Brothers-marked saddlery items are rare; this is one of the three or four differently sized and configured marks that they used.

Figure 2.16.
Photograph by R. C. Morrison of ***Moran Bros. Saddlery*** sign in Miles City.

II. J. S. Collins

Already famous for his development of the Plains cowboy's stock saddle, also known as the "Cheyenne Rig," J. (John) S. Collins & Co. opened a saddlery in Glendive, Montana, in 1885 as a satellite shop to the Collins brothers' principal establishments in Cheyenne, Wyoming, and Omaha, Nebraska. In August 1885, the Glendive shop was moved to Miles City, M.T., where several skilled saddle makers were employed including Ten Eyck (see chapter 3) and George Robbins (see below). The merger of J. S. Collins & Co. and Moran Bros. (Miles City, 1887) was likely occasioned by the financial recession that occurred after the death of most of the area's cattle herds over the winter of 1886–1887. However, after seven months the partnership ceased and J. S. Collins & Co. returned to Cheyenne (figure 2.17).

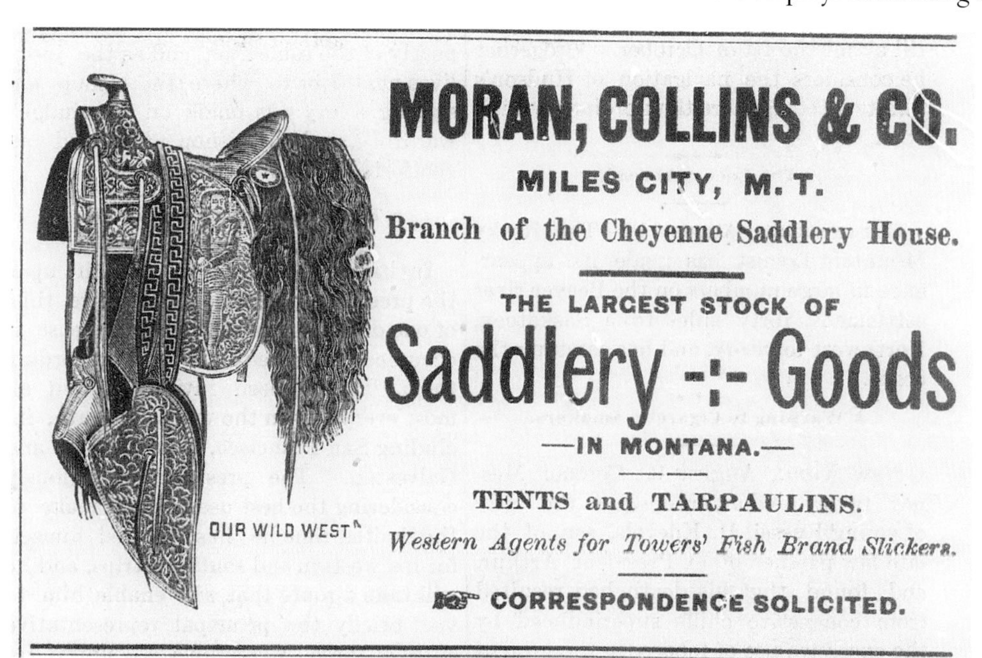

Figure 2.17.
Advertisement for ***Moran, Collins & Co.***, Miles City, M.T. From the *River Press* (Fort Benton, M.T.), August 17, 1887. This firm was in business for only seven months.

J. S. COLLINS, Omaha, Neb. | JOHN MORRISON, Cheyenne, Wyo. | CHAS. R. KELSEY, Miles City, Mont.

J. S. COLLINS & CO.,

MAIN STREET, MILES CITY, M. T.,

BRANCH OF THE CHEYENNE SADDLERY HOUSE.

NOW OPEN AND READY FOR BUSINESS.

BITS AND SPURS.

STOCK SADDLES,
BRIDLES,
REATAS,

STOCK SADDLES
Made to Order
ON SHORT NOTICE.

Repairing of all kinds on short notice.

TENTS,
WAGON COVERS.

SIDE SADDLES,
QUIRTS,
CHAPARAJOS,

SADDLES
Made to Order,
SINGLE RIGGED.

A full line of California Bits and Spurs of latest patterns.

SLICKERS,
TARPAULINS.

Our stock of Braided Bridles, Reins, Ropes, Etc., is very extensive, and of our own manufacture.

We also handle a full line of Colt's Revolvers and Ammunition: Rifles, Shot Guns, Etc.

Correspondence Solicited.

Figure 2.18.
Advertisement for ***J. S. Collins & Co.***, Miles City, M.T. Note that the Miles City firm was a branch of "The Cheyenne Saddlery House," with Chas. R. Kelsey at this location. From the *Yellowstone Journal*, September 23, 1885.

An advertisement for J. S. Collins & Co. (1887) is shown in figure 2.18. The six rare saddle advertising cards from J. S. Collins & Co. in Miles City (figures 2.19a through 2.19f) are the only ones known to exist. Several different types of saddle trees are shown, and the loop-seat saddles have iron horns (leather-covered), square skirts, and rigging for two cinches. The J. S. Collins, Miles City, M.T., mark is exceedingly rare, and is shown on a double-loop holster and on a pair of shotgun chaps with pockets (and trimmed fringes) in figures 2.20 and 2.22, respectively.

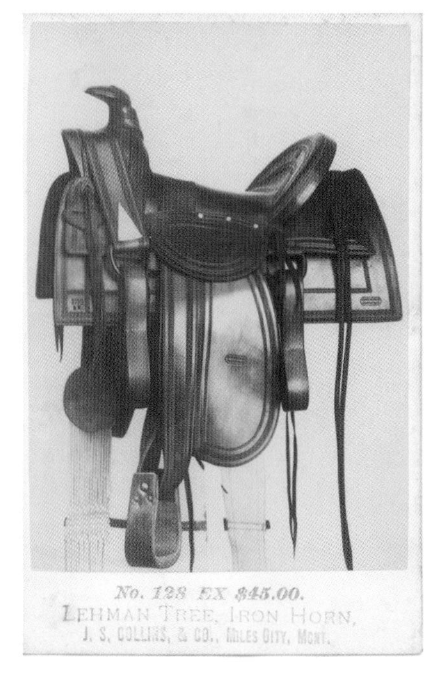

a.

Figure 2.19, a. through f. Cabinet cards from ***J. S. Collins & Co***., Miles City, Mont., depicting styles of loop-seat saddles built on different trees. a – No. 128, Lehman tree; b – No. 134x, Lehman tree; c – No. 131EX, "Little Dandy"; d – No. 130x, Long Freiseka tree; e – No. 130, short Freiseka tree; f – No. 125EX, Goodell tree.

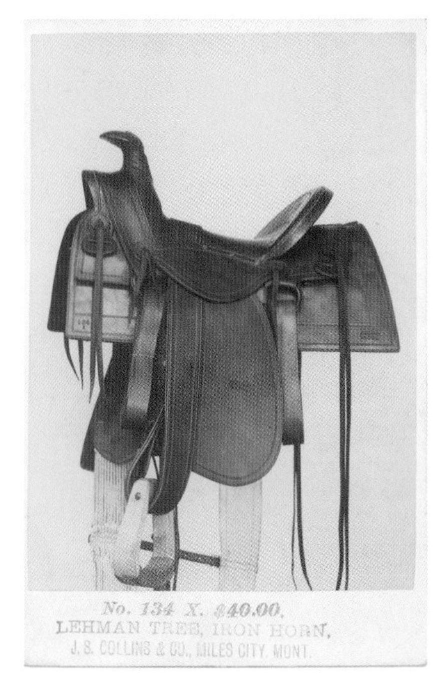

b.

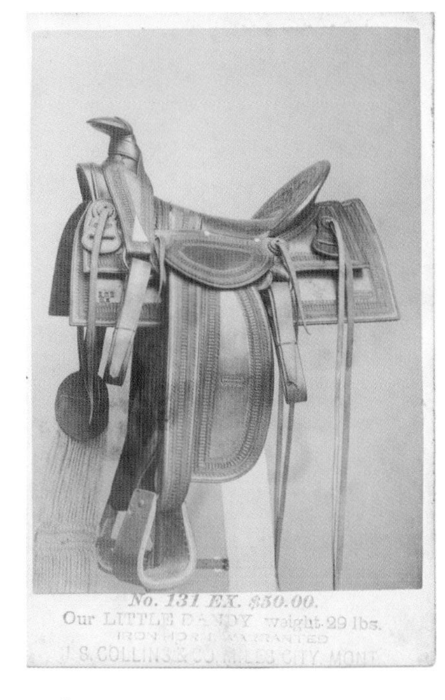

c.

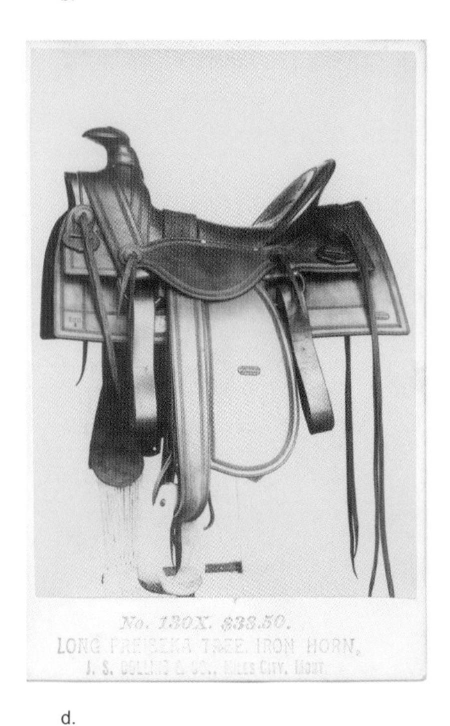

d.

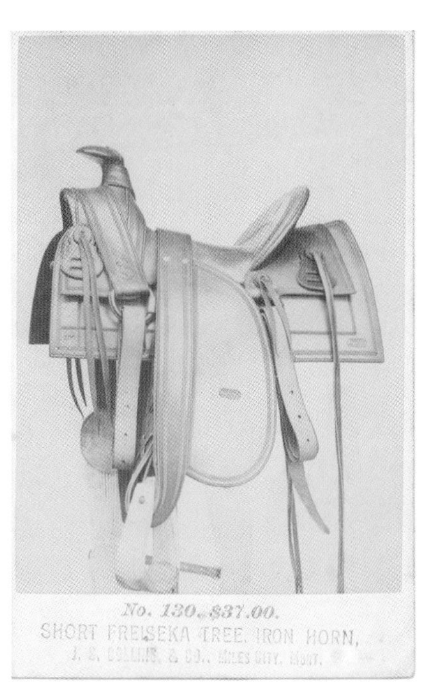

e.

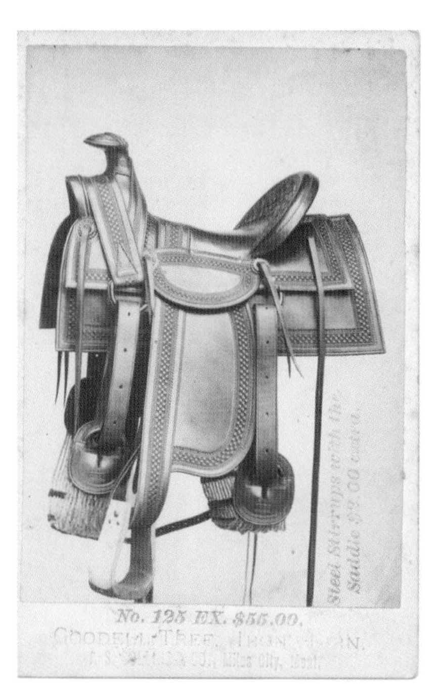

f.

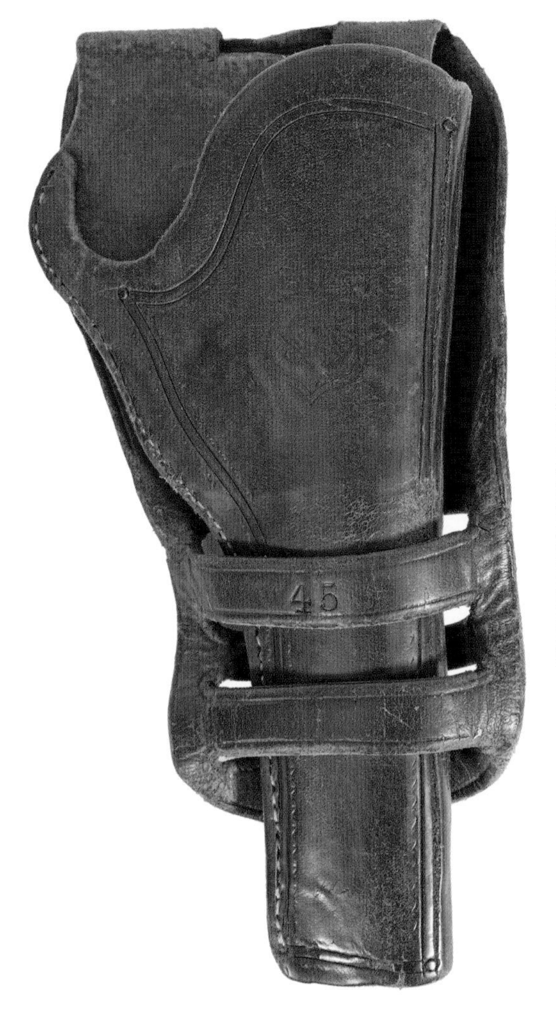

Figure 2.20.
The ***J. S. Collins*** Miles City saddlery was open for approximately one year. Marked items from the Montana shop are extremely rare. Holsters are always a desirable commodity. This holster is marked "45," which signifies it was made to fit a .45 caliber single-action Army Colt pistol. It is the best-conditioned piece of Collins shield Montana-marked leather that the author has had the opportunity to view.

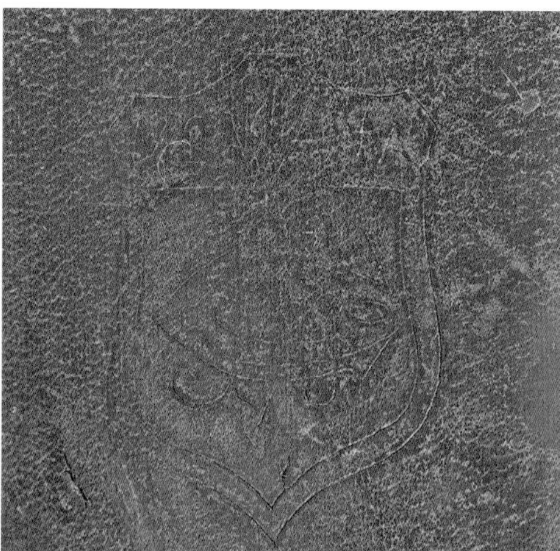

Figure 2.21.
This mark is difficult to read but is the same shield used by ***J. S. Collins*** in his Cheyenne, Wyoming shop, but the top reads "MONTANA" instead of the more common "CHEYENNE" (figure 2.20).

Figure 2.22.
An interesting pair of ***J. S. Collins*** shotgun chaps made with pockets of the style popular in the 1880s. They are in nice condition and would be even better if someone had not removed the fringes.

Figure 2.23.
One of the rarest Miles City Montana Territory marks is shown here. ***J. S. Collins*** came to Miles City in 1885 and the saddlery closed in early 1887, after having merged with Moran Bros. (see text). Only about a dozen items that Collins produced survived (figure 2.22).

Also shown are three different items marked "J. S. COLLINS & CO., MILES CITY, M.T.": a single wide-loop holster and cartridge belt (figures 2.24 and 2.25), a cartridge belt with two holsters of slightly different design (figures 2.26 and 2.27), and a set of saddle bags (figure 2.28). The *Daily Yellowstone Journal* (Miles City, Montana), dated September 27, 1885, describes the need for the Miles City branch, managed by Charles Kelsey of J. S. Collins & Co., to supply the cattlemen recently arrived in the county who previously had taken their demand for cowboy and trail-driving equipment elsewhere: "A magnificent two-story brick building was erected to accommodate the largest [establishment] in Montana." Moreover, "all their saddles are of their own manufacture, and made from only the choicest selected leather made especially for this firm, who take the entire product of one tannery." Likely this supplier was a California concern: J. S. Collins & Co. also advertised bits and spurs purchased from San Jose, California. "Nothing is too good for the cowboys in Montana, and only the best and costliest goods are purchased [by this saddlery]."

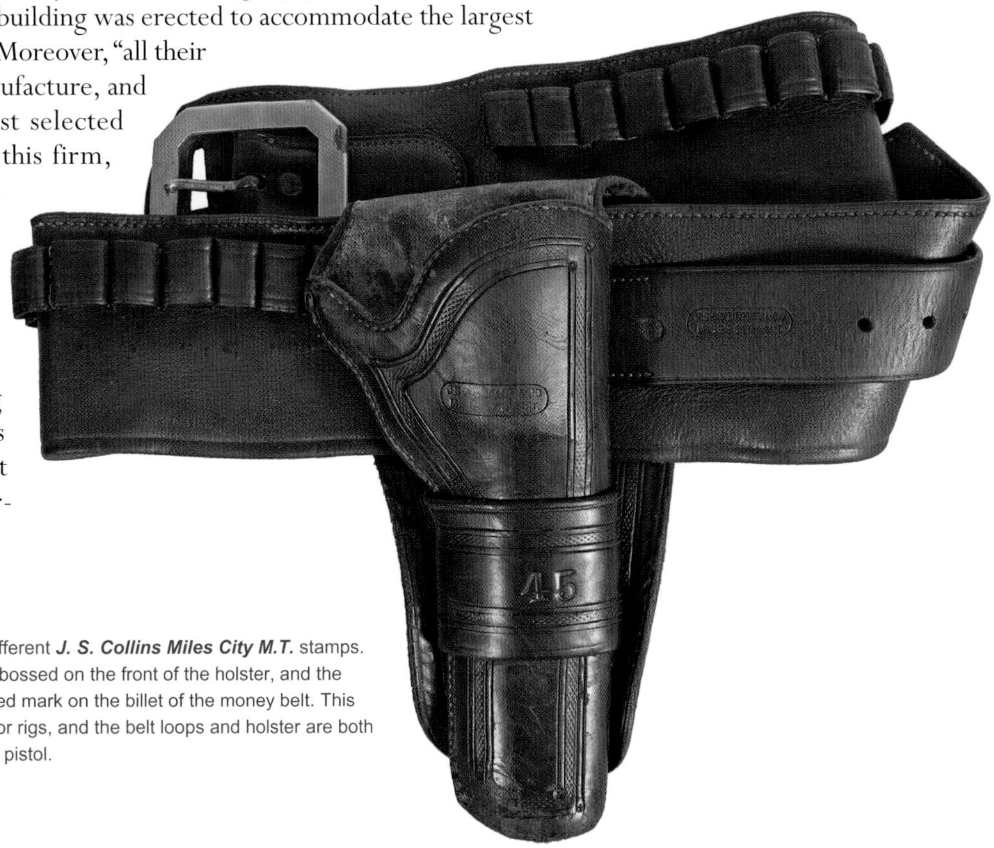

Figure 2.24.
This belt and holster rig has two different ***J. S. Collins Miles City M.T.*** stamps. The larger and longer stamp is embossed on the front of the holster, and the belt has the smaller Cheyenne-sized mark on the billet of the money belt. This is the most desirable of the collector rigs, and the belt loops and holster are both made for the .45 Colt single-action pistol.

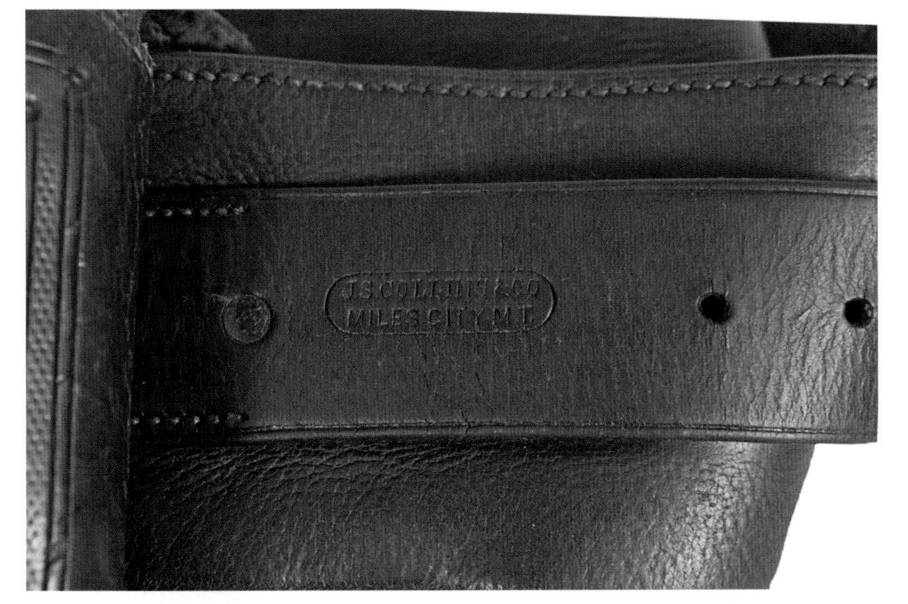

Figure 2.25.
The ***J. S. Collins Miles City*** saddlery used at least four different saddlery stamps while in business there. This one is the most common of the four and is almost exactly the same as their Cheyenne mark with "MILES CITY, M.T." on the bottom line in place of "CHEYENNE." Any Collins Montana saddlery items are rare and very collectible.

Figure 2.26.
Left-handed ***Collins Miles City*** holsters are much rarer than right-handed ones. Although it is unlikely that they were used together originally, they make an interesting display and are mounted on a ***Collins***-marked money belt as well. As would be expected, all of the items are extremely scarce.

Figure 2.27.
A better example of the ***Collins Miles City*** mark would be hard to find—this is the information collectors need to identify items that are for sale in the marketplace (figure 2.26).

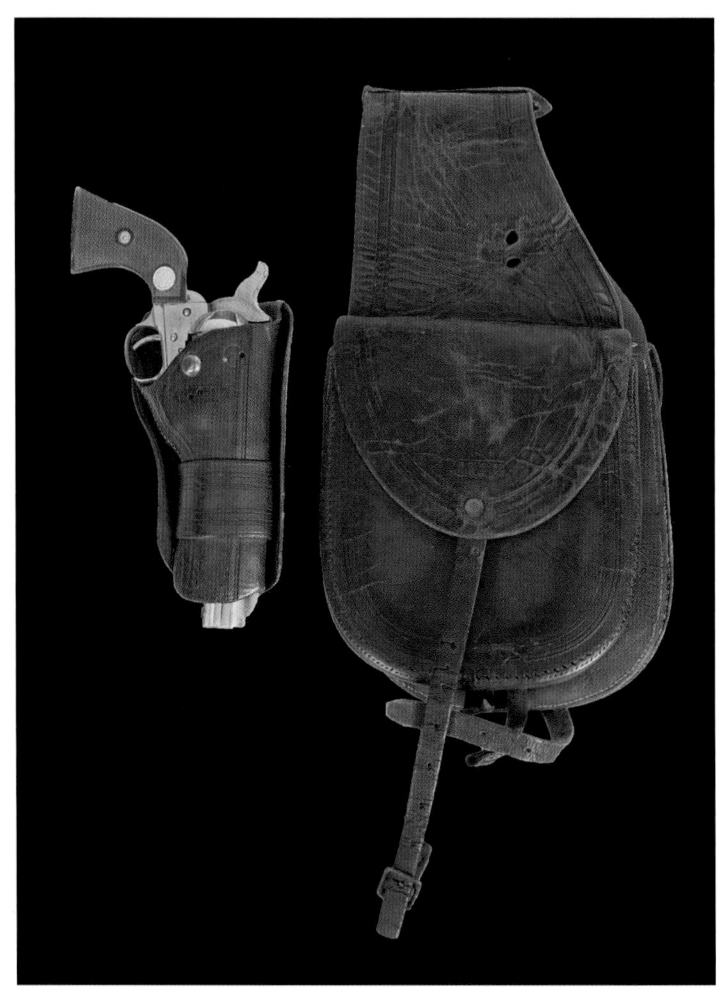

Figure 2.28.
The holster is altered from a standard single wide-loop Montana-style holster made by ***J. S. Collins, Miles City M.T.*** and is known as a "tip up holster." The holster is cut down both at the trigger guard and at the end of the barrel, such that the gun can be fired without drawing (removing the gun from the holster) by just "tipping up" the gun and firing from inside the holster. Obviously the owner of this holster saw the "need for speed" in his line of work. The saddle bags are also made by the ***Collins Miles City*** shop and marked M.T. as well.

III. Ernest Goettlich

Ernest Goettlich and William De Bord were partners in the saddle and harness business in Miles City from 1880–1881. From 1881–1885, Goettlich had his own shop, which was destroyed by fire in 1885 and left him in severe financial straits (*Daily Yellowstone Journal*, May 22, 1885). Previously he had established the Pioneer Harness Shop in Livingston, managed by J. F. Long (see chapter 8) (*Daily Yellowstone Journal*, Dec. 3, 1883). The advertisement shown in figure 2.29 (Miles City) was placed shortly before he became established in Livingston.

Figure 2.29.
Advertisement for ***Ernest Goettlich***, Miles City, M.T. From the *Daily Yellowstone Journal*, December 23, 1883.

Figure 2.30.
The saddle with the ***Goettlich*** mark is shown here and, as expected, is an early-style Sam Stagg double-rigged, square skirt saddle made for the cowboy's work of the time. It has a small amount of restoration but survives in remarkable condition for the use it received.

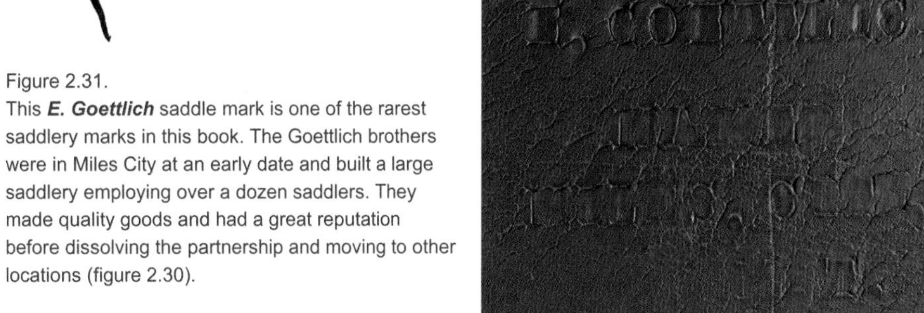

Figure 2.31.
This ***E. Goettlich*** saddle mark is one of the rarest saddlery marks in this book. The Goettlich brothers were in Miles City at an early date and built a large saddlery employing over a dozen saddlers. They made quality goods and had a great reputation before dissolving the partnership and moving to other locations (figure 2.30).

Items marked by E. Goettlich, Miles City, M.T., are scarce. A loop-seat saddle with two cinch rings (double-rigged) is shown in figures 2.30 and 2.31, and a very attractive cartridge belt and holster, both marked, can be seen in figures 2.32 and 2.33.

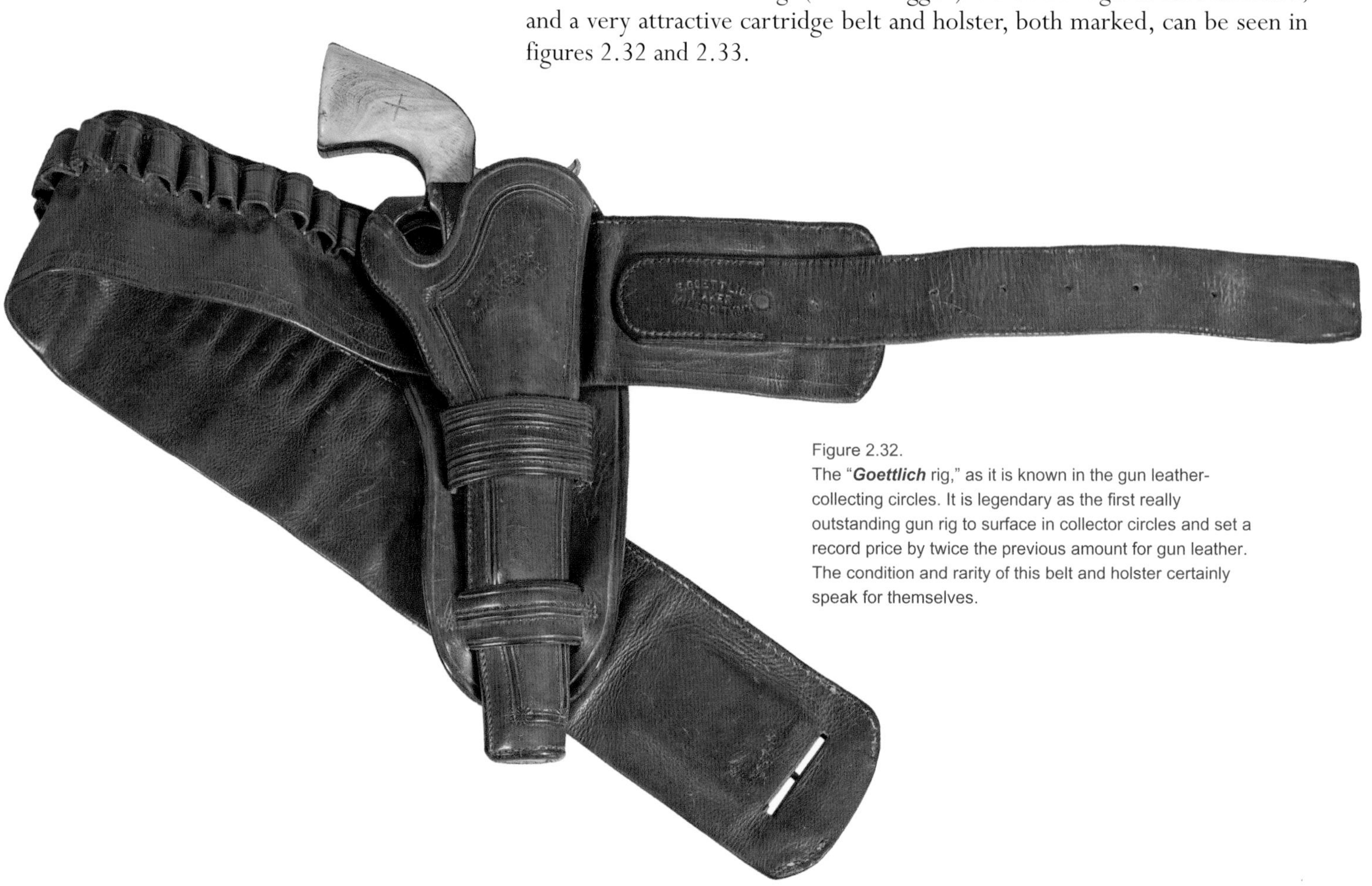

Figure 2.32.
The "***Goettlich*** rig," as it is known in the gun leather-collecting circles. It is legendary as the first really outstanding gun rig to surface in collector circles and set a record price by twice the previous amount for gun leather. The condition and rarity of this belt and holster certainly speak for themselves.

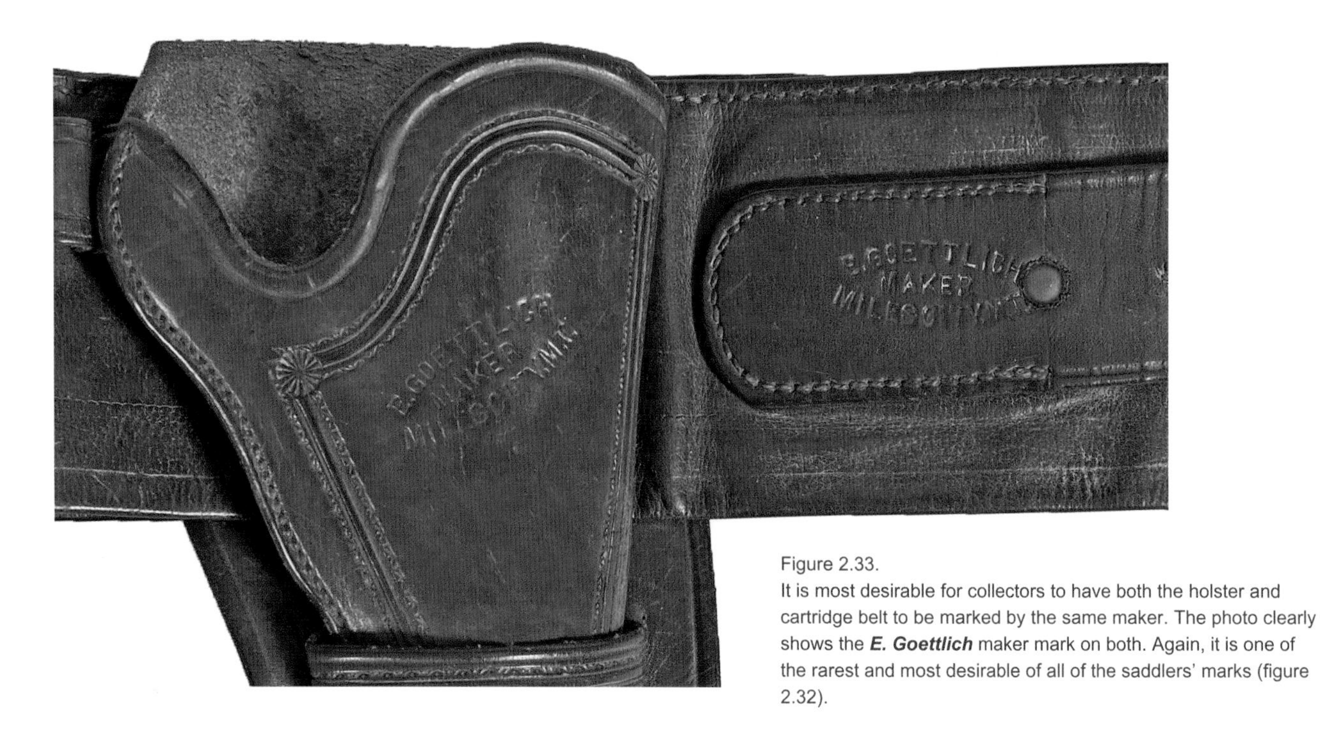

Figure 2.33.
It is most desirable for collectors to have both the holster and cartridge belt to be marked by the same maker. The photo clearly shows the ***E. Goettlich*** maker mark on both. Again, it is one of the rarest and most desirable of all of the saddlers' marks (figure 2.32).

IV. Robbins & Lenoir and George E. Robbins

George E. Robbins was a saddle maker and skilled leather carver who worked for J. H. and J. S. Collins & Co. from 1880–1884, in Cheyenne, Wyoming. He continued his association with J. S. Collins in 1886 after the branch opened in Miles City (Moran, Collins & Co., and later, Moran & Co.). In contrast, Charles (Charley) Lenoir was a Texas cowboy who arrived in Montana with a trail herd and remained in the area (at one point with the Hashknife outfit) for several years. When the firm of Robbins & Lenoir was formed in 1891, Lenoir was a deputy sheriff and Robbins assumed the role of saddle maker and business manager. In addition to a large stock of tack, range clothing, and their own saddles and harnesses, Robbins employed skilled workers that included Al Furstnow. By 1894, Lenoir left the business and it was sold to their harness foreman, J. R. Gerhart.

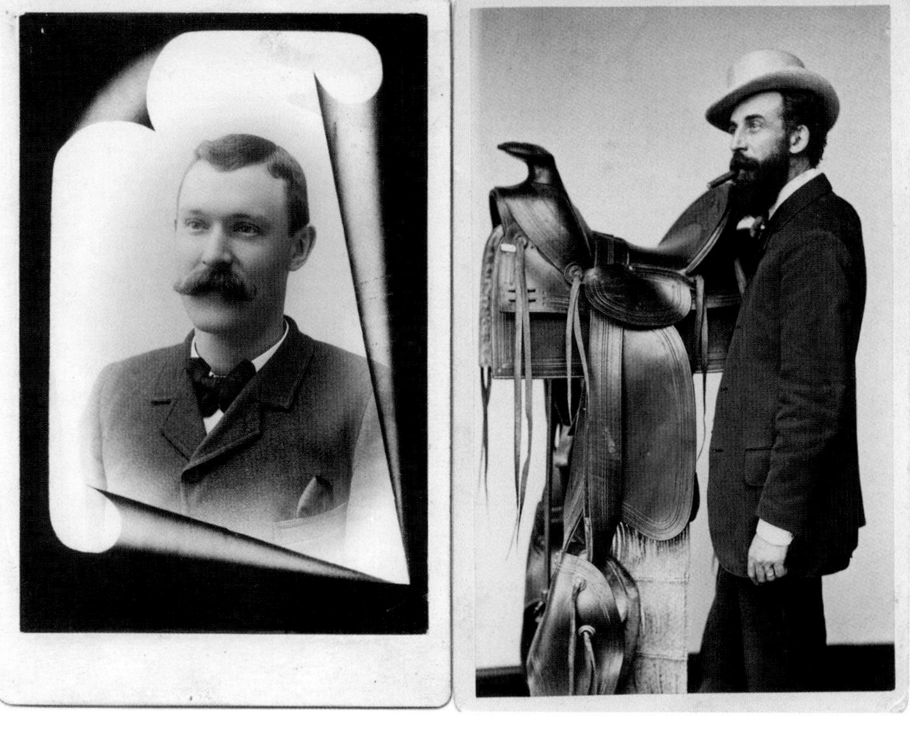

Figure 2.34.
Early photographs of ***George E. Robbins*** (*left*) and ***Charles (Charley) S. Lenoir*** (*right*).

At that point, Robbins started his own business in Miles City, known as George E. Robbins, which remained viable until 1902, when he was elected as Custer County treasurer. As a master saddle maker, Robbins's saddles and tack were of the highest quality and very much in demand.

Photographs of Robbins & Lenoir and their advertisement are shown in figures 2.34 and 2.35, with Lenoir standing next to a particularly handsome saddle. Their shop (figure 2.36) and its interior with an impressive inventory (note side saddle, blankets, cinches, and bridles) (figure 2.37) reveals a thriving and diversified business. Two saddles of different styles, but equal elegance, can be seen in figures 2.38 and 2.39. The former shows a fancy stitched Sam Stagg rigging, square-cornered skirts, and a roll cantle on a Goodell tree (No. 888), whereas the latter lacks the diamond-laced cinch rig, and has slightly rounded skirts and a different style of tooling. The custom-ordered saddle shown in figure 2.40 reveals not only the master carver's artistry, but also his sense of humor; the elk on the side jockey and the woman on the fender are a related theme—perhaps a fantasized huntress?

Figure 2.35.
Advertisement for ***Robbins & Lenoir***, Miles City, Mont.

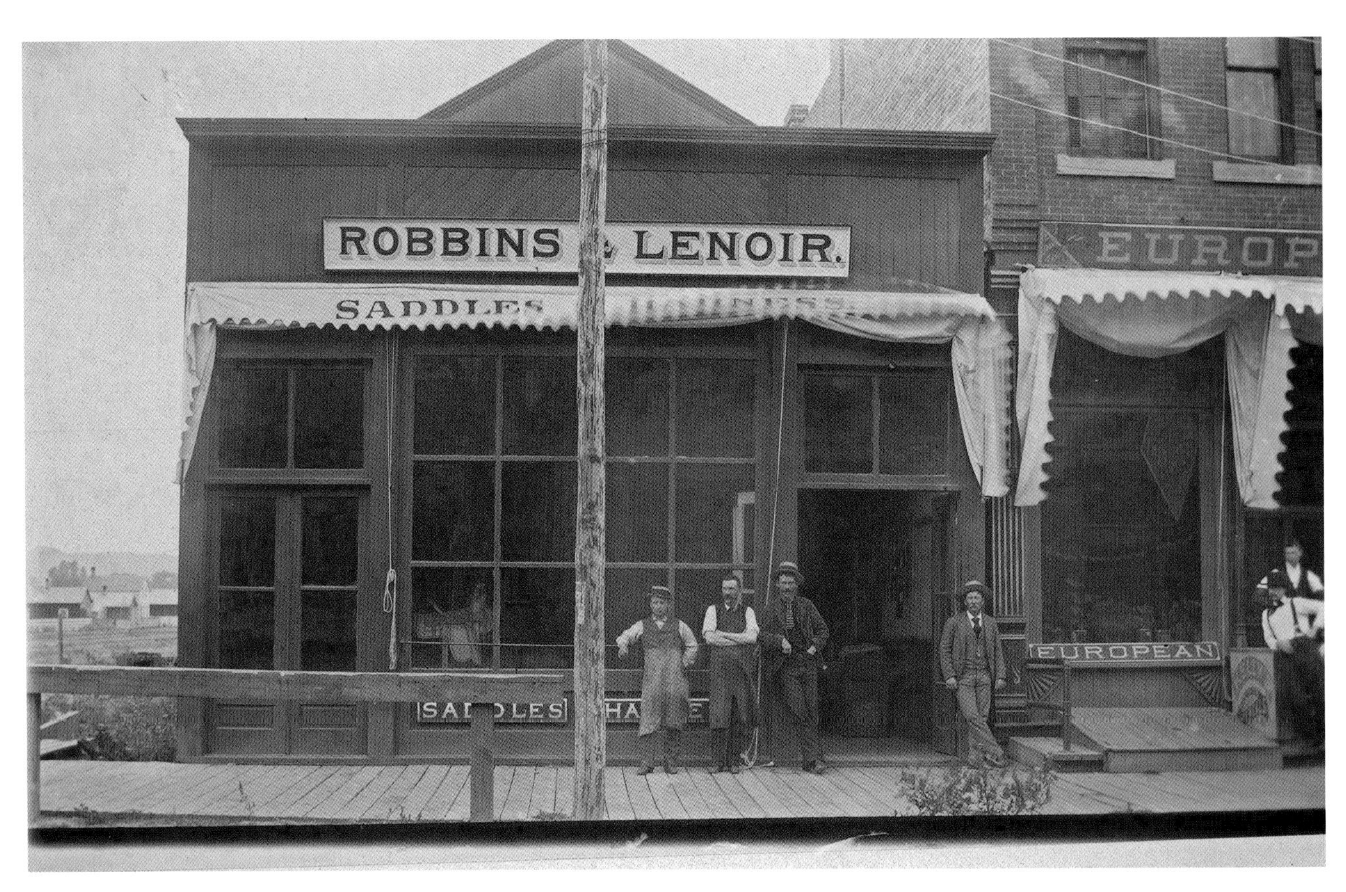

Figure 2.36.
Early photograph of the storefront of ***Robbins & Lenoir***, Miles City, Montana.

Figure 2.37.
Two early photographs of the interior of the ***Robbins & Lenoir*** shop. *Top*: "West side view Robbins & Lenoir repair shop." *Right*: Stock; note saddles, blankets, bridles, cinches, and harness.

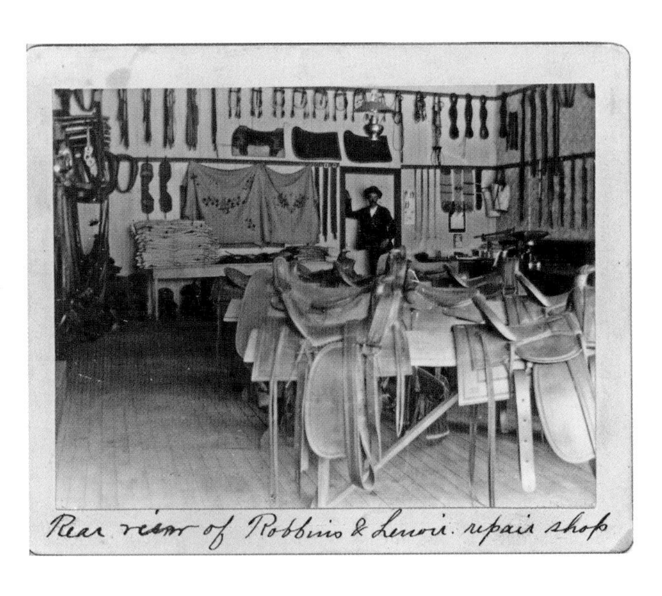

No. 888.
GOODELL TREE, (Iron Horn,)
Price
Roll Cantle, Square Housings, Side Jockeys, Half Seat. Diamond laced Cinch Rig Fancy cut and wheeled, complete with stirrups and Cinches. Also made on Lehman Tree.
ROBBINS & LENOIR,
Miles City,
Mont.

Figure 2.38.
Cabinet card from ***Robbins & Lenoir***, showing elegant loop-seat saddle, No. 888, made over a Goodell tree.

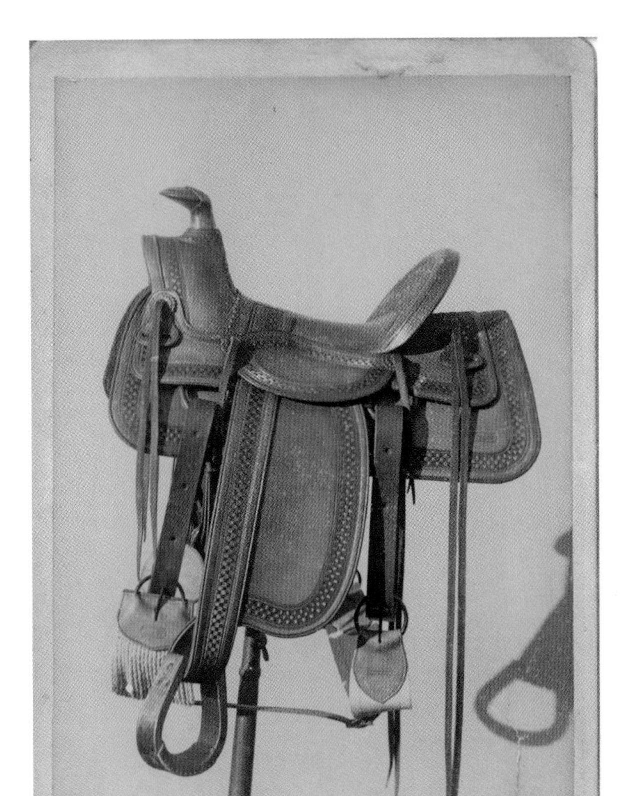

Figure 2.39.
R. C. Morrison photograph of a loop-seat saddle with the ***ROBBINS & LENOIR*** mark on the safe (leather ring cover) of the front mohair cinch.

Robbins. & Lenoir
$ 85.00
Miles City
1893.
Mont.

Figure 2.40.
1893 photograph of a custom-tooled loop-seat saddle by ***Robbins & Lenoir*** of Miles City, decorated with an elk and a fantasy huntress, clearly a custom order.

Further work marked by Robbins & Lenoir includes a transitional half-seat saddle, with a Sam Stagg rigging and two cinches (figures 2.41 and 2.42), a uniquely tooled pair of cowboy cuffs (figures 2.43 and 2.44), and a holster (figures 2.45 and 2.46). Photographed with a lion's head cap gun, the holster was purchased from the estate of Robbins's son Frank, for whom it was made on the occasion of his seventh birthday. The two filigreed leather belts (figures 2.47 through 2.50) marked "ROBBINS & LENOIR/MILES CITY MONT" exhibit fine craftsmanship and design, and would be coveted articles of apparel even today, approximately 120 years after they were produced.

Figure 2.41.
A beautiful example of a transitional half-seat saddle with separate side jockeys and a Sam Stagg rigging, made by ***Robbins & Lenoir***. This double-rigged saddle is in fine condition. In response to Coggshall's advertising of his saddles, Al Furstnow stated in his contemporaneous catalog that Moran Bros., George Robbins, and himself were the only owners in the business that could make a saddle, even if their competitors' lives depended on it. This statement might have been a slight exaggeration because many fine saddlers worked for all of the firms in Miles City. However, it reflected Furstnow's opinion of competitors like C. E. Coggshall, who was not a saddler but a businessman.

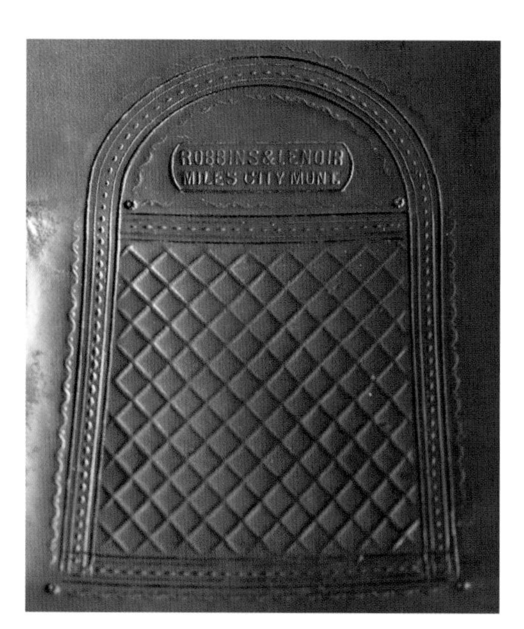

Figure 2.42.
Robbins & Lenoir used a mark (figure 2.41) very similar in shape to the mark used by Furstnow & Coggshall when they were in business. Robbins & Lenoir had already dissolved their partnership when Furstnow & Coggshall joined forces in 1894. It is distinctive and easy to recognize.

Figure 2.44.
A rare saddlery mark from Miles City, these cuffs were stamped by ***Robbins & Lenoir***. They are uniquely tooled, in good condition, and a fine example of a pair of cowboy cuffs that would have been used around 1900 (figure 2.43).

Figure 2.43.
Cowboy cuffs are designed and stamped in many different ways. ***Robbins & Lenoir*** made these cuffs with a minimum of taper and a unique stamping design that covers a lot of space. Another good example of what the well-dressed cowboy might wear.

Figure 2.45.
This holster and the lion's head cap gun are from the estate of Frank Robbins, George Robbins's son. It was made for Frank on his seventh birthday by his father George. It is marked with the ***Robbins & Lenoir*** saddle stamp and would make a great birthday present for a young cowboy even today. The belt is unmarked and was probably added later to match the holster.

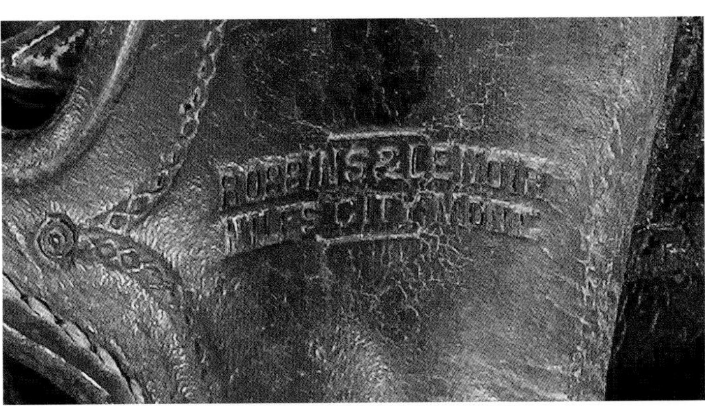

Figure 2.46.
A closer view of the ***Robbins & Lenoir*** saddle stamp from Miles City that is prominent on the holster for the cap gun (figure 2.45).

Figure 2.47.
A filigreed ladies' leather belt with a unique closure—a striking example of the leather artists' work. George Robbins (***Robbins & Lenoir***) was certainly one of the best of the leather carvers of his time, although both the Furstnow and Miles City Saddlery catalogs advertised similar items.

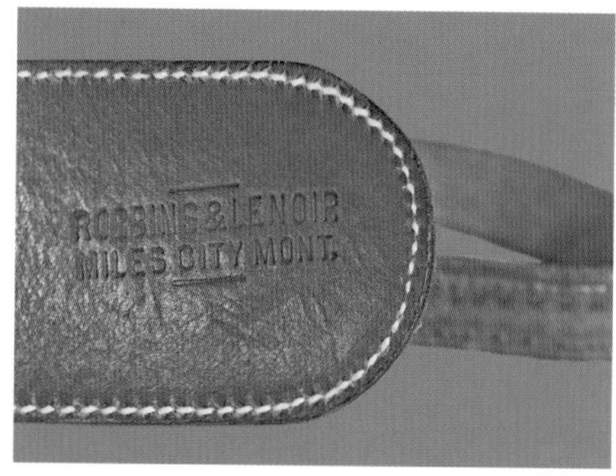

Figure 2.48.
An extremely clear example of the ***Robbins & Lenoir*** mark applied to a new belt as it left the shop (figure 2.47).

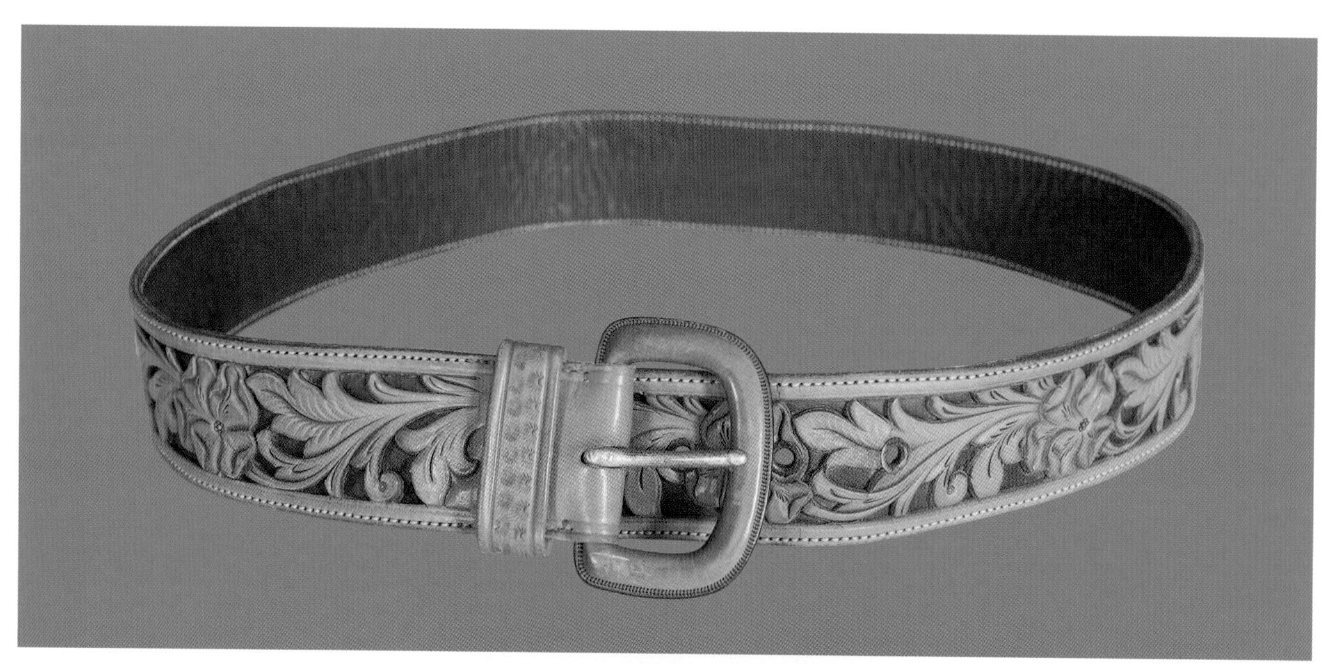

Figure 2.49.
The ***Robbins*** archive included several unused items—this is an example of a 110-year-old piece in new condition. The leather is actually filigreed, with the leather cut, removed, and subsequently backed with the brown lining to accentuate the pattern—leatherwork as a true western art form.

Figure 2.50.
Another of the crisp marks that were in the ***George Robbins*** and ***Robbins & Lenoir*** archive is shown here (figure 2.49).

The following figures in this section relate to the work of George E. Robbins (Miles City, 1895–1902). His catalog cover and mailer are shown in figure 2.51. A letter of thanks to Robbins (figure 2.52) was sent in 1902 from Forsyth, Montana, by W. H. Lyndes, the great uncle of author and rancher Jay C. Lyndes.

Figure 2.51.
Catalog cover for the ***Geo. E. Robbins Saddlery***, Miles City, Montana, with its matching mailer.

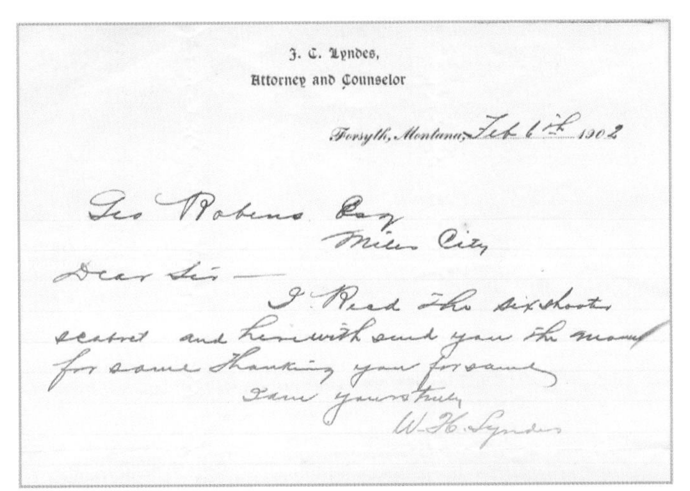

J. C. Lyndes,
Attorney and Counselor

Forsyth, Montana, Feb 6th 1902

Geo Robins Esq
Miles City

Dear Sir—
I Recd the six shooter scabard and herewith send you the money for same thanking you for same
I am yours truly
W. H. Lyndes

Figure 2.52.
Letterhead from J. C. Lyndes, Attorney and Counselor, Forsyth, Montana, dated Feb. 6, 1902, written by his brother (under-sheriff W. H. Lyndes) to ***Geo. Robins*** [*sic*] Esq., Miles City. W. H. Lyndes was the great uncle of author and rancher Jay C. Lyndes.

Figure 2.53.
A ***George Robbins***-marked ladies' sidesaddle in somewhat rough condition. Early sidesaddles had an extremely low survival rate, and this one might be the only one of its kind that still exists. Items marked by George Robbins are difficult to find in any condition.

Figure 2.54.
The offside of the ***George Robbins*** ladies' sidesaddle (figure 2.53) showing an interesting saddlebag as an accessory.

Figure 2.55.
A well-marked tapadero by ***Geo. E. Robbins*** that is part of the ladies' sidesaddle shown in figure 2.53.

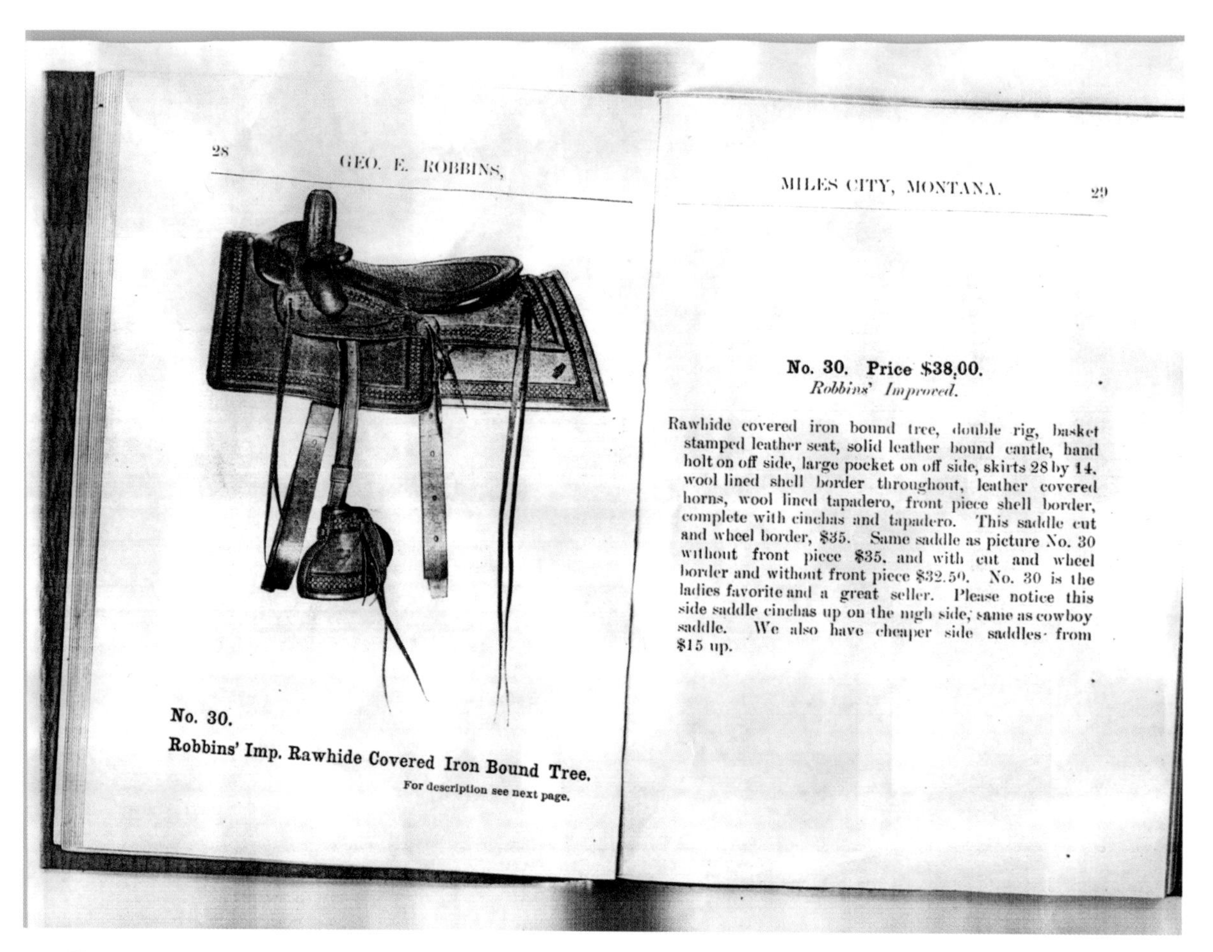

28 GEO. E. ROBBINS,

No. 30.

Robbins' Imp. Rawhide Covered Iron Bound Tree.

For description see next page.

MILES CITY, MONTANA. 29

No. 30. Price $38,00.

Robbins' Improved.

Rawhide covered iron bound tree, double rig, basket stamped leather seat, solid leather bound cantle, hand holt on off side, large pocket on off side, skirts 28 by 14. wool lined shell border throughout, leather covered horns, wool lined tapadero, front piece shell border, complete with cinchas and tapadero. This saddle cut and wheel border, $35. Same saddle as picture No. 30 without front piece $35. and with cut and wheel border and without front piece $32.50. No. 30 is the ladies favorite and a great seller. Please notice this side saddle cinchas up on the nigh side, same as cowboy saddle. We also have cheaper side saddles from $15 up.

Figure 2.56.
Catalog pages from ***Geo. E. Robbins Saddlery***, showing No. 30 side saddle (compare with figure 2.53 and see text for details).

Although surely not a high-volume sales item and therefore ignored by many Montana saddleries, Robbins produced side saddles, one of which is shown in figures 2.53 through 2.55. This model is very similar, if not identical, to the one described in the catalog as "Robbins' [*sic*] Improved" No. 30, with its leaping horn, tapadero, border tooling, and offside pocket (figure 2.56).

George Robbins also produced the standard "Montana cowboy" loop-seat saddle with a very clear stamp (figures 2.57 and 2.58). An intriguing color drawing by Robbins of what is likely a saddle designed for a client can be seen in figure 2.59; this nearly life-sized rendition was drawn on the back of an advertising broadside of the merchants I. W. Orschel & Bro., who were located in the same building as the Robbins Saddlery (figure 2.60).

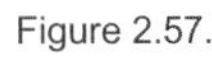

Figure 2.57.
This ***Robbins*** saddle was likely made by Robbins himself in the Miles City shop. It is not fancy and has some restoration but is what the cowboys of the time wanted.

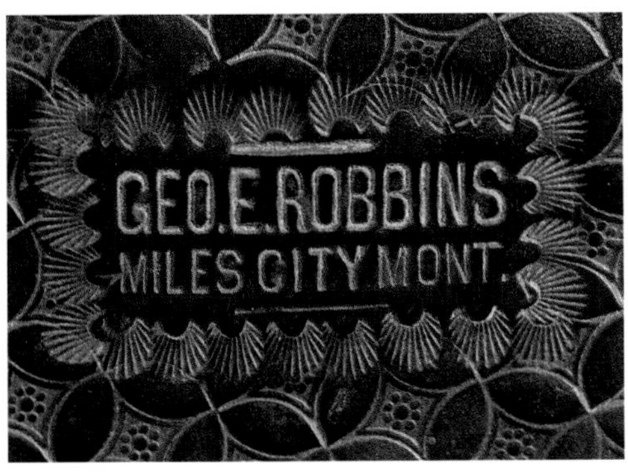

Figure 2.58.
A clear view of the standard ***George Robblns*** saddle stamp with a tooled border applied by Robbins to frame it nicely for the best artistic effect (figure 2.57).

Figure 2.59.
A large framed hand-drawn image of a saddle that ***George Robbins*** drew and signed presumably at a client's request. The colors are unique for a saddle, even a custom-ordered one. It is unknown if the saddle was ever made or if this was something done for display. The size is a 30" by 36", almost a "life sized" rendering of the proposed saddle.

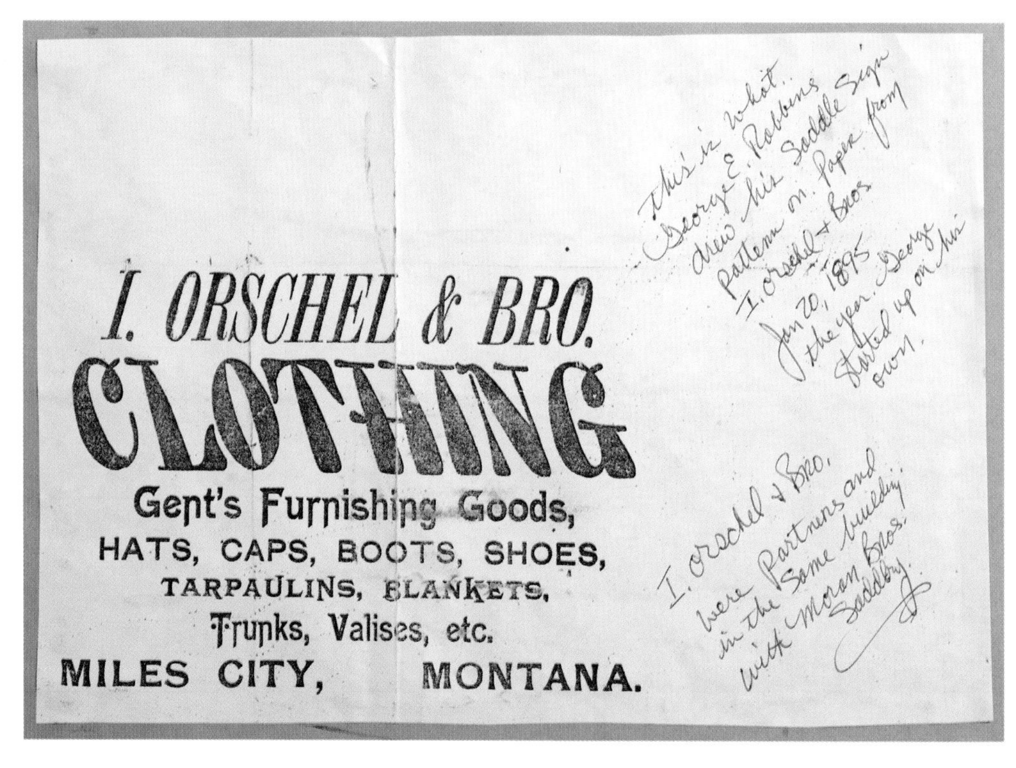

Figure 2.60.
When ***Robbins*** drew the saddle he used the best paper "canvas" available, the advertising broadside of the local merchant I. W. Orschel & Bros. They started in business in 1895, the year Robbins started, and were located in the same building as the Robbins saddlery (figure 2.59).

Concluding this section are examples of a single-loop holster (figure 2.61) and a small pair of cuffs made for Frank Robbins for his seventh birthday (figures 2.62 and 2.63) (accompanying the holster shown in figure 2.45, which is interestingly marked "ROBBINS & LENOIR"). A famous customer of the George E. Robbins establishment was the Miles City, M.T., photographer L. A. Huffman, for whom the photographic slide case pictured in figures 2.64 and 2.65 was made (and the slides have remained in the case). A photograph of Geo. Robbins (far right) shows him in his prime of life (figure 2.66).

Figure 2.61.
A fine example of the "single wide loop" construction of the holsters from Montana and specifically the Miles City saddlers. This would be the "standard" style of the holsters made in Miles City at the time, this one made by ***George Robbins***.

Figure 2.62.
This little pair of cuffs was made by ***George Robbins*** for his son Frank on his seventh birthday. He also made him a little holster with a cap gun inside (figure 2.45). These cuffs are wool-lined and would have been the envy of any young cowboy of the time.

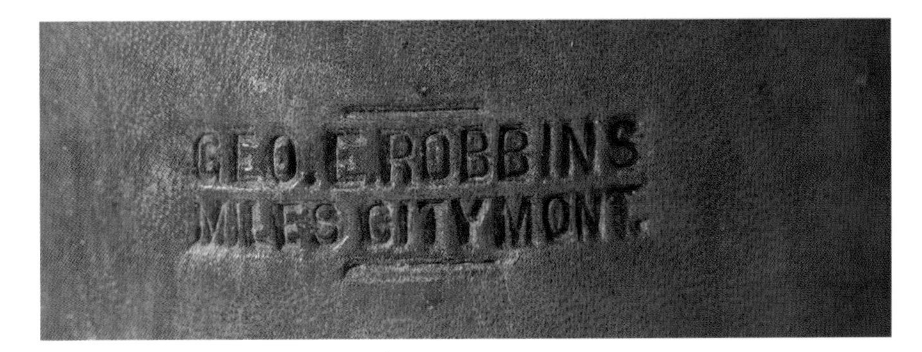

Figure 2.63.
George Robbins used a simple, straightforward saddle stamp that rendered his items easy to identify (figure 2.62).

Figure 2.65.
A unique combination: a rare photographer's blindstamp from L. A. Huffman, and his custom slide case made by the rare saddler ***Geo. E. Robbins*** of Miles City, MT (figure 2.64).

Figure 2.64.
An example of a product made to the customer's specifications. The customer was the famous photographer from Miles City, Montana, L. A. Huffman. Huffman obviously requested this case be constructed to contain photographic slides for one of his cameras (the slides are still in the case). ***George Robbins's*** saddle stamp is visible in the center of the case. On the upper right of the case lid are the blind stamps Huffman used to mark his photographs.

Figure 2.66.
Photograph of ***George Robbins*** (stamped *verso* C. A. Wiley-Miles City, Mont.) in Miles City, Montana.

V. William J. Zimmerman

An elusive saddle maker with an interesting background, Zimmerman had an extremely limited output and items marked by him are nearly impossible to find. He moved from his native Pennsylvania, where he learned the saddlery trade from his father, to Miles City, M.T., in 1886 and worked for Moran Bros. for one year. Following an unsuccessful venture with an untrustworthy partner in North Dakota, Zimmerman returned to Moran Bros. and worked there until 1887. He subsequently served as clerk of the District Court for Custer County and in 1895 purchased the Moran & Co. business, renamed "W. J. Zimmerman." Within nine months a partnership was formed between Zimmerman and Hugh Moran (see table 2.1) but within the year (1896) they were foreclosed upon, with their stock sold at a sheriff's sale to Furstnow & Coggshall (see below). Zimmerman eventually opened a saddlery in Dickinson, North Dakota.

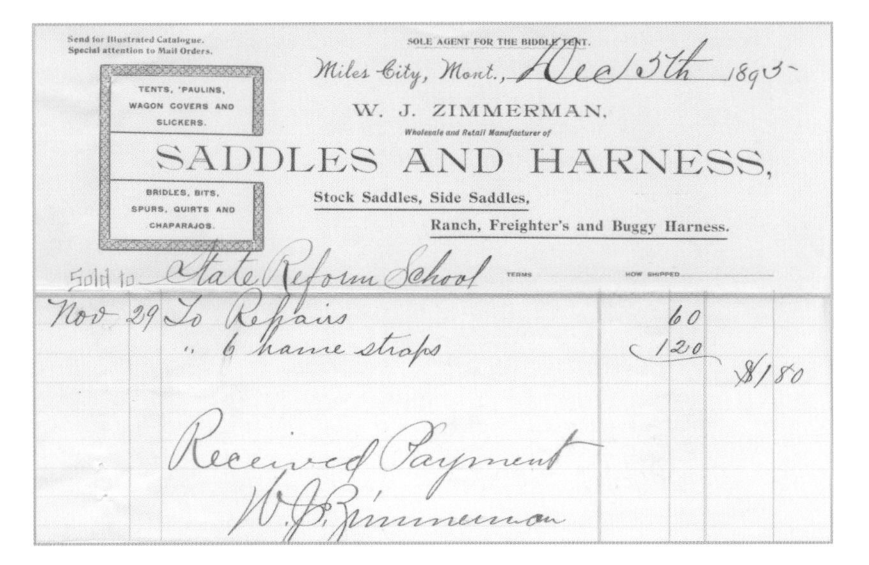

Send for Illustrated Catalogue.
Special attention to Mail Orders.

SOLE AGENT FOR THE BIDDLE TENT.

Miles City, Mont., Dec 5th 1895

TENTS, 'PAULINS, WAGON COVERS AND SLICKERS.

W. J. ZIMMERMAN,
Wholesale and Retail Manufacturer of
SADDLES AND HARNESS,
Stock Saddles, Side Saddles,
Ranch, Freighter's and Buggy Harness.

BRIDLES, BITS, SPURS, QUIRTS AND CHAPARAJOS.

Sold to State Reform School TERMS HOW SHIPPED

Nov	29	To Repairs	60	
		" 6 hame straps	1 20	
				$1 80

Received Payment
W. J. Zimmerman

Figure 2.67.
Invoice/letterhead from ***W. J. Zimmerman***, Miles City, Mont., dated Dec. 5, 1895, for which repairs and hame (harness) straps were sold to the State Reform School.

An invoice from W. J. Zimmerman dated 1895 is shown in figure 2.67. The State Reform School was the purchaser of harness equipment and repairs. Regrettably, only one item made and marked by Zimmerman is known at this time—a cartridge belt showing good workmanship and construction (figures 2.68 and 2.69). The combination of the 1886–1887 winterkill and significant competition from other Miles City saddleries likely accounted for the demise of W. J. Zimmerman and the Moran and Zimmerman establishments.

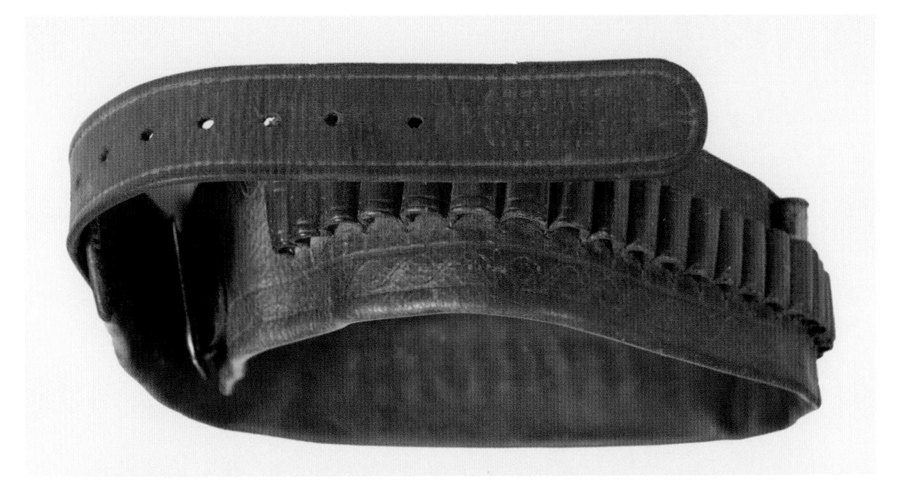

Figure 2.68.
This image gives a nice perspective of a ***W. J. Zimmerman*** Miles City cartridge belt made c. 1887. To the authors' knowledge it is the only example of his work that exists. The belt is extremely well made with borders on the cartridge loops and on the belt itself. The winter of 1886–1887 was brutal and killed a huge number of cattle on the Montana ranges. The next year (1887) saw several saddleries in Miles City alone go out of business. It is certain that the loss of the cattle and the reduction in the number of cowboys on the range reduced the demand for saddlery products. Moran Brothers, W. J. Zimmerman, and J. S. Collins were all 1887 casualties resulting from the loss of cattle in Montana.

Figure 2.69.
W. J. Zimmerman marked this cartridge belt while he was in business in Miles City in 1887. This is the only known example of anything Zimmerman made while he was there, despite reports of a surviving saddle that remains elusive (figure 2.68).

VI. Furstnow & Coggshall and C. E. Coggshall

Figure 2.70.
R. C. Morrison photograph of the ***Furstnow & Coggshall*** Saddlery sign, Miles City, Montana.

Al Furstnow left the Omaha firm of J. S. Collins in 1885 and worked in Miles City for both the Moran Bros. and Robbins & Lenoir saddleries. By 1894 he started his own business, Al. Furstnow, which lasted only five months before he formed a partnership with Charles Coggshall, and the firm was known as Furstnow & Coggshall Saddlery. It was a prosperous endeavor, facilitated by a saddlery catalog that enlarged the sales venue beyond the state of Montana. This partnership lasted from 1894–1899, at which point Coggshall established his own firm (C. E. Coggshall Saddlery, 1899–1909), which eventually was bought by the Miles City Saddlery (see section VIII). Furstnow also established a separate company in 1899, Al. Furstnow Saddlery (see section VII).

A photograph by R. C. Morrison of the Furstnow & Coggshall saddlery sign in Miles City (1890s) is shown in figure 2.70, and a cabinet card photograph of an exotic and highly embellished transitional loop-seat saddle made by the firm, in figure 2.71. Because the men were partners for only five years, finding items with their mark is difficult. A rare marked holster belt is shown in figures 2.72 and 2.73, and two pairs of cuffs, in figures 2.74 through 2.77. The former pair is highly ornate with skilled and detailed carving motifs and a very clear stamp—the condition is pristine. Fine examples of leatherwork from Furstnow & Coggshall appear in figures 2.78 through 2.81: a marked holster and cartridge belt, and a rare set of "sock protectors" (see captions). A pair of chaps clearly made for and used by a working cowboy is shown in figures 2.82 and 2.83. Although tapaderos were not commonly used on the northern ranges, it is clear that several saddleries produced them and offered them as options on many of their saddles; Furstnow & Coggshall's are shown in figures 2.84 and 2.85.

Figure 2.71.
Cabinet card photograph from ***Furstnow & Coggshall***, Miles City, Montana, showing a very elaborately tooled loop-seat saddle, single-rigged, with square skirts and an exposed nickel horn. A cowboy riding a bronc has been carved on the fender.

Figure 2.72.
Many consider the holy grail of collecting to be the marked belts and holsters that were used by cowboys working in areas that required their being armed at all times. This rare marked belt was made by ***Furstnow & Coggshall*** between 1894 and 1899.

Figure 2.73.
Because the ***Furstnow & Coggshall*** partnership didn't last long, finding their marked items is difficult. This is a good example of their flat mark with a border which has a double stamp appearance. Apparently the first attempt accidentally hit the rivet and the stamp was repositioned before the second try, which was successful (figure 2.72).

Figure 2.74.
How this pair of cuffs survived in this condition is anyone's guess. When collectors look for something that "it is difficult to improve upon," these cuffs are what they are talking about. They appear in the ***Furstnow & Coggshall*** catalog and were made between 1894 and 1899.

Figure 2.75.
It is our opinion that the early ***Al Furstnow*** mark that looks almost exactly the same as this mark is indeed Furstnow's earliest mark. If one puts "Furstnow" in the place of "Furstnow & Coggshall" on this mark, the same shape and configuration would be seen. It is reasonable that Furstnow changed his original mark to add "& Coggshall" when the partnership was formed (figure 2.74).

Figure 2.76.
Furstnow & Coggshall cuffs that are clearly marked with the flattened semi-rectangle stamp, used randomly on smaller items but rarely seen on saddles. They seem to be cowboy customized with a couple of added studs that do not detract from their look.

Figure 2.77.
Furstnow & Coggshall had at least two marks for the saddlery—this is the second and lesser used of the two. The mark is a long semi-rectangle with rounded ends and seemed to be used by the saddlery on a random basis. That there are not many surviving examples of their production makes it difficult to generalize why a given stamp was used on an item (figure 2.76).

Figure 2.78.
Matching belt and holster "rigs" are highly prized by collectors, and this pair was made by ***Furstnow & Coggshall*** between 1894 and 1899. The pistol was owned and used by one of the Montana Territorial marshals.

Figure 2.79.
Furstnow & Coggshall were not long in partnership in Miles City, but a fair amount of their products survived. This holster is a fine example of their mark and work. The condition is so good that one can still see the original price of $1.50 that was written in pencil on the front of the holster before it was sold (figure 2.78).

Figure 2.80.
Produced by ***Furstnow & Coggshall***, these may be the rarest of all the items in this book. Made to be worn with shoes (not boots), the purpose was to protect the socks of the wearer from being soiled by the stirrup leathers while riding to the bank or church. It is unlikely the range cowboys saw any need for a pair of these in their wardrobe.

Figure 2.81.
Furstnow & Coggshall used several marks during their tenure—this is one of the most common (figure 2.80).

Figure 2.82.
Furstnow & Coggshall made and marked this exciting example of the early shotgun chaps used on the Northern ranges. They are complete, in fine condition, and typical of the style popular in the mid-1890s. Although the chaps could have been ordered without fringes, it is likely that the narrow spaghetti fringes used on the early chaps became tattered and were subsequently removed by an image-conscious cowboy many years ago.

Figure 2.83.
The ***Furstnow & Coggshall*** semi-elliptical mark shows well on the belt of these chaps (see figure 2.82).

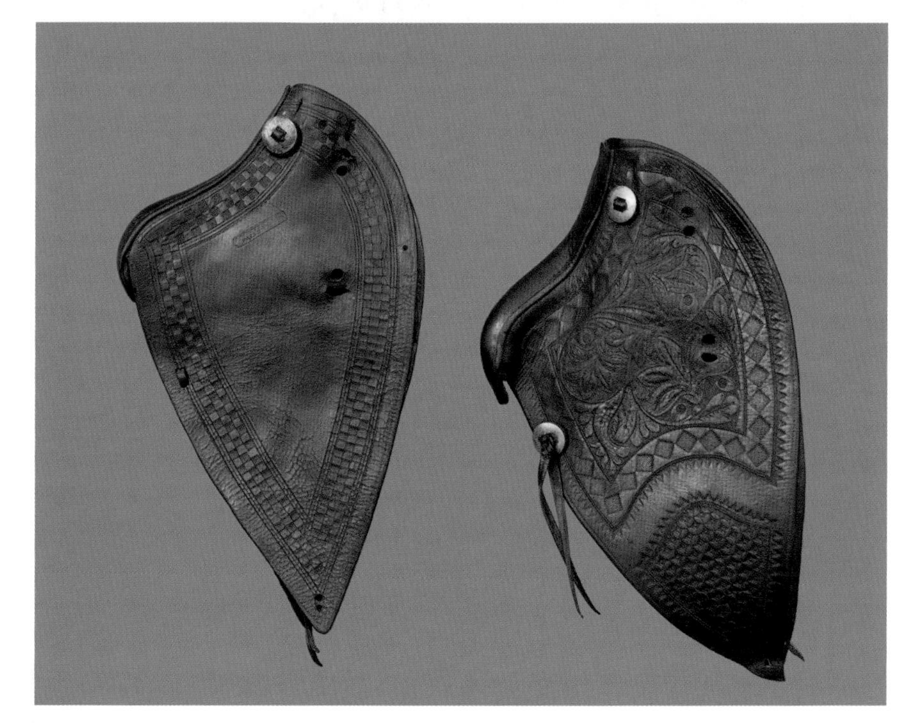

Figure 2.84.
Tapaderos are not commonly seen on the Northern cattle ranges but were considered an option on almost all of the saddles that Montana makers produced. This pair of tapaderos made by ***Furstnow & Coggshall*** was probably offered for one of their catalog saddles. Tapaderos were not especially useful in the North country, as they were designed to ward off thorny brush such as mesquite, which was common in the South. That these were likely removed from the saddle could explain why they survived in such good condition.

Figure 2.85.
The long, semi-elliptical ***Furstnow & Coggshall*** Miles City, Montana, mark (figure 2.84), which was in use for only a short time; items carrying it are therefore rare.

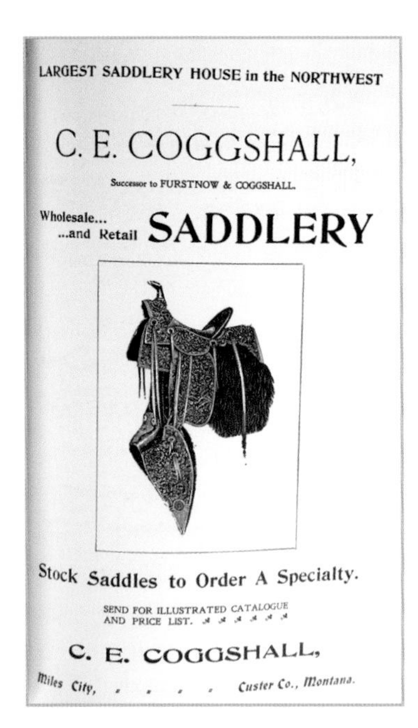

Figure 2.86.
Advertisement for ***C. E. Coggshall***, Saddlery, Miles City, Montana. Note: "Successor to Furstnow & Coggshall." From Van Dersal & Conner (1900).

Charles Coggshall arrived in Miles City as an associate in his father's cattle business, but in December 1894 he purchased a half-interest in Al Furstnow's saddle shop, which was likely in financial straits. Furstnow, the saddle maker, and Coggshall, the business manager, were successful for a short time, after which each founded his own business, in Miles City, in 1899. Coggshall produced high-quality merchandise and employed talented leather workers, but after a decade sold his business to three employees representing the Miles City Saddlery, with Coggshall's retaining a small interest in this new venture.

An advertisement for the C. E. Coggshall Saddlery, c. 1899–1900, is shown in figure 2.86. Examples of two of his firm's saddles, No. 44 and No. 404, appear in figures 2.87 through 2.90. The former, with its brass horn, is a typical Miles City–style saddle used at the turn of the nineteenth century; "44" refers to the catalog number. No. 404 is a beautifully preserved saddle with a high cantle, single cinch, and a clear mark. Another catalog item, No. 22, is a rather plain pair of cuffs with border tooling and the clear C. E. Coggshall mark, with a star (figures 2.91 and 2.92). A very rare item, a cotton-cord cinch, bears the Coggshall mark on the leather safe (figure 2.93). This section ends with a sampling of Coggshall's catalogs (figure 2.94).

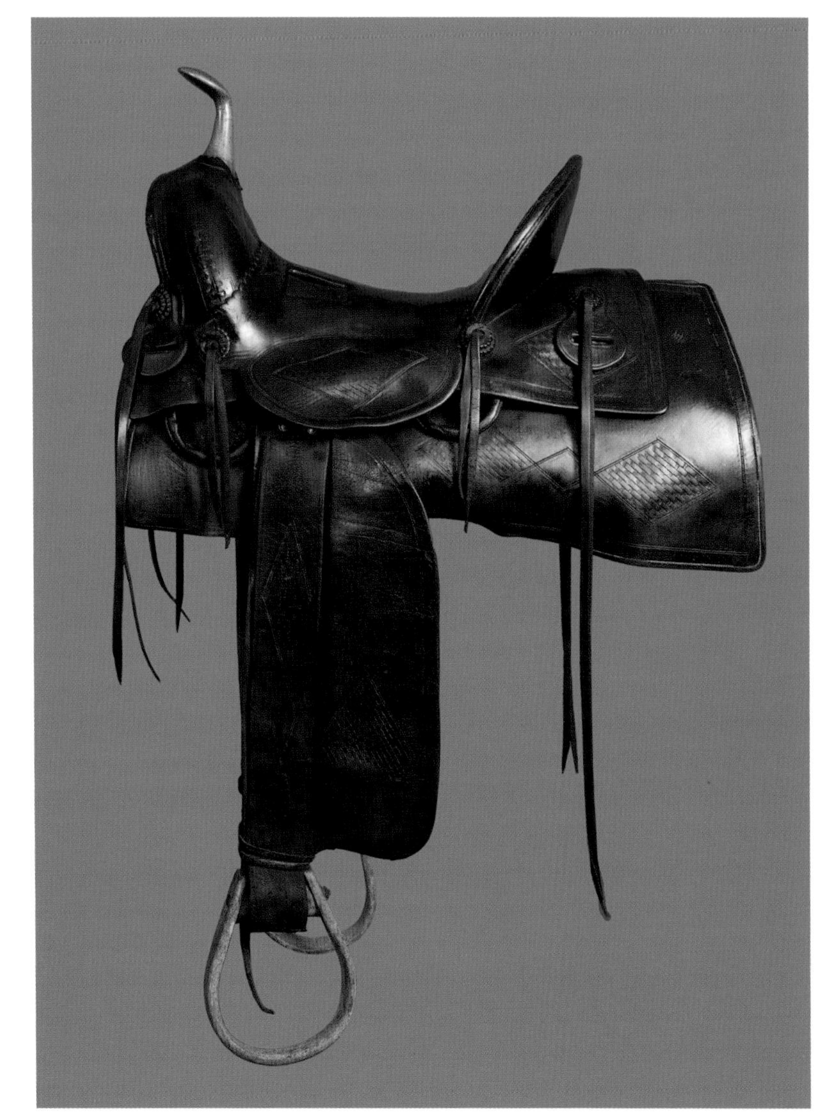

Figure 2.87.
This ***C. E. Coggshall Saddlery*** No. 44 saddle has an optional brass horn, and was made between 1899 and 1909—a nice example of the Miles City–style saddle of that time.

Figure 2.88.
C. E. Coggshall used this mark on all the saddles that were made after the dissolution of his partnership with Furstnow. It is embossed in a unique diamond with the catalog number "44" inside, consistent with the tooling on the rest of the saddle (figure 2.87).

Figure 2.89.
The ***C. E. Coggshall Saddlery*** was in operation from 1899 to 1909; therefore, there are not many examples of their work. This No. 404 saddle was probably ordered directly from the catalog and delivered to an owner who took incredibly good care of his prized possession. It is an excellent example of the high-quality work that all of the Miles City saddlers produced.

Figure 2.90.
The seat of the ***C. E. Coggshall*** No. 404 loop-seat saddle shows nice tooling and is well-marked for its age (figure 2.89).

Figure 2.91.
C. E. Coggshall saddlery made this rather plain pair of cuffs in the period from 1899 to 1909. They are shown in the catalog as No. 22 and would have cost the princely sum of $0.75. They have survived quite well and are a good example of what the average cowboy would have worn.

Figure 2.92.
A good example of the ***C. E. Coggshall*** mark that appears on the cuffs shown in figure 2.91. It is plain, concise, and easy to read with a clear border.

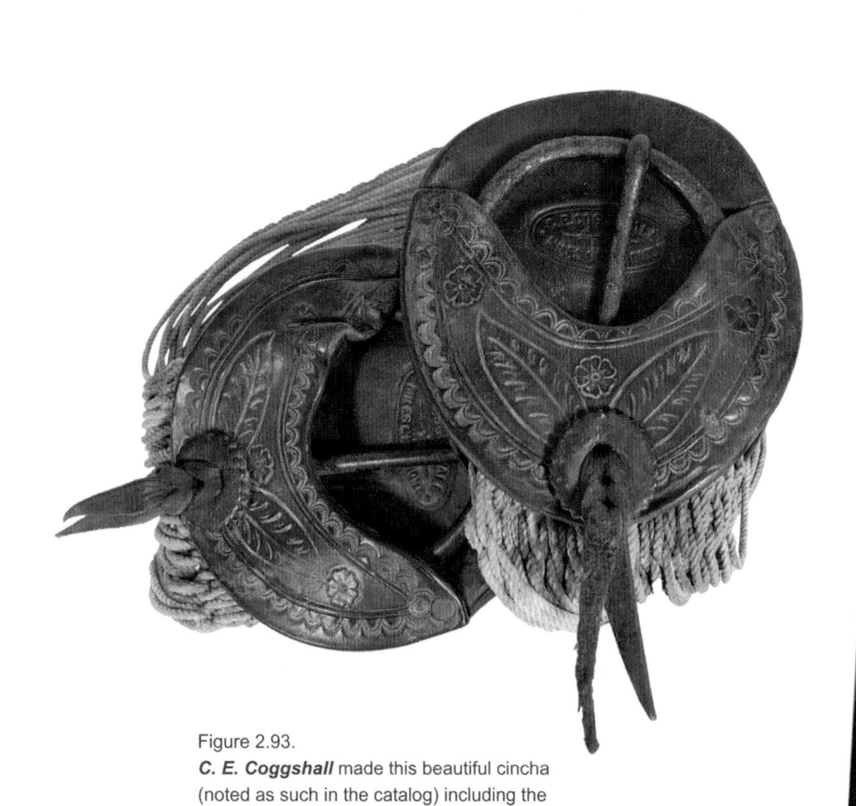

Figure 2.93.
C. E. Coggshall made this beautiful cincha (noted as such in the catalog) including the early tooling pattern on the leather covers or safes. This is the rare item that collectors always seek and is the only one of which we are aware. *Courtesy of T. Leland.*

Figure 2.94.
Four examples of ***Coggshall***'s catalogs.

VII. Albert Frank Furstnow

After the demise of Furstnow & Coggshall (see section VI), Al Furstnow established his own business, Al. Furstnow Saddlery, in Miles City, in 1899. It became a real presence in the town and one of the dominant saddleries in all of Montana. His catalogs were detailed, informational, and interesting because of the photographs of himself, his shop and workers, rodeo champions, and political figures. A Furstnow-made saddle was claimed to be "the saddle that made Miles City famous," a slogan that served as an excellent marketing tool, as Furstnow saddles were sold to movie stars (Jack Hoxie, Tim McCoy, Tom Mix, and the Cisco Kid), to Governor Stewart of Montana (1913), as trophies for competitions such as the Miles City Roundup, and as range equipment used in the American West, Canada, Mexico, and South America (*Furstnow Saddlery Catalog,* No. 31).

VerBeck (1998) states that by 1908, the Al. Furstnow Saddlery was producing approximately 700 saddles per year, and approximately 1,000 saddles each year from 1914 through 1919. Leather items, including bridles, cuffs, chaps, and harnesses, were also important stock that enjoyed high-volume sales. The decline in production began around 1920, with the advent of increasing numbers of automobiles and decreasing numbers of cowboys and cattlemen. In 1921, Al Furstnow opened a saddlery in Los Angeles, California, details about which are not clear, and the rare "Hollywood" stamp was used to mark his output. During this interval Al Moreno, Furstnow's acclaimed leather worker and, later, his son-in-law, assumed ownership of the Al. Furstnow Saddlery in Miles City. The saddle shop was closed in 1946, but western wear was sold until 1982, when the Al. Furstnow Saddlery closed permanently, after eighty-three years in business. Furstnow himself died in Los Angeles in 1925 at the age of 63. Photographs of his famous business in Miles City are shown in figures 2.95 and 2.96, and advertising ephemera, including "The Saddle that Made Miles City Famous," are shown in figures 2.97 through 2.103.

Figure 2.95.
Early photograph of ***Al. Furstnow's Saddlery***, Main St., Miles City, Montana. Photo by Morrison, 1895.

Figure 2.96.
Photo-postcard of ***Al. Furstnow Saddlery***, Miles City, 1909.

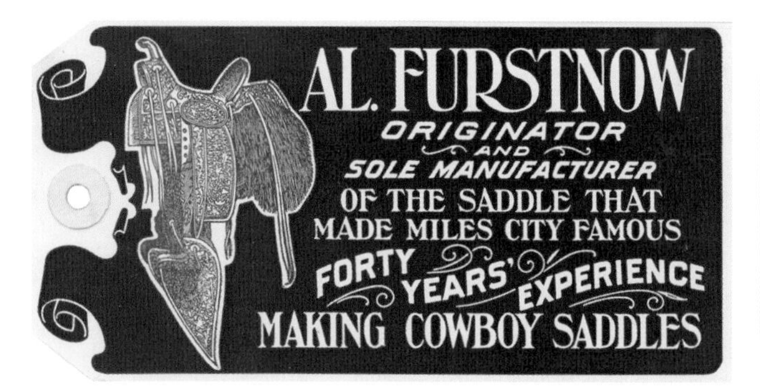

Figure 2.97.
Hang tag for ***Al. Furstnow***—"ORIGINATOR AND SOLE MANUFACTURER OF THE SADDLE THAT MADE MILES CITY FAMOUS."

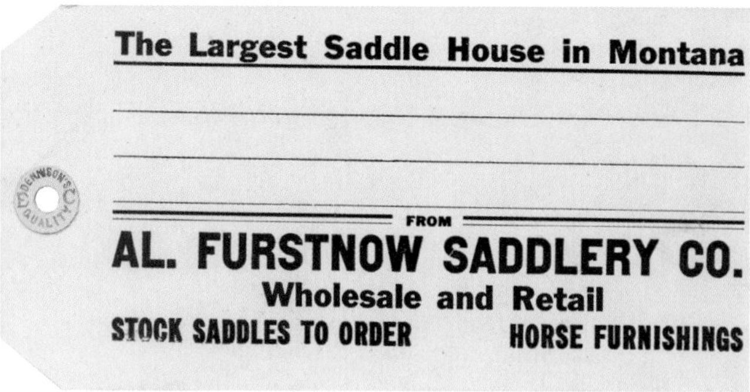

The Largest Saddle House in Montana

FROM

AL. FURSTNOW SADDLERY CO.

Wholesale and Retail

STOCK SADDLES TO ORDER HORSE FURNISHINGS

Figure 2.98.
Verso of the tag shown in 2.97, ***Al. Furstnow Saddlery Co.***

Figure 2.99.
Sign advertising ***Al Furstnow*** establishment.

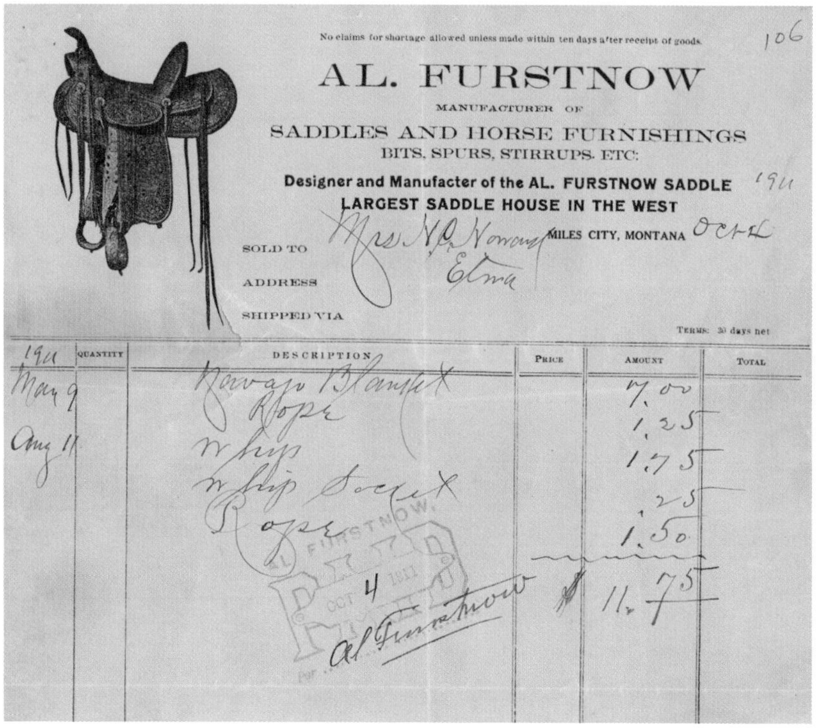

No claims for shortage allowed unless made within ten days after receipt of goods. 106

AL. FURSTNOW

MANUFACTURER OF

SADDLES AND HORSE FURNISHINGS

BITS, SPURS, STIRRUPS, ETC.

Designer and Manufacter of the AL. FURSTNOW SADDLE 1911

LARGEST SADDLE HOUSE IN THE WEST

MILES CITY, MONTANA Oct 4

SOLD TO Mrs. H. D. Noward

ADDRESS Elma

SHIPPED VIA

TERMS: 30 days net

1911	QUANTITY	DESCRIPTION	PRICE	AMOUNT	TOTAL
May 9		Navajo Blanket		7.00	
		Rope		1.25	
Aug 11		Whip		1.75	
		Whip Socket		.25	
		Rope		1.50	
				$ 11.75	

Al Furstnow

Figure 2.100.
Invoice/letterhead from ***Al. Furstnow***, Miles City, Montana, dated Oct. 4, 1911.

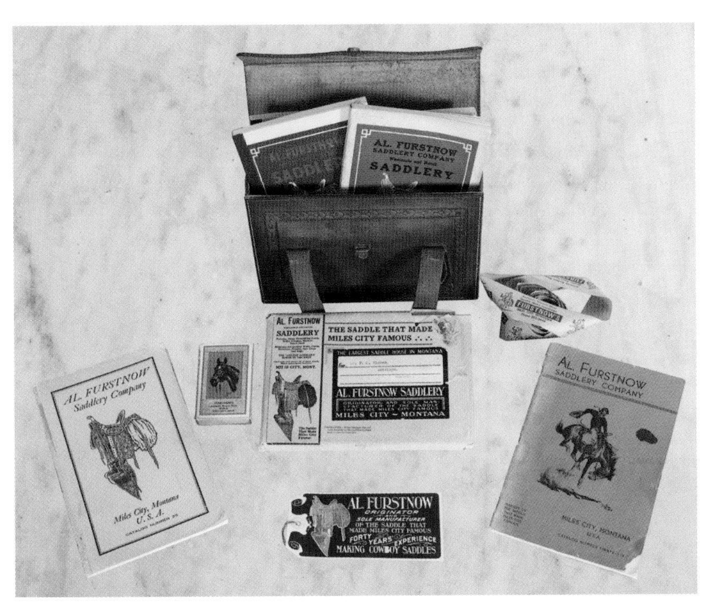

Figure 2.101.
Collection of catalogs, in custom leather case, from ***Al. Furstnow Saddlery***.

Figure 2.102.
Ten catalogs issued by ***Al. Furstnow Saddlery***. Note attractive and different covers for each year or catalog number.

Figure 2.103.
Marked ***Al. Furstnow Saddlery*** leather satchel, functional and nicely tooled.

Al Furstnow was indeed known for his saddles, examples of which appear, with their marks, in figures 2.104 through 2.105. A saddle made for E. H. "Doc" Rowen (figures 2.106 through 2.108) is truly a work of art, with its complete tooling, silver conchos, and name plate with Rowen's initials. Rowen was president of the Sage Riders Club in Miles City, a group organized in 1939 that participated in local parades, gymkhanas, horse shows, and overnight rides. Both E. H. and Mrs. Rowen rode in a Miles City parade in the summer of 1949, "Doc" mounted on a "three-quarter bred American Saddler named Topper and his famous modified 'Silver King' Furstnow saddle" (*The Bit and Spur*, December 1949).

Figure 2.104.
The number two ***Furstnow*** saddle is an epitome of the western saddle maker's art. It has about everything one could order on a saddle: fully floral-carved throughout, with full-sized tapaderos, and double-rigged with both cinches marked. The conchos on the saddle are ringed by a sterling silver "wreath" that is only seen on the best of the Miles City saddles. This saddle was made to be a showpiece and certainly accomplished its purpose.

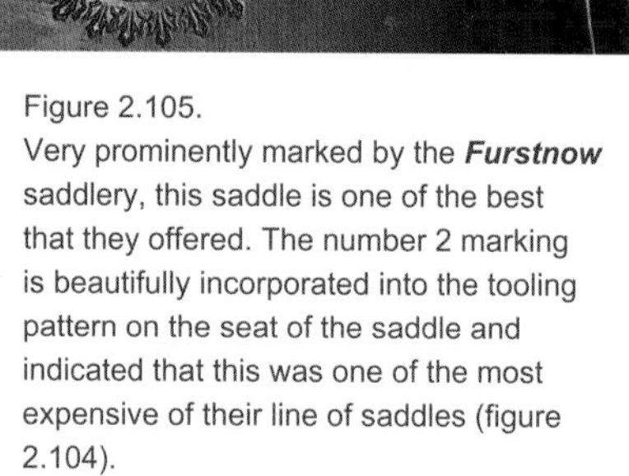

Figure 2.105.
Very prominently marked by the ***Furstnow*** saddlery, this saddle is one of the best that they offered. The number 2 marking is beautifully incorporated into the tooling pattern on the seat of the saddle and indicated that this was one of the most expensive of their line of saddles (figure 2.104).

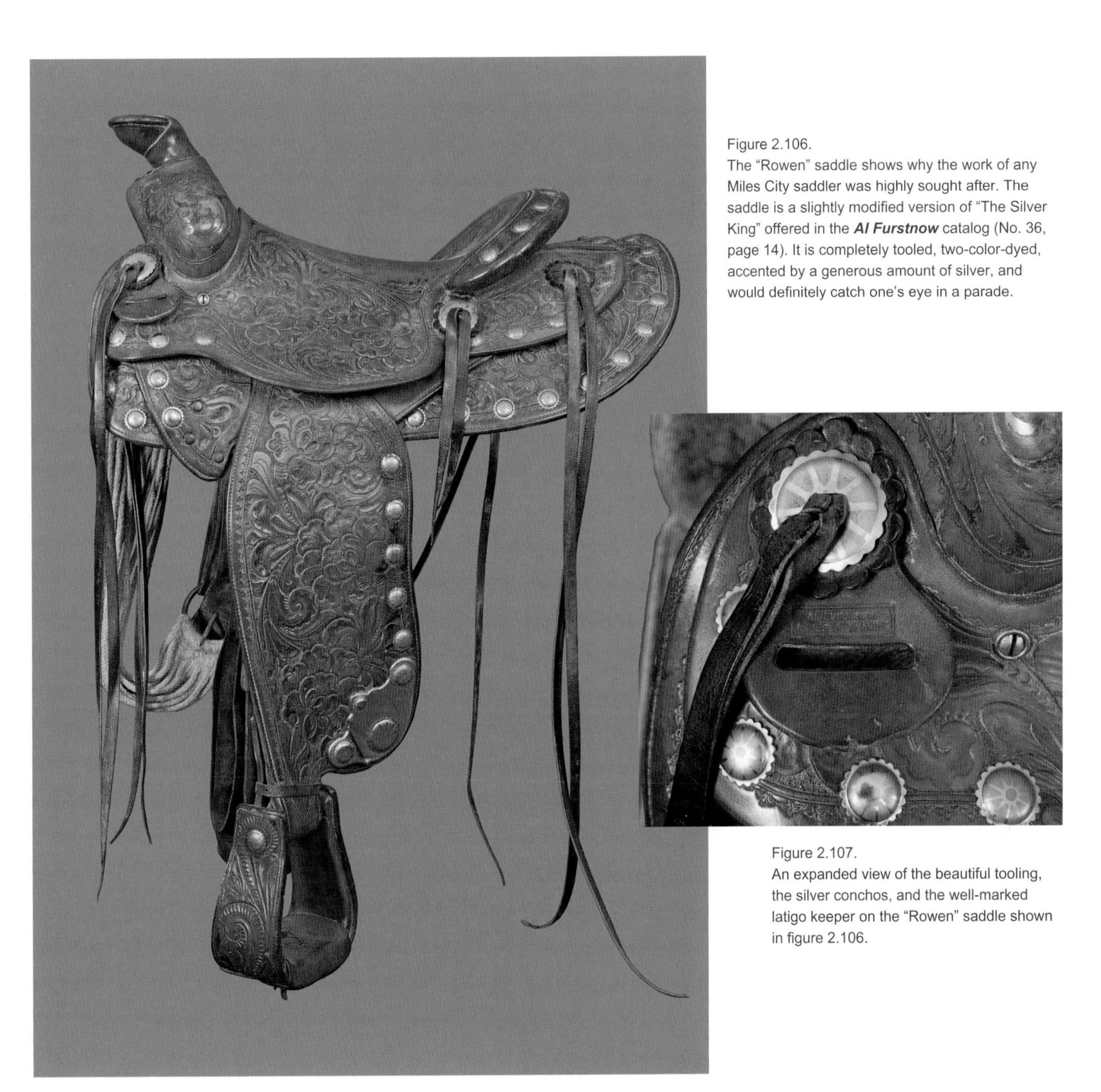

Figure 2.106.
The “Rowen” saddle shows why the work of any Miles City saddler was highly sought after. The saddle is a slightly modified version of “The Silver King” offered in the ***Al Furstnow*** catalog (No. 36, page 14). It is completely tooled, two-color-dyed, accented by a generous amount of silver, and would definitely catch one’s eye in a parade.

Figure 2.107.
An expanded view of the beautiful tooling, the silver conchos, and the well-marked latigo keeper on the “Rowen” saddle shown in figure 2.106.

Figure 2.108.
E. H. “Doc” Rowen was the proud owner of this ***Al Furstnow*** high-quality saddle (figure 2.106). He was a dentist in Miles City, the president of the Sage Riders of Miles City, and leader of their parade group. An article in the *Bit and Spur* magazine (December, 1949) shows the group on parade and lists many of the members (see text).

The "Powder River" saddle (premium model 1X) (figures 2.109 through 2.112) is equally elegant (though without the silver of the Rowen saddle), and the Power River motif recurs in Furstnow's output as a testimony to the early Miles City rodeos, called Powder River Roundups. The saddle in figures 2.113 and 2.114 bears a very early Furstnow mark (with no border) dating to the pre-partnership with Coggshall in 1894 (Furstnow was on his own for five months in 1894 as Al. Furstnow). This rare mark is highly sought after by collectors and scholars of the early west. Concluding this subsection is the Hollywood-marked Furstnow masterpiece, a silver saddle made for "Two Gun Bill Hart," the famous silent movie star (figures 2.117 and 2.118).

Figure 2.109.
A profile view of the ***Al Furstnow*** Premium 1X saddle, which was one of the two best saddles offered in their catalog. The tooling is exceptional, and the bucking horse rider on the fender, "Powder River," make this saddle truly outstanding. Only a limited quantity was produced.

Figure 2.110.
It is difficult to overstate the quality and artistic talent shown in making this saddle (shown in figure 2.109). The photo shows the Powder River cowboy embossed on the fender. The Powder River flows into the Yellowstone River near Miles City; hence the early Miles City rodeos were called Powder River Roundups. The saying that one hears around the Miles City area at rodeo time is still "Powder River, Let'r Buck."

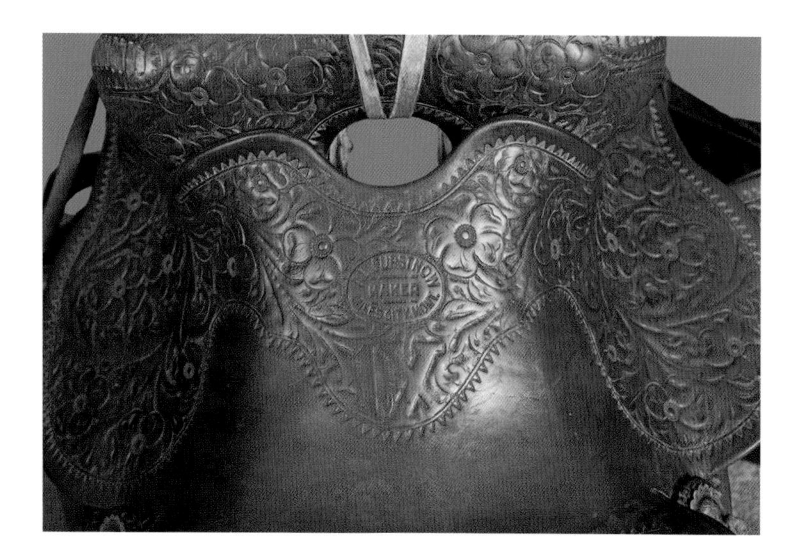

Figure 2.111.
The ***Al Furstnow*** saddle stamp and the designation of the model 1X indicates that this is one of the best saddles Furstnow offered in his catalogs. These marks are skillfully incorporated into the tooling pattern but are sufficiently prominent to identify the saddle maker.

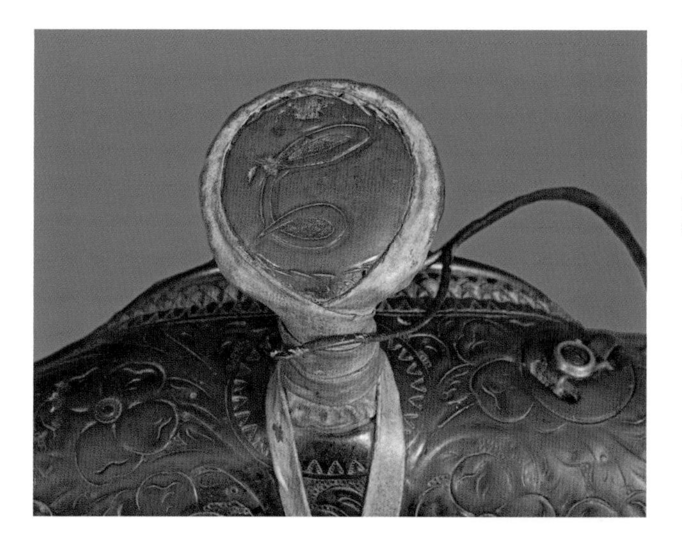

Figure 2.112.
The only damage to this saddle (figure 2.109) is the rope slide around the horn, which cut the leather and allowed the horn cap to come off. Someone later "cowboy modified" the saddle with a replacement horn cap of different leather and a rawhide wrap to hold it in place. The top of the horn has a stylized "C" embossed into it, likely the cowboy's initial.

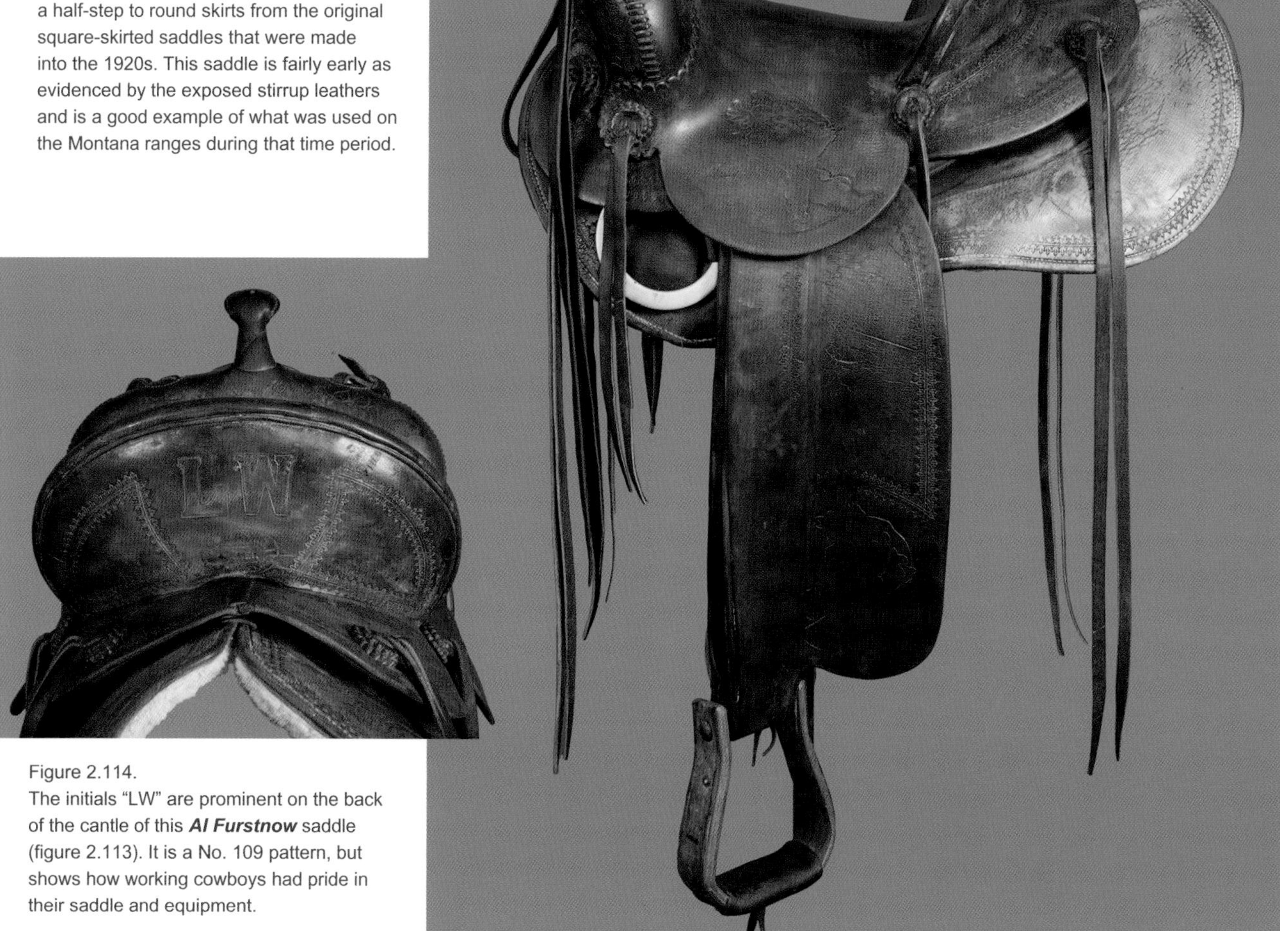

Figure 2.113.
A rather plain No. 109 ***Al Furstnow*** saddle has semi-rounded skirts, a sort of a half-step to round skirts from the original square-skirted saddles that were made into the 1920s. This saddle is fairly early as evidenced by the exposed stirrup leathers and is a good example of what was used on the Montana ranges during that time period.

Figure 2.114.
The initials "LW" are prominent on the back of the cantle of this ***Al Furstnow*** saddle (figure 2.113). It is a No. 109 pattern, but shows how working cowboys had pride in their saddle and equipment.

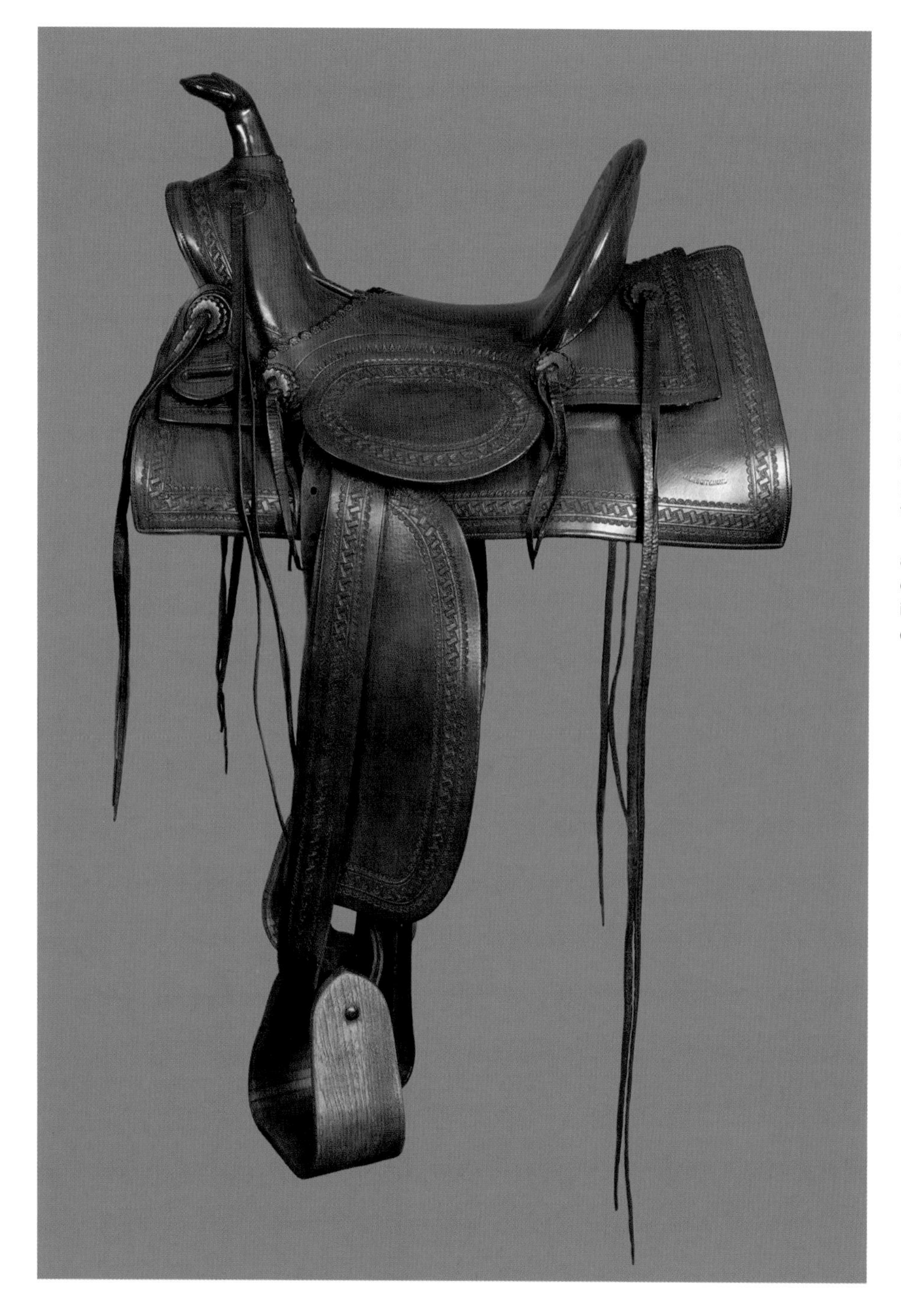

Figure 2.115.
An extremely interesting early Montana saddle for a number of reasons: First, it is in extraordinarily fine collector's condition. Second, it is an A-fork saddle of light construction like most saddles made in the mid-to-late 1880s, with that early "cowboy look." Third, it has an unusual seat construction, with the front of the seat cut back in the form of a triangle, a design leading one to believe that it was not far removed from the half-seat construction popular in the 1870s to the mid-1880s. Fourth, it is marked with the ***Al Furstnow*** flat mark with the dividing bar and no circular border (figure 2.116). This saddle dates to the period after Furstnow purchased Moran's assets and before the Coggshall partnership was formed in 1894. All the factors considered in the age and construction of this saddle point to the conclusion that the early unbordered mark is the first saddle mark that Furstnow used during his long career in Miles City.

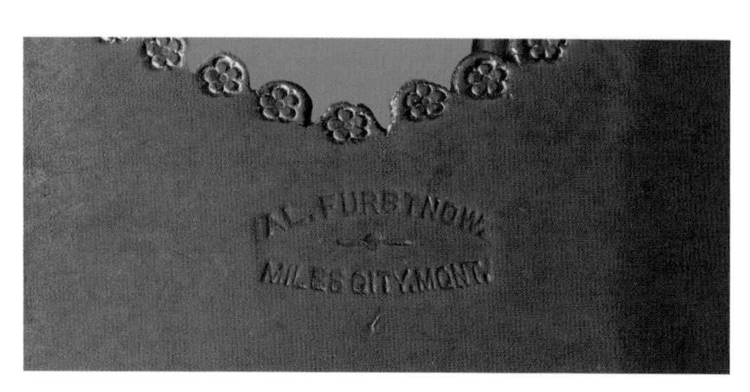

Figure 2.116.
Al Furstnow came to Miles City early and stayed late. He worked for several saddlers in town before he started his own shop. In the authors' opinion, this is the first mark that he used on his production after he bought the assets of the bankrupt Moran Brothers, and that he used this mark until he entered into partnership with C. E. Coggshall in 1894. It is a simple mark with no border and is highly similar to the later mark that was used by the Furstnow & Coggshall saddlery (figure 2.115).

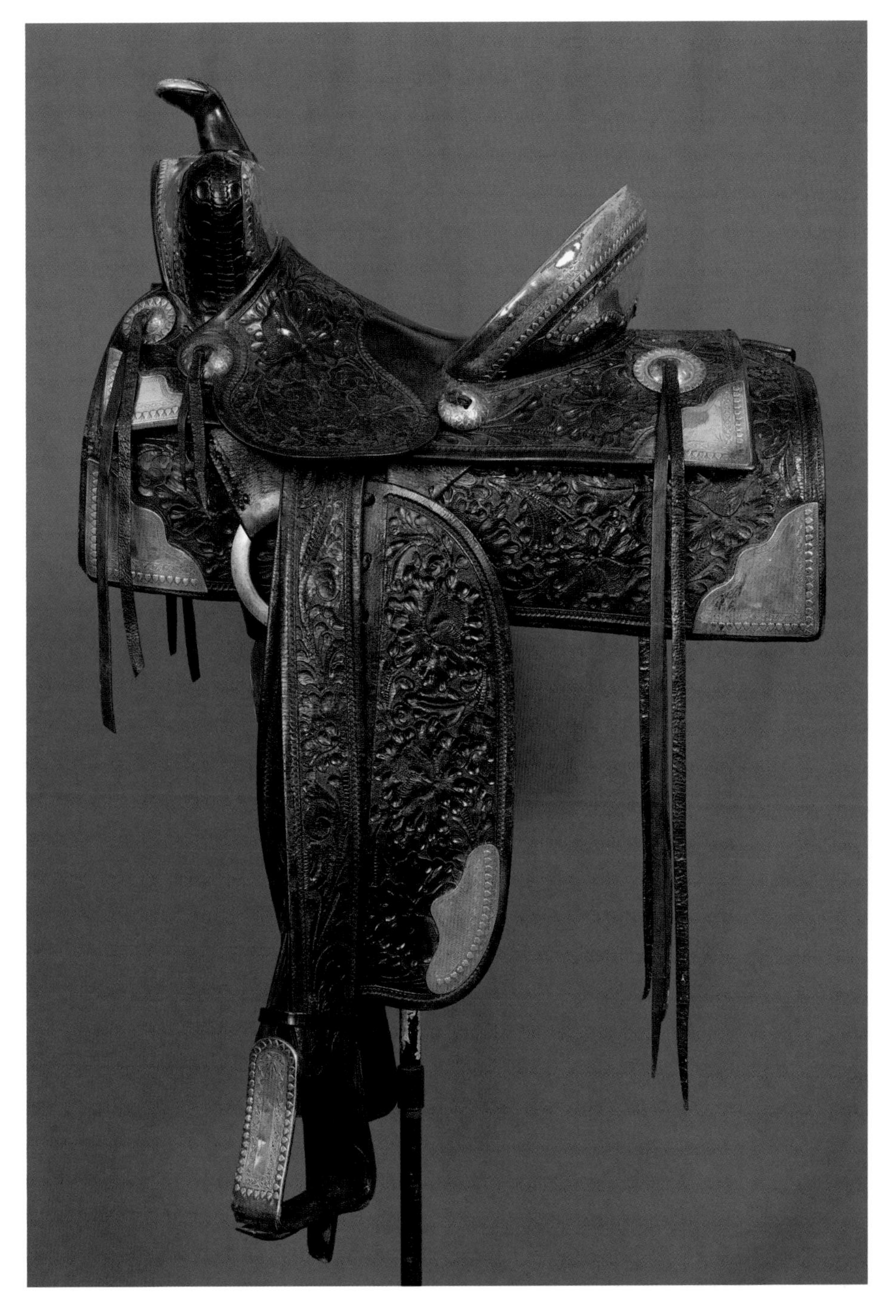

Figure 2.117.
It is quite rare to find ***Al Furstnow***–marked items from his time in Hollywood. He moved from Miles City to Hollywood later in his life for health reasons. He had known Ed Bohlin for many years as Bohlin had started making saddles in Cody, Wyoming, prior to his move to Hollywood many years earlier. It is likely that Bohlin ordered highly finished saddles and other goods from Furstnow that he subsequently had silver mounted in his shop. This connection could have certainly led to Furstnow's starting the Hollywood saddle shop and producing pieces for several movie stars. This saddle was made for and owned by "Two Gun Bill Hart," a famous early silent movie star. A statue commemorating him, titled "Range Rider of the Yellowstone," is located at the entrance to the airport in Billings, Montana. Bill Hart apparently did not have a great "movie voice" for "talkies" and faded into obscurity. His estate home containing early Western art and artifacts is a public museum in Valencia, California. This saddle was previously in the collection of one of the famous early cutting horse breeders and competitors, Rex Cauble.

Figure 2.118.
Furstnow's Hollywood Saddlery mark is clearly shown by this photo although it is an odd location on the saddle, directly under the stirrup leathers. The authors are aware of only a handful of surviving items from the time the Hollywood saddlery operated (figure 2.117).

Chaps from the Al. Furstnow Saddlery are shown in figure 2.119 through 2.138. These examples are representative of the times and of Furstnow's work, and in certain cases are not only exciting in design and materials, but also historically important. Woollies—card-suit or emblem-decorated, working-style or showy—the Al. Furstnow Saddlery made them all. We call attention in particular to chaps marked and worn by Curley, the Crow Scout who served during the Battle of the Little Bighorn (figures 2.134 through 2.136), and to perhaps the most outstanding pair of hand-made, decorative, pre-1900 chaps, marked "AL. FURSTNOW/MILES CITY, MONT." (figures 2.137 and 2.138).

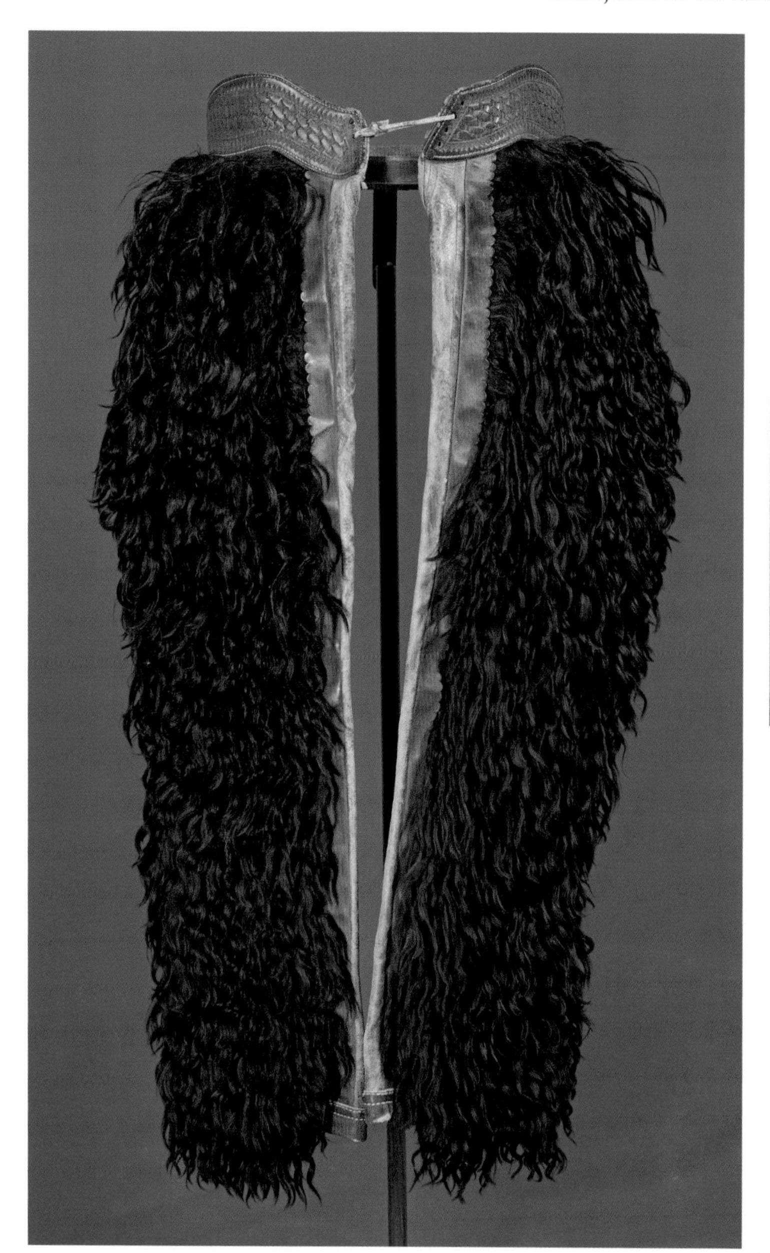

Figure 2.119.
A pretty pair of black shotgun woollies shown as No. 2 in the ***Furstnow*** catalog (No. 20). The basket-stamped belt was one dollar less than any of the five flower-stamped belts that could be ordered.

Figure 2.120.
The basket-stamped belt offered on all of the ***Al Furstnow*** chaps with a clear readable stamp in the usual location (figure 2.119).

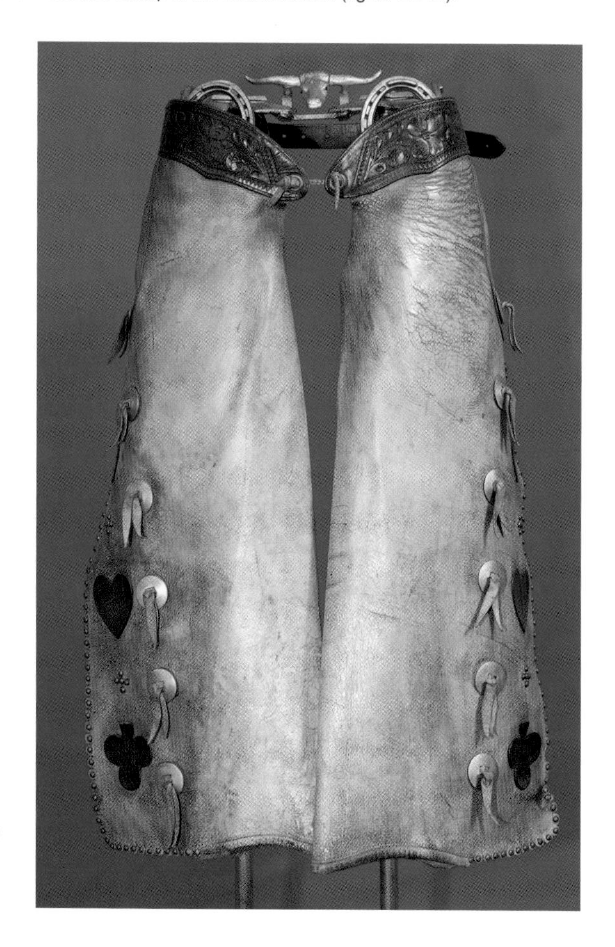

Figure 2.121.
Chap style No. 11, catalog No. 20. The "No. 1 regular" belt with metal grommets was used frequently by the saddlery throughout the years after World War I. Although there were four other belt options offered, many customers chose this one, a good indication that the chaps were made by ***Furstnow***. A couple of other saddleries used grommets but generally much later in the 1940s.

Figure 2.122.
Shown exactly as pictured in the ***Furstnow*** catalog (No. 20), "Chaparejos" style No. 11 could also be ordered with the suits of cards dyed red or black and were offered in either kip or horse hide. They were priced at $30 per pair; eight other styles were offered, of which four were more expensive. Catalog No. 20 contained a wide range of goods and was indicative of the relative economic boom that followed World War I. Catalogs in the late 1920s and throughout the 1930s generally offered smaller selections of goods, and at lower prices (figure 2.121).

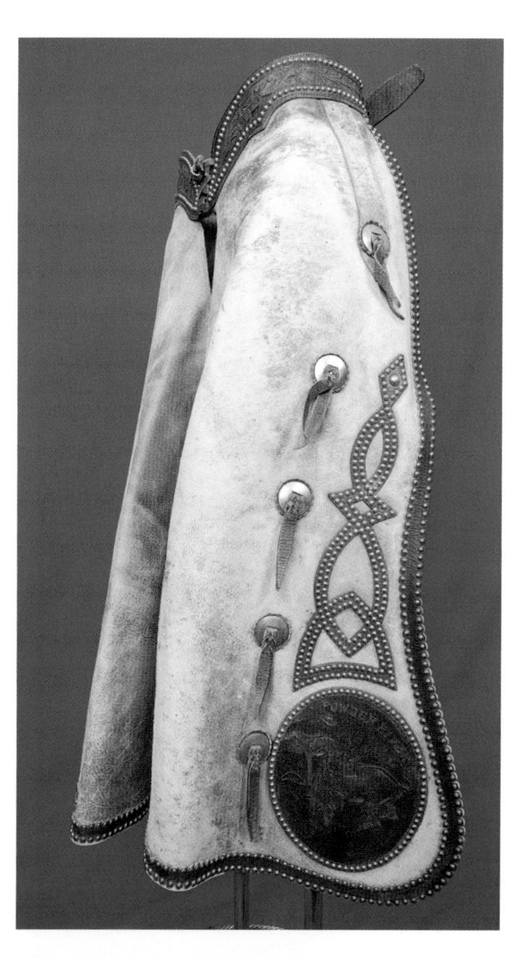

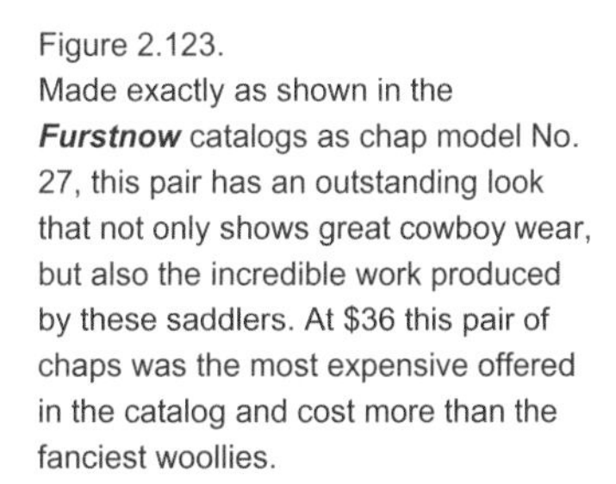

Figure 2.123.
Made exactly as shown in the ***Furstnow*** catalogs as chap model No. 27, this pair has an outstanding look that not only shows great cowboy wear, but also the incredible work produced by these saddlers. At $36 this pair of chaps was the most expensive offered in the catalog and cost more than the fanciest woollies.

Figure 2.124.
The tooled and carved panel mounted on the No. 27 chap is a fine example of the artistic ability and talent required to produce the high-quality items that were offered in the ***Furstnow*** catalog. It was noted in the catalog that this panel could be changed to incorporate names or brands requested by prospective purchasers (figure 2.123).

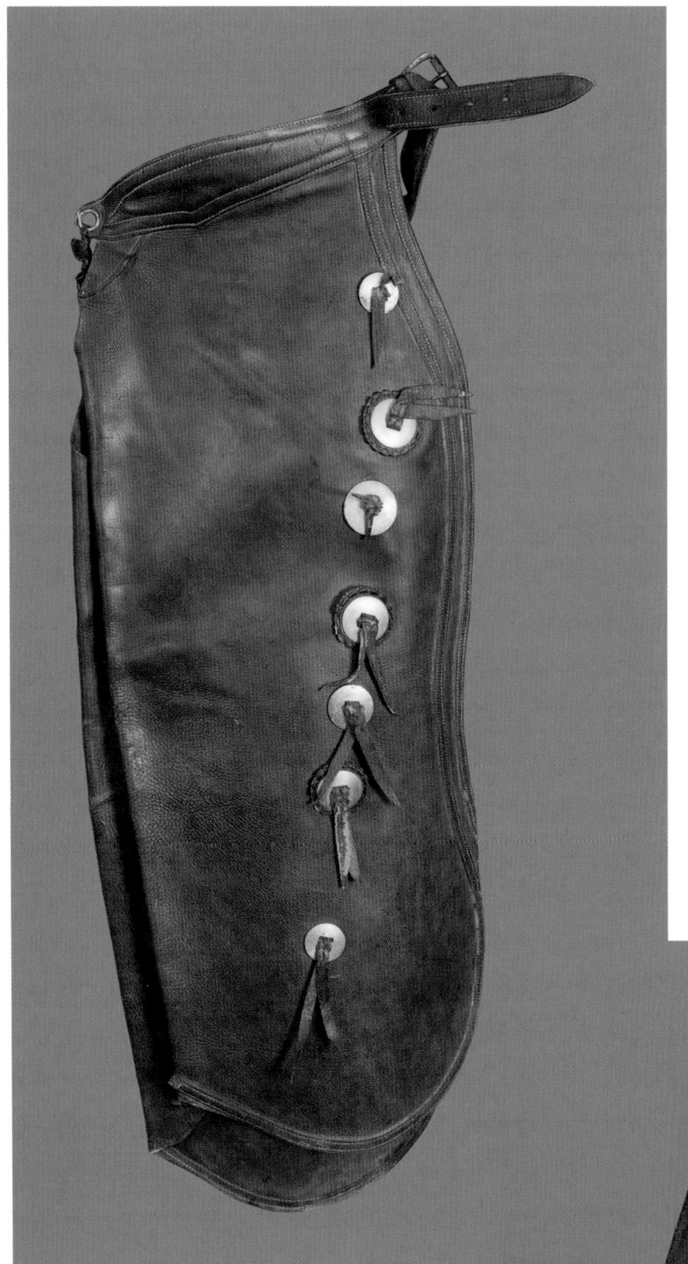

Figure 2.125.
Obviously the owner of this pair of chaps did not like big heavy batwings that flopped around when he rode and walked. He told the ***Furstnow*** saddlery to reduce the size of the batwing, and, as a result, these look almost like a pair of shotgun chaps. Other than their unique shape, these chaps appear to have been made in the 1940s or '50s.

Figure 2.126.
These chaps are a unique example of the sort of custom orders that the saddleries could produce. This pattern does not appear in the ***Furstnow*** catalogs and was therefore a custom job. The customer probably showed up with a hand-done drawing with no scale, and the saddlery measured the customer, laid out the patterns, and made a great pair of chaps that collectors today fight over to own.

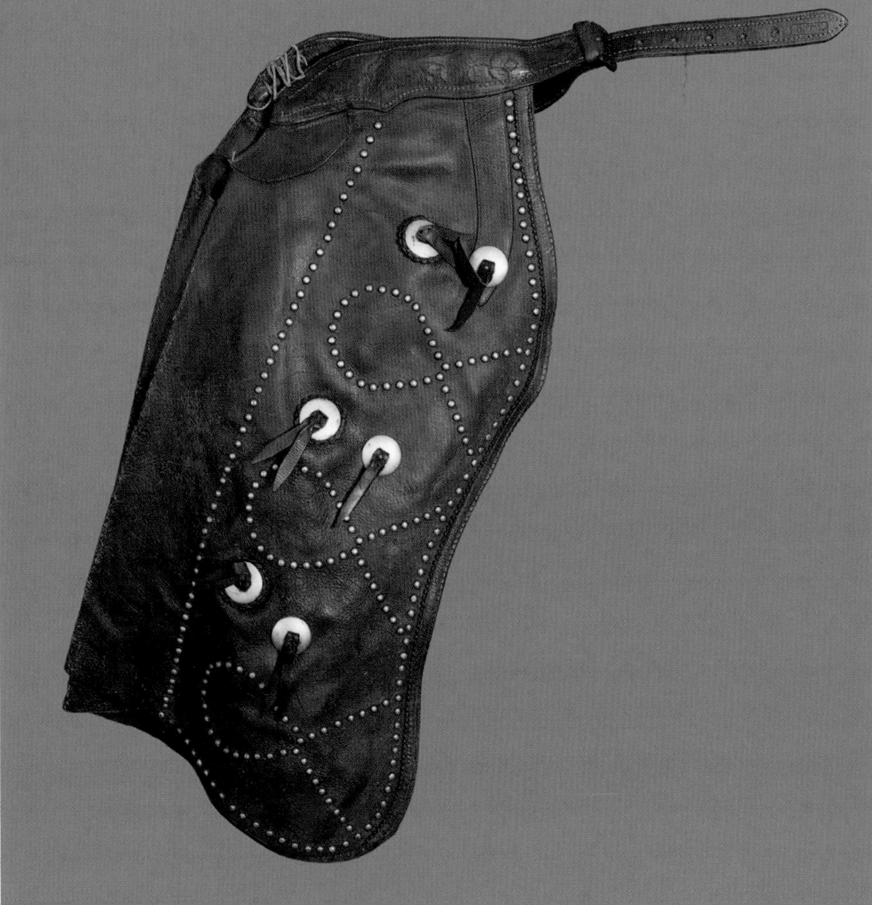

Figure 2.127.
A pair of black-and-white woollies made by the ***Furstnow Saddlery***. They are quite rare and were likely special ordered.

Figure 2.128.
These woolly chaps (***Furstnow***) went to work with a cowboy, did their job, and kept him warm. Woolly chaps did not survive well because about everything in the barn either ate them, made nests in them, and/or chewed on them (their worst enemy was probably the grandma who disliked the odor and burnt them up in the stove). Collectors appreciate woollies for the pure part of Western Americana they represent.

Figure 2.129.
Made to match the offering from the ***Furstnow*** catalog (with a couple of added touches), these chaps have both the look and outstanding condition desired by collectors.

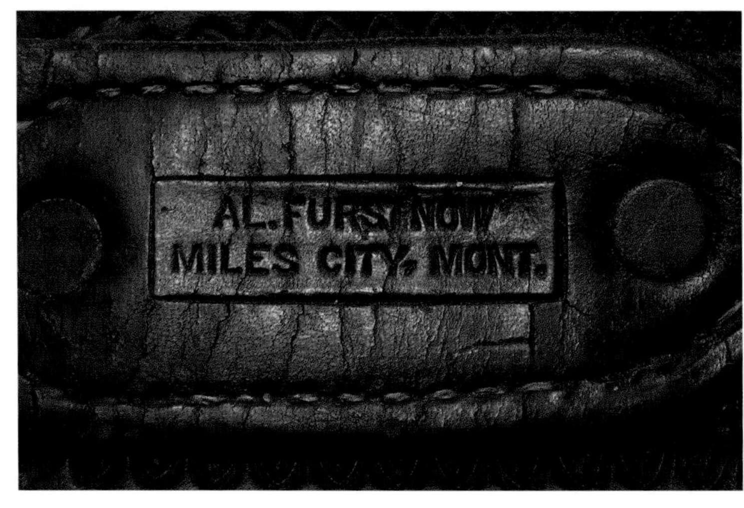

Figure 2.130.
Looking at this maker's stamp (***Furstnow***) gives a collector an immediate frame of reference as to what an original mark on an early leather item should look like. It is virtually impossible to make a fraudulently-marked item look like this one (figure 2.129).

Figure 2.131.
The first thing one notices about this pair of chaps is the ancient symbol, later used by certain Native American tribes and termed the "whirling log." When the Third Reich rose to power in Germany in the 1930s, this symbol was abandoned. The pre-1895 ***Furstnow*** stamp seems to have been used on items that were produced later, as seen on these chaps. That this pattern does not appear in the catalogs indicates a special order.

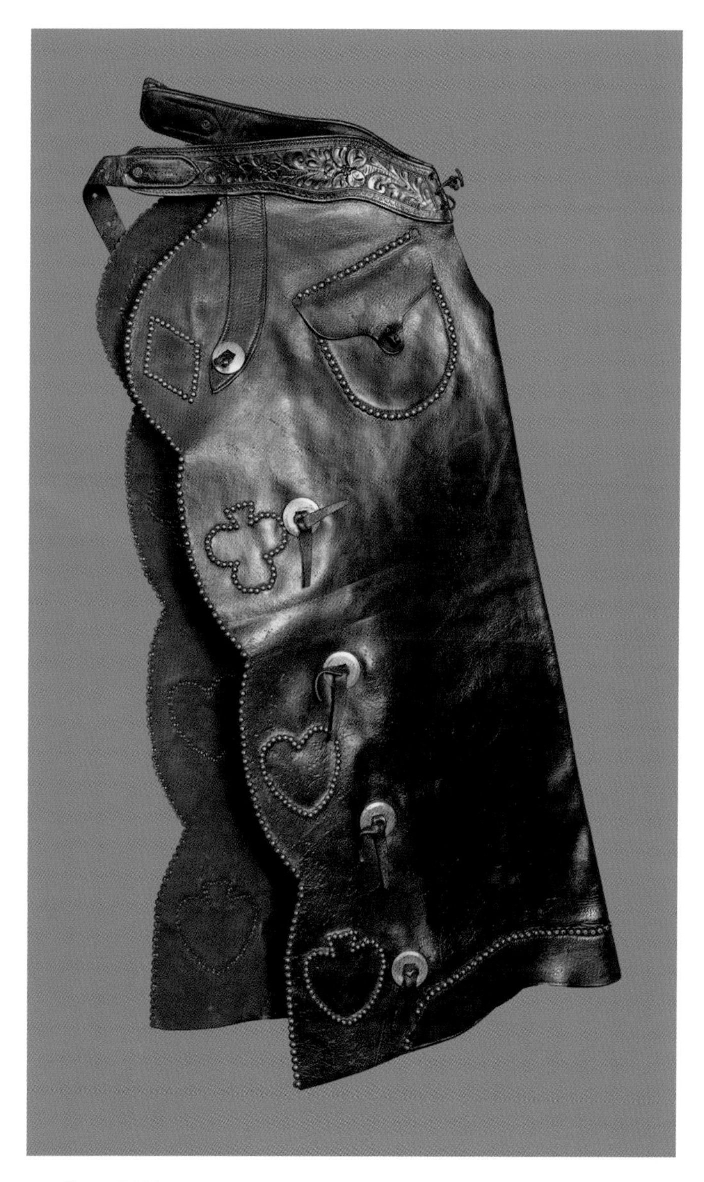

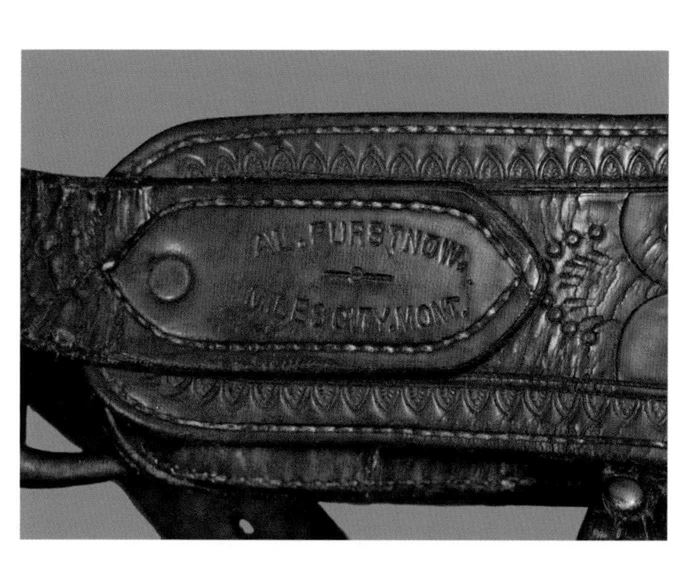

Figure 2.132.
The early ***Furstnow*** mark on a striking pair of chaps. This appears to be the earliest Furstnow mark, which would have been used from August 1894 to December 1894, when he began the partnership with C. E. Coggshall (see figure 2.131).

Figure 2.133.
This pair of chaps possesses a truly unique look. They are in extremely fine condition, and the scallops around the suit of cards studs made them special. A cowboy in the early 1900s wearing this pair of chaps at a rodeo drew the notice of all the girls.

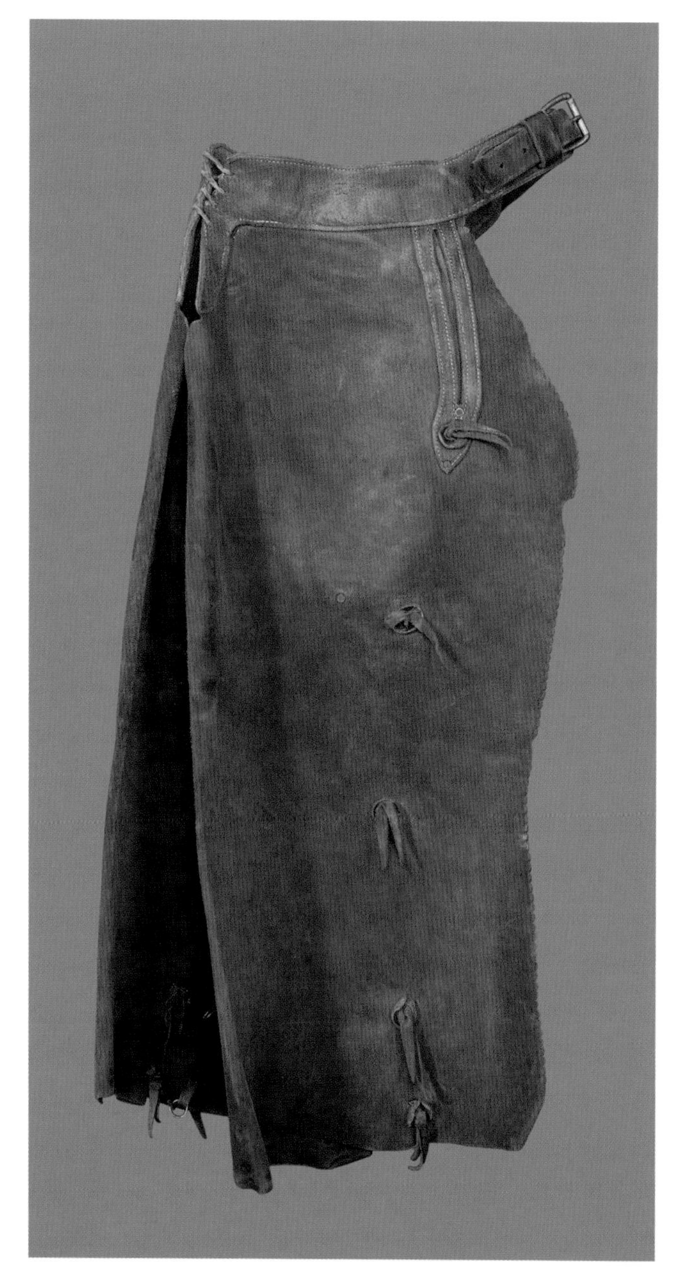

Figure 2.134.
This pair of historic chaps came to the collector in a unique way. About thirty years ago a box was delivered to him that was dripping some black oily "junk." It had a return address from the Lame Deer Trading Post, but was so nasty that it was questionable whether to open it at all. Curiosity, however, prevailed: a pair of chaps was crammed into the smallest box possible. The chaps were coal black and dripping with used motor oil. Just by chance the collector noticed the chaps were made by ***Furstnow*** and by pure luck (because every place the chaps touched instantly became covered with motor oil) he decided to look at the inside of the belt. After removing some of the oil and grime, the collector saw the name "Curley" and the year "1915" carved into the leather. Because it became obvious that these chaps were very special, the first step was to contact the Trading Post to determine the source. A phone call established that "one of the Curley boys" (grandchildren of the Crow Scout who served with General Custer) had sold them for gas money to get to a rodeo. Now they have been cleaned and are shown here for others to enjoy.

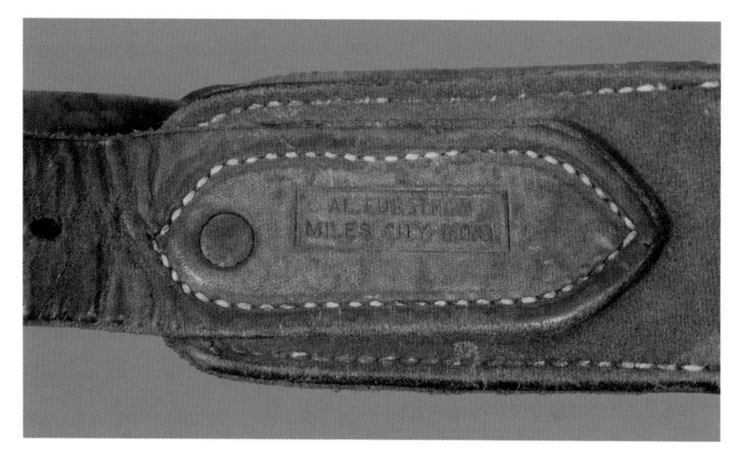

Figure 2.135.
The photo of the outside of the belt of the chaps (figure 2.134) clearly shows the ***Al Furstnow*** saddle stamp.

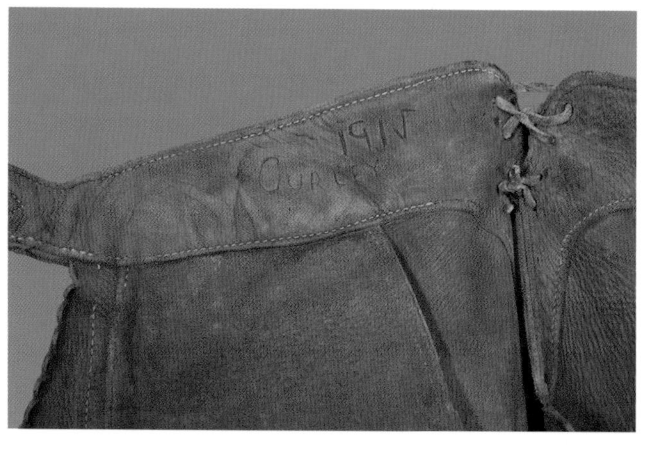

Figure 2.136.
The photo of the inside of the belt of the chaps (figure 2.134) shows the name "Curley" and the date "1915."

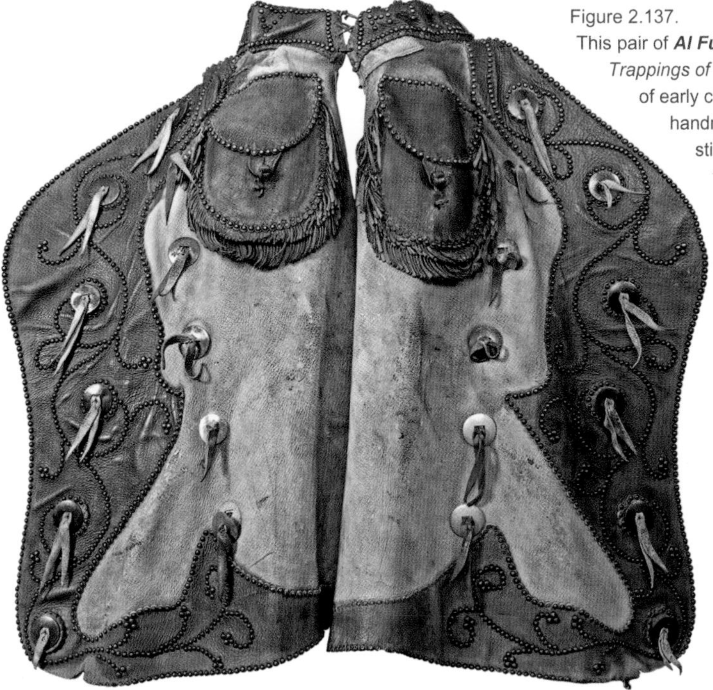

Figure 2.137.
This pair of ***Al Furstnow*** chaps is pictured on the cover of *Cowboys and the Trappings of the Old West* (1997) and is considered one of the finest pairs of early chaps discovered by collectors. They are pre-1900 and truly handmade, constructed with only "hand buckstitching" with no machine stitches in any part of the chaps. This is the only pair produced by this method known to the author.

Figure 2.138.
The ***Furstnow*** maker's mark embossed into the belt of the chaps shown in figure 2.137 and a very nice example of the stitching used for the construction.

In addition to the "Furstnow flat sap" (figures 2.139 and 2.140), another important item made by this firm was gun leather: rifle scabbards, rigs, and holsters (figures 2.141 through 2.146). Furstnow's "Hollywood" mark is shown on the "movie rig" (AL. FURSTNOW/MAKER/HOLLYWOOD, CAL.) in figure 2.144 and on the holster (FURSTNOW SADDLERY CO./MAKERS/ HOLLYWOOD, CALIF.) in figure 2.145 (compare with the Miles City mark in figure 2.146).

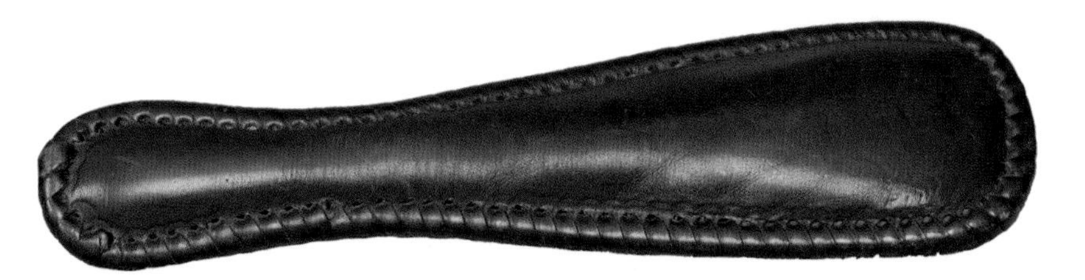

Figure 2.139.
Identified as the "***Furstnow*** Flat Sap," this item was available for sale in catalog No. 36. Catalog numbers were loosely attached to the year of their publication but were never exact. This sap was likely made earlier than 1936 because most of the items were included in catalogs due to previous demand. The catalog noted saps could be made with either sewn or laced edges, this one obviously laced.

Figure 2.140.
The standard ***Furstnow*** rectangular mark shows well on the "sap."

Figure 2.141.
Saddle scabbards that are completely basket stamped are unusual. Scabbards that have excessive amounts of tooling were often added to a saddle outfit when originally purchased. This is a large scabbard and attractively done by the maker, ***Al Furstnow.***

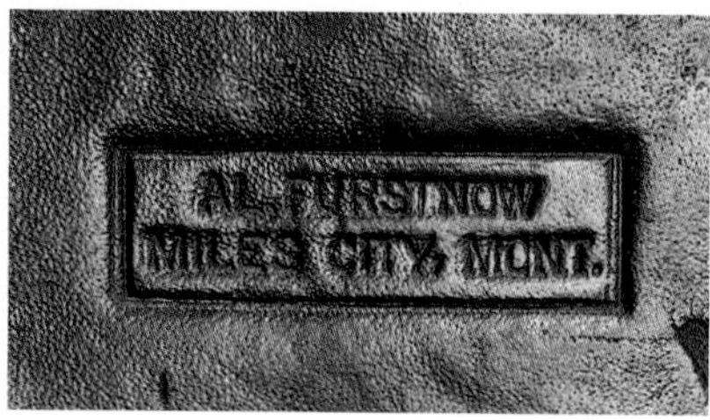

Figure 2.142.
A deeply embossed ***Al Furstnow*** rectangular mark is clearly shown. Depending on the item and the individual doing the stamping, these marks can vary from very light and nearly illegible to very deeply incised, as seen on this one (figure 2.141).

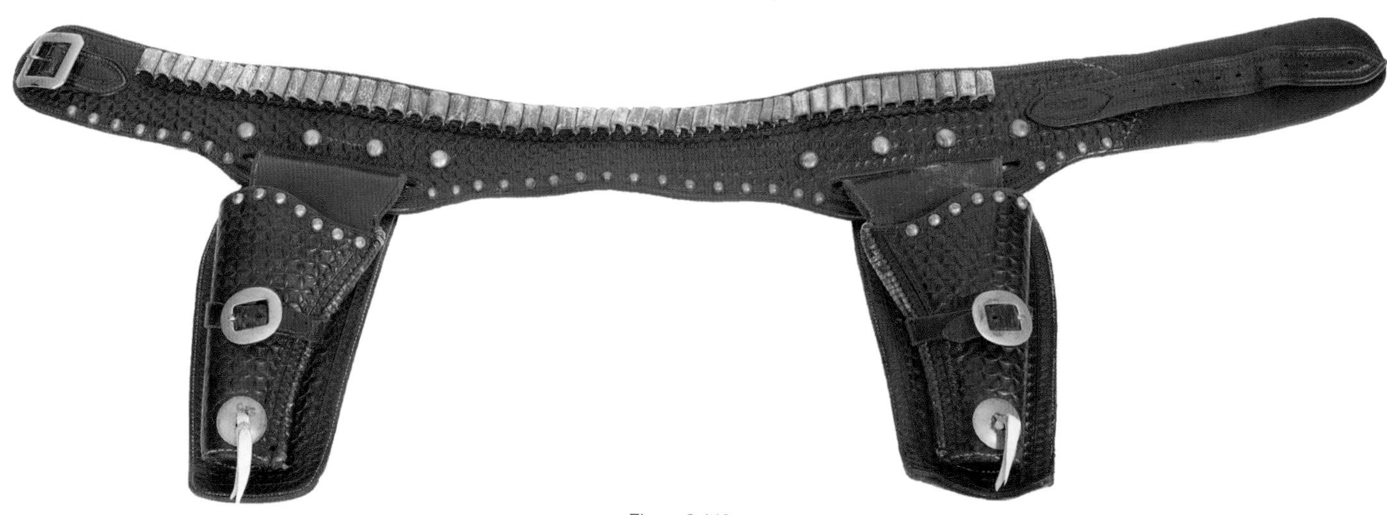

Figure 2.143.
A well-marked "movie rig" always starts collectors on a photo hunt to determine for whom it was made. This ***Al Furstnow Hollywood California***-marked movie rig is well used, but we have been unable to identify the actor or the movie in which it was used.

Figure 2.144.
The ***Furstnow*** mark from the Hollywood Saddlery is unique and different from the earlier marks used in Miles City. Both the belt and the holsters are marked on this fancy movie rig (see figure 2.143).

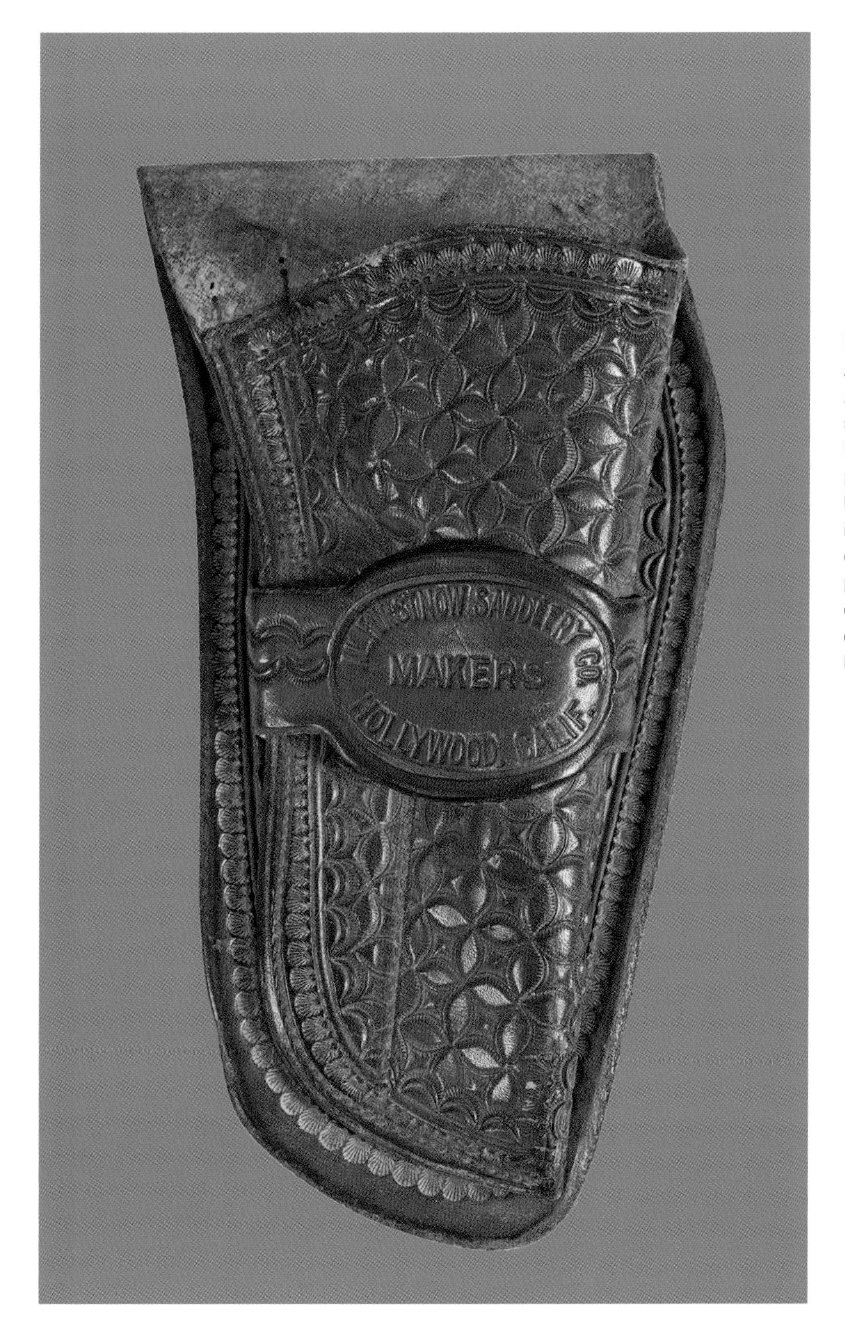

Figure 2.145.
An example of the larger of the ***Furstnow Saddlery Company*** stamps used when he moved to Hollywood, California. The tooling pattern is different from those used by the saddlers at his original shop in Miles City and might have been done intentionally to differentiate products from the two shops (or it could have been a function of the different personnel he employed in Hollywood).

Figure 2.146.
The master carvers at the ***Furstnow*** saddlery have skillfully incorporated a rather blasé lettered stamp into the gorgeous tooled background of the item, a practice requiring years of experience.

Other collectible and/or rarely-seen pieces produced by this firm include highly decorated leather cuffs (figures 2.147 through 2.149), a set of pre-1920 saddle bags (figures 2.150 and 2.151), an ornate riding martingale with celluloid rings and fancy studding (figure 2.152), spur straps (figures 2.153 through 2.155), and an interesting tooled leather collar, made for dressy occasions (figures 2.156 through 2.157).

Two highly unusual Furstnow products can be seen in figures 2.258 and 2.159 (a leather dice cup marked by Furstnow and embossed with the owner's name, Geo. Myers, and in figures 2.160 and 2.161 (a leather cribbage board made for the Bullard Block Bar in Miles City).

The presentation saddle "Pride of the Yellowstone" was awarded to the winner of the Montana Riding Contest at the 1914 Miles City Roundup. Figures 2.162 through 2.165 illustrate the magnificent tooling, fine lines, silver conchos, and corner elements, and inscriptions worked into the leather on the front and back of the cantle. This saddle, with a bucking bronc on the side jockey and a flying eagle on the fender, was won by Lee Caldwell in 1914. Prior to the presentation, both Charles Russell and the Governor of Montana rode the saddle in the daily parades associated with the Rodeo. Lee Caldwell, making a stunning ride on "Flying Devil," appears in the photograph in figure 2.166, as he won the Bucking Horse Contest at the Miles City RoundUP [*sic*] in 1914.

Figure 2.147.
Al Furstnow catalogs show this as cuff No. 48 in the catalogs from No. 9 through No. 31—the cuff shown in the photo matches exactly the example shown in the catalog. This catalog showed five styles of cuffs: two studded, two floral tooled, and one relatively plain with a border design. The full floral was the most expensive, followed by this studded pair, which cost $2.75 c. 1932.

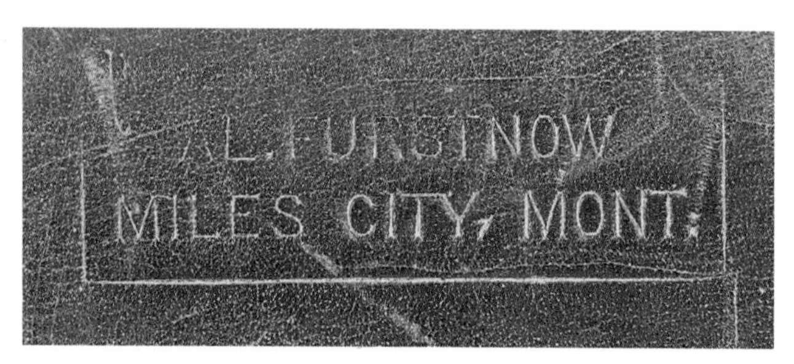

Figure 2.148.
The ***Al Furstnow*** stamp on this pair of cuffs was applied very lightly—if the cuffs had suffered significant wear it would probably not be visible (figure 2.147).

Figure 2.149.
These cuffs were intended to be a showpiece for the best-dressed cowboy or businessman. They were shown as item No. 51 in the ***Furstnow*** catalogs from No. 9 through No. 31. Obviously made by a master craftsman, these showcase almost every style of tooling and carving on one item.

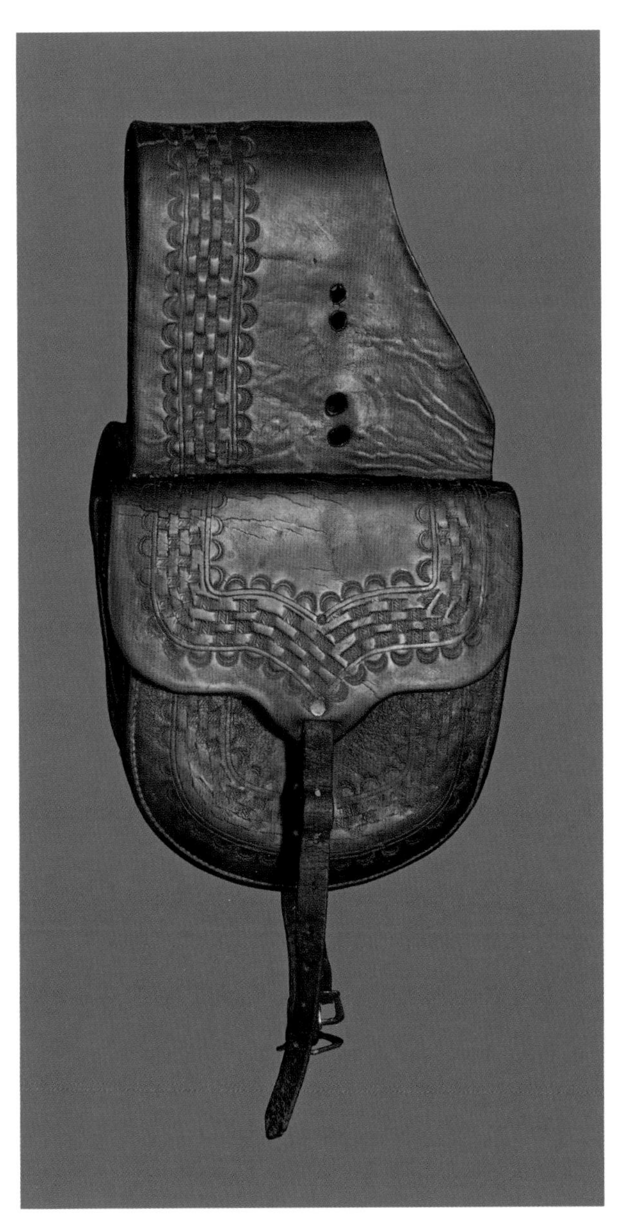

Figure 2.150.
Smaller-sized saddle pockets seem generally to have been made earlier; as time progressed cowboys must have wanted more room, necessitating larger bags. These nice little bags with exceptional hand tooling were made prior to about 1920 by ***Al Furstnow***.

Figure 2.151.
The ***Al Furstnow***, Miles City large saddle stamp that was used on a pair of fairly small saddle pockets (figure 2.150). It is rare to find this mark on something this small.

Figure 2.152.
Called a "Running Martingale" and listed as item No. 120 in ***Al Furstnow*** catalog No. 36, this equipment is a beautiful example of how to dress up your horse and make him more responsive at the same time. The celluloid rings were referred to as a "running martingale" by the cowboys in Montana. This item is rare because most saddlery items were passed down from generation to generation in the same family and eventually wore out.

Figure 2.153.
Al Furstnow spur straps that were sold as catalog pattern No. 3 in many of the catalogs. This pattern was made for many years and was very popular with the cowboys; only pattern No. 5 is more often found. This pair of straps has the owner's brand incised into the inside leather: "DD," with a quarter circle placed under the DDs.

Figure 2.154.
Al Furstnow-marked spur straps are difficult to find because they wore out quickly. This pair is still in decent condition; although Furstnow offered between 6 and 10 different spur strap options in every catalog, this tooling pattern we were unable to find.

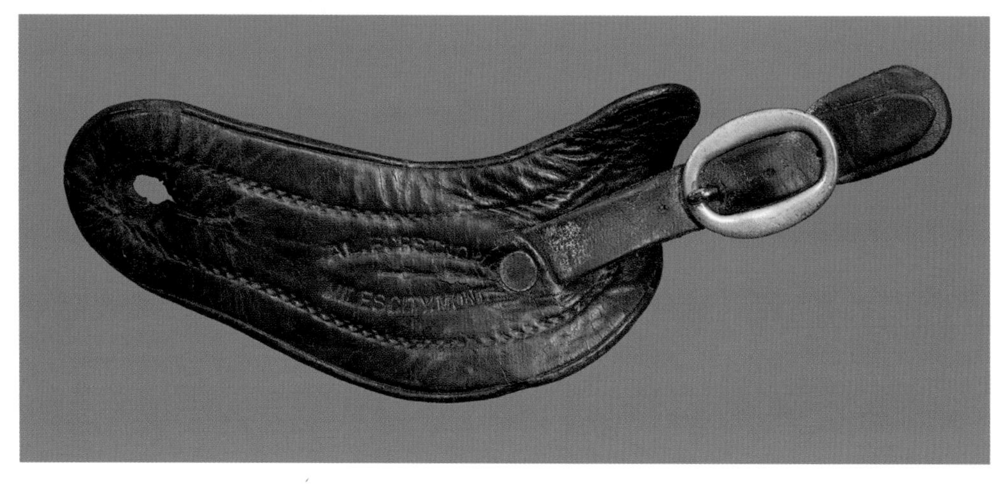

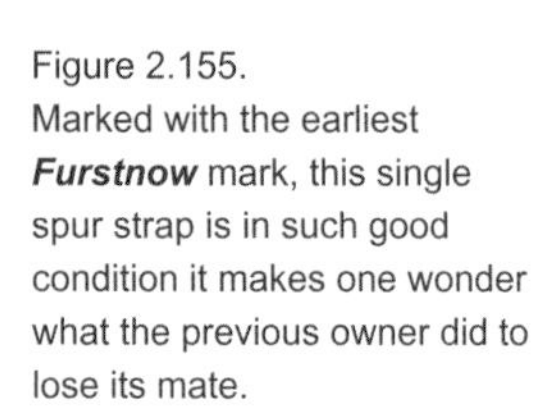

Figure 2.155.
Marked with the earliest ***Furstnow*** mark, this single spur strap is in such good condition it makes one wonder what the previous owner did to lose its mate.

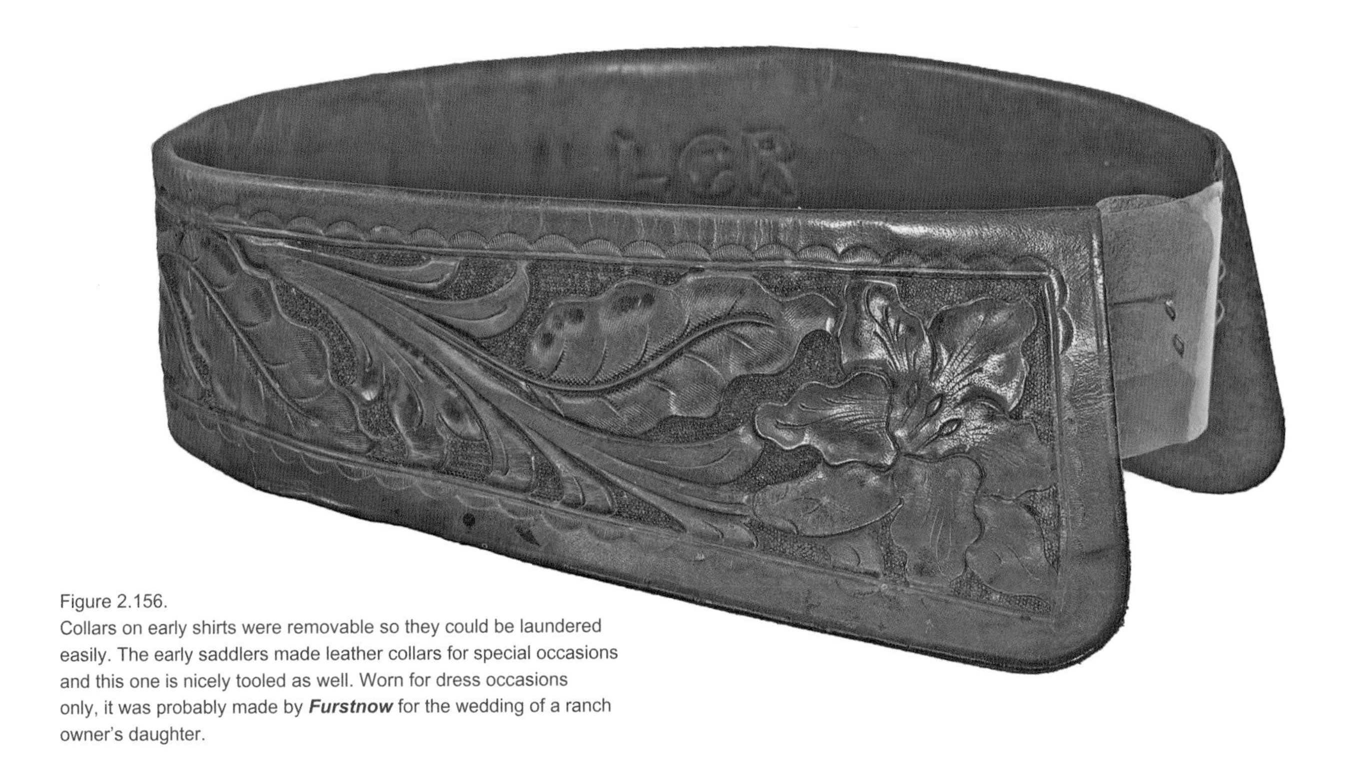

Figure 2.156.
Collars on early shirts were removable so they could be laundered easily. The early saddlers made leather collars for special occasions and this one is nicely tooled as well. Worn for dress occasions only, it was probably made by ***Furstnow*** for the wedding of a ranch owner's daughter.

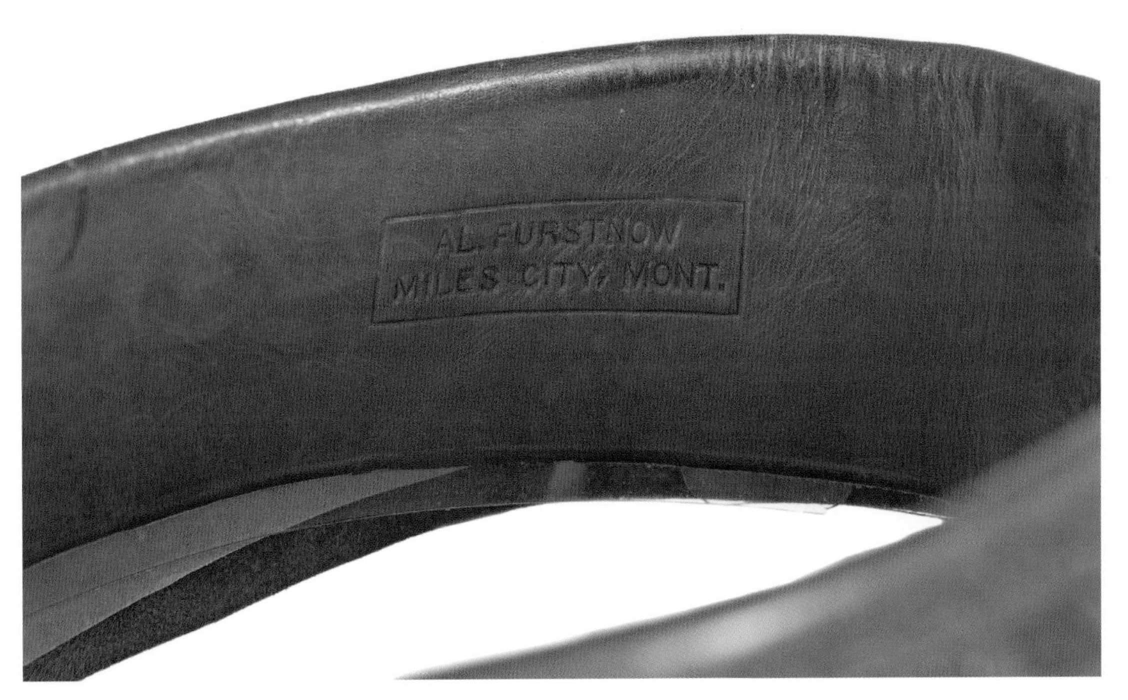

Figure 2.157.
Clearly but delicately marked inside the collar, this piece shows little use after ***Al Furstnow*** made it (figure 2.156).

Figure 2.158.
Dice cups were not unusual, especially around bars. They are generally used to gamble with the house for free drinks and occasionally for money. This cup is extremely rare (as it is stamped by ***Al Furstnow***), fully floral-carved, and embossed with the owner's name, Geo. Myers. George Myers and his brothers were in Miles City from early 1879 or 1880. They owned several ranches; eventually George also owned a bar from which this undoubtedly survives.

Figure 2.159.
A clever bit of advertising by ***Furstnow*** was to emboss the dice cup with this saddlery stamp and some tooling, in view every time the cup was tipped over (figure 2.158).

Figure 2.160.
It is always exciting to find items that the saddleries did not make as part of their day-to-day operation. In this case the item is a cribbage board and it is made for the Bullard Block Bar. The Bullard Block was made famous in an early 1880s photograph by the famed photographer L. A. Huffman. William (Bill) Bullard arrived in Milestown in 1877 and was with Nelson Miles at both the Lame Deer fight and the capture of Chief Joseph at the battle of the Bear Paw. He became sheriff in c. 1879 and operated Bullard's, after which the block is named. The Bullard Block Bar was associated with his brewery. This cribbage board was probably used by the patrons to win both drinks and money.

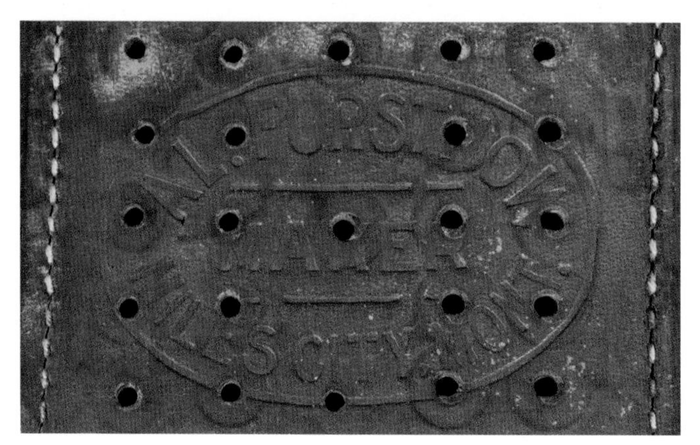

Figure 2.161.
The early "saddle stamp" that ***Furstnow*** used on most of his larger production items—it is unusual to find it on something as small as a cribbage board (see figure 2.160). The early catalogs do not show a cribbage board, however; in catalog 31 it is shown as item No. 171 and described as "skirting leather doubled and stitched"; it could be purchased for $2.

Figure 2.162.
Al Furstnow made this saddle for presentation to the winner of the Montana Riding contest at the 1914 Miles City Roundup. The saddle, shown in the Furstnow catalogs of the period, is the finest saddle they offered. Called "The Pride of the Yellowstone," it cost about $500 at the time it was awarded to the winner, Lee Caldwell. The saddle is beautifully tooled, and has silver mounted corners on the skirts and borders on the conchos. It should be noted that prior to 1914 the Miles City Rodeo was a more local event and was known as the "Powder River Roundup" (where the battle cry "Powder River, Let'r buck" originated). In 1914 additional prize money was raised and the city fathers tried to make Miles City a part of the rodeo circuit that included Cheyenne, Pendleton, and Calgary. The prize saddle and the attendance of the governor and Charlie Russell were also part of the promotion.

Figure 2.163.
A profile view of the "Pride of the Yellowstone" saddle (figure 2-136), the most expensive saddle in the ***Furstnow*** catalog for many years. It shows the finest in tooling, with the bucking bronc on the side jockey and the flying eagle on the fender. This very saddle was won by Lee Caldwell in the 1914 Rodeo and was ridden in the daily parades before the presentation by Charlie Russell and the Governor of Montana, both of whom were present at the Rodeo.

Figure 2.164.
The back of the seat (figure 2.163) is beautifully tooled. Prior to 1914, the Miles City Rodeo was known as the "Powder River Roundup," and its logo therefore appears on the saddle seat.

Figure 2.165.
An example of the leather carver's unique skill. The photo is self-explanatory and one can enjoy the work for the artistry it exhibits (figure 2.62).

Figure 2.166.
The real photo postcard shown here is one of the more famous early rodeo cards and has been reproduced extensively over the years. It shows the rodeo rider Lee Caldwell winning the "Bucking Horse Contest" at the 1914 Miles City Roundup and, in the process, the "Pride of the Yellowstone" trophy saddle presented by the ***Furstnow Saddlery*** (figure 2.162). Almost every collector has seen this image at one time or another. Lee Caldwell when interviewed some years later said it was the best and most difficult ride he had made during his rodeo career.

VIII. Miles City Saddlery

The Miles City Saddlery was created in 1909, when C. E. Coggshall sold his business to Frank Jelinek, Bert Coleman, and Clem Kathman for approximately $9,500. Kathman, the only leather worker of the trio, had been Coggshall's shop foreman. The zenith of their manufacturing era spanned the years 1910–1919, similar to the Al. Furstnow Saddlery, its major competitor in Miles City. Glenn VerBeck reports that in 1919, a record-high number of over 1,900 saddles were made; the average number in the period from 1913–1917 was 1,557, a low estimate (VerBeck, 1998). Following the death of Klathmann in 1936 (Coleman had died in 1917), at a time when the firm was struggling to remain viable, Pete VerBeck assumed the roles of shop foreman and manager. A highlight of the saddlery's output was the silver outfit (saddle, bridle, martingale, et al.) created for Crown Prince Olaf of Norway, upon his visit to the United States in 1939.

Figure 2.167.
R. C. Morrison photograph of the ***Miles City Saddlery***, on 6th Street, Miles City, Montana.

After the deaths of his two partners, Frank Jelinek and the firm's bookkeeper Joe Conway became joint owners of the Miles City Saddlery until 1939, at which point Conway and his sons assumed ownership until 1962. The saddle shop, which had subsequently become a western store, was formally closed in 1961, with the transfer of the equipment and the stamp "Coggshall Saddle" to Carl Wilson, their last saddle maker.

The Miles City Saddlery printed mail-order catalogs that were the envy of the industry. They advertised themselves as "Makers of the Original Coggshall Saddles" and included lengthy descriptions, photographs, and illustrations of Coggshall's Improved Saddle Trees in a number of styles (for example, Montana, Nelson, Taylor, Visalia, Ladesma), several of which are shown as finished saddles in the figures in this section. The firm emphatically stated, "We positively use no Penitentiary made Trees" in bold type.

A major contributor to the early success of the Miles City Saddlery was World War I and the attendant need for horses and their equipment; Montana was a target state for the purchase of horses, and the eastern Montana saddleries especially profited from government contracts. Catalog No. 29 (approximately 1928–1930), published during the Depression years, featured a strong selection of team and work harness, as well as men's outdoor/ranch clothing, Fish brand slickers, and eleven pages of men's Stetson hats.

An early photograph by R. C. Morrison of the Miles City Saddlery, on 6th Street, Miles City, Montana, is shown in figure 2.167, and the Miles City Saddlery safe, in figure 2.168. A letter and envelope from the firm to Mr. R. J. Scates (figures 2.169 and 2.170) illustrates its stationery and advertising, and includes a lengthy description of the saddlery, its history, products, reputation, and guarantee.

Figure 2.168.
A safe from the ***Miles City Saddlery Co.***, decorative and very sound.

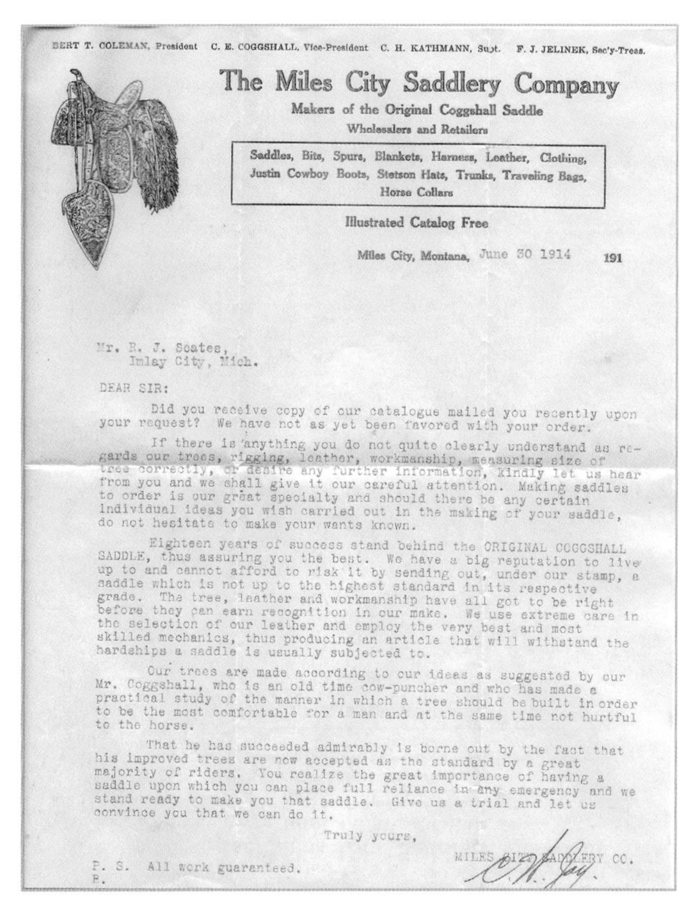

BERT T. COLEMAN, President C. E. COGGSHALL, Vice-President C. H. KATHMANN, Supt. F. J. JELINEK, Sec'y-Treas.

The Miles City Saddlery Company

Makers of the Original Coggshall Saddle

Wholesalers and Retailers

Saddles, Bits, Spurs, Blankets, Harness, Leather, Clothing, Justin Cowboy Boots, Stetson Hats, Trunks, Traveling Bags, Horse Collars

Illustrated Catalog Free

Miles City, Montana, June 30 1914 191

Mr. R. J. Scates,
Imlay City, Mich.

DEAR SIR:

Did you receive copy of our catalogue mailed you recently upon your request? We have not as yet been favored with your order.

If there is anything you do not quite clearly understand as regards our trees, rigging, leather, workmanship, measuring size of tree correctly, or desire any further information, kindly let us hear from you and we shall give it our careful attention. Making saddles to order is our great specialty and should there be any certain individual ideas you wish carried out in the making of your saddle, do not hesitate to make your wants known.

Eighteen years of success stand behind the ORIGINAL COGGSHALL SADDLE, thus assuring you the best. We have a big reputation to live up to and cannot afford to risk it by sending out, under our stamp, a saddle which is not up to the highest standard in its respective grade. The tree, leather and workmanship have all got to be right before they can earn recognition in our make. We use extreme care in the selection of our leather and employ the very best and most skilled mechanics, thus producing an article that will withstand the hardships a saddle is usually subjected to.

Our trees are made according to our ideas as suggested by our Mr. Coggshall, who is an old time cow-puncher and who has made a practical study of the manner in which a tree should be built in order to be the most comfortable for a man and at the same time not hurtful to the horse.

That he has succeeded admirably is borne out by the fact that his improved trees are now accepted as the standard by a great majority of riders. You realize the great importance of having a saddle upon which you can place full reliance in any emergency and we stand ready to make you that saddle. Give us a trial and let us convince you that we can do it.

Truly yours,

MILES CITY SADDLERY CO.
C. W. Jay.

P. S. All work guaranteed.
B.

Figure 2.169.
Letter from ***Miles City Saddlery*** dated June 30, 1914, describing the firm's history, products, reputation, and guarantee. *Courtesy of Brian Lebel.*

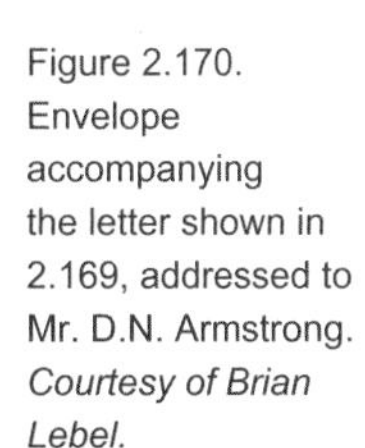

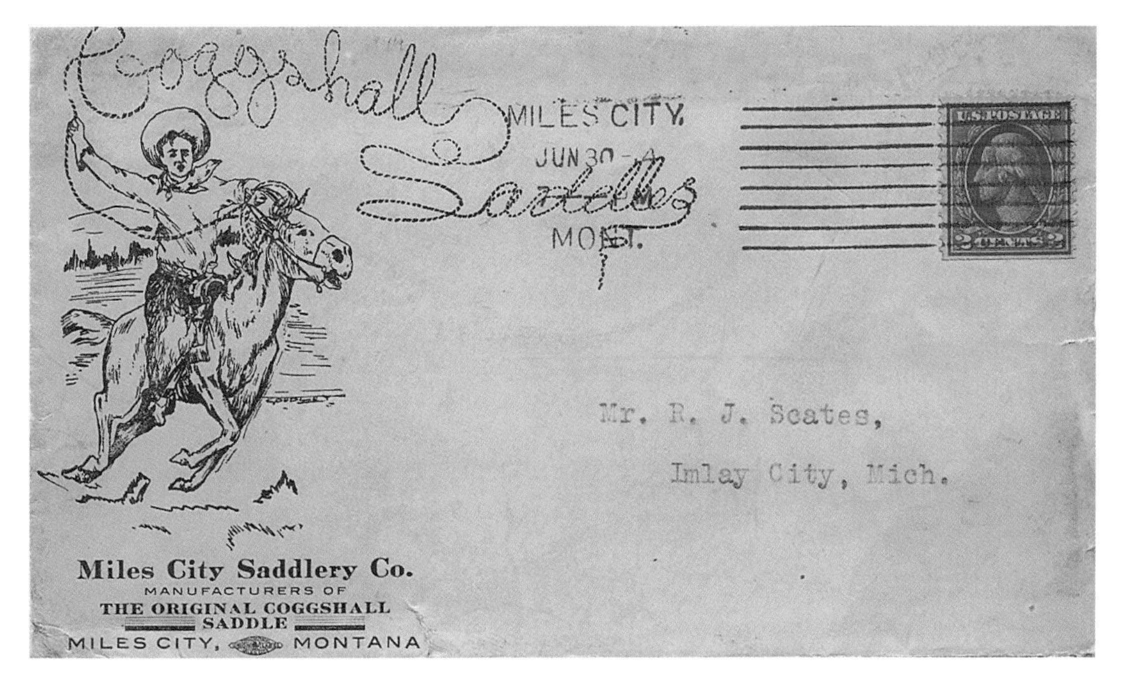

Figure 2.170.
Envelope accompanying the letter shown in 2.169, addressed to Mr. D.N. Armstrong. *Courtesy of Brian Lebel.*

The Miles City Saddlery Co. advertised itself as "the manufacturers of the original Coggshall Saddle." Indeed they were known for their beautiful and well-constructed saddles, several of which are shown in figures 2.171 through 2.191. It is important to note that the saddlery imported fair skirting from out-of-state tanneries such as S. H. Frank & Co. of San Francisco, as well as California-made spurs and bits (Griff Durham, personal communication). An extraordinary saddle, decorated with heart-shaped silver pieces engraved by the famous Miles City silversmith and jeweler Ed Klapmeier (1896–1983), was custom-made for William S. Hart (figures 2.171 through 2.174). Figures 2.175 through 2.179 show a pair of fancy saddles made for Gus and Helen Albert of Miles City. Although these ornate and beautifully tooled saddles appear identical, Helen's saddle (unsurprisingly) was smaller. Probably used for parades, both saddles were finished with the "Lazy H" brand, belonging to the Alberts.

Another historically interesting saddle appears in figures 2.184 and 2.185. A one-of-a-kind Rodeo Presentation saddle, the date "July 1-2-3 1920" has been tooled onto the back of the cantle, and on the front, "BUCKING CONTEST FIRST PRIZE." In addition to personalizing some of their saddles with, for example, the owner's initials (figure 2.187 and 2.189), the saddlery also fabricated custom-order saddles, with an unusual horn or special tree, for their clients (figure 2.190). To accompany certain saddles, Miles City Saddlery sold tapaderos of different styles, although these fittings were not frequently requested and, hence, are rare (figures 2.192 through 2.194).

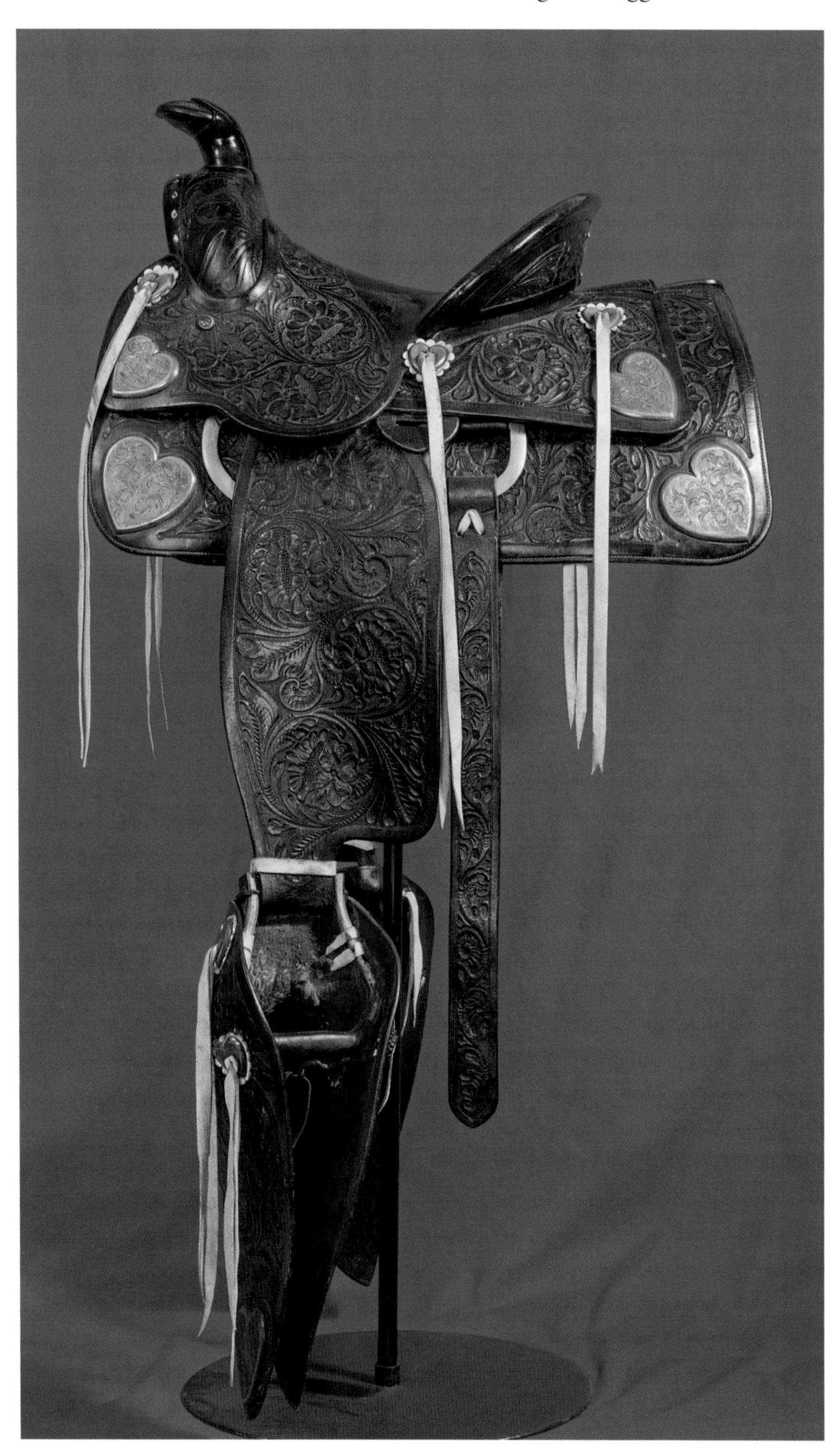

Figure 2.171.
The ***Miles City Saddlery*** made a fine custom-silver-mounted saddle for the famous silent movie star William S. Hart. Hart certainly had this saddle, bridle, spurs, and other accessories made during the height of his popularity. He rode it in movies, during photo shoots, and in the many parades of the era that were used to publicize his films. Several of the silver pieces on the saddle were made and marked by Klapmeier, a renowned Miles City silversmith (it is possible he did the hearts as well). William S. Hart was a popular western hero during the entire silent move era and was a friend of both Will Rogers and C. M. Russell. Hart's home in Valencia, California, is now a public museum—the house contains some priceless Russell, Remington, and J. H. Sharp art hung ceiling-to-floor throughout. The stable is also open to viewing and contains several incredible Deer Lodge horsehair bridles.

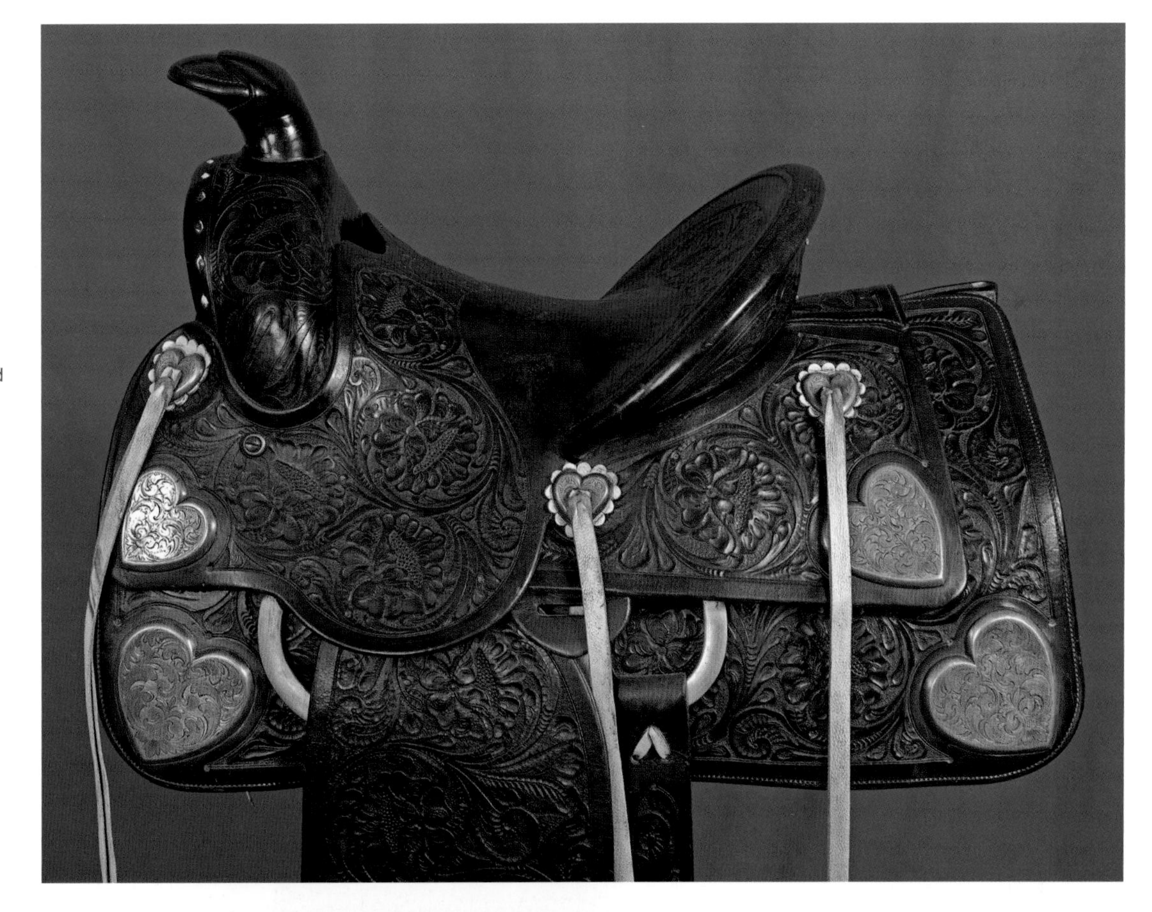

Figure 2.172.
William S. Hart's ***Miles City Saddlery*** silver saddle (figure 2.171), showing the heart-shaped silver decorations by Klapmeier.

Figure 2.173.
Miles City Saddlery mark, which includes "ORIGINAL COGGSHALL SADDLES," on the William S. Hart saddle (figure 2-144). The number "673" is marked prominently under the cartouche.

Figure 2.174.
William S. Hart's name is prominent on the silver cantle plate shown in this photo. As described at figure 2.171, there is quite a bit of marked ***Klapmeier*** silver on the saddle.

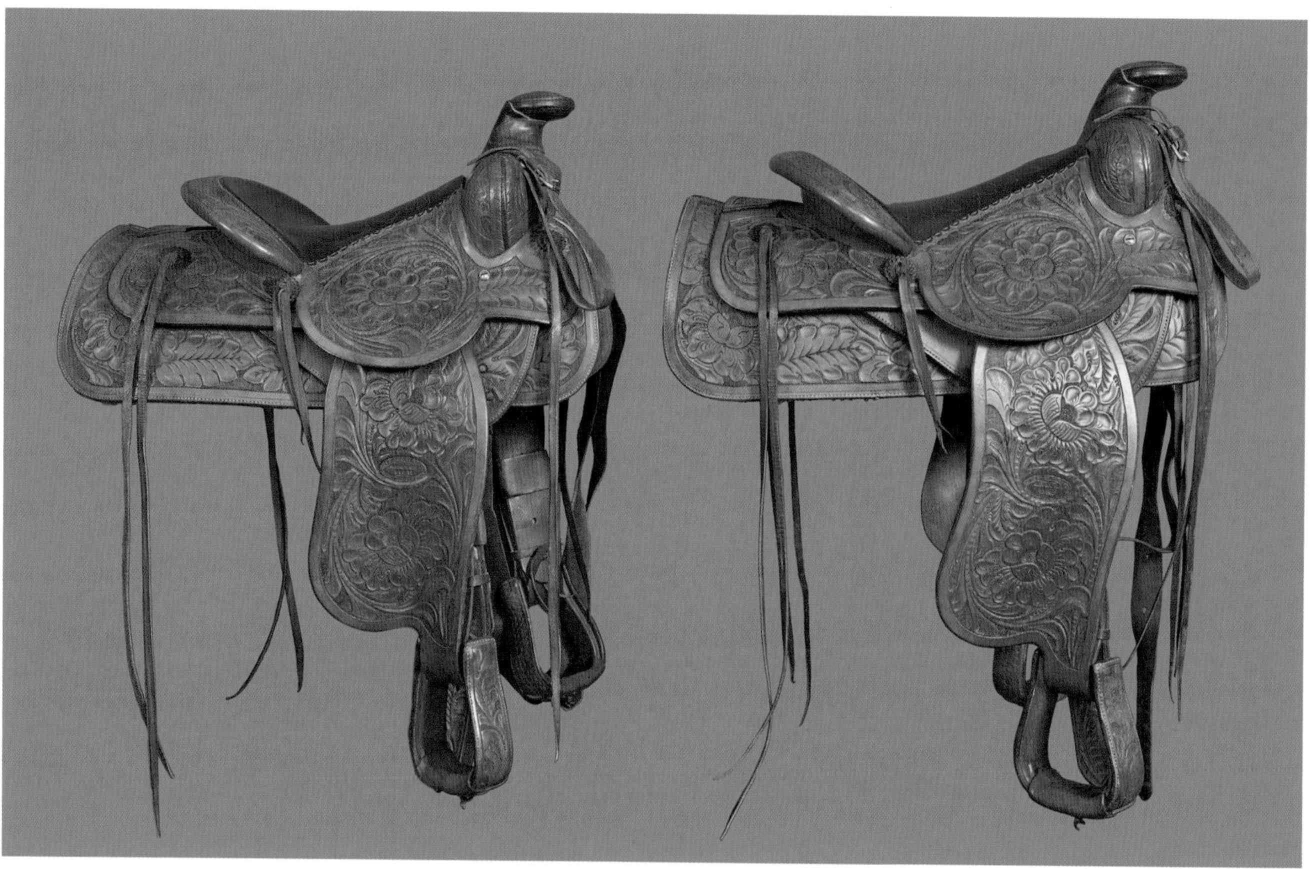

Figure 2.175.
These views of the Albert saddles allow one to appreciate the ability of the saddler to make two items that are mirror images of each other except for the size. The ***Miles City Saddlery*** Catalog No. 32 (red cover) shows these saddles to be style 169 with a slightly different tooling pattern from that shown in the catalog. It was called the "duck bill roper," one of the worst names imaginable for a saddle.

Figure 2.176.
These saddles were made for Gus and Helen Albert of Miles City by the ***Miles City Saddlery***. This view of the saddles shows how closely they matched, the only difference being the smaller size of Helen's saddle.

Figure 2.177.
This view of the ***Miles City*** maker's mark on the fender of the saddle (figure 2.175) shows how much effort went into the tooling. The mark is intertwined with leaves and flowers, and the stamping in between is dyed a darker color such that the tooling stands out prominently.

Figure 2.178.
This profile of the Helen Albert saddle shows a fully floral-carved ***Miles City Saddlery*** saddle with a padded seat. It was obviously made to ride in a parade and might have occasionally gone out with the cowboys when they were "moving a few cows" (figure 2.175).

Figure 2.179.
The back of the cantle shows the "lazy H" brand and the sequential numbering system that was adopted by both the ***Miles City Saddlery*** and Al Furstnow around the end of World War II. The number is 28, i.e., the 28th saddle that the Miles City Saddlery made in 1954 (figure 2.175).

Figure 2.180.
Many times people that did not own cattle made up their own rather unique and sometimes humorous brands. In this case, the "lazy H lazy G" rafter brand is a statement on the employment status of Helen and Gus Albert, who were probably retired when they belonged to the Sage Riders; it was not a working cattle brand.

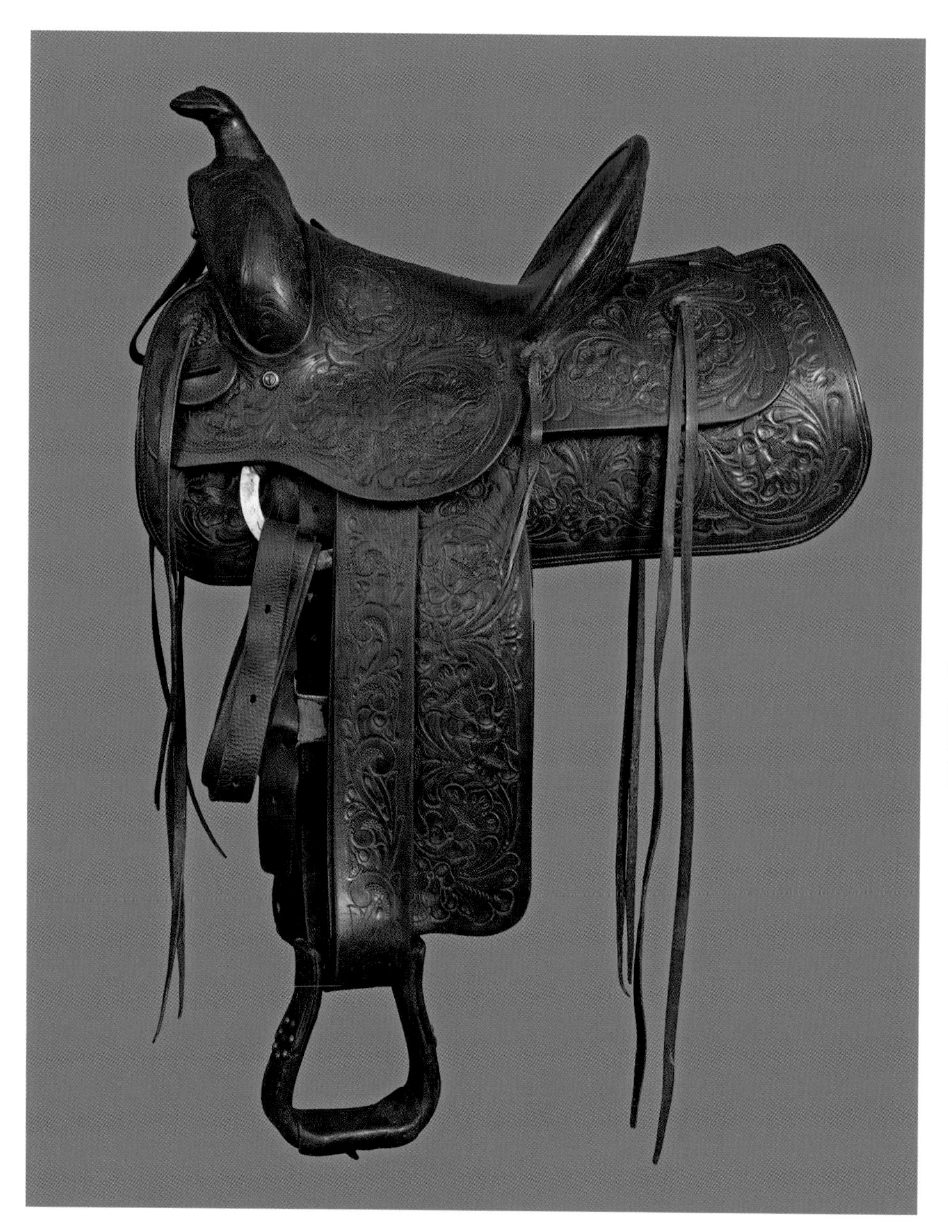

Figure 2.181.
The exposed stirrup leathers, extensive tooling, and studded leather-bound stirrups identify this item as one of the higher-quality saddles made by the ***Miles City Saddlery***.

Figure 2.182.
The seat mark on the ***Miles City Saddlery*** No. 3 saddle shows the artistry that the saddle stampers used to incorporate their maker's mark and the model number into a pleasing group of "leaves" that highlight the quality of the saddle (figure 2.181).

Figure 2.183.
The back of the cantle of the No. 3 saddle done by ***Miles City Saddlery*** (figure 2.181). The size of the initials *J.W.* and their location over the place where the saddlery stamp would normally appear are indicative of a special order. It is rare that the saddlery identification stamp was moved or obscured to accommodate the initials of the new owner.

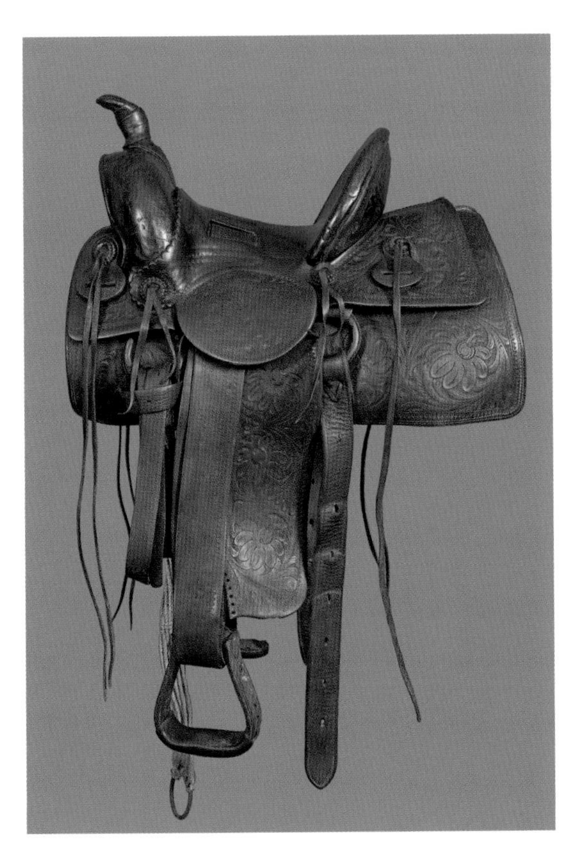

Figure 2.184.
A side view of the 1920 presentation saddle (figure 2.185) shows the loop seat with the exposed stirrup leathers and some minor restoration. "BUCKING CONTEST FIRST PRIZE" is tooled on the front of the cantle.

Figure 2.185.
This photograph highlights the outstanding work of the ***Miles City Saddlery*** and indicates that they routinely donated their work as rodeo prizes. In 1920 there was no better way to show off one's skills than to produce the saddle destined for the winner of the Montana riding contest during the largest rodeo in Montana. This saddle was given to the winner of the Fourth of July rodeo in 1920. It is in excellent condition considering that it was awarded to a bronc rider who undoubtedly took it out on the range and subjected it to heavy use.

Figure 2.186.
A ***Miles City Saddlery*** No. 1 was the best saddle offered by this saddlery. It is a loop-seat saddle with 21-inch swells, an extremely wide and unusual tree for this saddle. It is highly tooled and ornate and would have been one of the most expensive saddles that Miles City Saddlery would have built, c. 1915.

Figure 2.187.
The back of the cantle of the ***Miles City Saddlery*** catalog No. 1 saddle (figure 2.186) is personalized for the original owner with the initials "DM." The mark was used for most of the time the saddlery was in business.

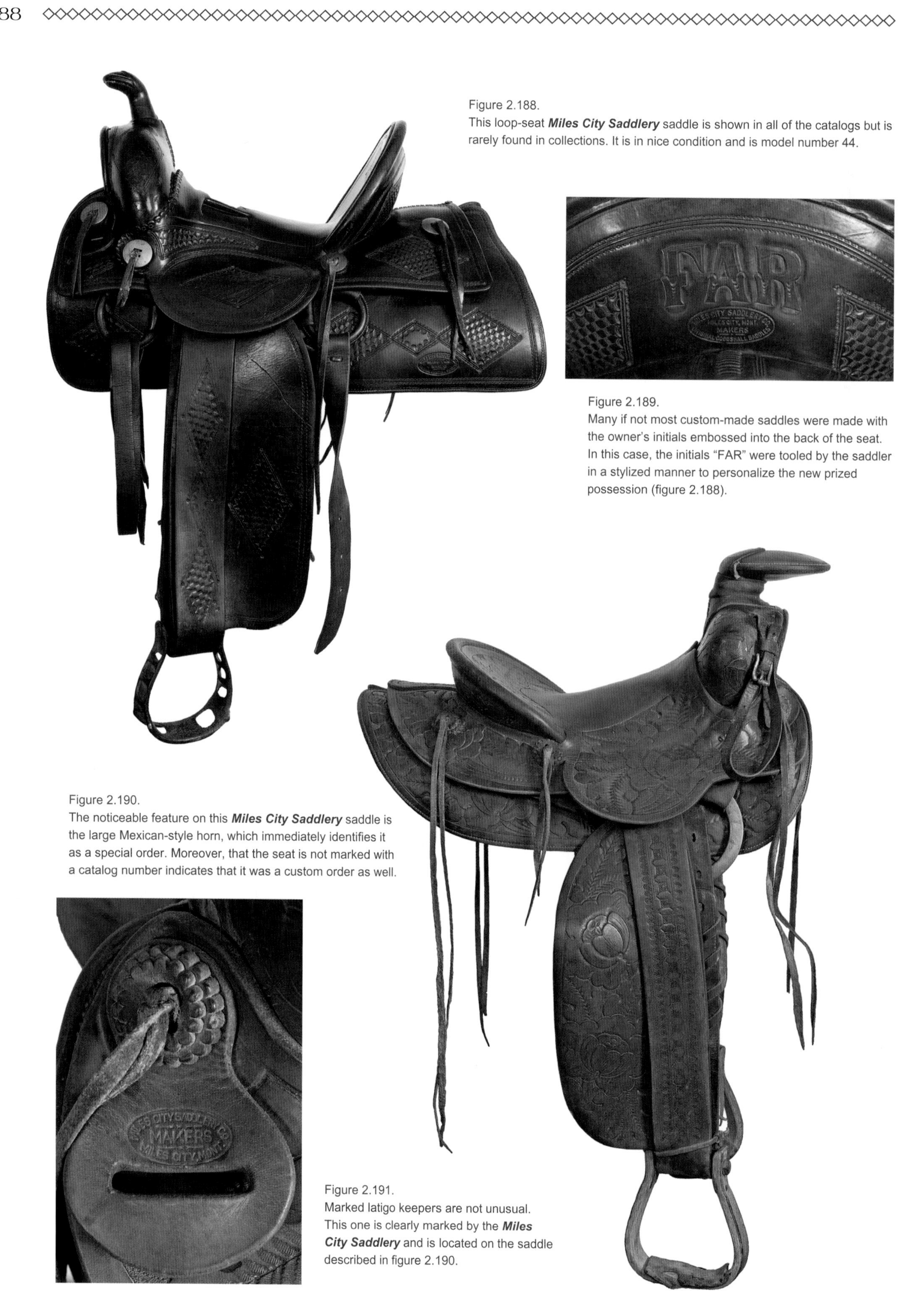

Figure 2.188.
This loop-seat ***Miles City Saddlery*** saddle is shown in all of the catalogs but is rarely found in collections. It is in nice condition and is model number 44.

Figure 2.189.
Many if not most custom-made saddles were made with the owner's initials embossed into the back of the seat. In this case, the initials "FAR" were tooled by the saddler in a stylized manner to personalize the new prized possession (figure 2.188).

Figure 2.190.
The noticeable feature on this ***Miles City Saddlery*** saddle is the large Mexican-style horn, which immediately identifies it as a special order. Moreover, that the seat is not marked with a catalog number indicates that it was a custom order as well.

Figure 2.191.
Marked latigo keepers are not unusual. This one is clearly marked by the ***Miles City Saddlery*** and is located on the saddle described in figure 2.190.

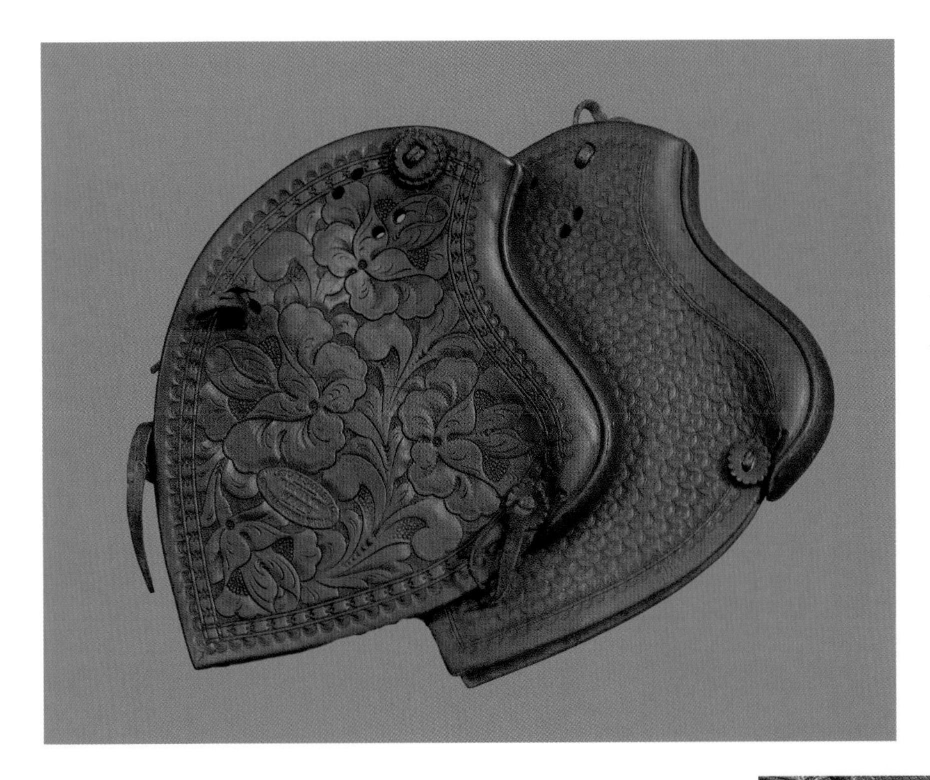

Figure 2.192.
Bulldog or monkey-nose tapaderos were offered as an option on any of the ***Miles City*** saddles, but were rarely ordered unless they were part of a deluxe saddle package. These show off nearly every one of the saddlers' talents in the manner of tooling, stamping, and border design. The longer Mexican style tapaderos were also available but are even more rare than this pair.

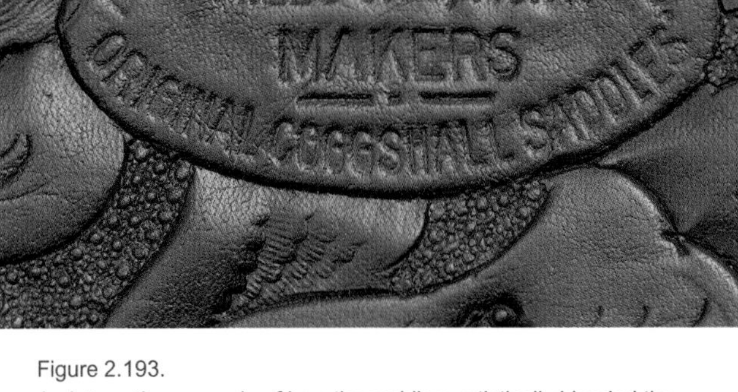

Figure 2.193.
An interesting example of how the saddlers artistically blended the standard maker's stamp into the tooling motif present on the rest of the saddle (figure 2.192). Each saddlery and its workers had their own unique way of making the entire product outstanding.

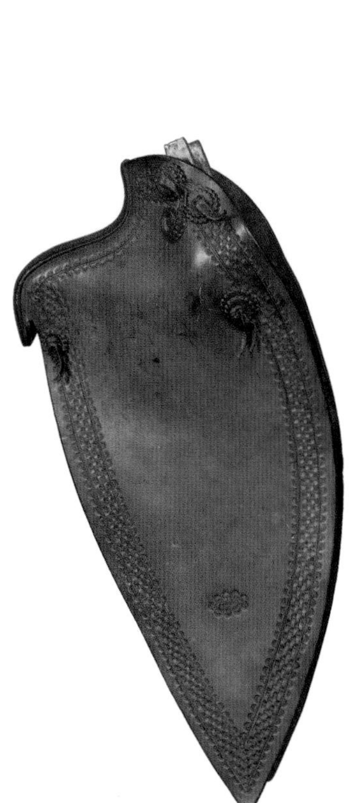

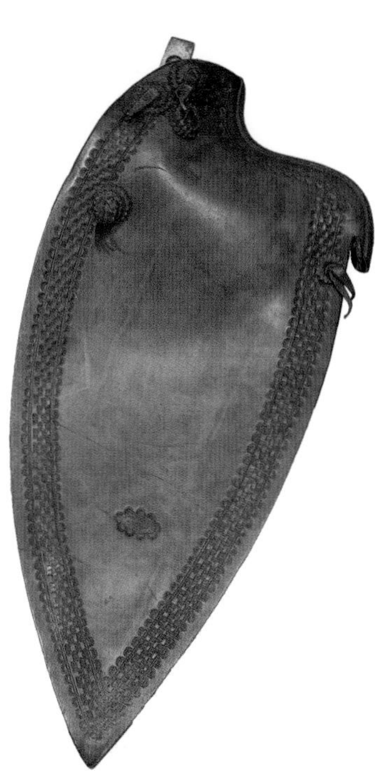

Figure 2.194.
Tapaderos could be made in any size the customer wanted—whoever ordered these wanted them LARGE. This pair of eagle beak taps was the only border-tooled model by the ***Miles City Saddlery***, and are the largest we have encountered.

A favorite collector's item is the chaps that cowboys wore, both for range/ ranch work and for rodeos and parades. A grouping of five Miles City–marked chaps is shown in figures 2.195 and 2.196. This mark was for the most part standard on chaps produced by the saddlery. Studded card-suit, plain, woolly, and extra-fancy designs appear in figures 2.197 through 2.202.

Other pieces produced by this long-standing saddlery and pictured here include gun leather, a bridle, and a studded bronc belt (figures 2.203, 2.204, 2.205, and 2.206, respectively). This section ends with photographs of three highly unusual pieces marked by the Miles City Saddlery and extremely rare: a stirrup leather protector (figure 2.207), a document case for transport of rolled-up maps or papers (figure 2.208 and 2.209), and a leather binder engraved across the front diagonal "MILES CITY/MONTANA" (figure 2.210).

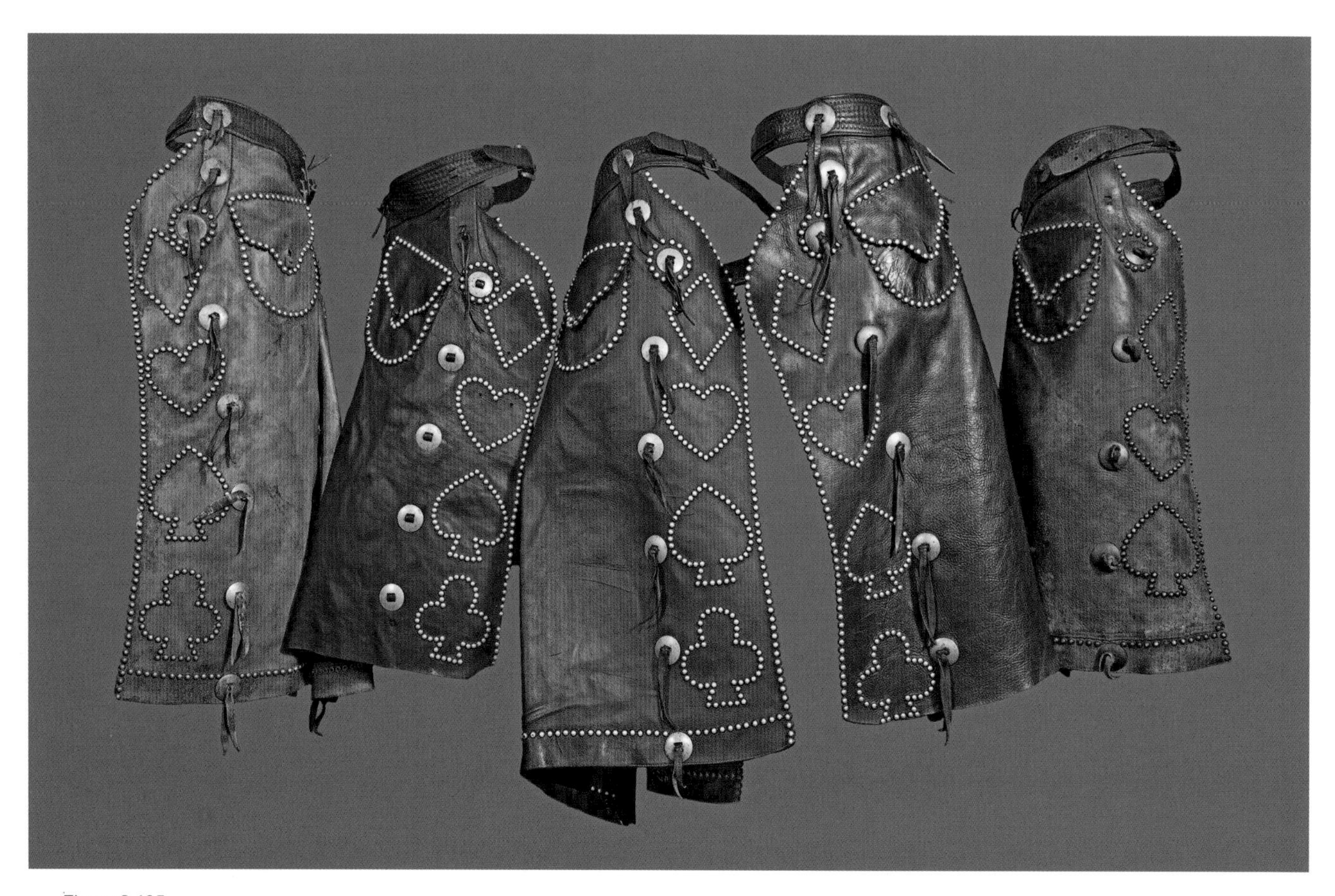

Figure 2.195.
This interesting grouping of the ***Miles City Saddlery*** Catalog No. 20 studded card suit chaps shows almost everything that could be special-ordered on this one item. The pair on the *left* of the photo is light in color and likely made of horsehide rather than the standard cowhide leather. The *center* pair is the standard catalog offering but made for a much larger person than most of the others. The pair on the *right* has seen hard use and was made for a much smaller cowboy (the legs are so short that one of the card suits [the club] was not applied). That these chaps have the original cuff on the bottom indicates that they were deliberately made this way. The *second* and *fourth* pairs were also made for a larger and smaller cowboy, respectively, and have had the cuff trimmed off when a different owner "cowboy customized" them. The saddlery records indicate that only six pairs of these chaps were made, but it is obvious that more had to have been produced given the low survival rate of saddlery items in general.

Figure 2.196.
A close look at this mark shows that it is slanted as well as off center both horizontally and vertically (figure 2.195). The mark is correct but even the stitching lines are sloppy. This carelessness happened very rarely with the big saddleries and is not always a sign that the piece was forged. Our discussions with Glenn VerBeck indicated that the saddlers all retired to the local pub for refreshments after work and this mark might have been the result of a night of drinking.

Figure 2.197.
These chaps were a standard offering in the ***Miles City Saddlery*** catalogs for many years. A search of the records several years ago showed a total production of about six pairs in all of those years. They were item number 20 in catalog No. 30. Advertised that they had "upwards of 700 German silver spots," this was the most expensive pair of chaps in the catalog.

Figure 2.198.
Two child-sized pairs of chaps, both of which were offered in most of the ***Miles City Saddlery*** catalogs. Children's cowboy items are rare as they were expensive and the child outgrew them very quickly.

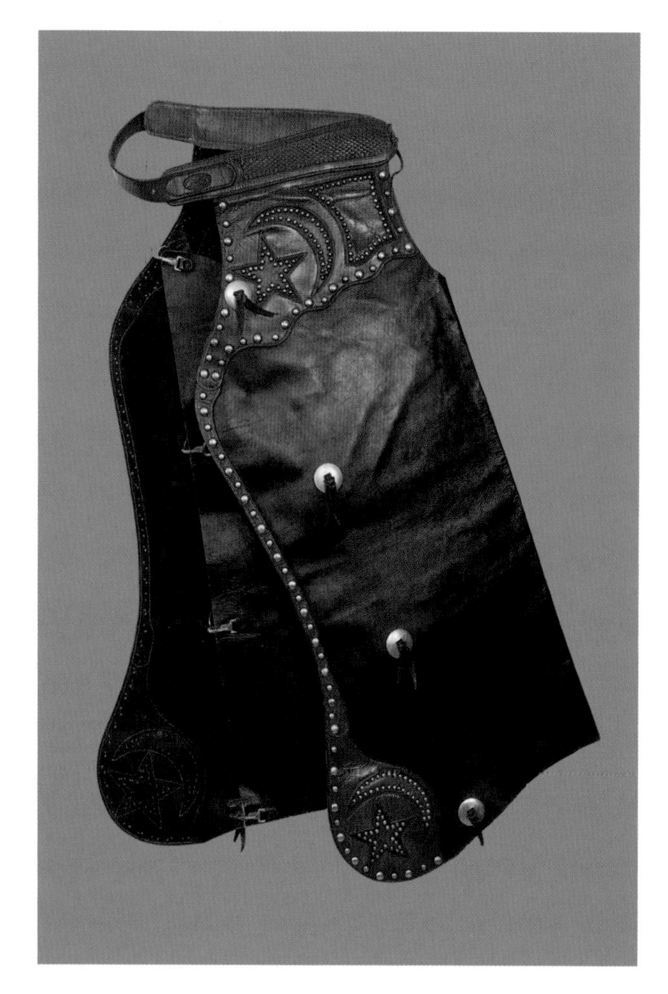

Figure 2.199.
An extremely rare example of custom-made studded chaps by the ***Miles City Saddlery*** artisans. These chaps are in extremely fine condition and are probably one of a kind. They exemplify the range of the custom orders made by the saddlery during its years of operation.

Figure 2.200.
A rare and very ornate pair of ***Miles City Saddlery*** chaps. They show the wide range of options available on custom-ordered items (figure 2.199).

Figure 2.201.
The smaller ***Miles City Saddlery*** mark that was used for chaps, belts, holsters, and other small saddlery production (figure 2.199).

Figure 2.202.
A pair of ***Miles City Saddlery*** chaps that were available for order and are shown as an option in most of the catalogs. This particular studded chap pattern is rarely seen.

Figure 2.203.
Miles City Saddlery made and stamped this large single-action holster. Holsters were made to order and the studs were added at extra cost. *Courtesy of T. Leland.*

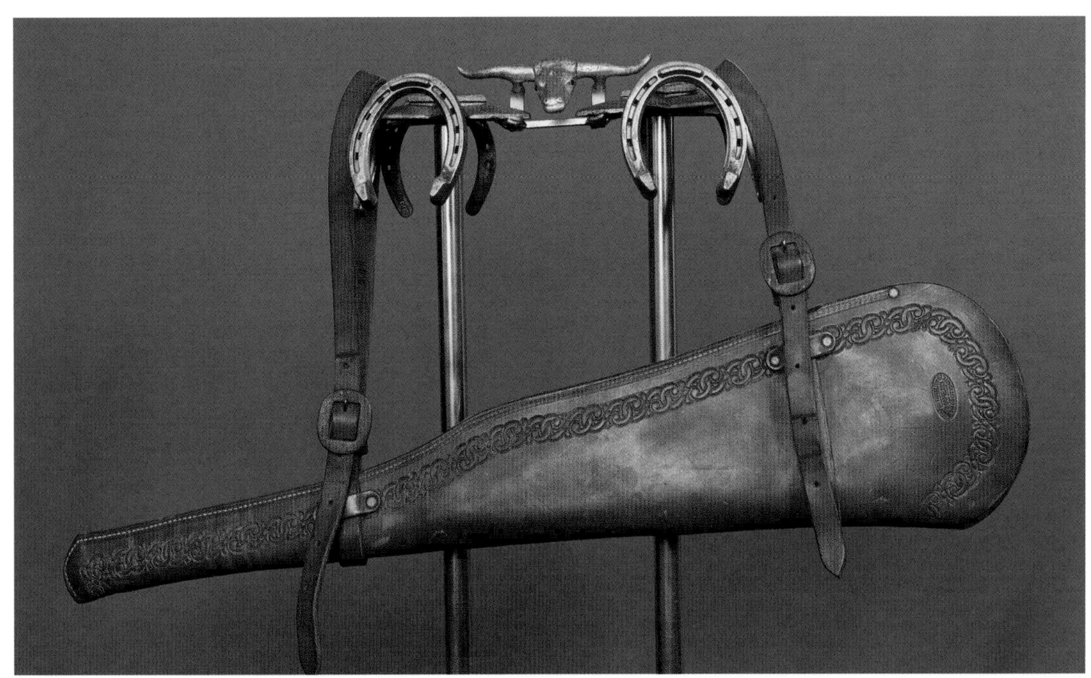

Figure 2.204.
This scabbard is a unique design and is not made like the standard saddle scabbards for a Winchester or Marlin. ***Miles City Saddlery***, like all of its competitors, made whatever its customer wanted. In this case the buyer wanted a scabbard that would fit whatever rifle he carried on his saddle; hence, this odd-looking scabbard was designed for a singular use.

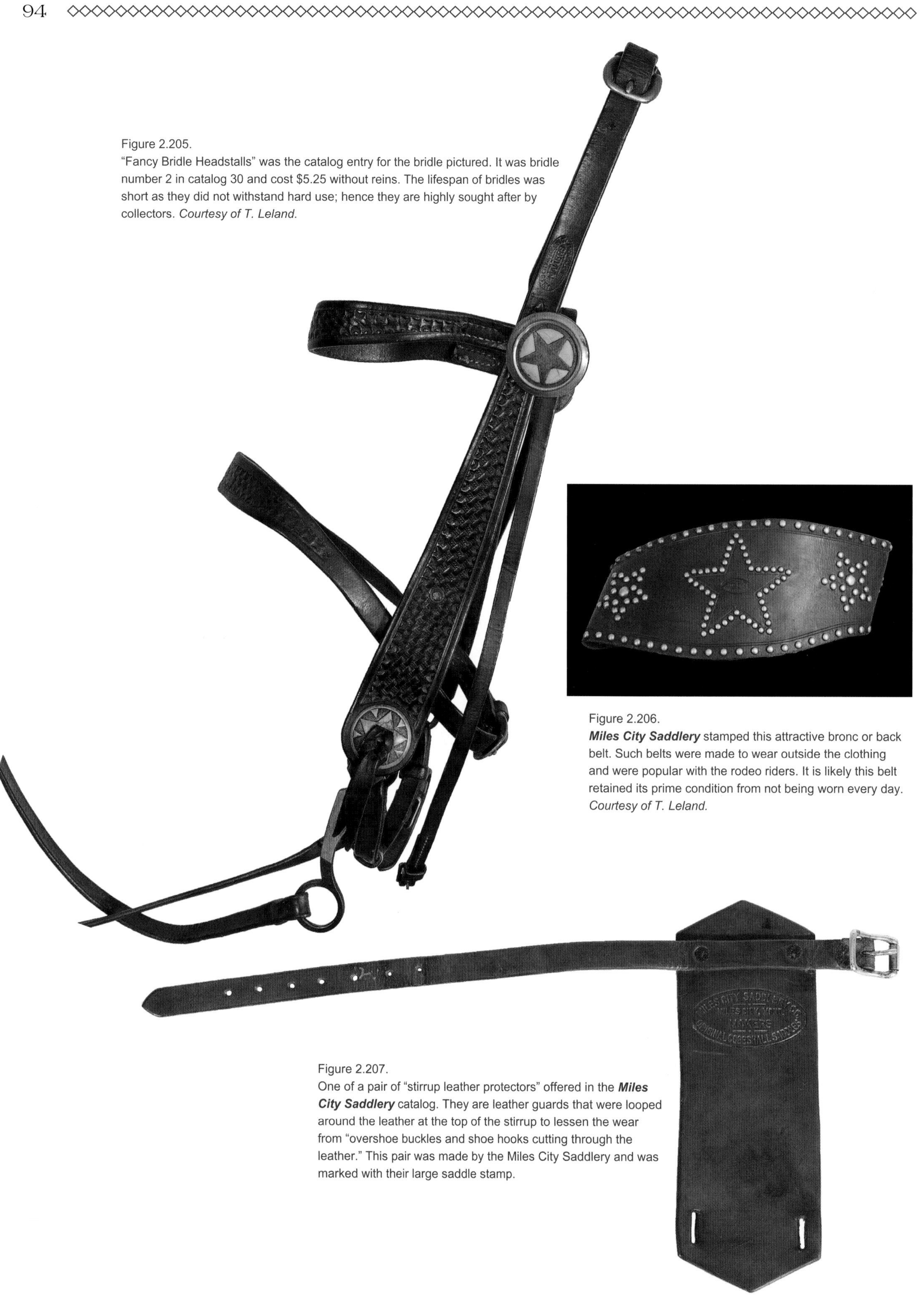

Figure 2.205.
"Fancy Bridle Headstalls" was the catalog entry for the bridle pictured. It was bridle number 2 in catalog 30 and cost $5.25 without reins. The lifespan of bridles was short as they did not withstand hard use; hence they are highly sought after by collectors. *Courtesy of T. Leland.*

Figure 2.206.
Miles City Saddlery stamped this attractive bronc or back belt. Such belts were made to wear outside the clothing and were popular with the rodeo riders. It is likely this belt retained its prime condition from not being worn every day. *Courtesy of T. Leland.*

Figure 2.207.
One of a pair of "stirrup leather protectors" offered in the ***Miles City Saddlery*** catalog. They are leather guards that were looped around the leather at the top of the stirrup to lessen the wear from "overshoe buckles and shoe hooks cutting through the leather." This pair was made by the Miles City Saddlery and was marked with their large saddle stamp.

Figure 2.208.
When this unusual piece was sold at auction recently, only a couple of us there had ever seen one before. It is identified in one of the early C. E. Coggshall catalogs as a "music roll," it was apparently used for transporting documents or maps rolled up inside. This example is marked ***Miles City Saddlery*** but it has not been found in their catalogs. The same people who had worked previously for C. E. Coggshall and were familiar with their product line most likely made a case after the sale of Coggshall Saddlery and subsequent beginning of the Miles City Saddlery.

Figure 2.209.
A clear example of the ***Miles City Saddlery*** stamp that identifies the "music roll" or document case (figure 2.208).

Figure 2.210.
A unique binder made as a custom order by the ***Miles City Saddlery***. Because the company would make just about anything on request, the saddlery developed a loyal customer base.

IX. Pete VerBeck and Glenn VerBeck

Pete and his son Glenn VerBeck were well-respected Miles City saddle makers. At the age of fifteen, Pete apprenticed in the Al. Furstnow Saddlery in 1915. Furstnow's son-in-law, Al Moreno, was his mentor, under whom Pete learned the art of raised flower stamping or tooling in floral designs on many types of leather items. He continued his training at the Miles City Saddlery under Rudy Mudra, from 1919–1920. Until 1946, when he purchased the shop equipment of the Al. Furstnow Saddlery and started his own saddlery business, Pete worked for both the Miles City Saddlery (he became foreman and saddle maker in 1936 after Clem Kathmann's death; see section VIII) and for Al Furstnow Saddlery (by this date owned by Al Moreno) in 1944. Pete VerBeck's Saddle Shop was in business from 1946 to 1976 and was terminated at his death. A one- or two-man shop (with son Glenn) could not approach the output of a major saddlery firm, and the VerBecks concentrated on custom-made saddles for individual patrons with whom they developed an understanding of their particular needs. Glenn VerBeck claims that there were more than 1,000 saddles made with the PETE VERBECK mark, and that in his career Pete produced over 2,000 saddles as well as other leather items (VerBeck, 1998), an accomplishment impossible today.

A saddle from this firm is shown in figures 2.211 and 2.212. No. 555 saddle was beautifully tooled and was marked with the clear PETE VERBECK stamp, as well as "1649," the latter indicating that this item was the 16th saddle made by this firm in 1949.

Glenn VerBeck continued to work with his father and made saddles from approximately 1944 into the late 1950s. A recent photograph of him with one of his custom saddles is shown in figure 2.213.

Figure 2.213.
Recent photograph by Steve Allison (*Miles City Star*) of ***Glenn VerBeck*** in his workshop, displaying one of his exquisite saddles.

Figure 2.212.
The mark ***Pete VerBeck*** used on all of his saddles. It is deeply stamped and easy to read.

Figure 2.211.
A ***Pete VerBeck*** No. 555 saddle in fine condition that was made by Pete himself in his own shop. The number "1649" on the back of the cantle indicates that it was the 16th saddle made by Pete in 1949. He was an extremely talented craftsman and did very detailed leatherwork and tooling on his saddles.

X. Saddleries in Glendive, Wibaux, Forsyth, and Sidney

There were several small cities and towns in Eastern Montana located outside Miles City, and in this ranching-focused Area 2, it would be expected that saddleries were doing business there. Glendive, now the seat of Dawson County, was founded by the Northern Pacific Railway during the construction of the northern transcontinental railroad from Minnesota to the Pacific coast. Glendive was not only the headquarters of the Yellowstone Division of the Railway, but was also a center for both ranching and farming enterprises in eastern Montana.

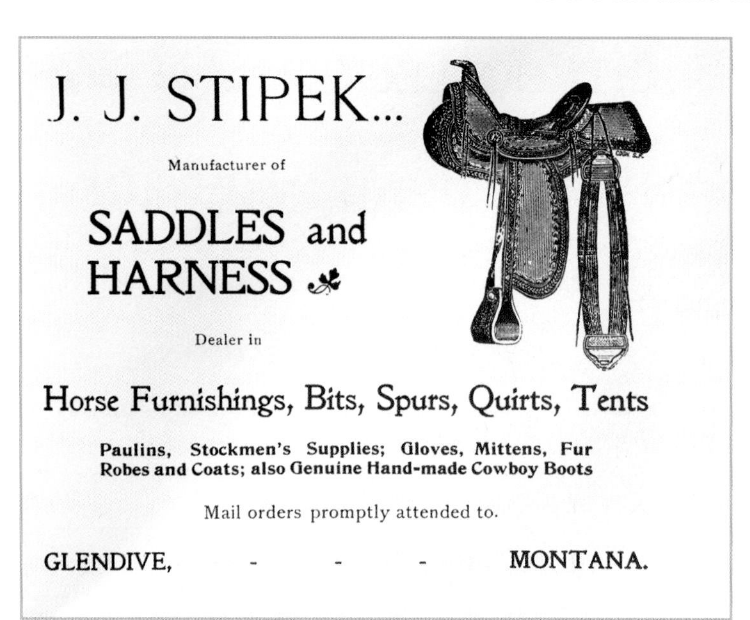

Figure 2.214.
Advertisement for ***J. J. Stipek***, Glendive, Montana, which appeared in the Van Dersal & Conner Directory of 1900.

The town of Wibaux, Montana, serves today as the seat of Wibaux County. In former times, it was called Beaver, Keith, and Mingusville, until it was renamed in 1895 for Pierre Wibaux, a prominent local cattleman. Wibaux himself promoted the town as a shipping center, via the Northern Pacific Railroad, for cattle from the local area as well as those from Medora, North Dakota ranches owned by Theodore Roosevelt (Maltese Cross and the Elkhorn). The trail drives in the 1880s from Texas to the Northern ranges sometimes passed by Wibaux and would thus have provided cowboy customers, not only for the saloons, but also for the saddleries.

J. J. Stipek was a prominent businessman in Glendive who manufactured saddles and harness and sold other horse furnishings (figures 2.214 and 2.215). His advertisements as proprietor of the Bee Hive Cash Store, Glendive, Montana (figures 2.216 and 2.217), and his stationery as "the founder and promoter of Townsite Sale, May 18, 1910" (figure 2.218) attest to his activities.

Figure 2.215.
Photograph of ***J. J. Stipek*** store, no date given.

J. J. Stipek founded the town of Stipek, known as the "Wheat City" of Dawson County, and he continued his saddlery in Glendive until 1937. He clearly imported items from other sources, as shown in figures 2.219 through 2.221, such as a pair of spaghetti-fringed chaps marked by the Miles City Saddlery and also stamped "FOR SALE BY/J. J. STIPEK/GLENDIVE, MONT." An interesting set of saddle bags (figures 2.222 and 2.223) stamped "J. J. STIPPEK" is assumed to be an early piece made by Stipek but an unusual error to have been made, perhaps by a careless worker who entered each letter by hand rather than using a fixed stamp. To complicate matters further, Stipek also formed a partnership with Lyon (figure 2.224), and extended his dealings to the town of Wibaux.

Figure 2.216.
Advertisement for The Bee Hive Cash Store, ***J. J. Stipek,*** Proprietor, Custom Harness and Saddle Maker. *Courtesy of T. Leland.*

Figure 2.217.
Victorian-style advertisement from J. J. Stipek to "Stockmen and Ranchmen of Dawson County."

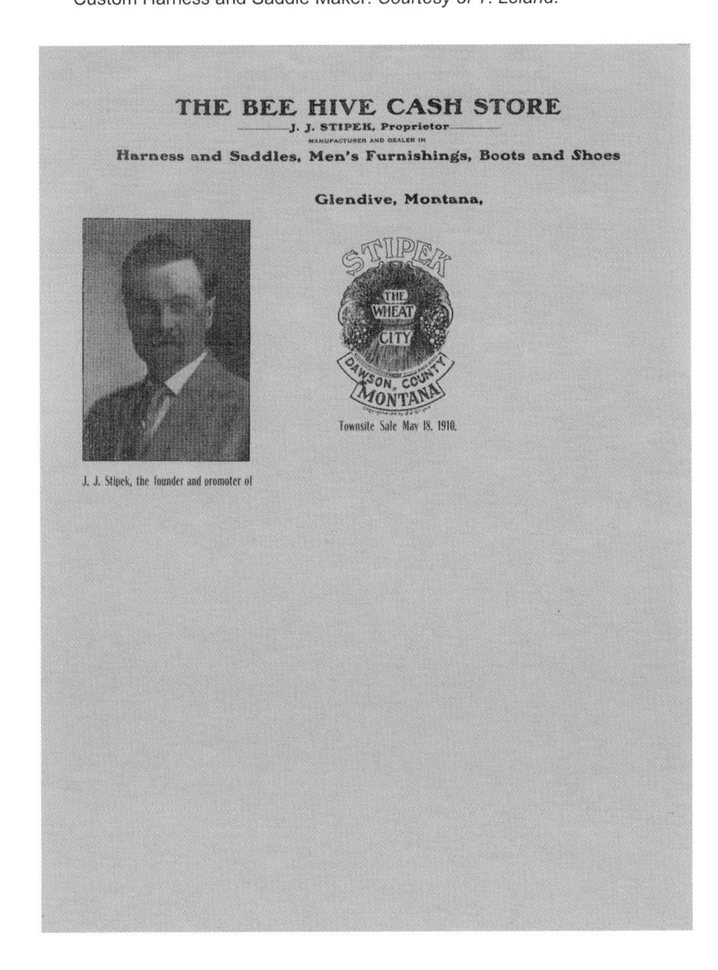

Figure 2.218.
Letterhead from the Bee Hive Cash Store, ***J. J. Stipek***, Proprietor, Glendive, Montana, dated May 18, 1910. A portrait of Stipek can be seen, with his notation as "the founder and promoter of the Townsite Sale May 18 1910." Stipek, Montana, was "The Wheat City" in Dawson County.

Figure 2.219.
This pair of chaps bears the maker's mark from ***Miles City Saddlery*** and is shown in their catalogs. It also has the stamp of ***J. J. Stipek*** stating they were sold by him. Stipek was the only saddler known to the authors to "fess up" to the practice.

Figure 2.220.
The chaps bearing the mark "sold by ***J. J. Stipek***" also bear the ***Miles City Saddlery*** stamp, indicating he purchased them from Miles City Saddlery for resale (figure 2.219).

Figure 2.221.
J. J. Stipek did not make all of the items he sold, and this is the mark he used on items he purchased for resale in his shop. It is not unusual for saddlers to sell goods purchased from elsewhere, but it is unusual for them to draw attention to the fact that they are doing it (figure 2.219).

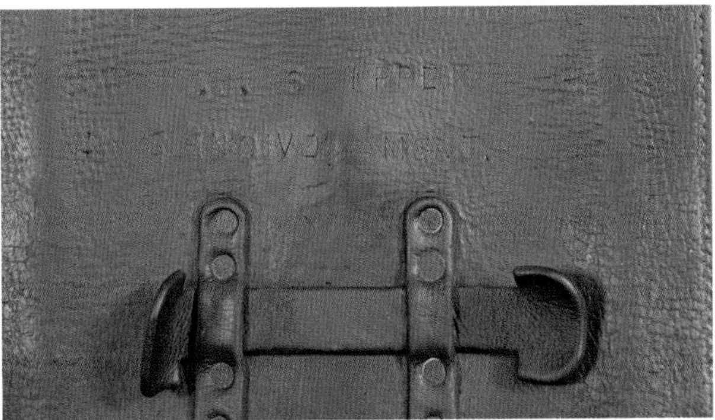

Figure 2.223.
This mark is from ***J. J. Stippek*** [*sic*] of Glendive, Montana. It is difficult to read but appears to be made by the use of individual letter stamps rather than the usual "gang stamp" (a single stamp with a border). It is probably one of his earlier marks as it likely took a while to receive a saddle stamp after it was ordered from a firm in the East (figure 2.222).

Figure 2.224.
Advertisement for ***Stipek & Lyon***, Glendive, Montana. *Courtesy of T. Leland.*

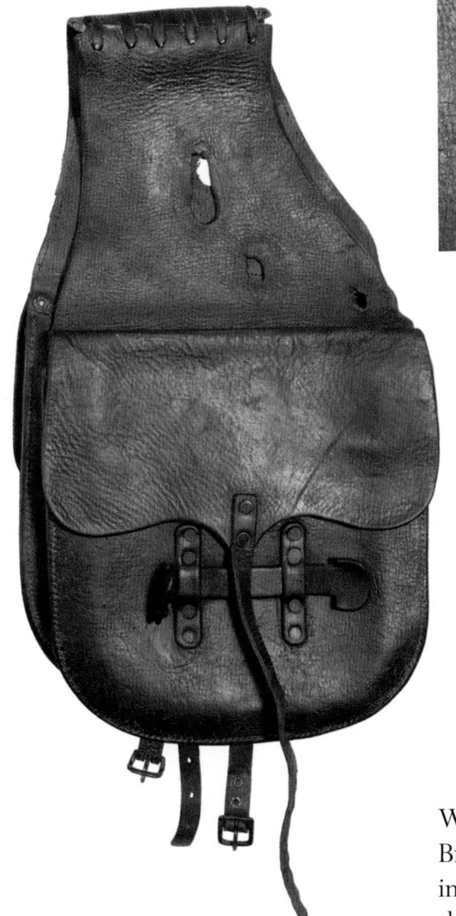

Figure 2.222.
A rare pair of saddle bags made and stamped by ***J. J. Stippek*** (note the misspelling) of Glendive, Montana. They have a unique closure using a combination of a handle and leather strap that buckles at the base of the bags. It is the only closure of this type found by the authors.

As shown in table 2.1, at least three saddle makers were in business in Wibaux around the end of the nineteenth century: Frank J. Stipek, Stipek Bros., and the Wynn brothers. F. J. Stipek (1868–1940) (his mark is shown in figure 2.225) was a brother of J. J. Stipek of Glendive and was engaged in the harness and saddlery business in Wibaux upon his arrival there in 1898 (*Wibaux Pioneer Gazette*, 1940). The two holsters shown in figure 2.226 bear different but related marks: "STIPPECK BROS./WIBAUX MONT." (figure 2.227, holster) and "J. J. STIPEK/GLENDIVE, MONT." (figure 2.228). Again, the spelling of "STIPPECK," in individually stamped letters, differs from "STIPEK" (inclusive stamp) and, interestingly, from the "STIPPEK" in figure 2.223. Was "Stippeck" an attempt to Anglicize "Stipek" (the brothers were from Czechoslovakia), or carelessness in spelling? We simply do not know. The grouping seen in figure 2.229 includes spur straps with the "J. J. STIPEK/GLENDIVE, MONT." mark and a holster with the "STIPEK BROS./WIBAUX, MONT." mark (figures 2.230 and 2.231, respectively). The last item shown here from Stipek Bros. of Wibaux is a set of saddle bags, with an unusual placement of the mark (figures 2.232 and 2.233).

Two Johns brothers, Charles and George, worked as saddle makers for J. J. Stipek in Glendive and later opened their own shop around 1908 (figure 2.234). Their leather goods were stamped "JOHNS BROS./MAKERS/GLENDIVE MONTANA" (figures 2.235 and 2.236). At some point prior to 1912 they returned to their native Canada, and George Johns's name alone appeared in the advertisement for the company in 1909 (figure 2.237). Later in the same year, George Johns formed a partnership with Hallinan (*Yellowstone Monitor*, November 11, 1909) (figure 2.238).

Figure 2.225.
The saddlery mark of ***P. J. Stipek*** of Wibaux is extremely rare and this is the only one we have encountered. *Courtesy of T. Leland.*

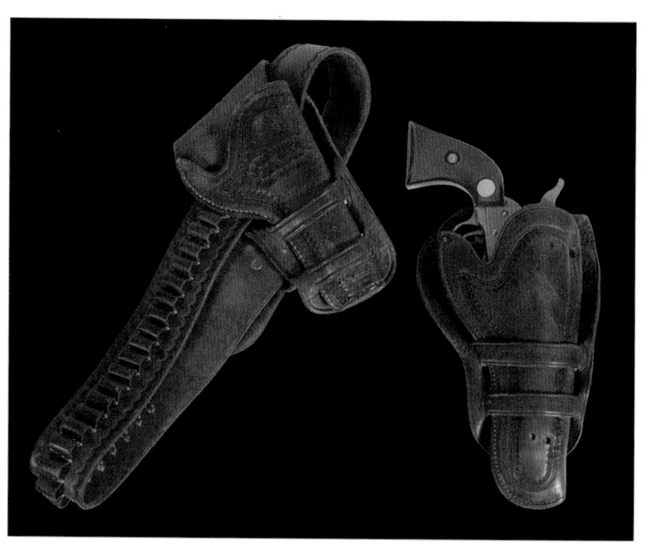

Figure 2.226.
This pair of holsters was made by ***Stipek*** or ***Stippek***, spelled differently on the stamps. It is possible that Stipek made both of these items but one is marked "Glendive" and one is marked "Wibaux Montana" (see text and figures 2.227 and 2.228).

Figure 2.227.
This double-loop holster is marked with hand-applied stamps. The name ***STIPPECK*** is spelled with two Ps and a C and it is marked "Wibaux Mont." This is the only case we have encountered of the saddler (or his employee) misspelling his own name on an item.

Figure 2.228.
This ***Stipek*** mark on this holster is spelled with one P and is different from that on the Wibaux holster. This mark is the only one we have found, but it seems that Stipek used several different marks before he went into the real estate business (see text).

Figure 2.229.
A nice grouping of ***Stipek*** items that show the versatility of their saddlers. The holster is marked "STIPEK BROS./WIBAUX" and the cartridge belt and spur straps are marked "J. J. STIPEK" from the Glendive shop.

Figure 2.230.
J. J. Stipek has had as many stamps as any saddler we researched. This Glendive mark is very simple, as were most of his stamps. *Courtesy of T. Leland.*

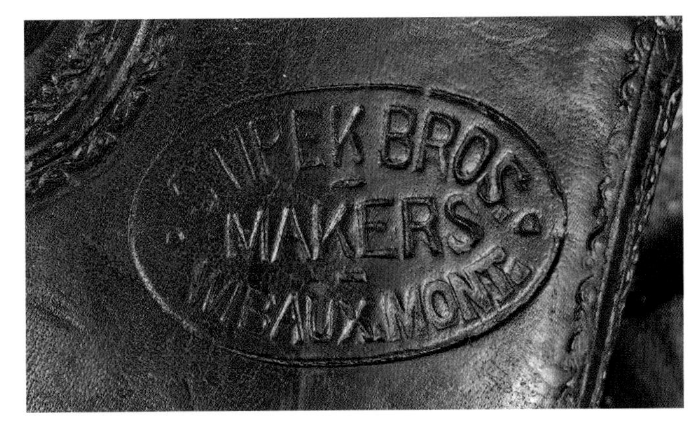

Figure 2.231.
Another extremely rare mark is that of ***Stipek Brothers*** from Wibaux, Montana. This is the first time we have seen this mark. *Courtesy of T. Leland.*

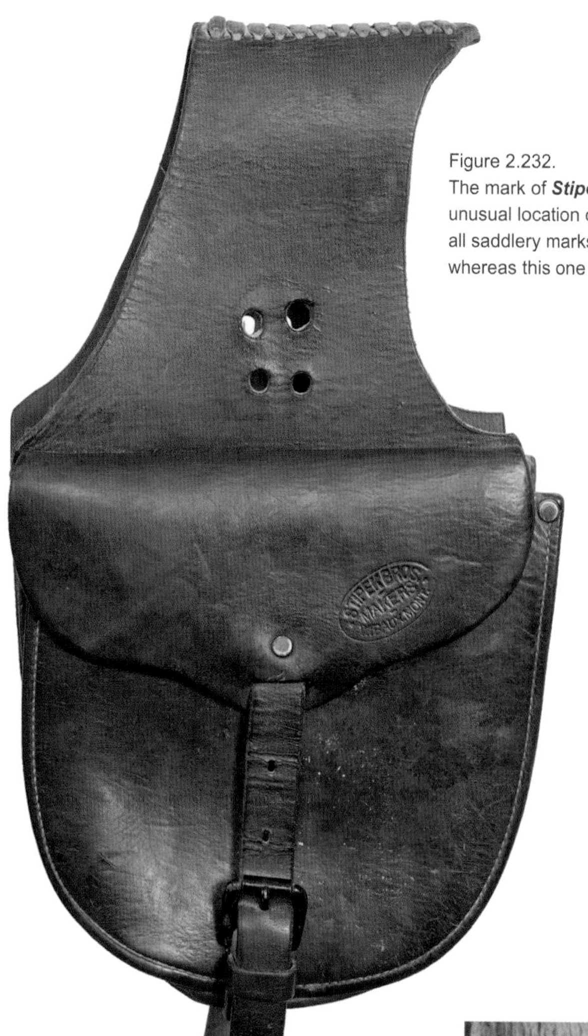

Figure 2.232.
The mark of ***Stipek Brothers*** was placed in an unusual location on this pair of saddle bags. Almost all saddlery marks are centered on the marked item, whereas this one was not. *Courtesy of T. Leland.*

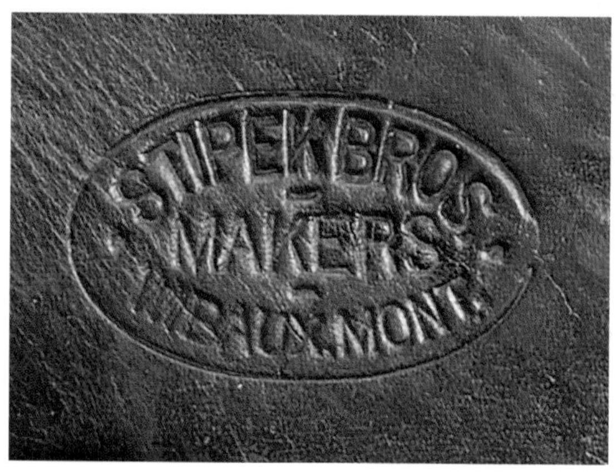

Figure 2.233.
A close-up view of the ***Stipek Brothers*** mark in Wibaux shows the difficulty in applying the mark uniformly by the deep impression at the top and the light impression at the bottom. In this case the stamp was not struck squarely with the mallet (figure 2.232). *Courtesy of T. Leland.*

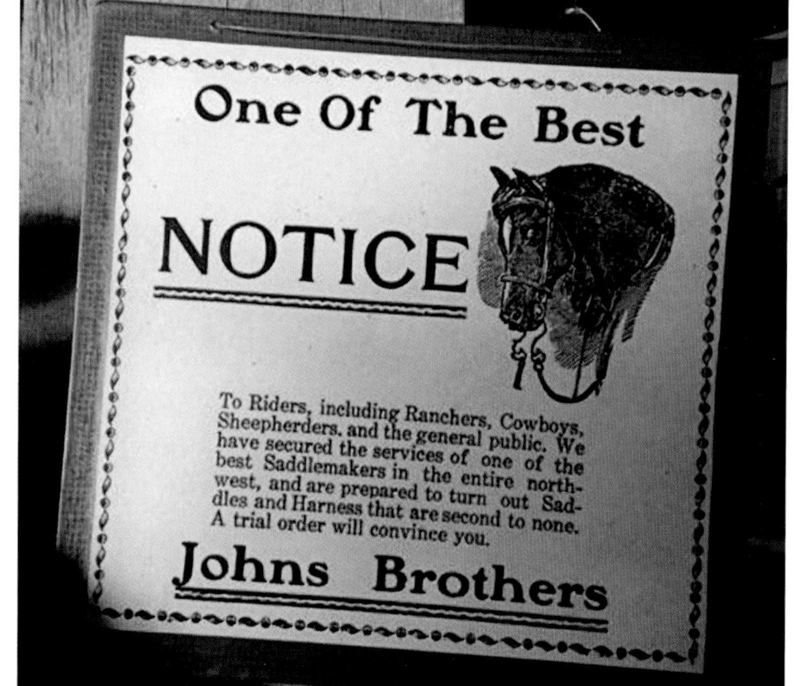

Figure 2.234.
Advertisement for ***Johns Brothers***, "One of the Best," Glendive, Montana, c. 1908–1912. *Courtesy of T. Leland.*

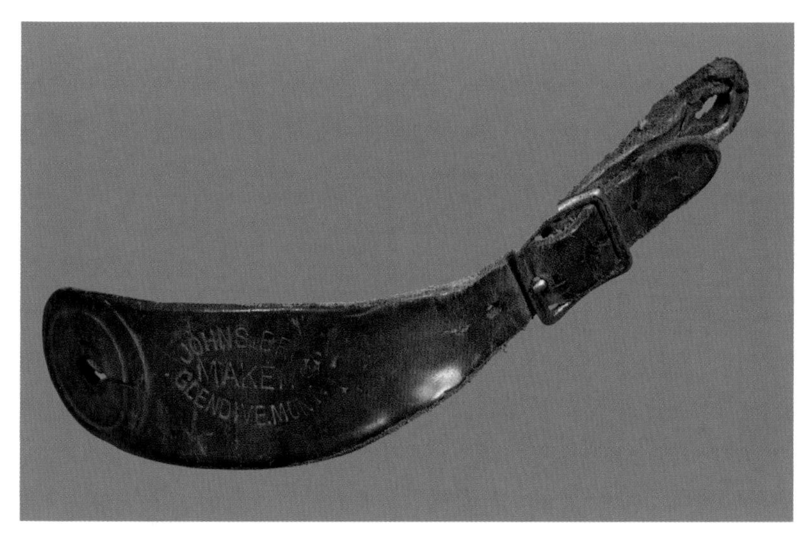

Figure 2.235.
Spur straps did not last with hard use, and only one of this pair survived. Made by ***Johns Bros***. in Glendive Montana, it is the only leather item marked by this saddlery that the authors have seen.

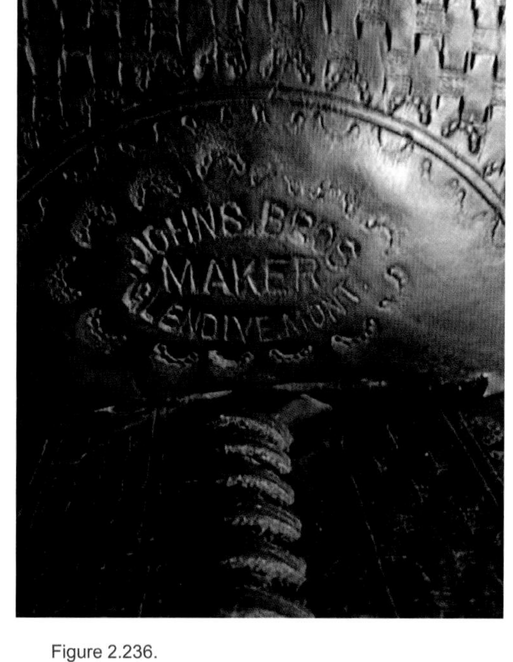

Figure 2.236.
JOHNS BROS. mark from Glendive, Mont.
Courtesy of T. Leland.

Heavy Farm Harness From $22 Up.

We make a specialty of this Harness and guarantee superior workmanship and best quality. A complete line of buggy harness, collars, etc. Past customers are the best advertisement.

We always have a complete line of our

Hand Made Saddles and Harness.

George Johns

Figure 2.237.
Advertisement for ***George Johns***, Glendive, Montana, from the *Yellowstone Monitor*, dated Aug. 12, 1909.

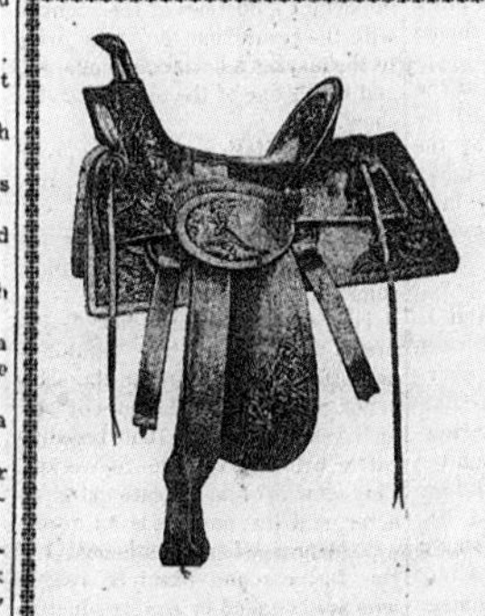

Mr. Hallinan has purchased a half interest in the saddlery business of George Johns of this city. Mr. Hallinan has had 20 years experience in the Saddle business in the leading saddle shops in the south and west, and along the coast, and is an expert in Mexican hand carved stamp work, such as high class pocket books, ladies stamped belts, high grade saddles, chaps and cowboy outfits. The citizens of Dawson county are cordially invited to call and examine his work.

Johns & Hallinan

Figure 2.238.
Advertisement for ***Johns & Hallinan***, Glendive, Montana. From the *Yellowstone Monitor*, November 11, 1909.

Forsyth, M.T., founded in 1876 as the first settlement on the Yellowstone River, served as a steamboat landing for the United States Army during the Indian Wars. The town itself was named for General Forsyth, who among other campaigns commanded the Seventh Cavalry during the infamous battle at Wounded Knee. In 1882 Forsyth also became a location point for the progress of the Northern Pacific Railroad. It is now the seat of Rosebud County, Montana.

At least seven saddleries were in business in Forsyth around the turn of the nineteenth century (table 2.1). A now fragile brochure from E. M. Huff's saddlery was complete with a portrait of him and photographs of several of his saddles (figures 2.239 and 2.240). The saddles show interesting variety—there are loop-seats built on different trees, with leather carving ranging from floral to geometric, with or without tapaderos. There is also a side saddle with a quilted calfskin seat, two cinches, and wool-lined tapaderos.

A double-loop holster with a badly-effaced E. M. Huff mark can be seen in figures 2.241 and 2.242. This piece is exceedingly rare. Huff was also a partner in the firm of Becker and Huff, in Forsyth, although by the appearance of the holster and belt shown in figures 2.243 through 2.246, the partnership was later. Yet the mark "BECKER & HUFF/MAKERS/FORSYTH, MONT." is also extremely rare—the tooling and construction of the holster are especially well done and attest to the expertise of this saddlery.

Although minimal information is available concerning the Wynn Brothers (James D. and Emmett L.), their establishment was operational from 1898–1903. We have no examples of their work. James Wynn, at the closing of the company, worked for Pierre Wibaux as a cowboy for two years before becoming a butcher and later a sheriff in Wibaux (Sanders, 1913).

The harness and saddle maker located in Sidney, Montana, H. B. Hudson (table 2.1), advertised in the Van Dersal and Conner Directory in 1909 (figure 2.247). However, examples of his work have not been found to date.

Figure 2.239.
Fold-out brochure for the saddlery of ***E. M. Huff***, Forsyth, Montana, showing photographs of Huff.

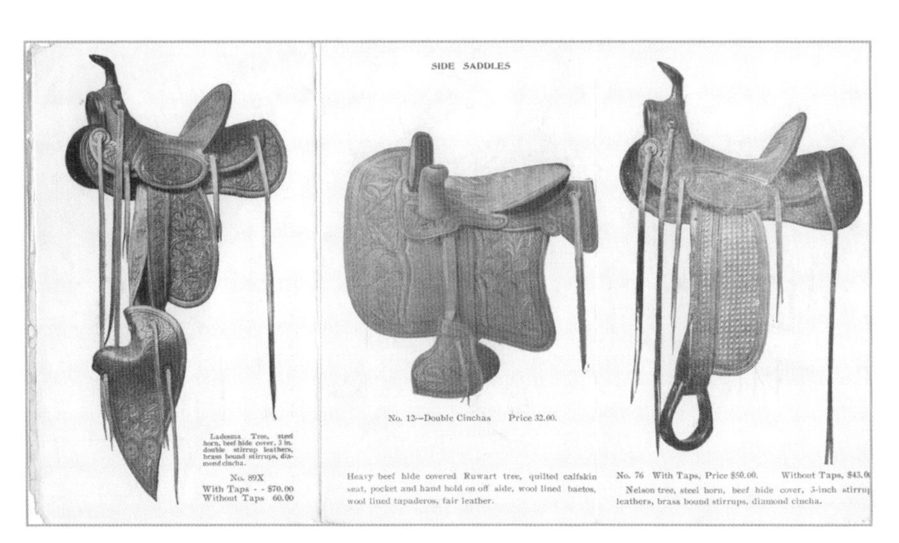

Figure 2.240.
Fold-out brochure with the photographs of three saddles made by ***E. M. Huff*** (figure 2.239). Note the use of different saddle trees for the ornate stock saddles, and the highly detailed side saddle with its quilted seat and wool-lined tapadero.

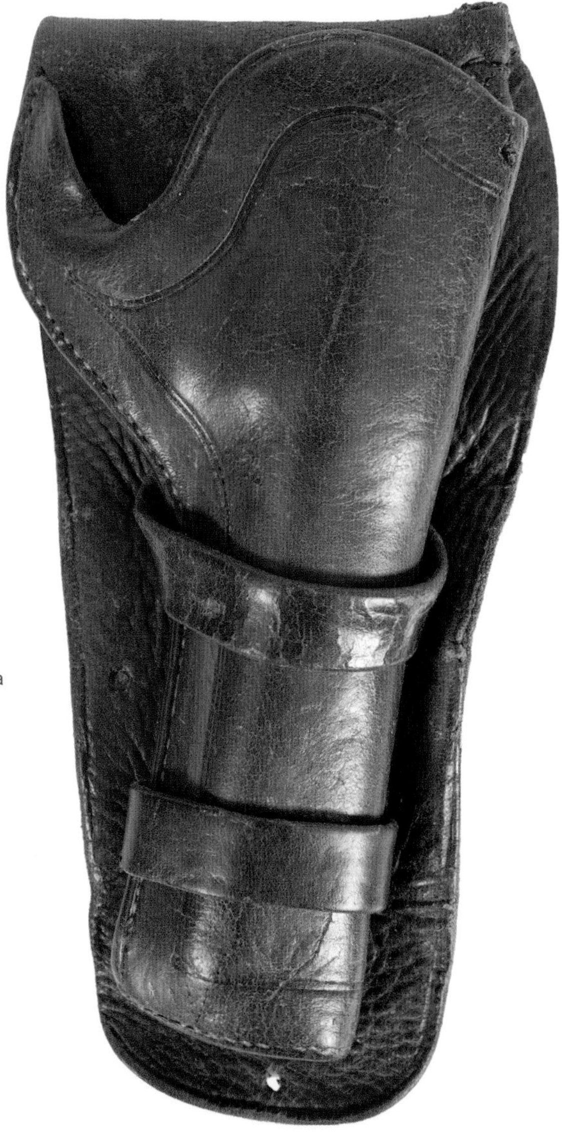

Figure 2.241.
The ***E. M. Huff*** marked holster is in reasonable shape, and the mark can be seen at the top center of the loop in the tooled line on the holster pouch. This is the smallest saddlery mark used by the Montana saddlers (figure 2-212).

Figure 2.242.
E. M. Huff worked for the Miles City Saddlery before he relocated to Forsyth, Montana. This mark is extremely small and is very hard to identify if a collector has not seen it. In fact, this holster is erroneously identified in *Packing Iron* (Rattenbury, 1993) because it was on a Furstnow & Coggshall gun belt and not viewed carefully for positive identification.

Figure 2.243.
Becker & Huff made this exquisitely carved and stamped holster. From the way the saddle stamp is framed and the look of the construction and workmanship, it is almost certain they made it in their shop. This item equals, if not exceeds, the quality of any other saddlery item photographed for this book.

Figure 2.244.
The mark on this ***Becker & Huff*** holster is deeply and clearly stamped and is extremely rare; only a couple of marked items from these makers are known to collectors (figure 2.243).

Figure 2.245.
Becker & Huff both worked for the Miles City Saddlery before moving to Forsyth, about 50 miles east of Miles City, to start a saddlery. This unique belt is one of only a couple of items of Becker & Huff-marked leather that the authors could find to photograph.

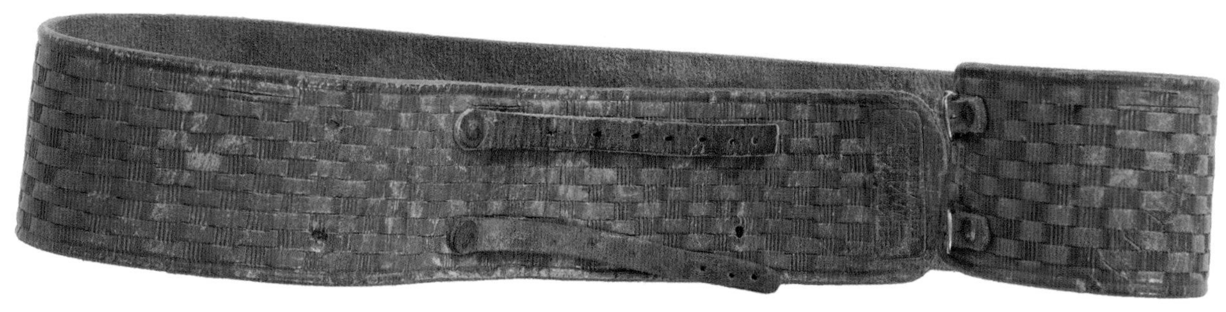

Figure 2.246.
It is always a temptation for dealers and collectors to consider any belt to be "gun leather." This belt is nicely tooled and in great condition, but is only a belt (figure 2.245).

Figure 2.247.
Advertisement for ***H. B. Hudson***, Sidney, Montana, dated 12/24/09.

Lincoln
Libby
Flathead
Kalispell
Glacier
Cut Bank
Toole
Shelby
Liberty
Chester
Hill
Havre
Chinook
Blaine
Malta
Phillips
Valley
Glasgow
Scobey
Daniels
Plentywood
Sheridan
Roosevelt
Wolf Point
Pondera
Conrad
Sanders
Thompson Falls
Lake
Polson
9
Teton
Choteau
5
Chouteau
Fort Benton
4
McCone
Circle
Sidney
Richland
Superior
Mineral
Missoula
Missoula
7
6
Lewis and Clark
GreatFalls
Cascade
Stanford
Judith Basin
Fergus
Lewistown
Petroleum
Winnett
Jordan
Garfield
Dawson
Glendive
Wibaux
Prairie
Terry
Wibaux
Hamilton
Ravalli
Granite
Philipsburg
Powell
Deer Lodge
Helena
Meagher
White Sulphur Springs
Wheatland
Harlowton
Golden Valley
Ryegate
Musselshell
Roundup
Hysham
Treasure
Rosebud
Forsyth
2
Miles City
Custer
Fallon
Baker
Anaconda
Deer Lodge
Silver Bow
Butte
Boulder
Jefferson
Townsend
Broad-water
Gallatin
Bozeman
Park
Livingston
8
Sweet Grass
Big Timber
Stillwater
Columbus
Yellowstone
Billings
3
Hardin
Big Horn
Carbon
Red Lodge
Ekalaka
Powder River
Broadus
Carter
Beaverhead
Dillon
Madison
Ennis

3

South-Central Montana

Billings

Big Timber

Billings, the seat of Yellowstone County, was founded as a railroad town in 1882. Named for Frederick Billings, a president of the Northern Pacific Railroad, the town became a major trading, shipping, and distribution area for most of Montana and portions of its contiguous states including the Dakotas and Wyoming. Once known as Clarks Fork Bottom, the settlement was planned as a hub for the transport of freight to the Judith and Musselshell Basins, as well as Fort Benton (see chapter 5). In 1877 the town of Coulson was founded by settlers and businessmen, in anticipation of its becoming the railroad center serving much of M.T. However, the rough and rather lawless town failed to secure this distinction because the railroad created a new town, approximately two miles west of Coulson, and named it Billings, on the banks of the Yellowstone River. Subsequently, many of the Coulson residents and businesses moved to the rapidly growing town of Billings, and by 1930 Coulson had effectively disappeared.

Billings is surrounded by no less than six mountain ranges that include the famous Bighorns, Pryors, and Beartooth. The area was by this time known for major ranches both north and west of the city, for example, near Big Timber. It is disappointing that items from saddlers located in Coulson have not surfaced. However, as seen in table 3.1, a number of saddleries were operating in Billings, a few of which were Territorial. Yegen Bros. was established in 1882 (figures 3.1 and 3.2) and did a wide range of business that included the distribution of Pabst beer. An advertisement from Rockwell & Tovey and a letterhead from Donovan and Spear, which handled Schlitz beer, are shown in figures 3.3 and 3.4.

Table 3.1. Saddleries of Montana[1]

MAKER	LOCATION	DATES[2]
Chapman, F. B.	Billings	(1901), 1905–1906
Connolly Bros. Saddlery: Jack & Pat	Billings	1912–1929
Pat Connolly Saddlery	Billings	1929–1950†
Donovan & Spear	Billings	(1897)
Racek Bros.	Billings	(1883)
Racek, C.	Billings	(1884)
Rockwell, Thomas D. & Tovey	Billings	(1883)
Schneider, Wm.	Billings	
Sentinel Butte Saddlery Co.	Billings‡	c. 1910–1920
Smith, C. E.	Billings	M.T.
Solberg, J. S.	Big Timber	1889, pre-1900–1907
Talmage, W. A.	Red Lodge	(1900)
Ten Eyck, W. B.	Billings, M.T.	(1899)
Yegen Brothers	Billings	1882, (1898), 1908 incorp.

1. Products made or sold by these saddleries included harness, saddles, bits, spurs, whips, boots, bridles, accessories (horse blankets, grooming tools, trunks, bags, and/or robes), vehicles (sleighs, buggies, wagons, carts), and Indian-made goods (e.g., saddle blankets).

2. Dates in parentheses are specified on the company letterhead or in a newspaper/journal advertisement. Inclusive dates for the tenure of the company have been provided where data are available and reliable.

† Continued by family members John T. (son) and Alice (daughter).

‡ Montana branches also in Glendive, Terry, Baker, and Lewistown.

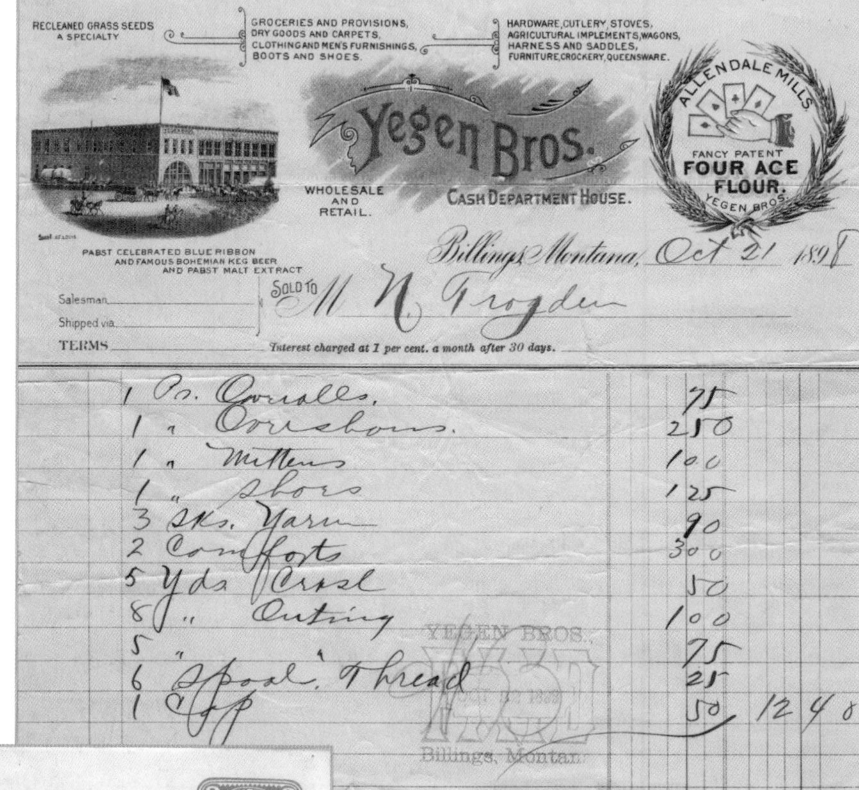
RECLEANED GRASS SEEDS A SPECIALTY

GROCERIES AND PROVISIONS, DRY GOODS AND CARPETS, CLOTHING AND MEN'S FURNISHINGS, BOOTS AND SHOES.

HARDWARE, CUTLERY, STOVES, AGRICULTURAL IMPLEMENTS, WAGONS, HARNESS AND SADDLES, FURNITURE, CROCKERY, QUEENSWARE.

Yegen Bros.

WHOLESALE AND RETAIL.

CASH DEPARTMENT HOUSE.

ALLENDALE MILLS
FANCY PATENT
FOUR ACE FLOUR.
YEGEN BROS.

PABST CELEBRATED BLUE RIBBON AND FAMOUS BOHEMIAN KEG BEER AND PABST MALT EXTRACT

Billings, Montana, Oct 21 1898

SOLD TO

Salesman

Shipped via

TERMS

Interest charged at 1 per cent. a month after 30 days.

Figure 3.1.
Letterhead/invoice from ***Yegen Bros.***, Billings, Montana, dated Oct. 21, 1898. The logo (showing a huge building) states that this firm represented "Pabst Celebrated Blue Ribbon and Famous Bohemian Keg Beer and Pabst Malt Extract." *Courtesy of Ken Hamlin.*

Figure 3.2.
Envelope from ***Yegen Bros.***, Billings, Mont. Note the logo stating their establishment in 1882 (M.T.) and their incorporation in 1902.

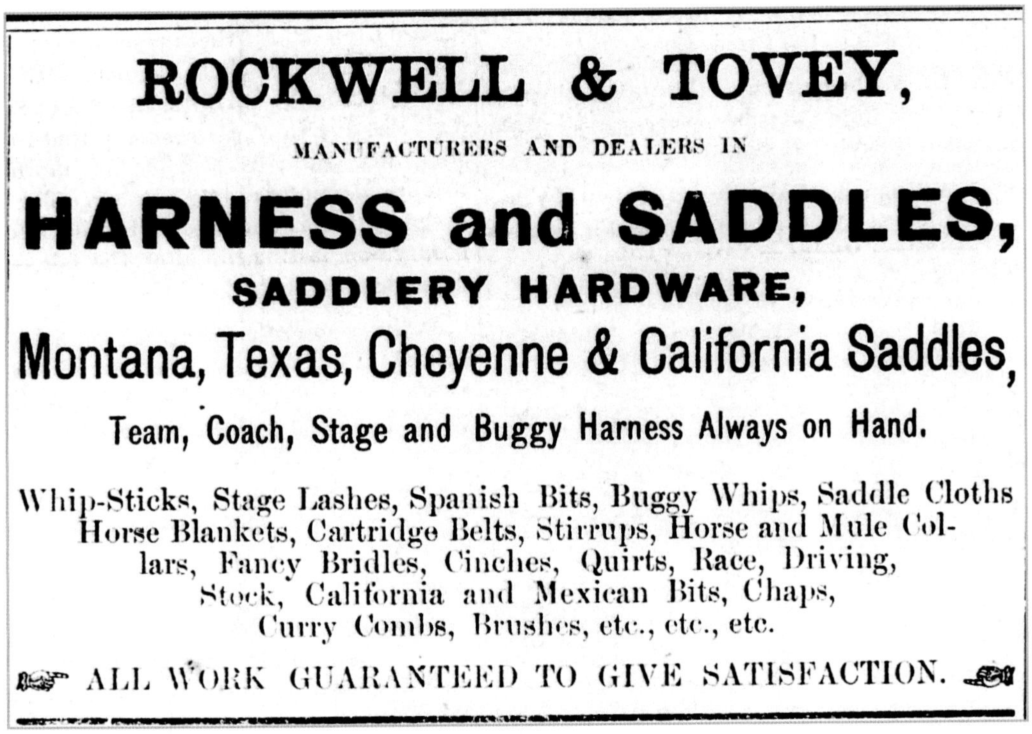

ROCKWELL & TOVEY,

MANUFACTURERS AND DEALERS IN

HARNESS and SADDLES,

SADDLERY HARDWARE,

Montana, Texas, Cheyenne & California Saddles,

Team, Coach, Stage and Buggy Harness Always on Hand.

Whip-Sticks, Stage Lashes, Spanish Bits, Buggy Whips, Saddle Cloths Horse Blankets, Cartridge Belts, Stirrups, Horse and Mule Collars, Fancy Bridles, Cinches, Quirts, Race, Driving, Stock, California and Mexican Bits, Chaps, Curry Combs, Brushes, etc., etc., etc.

ALL WORK GUARANTEED TO GIVE SATISFACTION.

Figure 3.3.
Advertisement for ***Rockwell & Tovey***, Billings, M.T. From the *Billings Herald*, September 1, 1883.

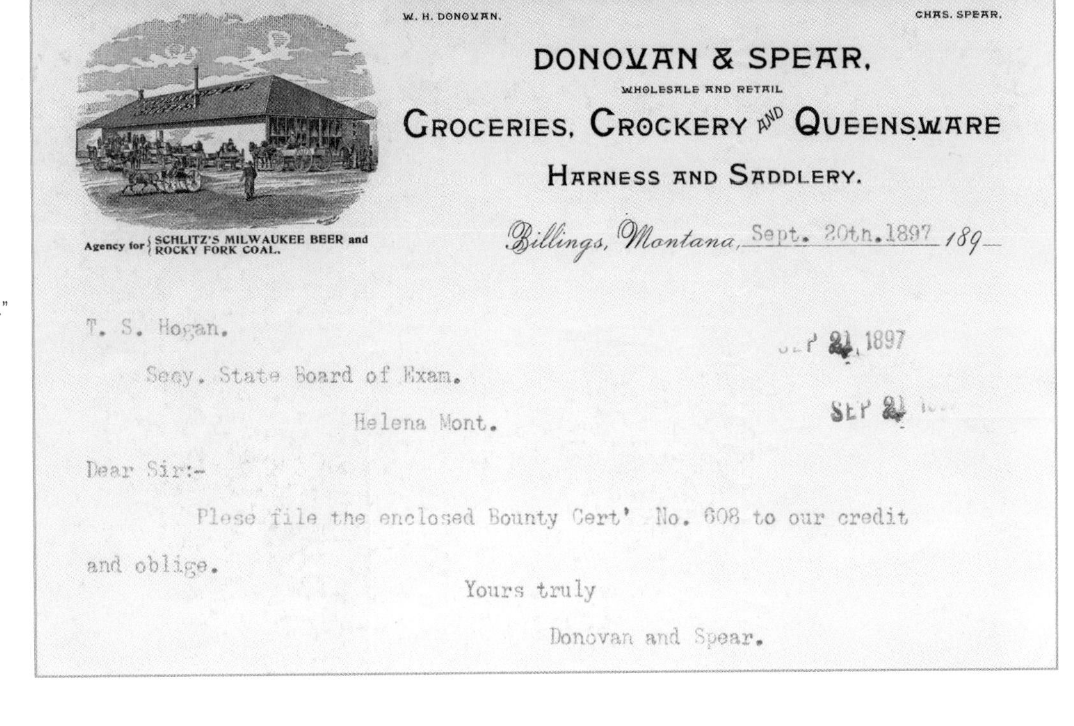
W. H. DONOVAN. CHAS. SPEAR.

DONOVAN & SPEAR,

WHOLESALE AND RETAIL

GROCERIES, CROCKERY AND QUEENSWARE

HARNESS AND SADDLERY.

Agency for { SCHLITZ'S MILWAUKEE BEER and ROCKY FORK COAL.

Billings, Montana, Sept. 20th.1897 189

T. S. Hogan.

Secy. State Board of Exam.

Helena Mont.

SEP 21 1897

SEP 21

Dear Sir:-

Plese file the enclosed Bounty Cert' No. 608 to our credit and oblige.

Yours truly

Donovan and Spear.

Figure 3.4.
Letter from ***Donovan and Spear***, Billings, Montana, dated Sept. 20, 1897, concerning a "Bounty Cert." Note that this firm acted as an agency for Schlitz's Milwaukee Beer.

C. Racek, who bought the firm of Rockwell & Tovey in 1884 (*The Billings Herald*, September 6, 1884) and was in partnership with Racek Bros. (figure 3.5), was an M.T. maker, and rare examples of his work are shown in figures 3.6 through 3.10. W. B. Ten Eyck, a contemporary of Racek whose output appears to be more extensive, based on items available today, produced holsters (figures 3.119 and 3.12), rifle cases (figure 3.13), chaps (figures 3.14 through 3.16), spur straps (figures 3.17 and 3.18), money/cartridge belts (figure 3.19), and harness (figures 3.20 and 3.21), as well as saddles, bridles, and other horse-related items not shown here. Ten Eyck's mark is not only distinctive, but also very attractive, as part of it is in script (figure 3.18, for example). However, most of Ten Eyck's tenure in Billings was *post*-Territorial, i.e., after 1889, yet he continued to use his M.T. mark until his business closed in the first decade of the twentieth century.

Two elusive Billings saddle makers about whom we know very little are C. H. Smith and Wm. Schneider. The former used an "M.T." mark, as shown on a belt in figures 3.22 and 3.23. An example of Schneider's work, marked "MONT.," is shown by a single wide-loop holster (figures 3.24 and 3.25).

Racek Bros.,

Harness Makers

AND SADDLERS.

Cheyenne Saddles, Chaps and Cow Boy outfits a specialty. Dealers in Collars, Whips. Lashes Brushes. Combs. Etc.

Billings, - Montana.

Figure 3.5.
Advertisement for ***Racek Bros.***, Billings, Montana. From the *Billings Herald*, September 1, 1883.

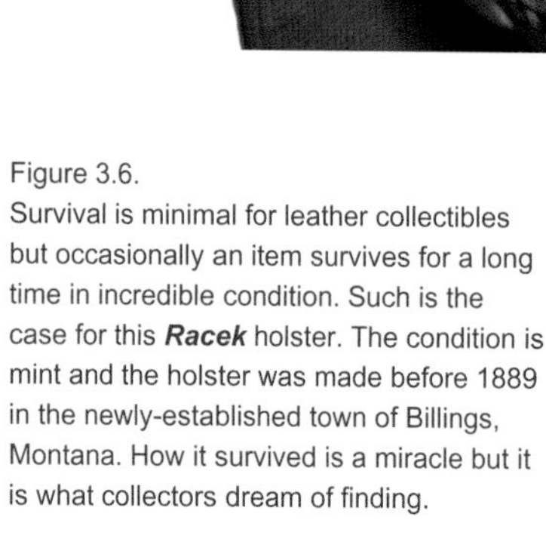

Figure 3.6.
Survival is minimal for leather collectibles but occasionally an item survives for a long time in incredible condition. Such is the case for this ***Racek*** holster. The condition is mint and the holster was made before 1889 in the newly-established town of Billings, Montana. How it survived is a miracle but it is what collectors dream of finding.

Figure 3.7.
From our experience this is the only mark used by ***Charles Racek*** during his tenure in Billings, M.T. It is absolutely essential to be able to reference the authentic marks of the saddlers. Charles Racek made this holster before 1889 and it is still in near-mint condition. Because the mark is absolutely crystal clear, it would be easy to identify on other items one may find (figure 3.6).

Figure 3.8.
A Territorial saddle with the half-seat and Sam Stagg rigging style that was popular with cowboys before 1890. This saddle is marked ***C. Racek***, Billings, M.T., and is extremely rare. Less than ten Racek items are known to the authors.

Figure 3.9.
Holster made by ***C. Racek***, Billings, M.T. The territorial mark is clearly shown.

Figure 3.10.
Pommel bags that fit over the saddle horn are generally considered early and rare because they only fit properly on the early A-fork saddles. This nice pair of bags was made by ***Racek*** and may be as early as 1882, when Billings was established.

Figure 3.11.
W. B. Ten Eyck made this beautiful tooled example of what is known as the single wide-loop Montana holster, the classic look in a holster made in Eastern Montana. As a general rule, this would be the standard style of single-action holster offered by any of the saddleries east of Bozeman in the period from 1880 to c. 1900. The mark is shown in figure 3.12.

Figure 3.12.
W. B. Ten Eyck has the authors' vote for the most attractive and interesting of all the saddle marks used in Montana. The beautiful script "Billings, M.T." and the unique corner borders make it a real eye-catcher. However, the age of this mark is a little deceiving. William Ten Eyck arrived in Billings approximately one year before Montana became a state and established his saddle shop. In November, 1889, Montana became a state and most saddleries slowly began to change their marks to reflect the new status. Apparently, William Ten Eyck never appreciated the need to make this change. All known items made by his saddlery have this territorial mark despite the fact that saddle-making continued after 1900.

Figure 3.13.
A well-used lever-action rifle scabbard produced by the ***Ten Eyck*** saddlery in Billings. This scabbard was made before 1900 and was well used by the cowboy that owned it. Although collectors' items today, scabbards were, and in some cases still are, used by the cowboys who purchased them.

Figure 3.14.
These ornate chaps are as heavy as they look and are in exceptional condition. In the early 1970s, a saddler who owned these chaps for a time replaced all of the small leather ties (collectors would have preferred the older ones instead). It is our opinion that these were "catalog chaps," available for saddleries to purchase unmarked, subsequently stamped with their own maker's mark, and sold from their business. Not all saddleries made the entirety of their sale merchandise in house, probably the case with these chaps. However, they were stamped by ***Ten Eyck*** and are early, although probably not pre-1889.

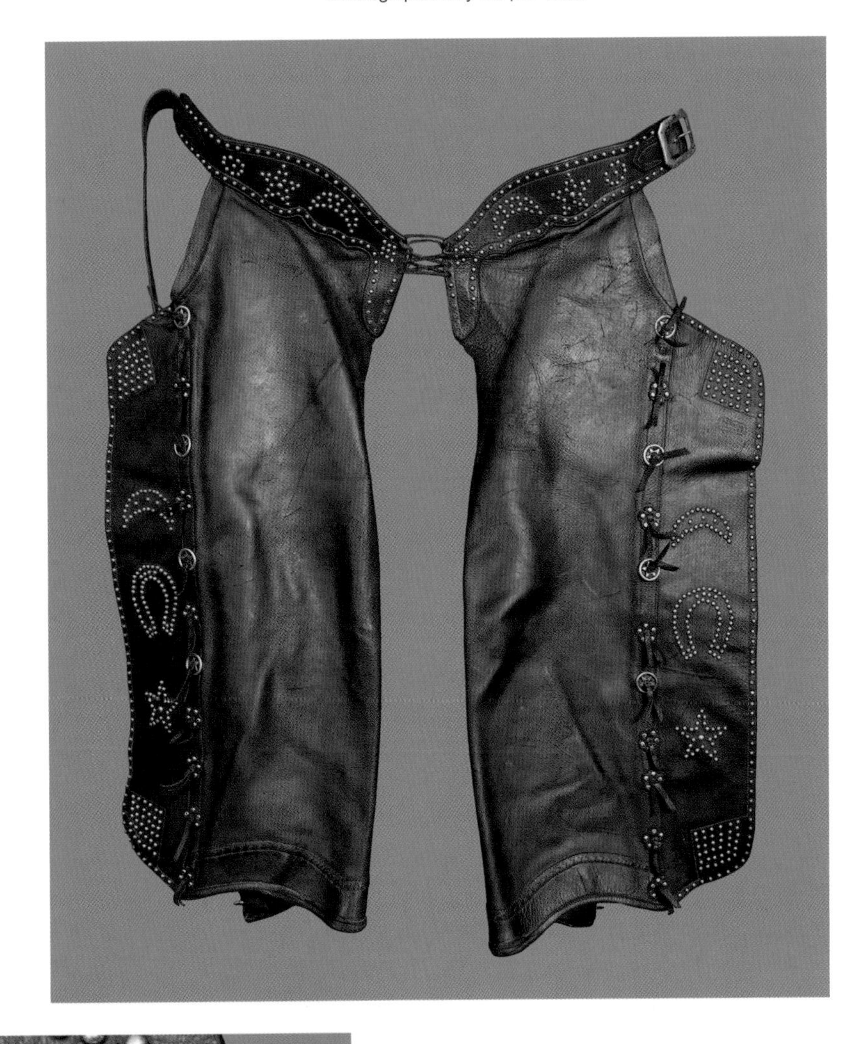

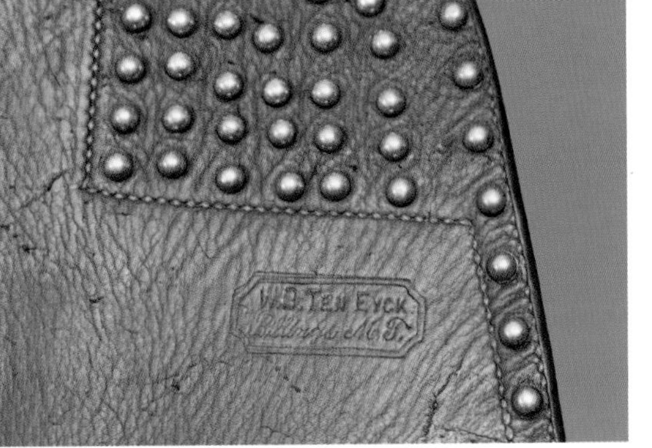

Figure 3.15.
William (W. B.) Ten Eyck marked this showy studded pair of cowboy chaps (figure 3.14) with his territorial mark. The Ten Eyck saddlery mark is one of the most unique and attractive of those used in early Montana. Although he worked in Billings until after the turn of the century, he never updated his mark. Consequently, all of his production bears this mark.

Figure 3.16.
An early pair of fringed shotgun chaps that were made by ***W. B. Ten Eyck*** of Billings, M.T. The chaps have the classic shape and a fine "spaghetti fringe," an indicator of early manufacture.

Figure 3.18.
W. B. Ten Eyck, Billings, M.T., mark on spur strap (figure 3.17). This mark is deep, crisp, and unmistakable.

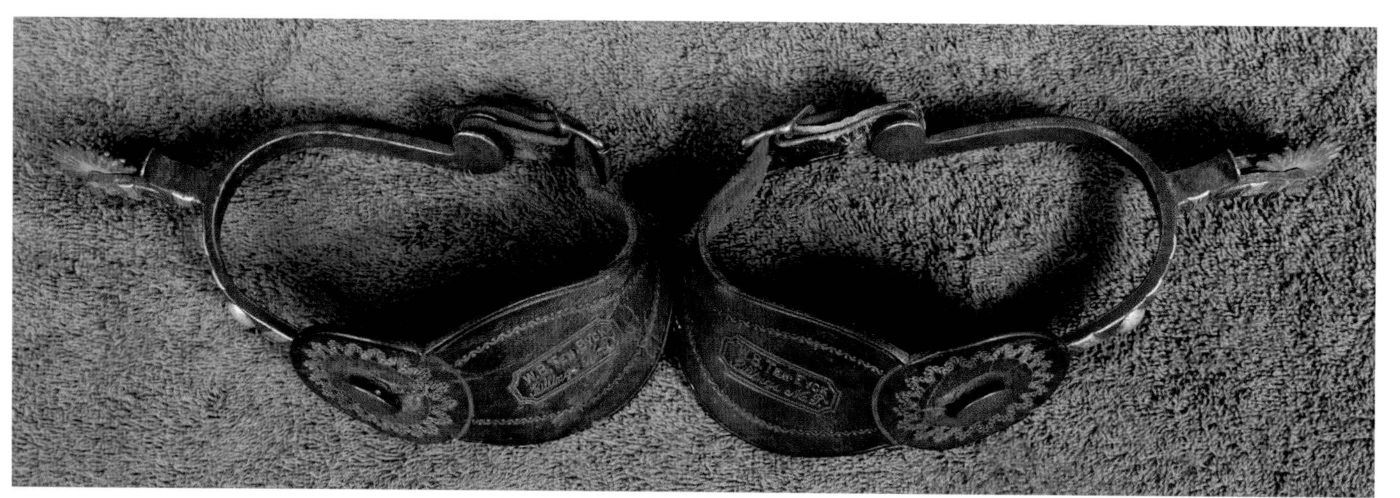

Figure 3.17.
A pair of spur straps made by ***W. B. Ten Eyck***—the mark is shown in figure 3.18 (one on each strap).

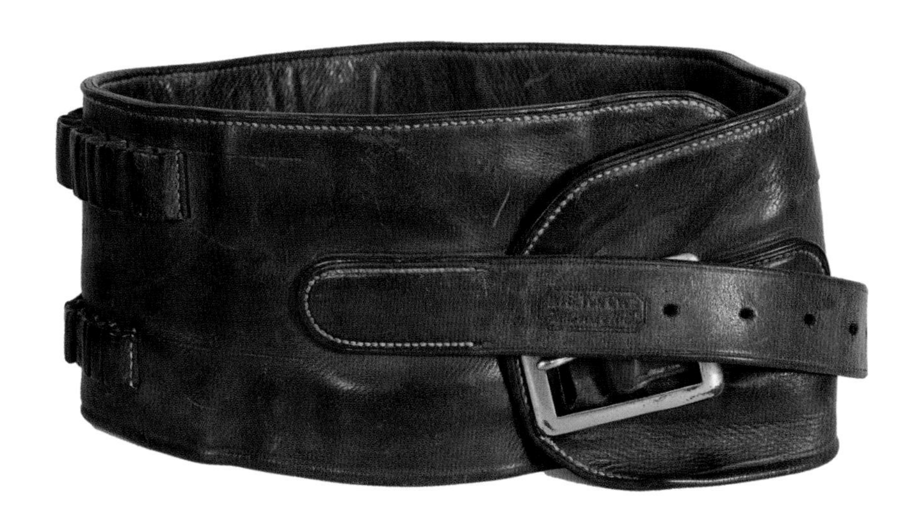

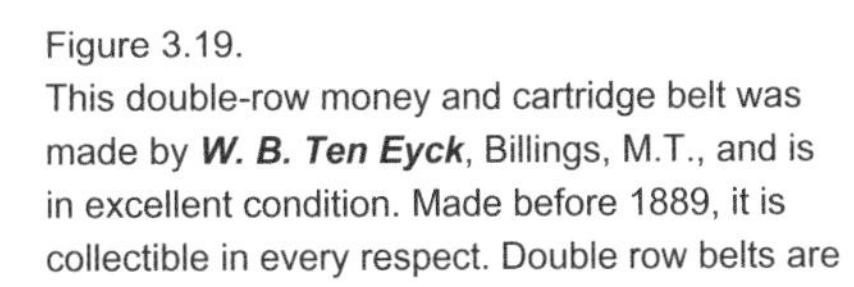

Figure 3.19.
This double-row money and cartridge belt was made by ***W. B. Ten Eyck***, Billings, M.T., and is in excellent condition. Made before 1889, it is collectible in every respect. Double row belts are very seldom encountered.

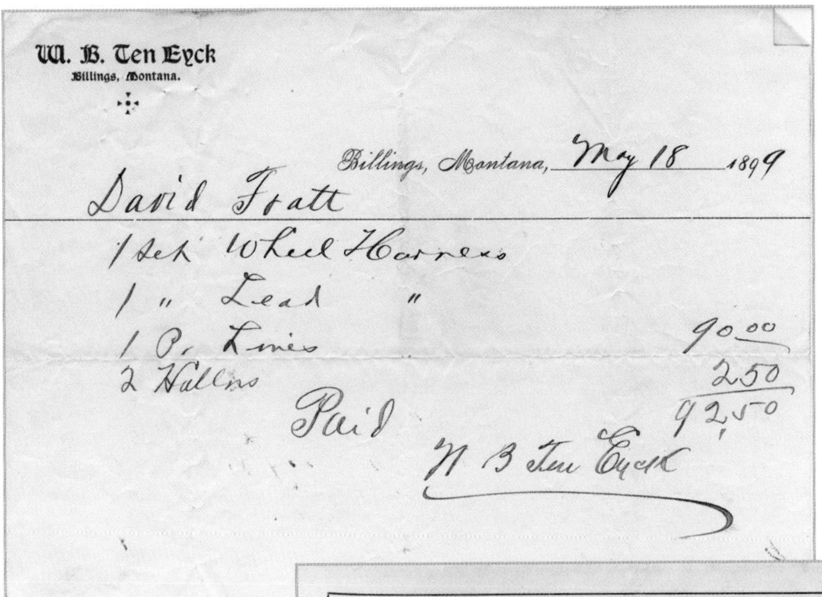

W. B. Ten Eyck
Billings, Montana.

Billings, Montana, May 18 1899

David Fratt

1 set Wheel Harness
1 " Lead "
1 Pr Lines 90.00
2 Halters 2.50
Paid 92.50

W B Ten Eyck

Figure 3.20.
Invoice from ***W. B. Ten Eyck***, Billings, Montana, dated May 18, 1899, to David Fratt, for harness sets.

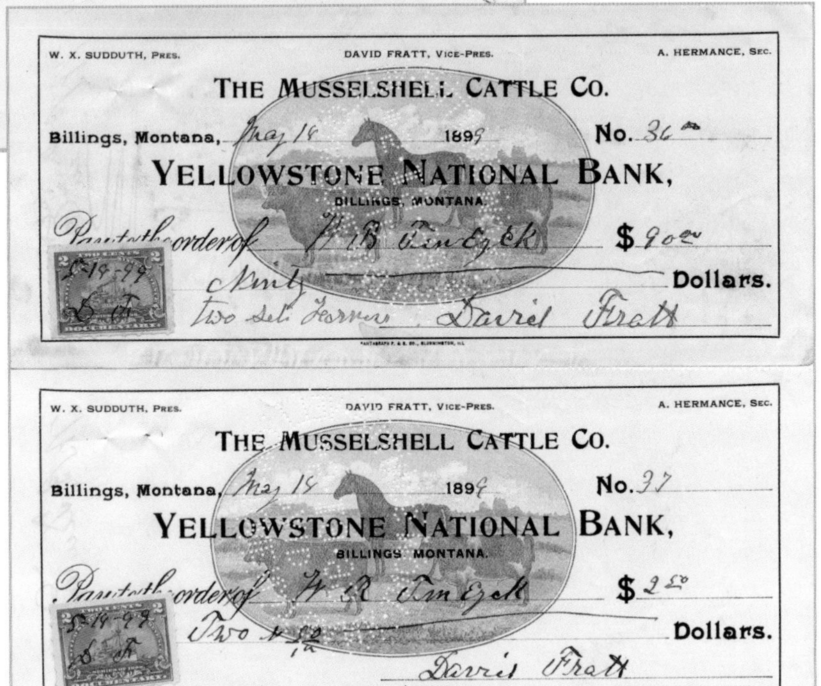

W. X. SUDDUTH, PRES. DAVID FRATT, VICE-PRES. A. HERMANCE, SEC.
THE MUSSELSHELL CATTLE CO.
Billings, Montana, May 18 1899 No. 36
YELLOWSTONE NATIONAL BANK,
BILLINGS, MONTANA
Pay to the order of W B Ten Eyck $90.00
Ninety Dollars.
two set Harness David Fratt

W. X. SUDDUTH, PRES. DAVID FRATT, VICE-PRES. A. HERMANCE, SEC.
THE MUSSELSHELL CATTLE CO.
Billings, Montana, May 18 1899 No. 37
YELLOWSTONE NATIONAL BANK,
BILLINGS, MONTANA.
Pay to the order of W B Ten Eyck $2.50
Two 50/100 Dollars.
David Fratt

Figure 3.21.
Two cancelled checks from David Fratt, vice-president of the Musselshell Cattle Co., to ***Ten Eyck*** in payment of the invoice shown in figure 3.20.

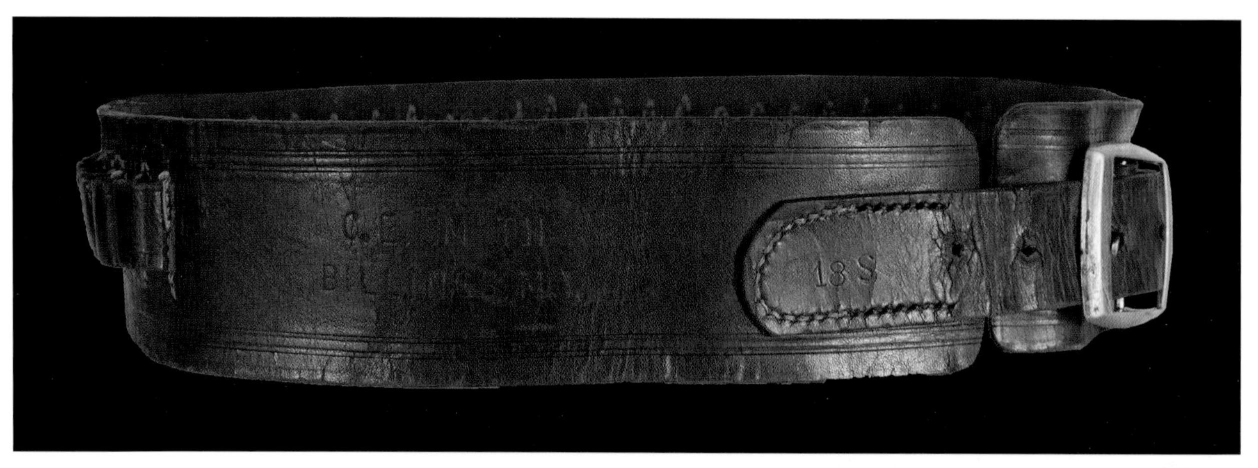

Figure 3.22.
We know virtually nothing about ***C. E. Smith***—this is the only saddlery item we can find that he produced.

Figure 3.23.
C. E. Smith made and marked this belt in Billings before 1889. It is the only example of this saddler and his mark that we know about (figure 3.22).

Figure 3.24.
The ***Schneider*** holster is made according to the standard single wide-loop holster construction technique made by the majority of the Montana makers, although all of the catalogs showed many different loop arrangements.

Figure 3.25.
Not much is known about ***William Schneider*** of Billings except the existence of this marked and nicely-tooled holster (figure 3.24).

A company from Sentinel Butte, North Dakota, the Sentinel Butte Saddlery Co., opened a short-lived satellite branch in Billings during the first decade of the twentieth century (figure 3.26), and employed Ten Eyck in this venture. Although they were in business in Billings for only a limited time (the dates are unclear but could be as late as 1918–1920), their output was not only impressive, but also outstanding with regard to its quality, beauty, and design. A set of orange woolly (angora goat) saddle drapes and their distinctive almond-shaped mark are shown in figures 3.27 through 3.29, and a set of bear-skin woolly chaps imprinted with the same mark is shown in figures 3.30 and 3.31. A rare, marked bridle (figures 3.32 and 3.33) bears the SENTINEL BUTTE SADDLERY CO. mark with no location of manufacture—possibly North Dakota or Billings, Montana. It is reported that Frank Lucas, of the Rafter E Ranch in Mosher, South Dakota, founded the firm on his ranch but moved it to Sentinel Butte. In 1910, it was sold to Lewis Crawford, who incorporated the business and hired W. F. Peterson as general manager and bookkeeper. Crawford, a Harvard graduate, opened satellite branches in North Dakota and in Montana—Glendive, Terry, Baker, and Lewistown. After the decline of the saddlery business (a general trend that occurred from about 1900 to 1920), the Sentinel Butte factory was closed and moved to Billings in 1918, where it ceased operations permanently two years later (Redmond, 1992). Other examples of Sentinel Butte, Billings–marked products are a custom-made saddle with the opening in front of the swells (pommel) covered by the leather seat (an unusual feature) (figures 3.34 and 3.35), and two holsters (figure 3.36).

A rifle scabbard (figures 3.37 and 3.38) with "P. SMITH" stamped above the Sentinel Butte mark (likely the owner's name) shows a more utilitarian design that would have been used on the Montana range. Items from this saddlery are considered quite rare; a satchel is shown in figure 3.39.

MAKERS OF THE FAMOUS SENTINEL BUTTE SADDLE

SENTINEL BUTTE SADDLERY CO.

SENTINEL BUTTE, N. D.
AND
BILLINGS, MONT.

PRESENTED BY
F. W. PETERSON,
MANAGER

Figure 3.26.
Business card for ***Sentinel Butte Saddlery Co.***, of Sentinel Butte, N.D. and Billings, Mont. *Courtesy of Brian Lebel.*

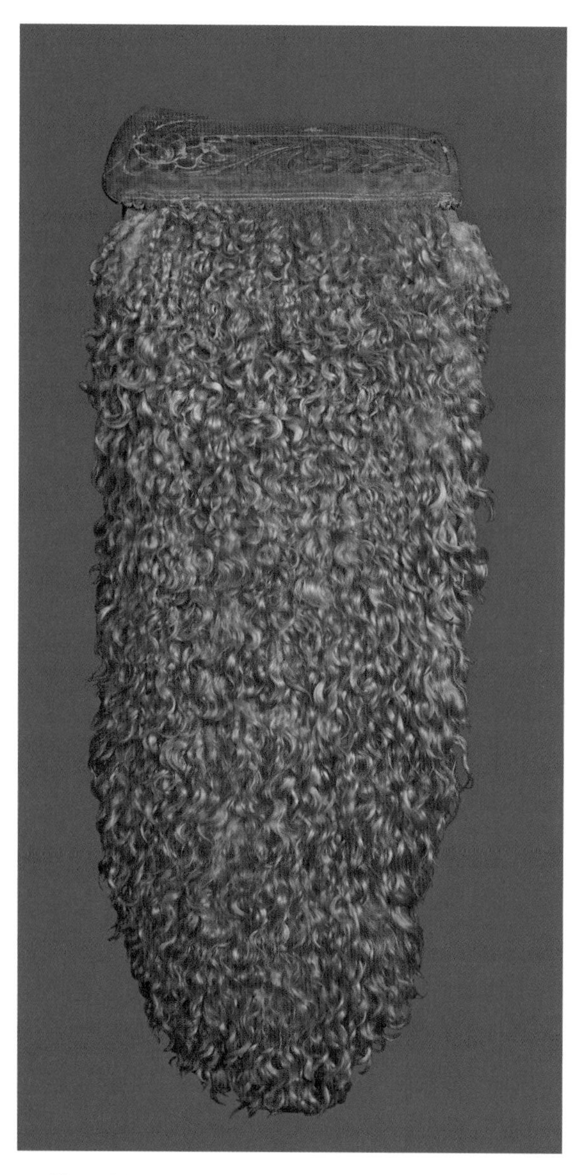

Figure 3.27.
This gorgeous pair of serapes or saddle drapes was made by the ***Sentinel Butte Saddlery*** during their short tenure in Billings. The black serapes on the back of Buffalo Bill's personal saddle (on display in the Cody Museum) are constructed and marked exactly as these. It is almost certain that the serapes on the Cody saddle and this set were custom made for use in the Cody Old West Productions. The serapes measure almost four feet from top to bottom and the leather at the top is floral-carved, a real showpiece.

Figure 3.28.
This side view of the serapes (figure 3.27) shows they are made without saddle bags and would not serve a useful purpose on a working cowboy saddle, again a good indication that they were made for "show and eye appeal" and likely used in Buffalo Bill's Wild West productions.

Figure 3.29.
Football-shaped saddlery marks are not unusual, yet the ***Sentinel Butte Saddlery Co.*** chose to use the shape when they started their shop in Billings. They were in business for only a limited time (the actual dates are unclear, see text). One of their employees was William Ten Eyck, whose shop had closed earlier. This was one of at least two different marks they used in their Billings location (figure 3.27).

Figure 3.30.
Chaps that are made of something other than leather or angora are rare indeed. This pair is made from the hide of a black bear by the ***Sentinel Butte Saddlery*** in Billings. Most of the time a client had shot something other than a cow and wanted to show off the hide by having chaps made from it. In the short time they were in Billlings, Sentinel Butte Saddlery made some very rare and unique items. Note the initials "W.M." on the belt.

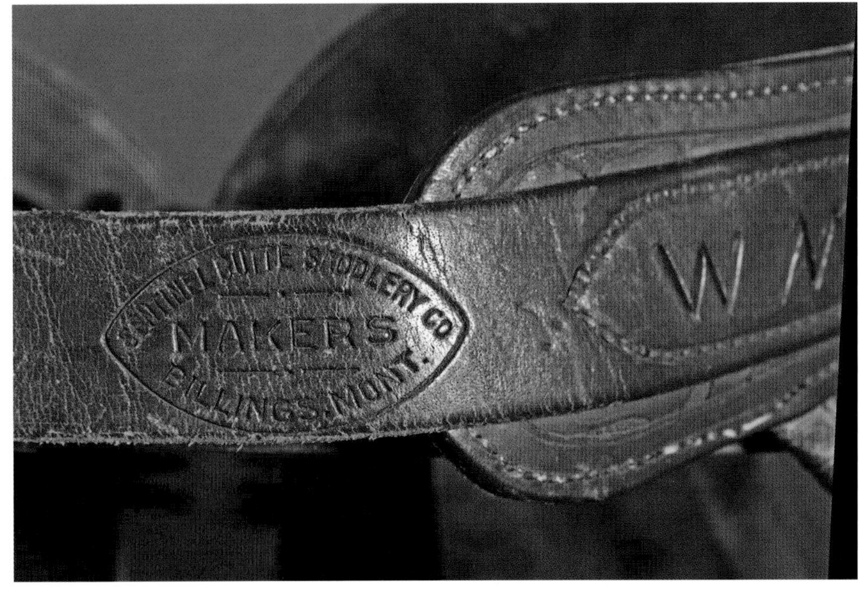

Figure 3.31.
A clear example of the standard mark used by ***Sentinel Butte Saddlery Co.*** during the short time they had their shop in Billings. Despite their good location across from the Post Office and near the large mercantile of Yegen Bros. on Montana Avenue, their shop closed (figure 3.30).

Figure 3.32.
Sentinel Butte Saddlery made this bridle but it is impossible to know whether it was made in Billings, Glendive, or in North Dakota (see text). *Courtesy of T. Leland.*

Figure 3.33.
The ***Sentinel Butte*** mark does not indicate the city of manufacture located on this bridle. It could have been made in Montana or North Dakota (figure 3.32). *Courtesy of T. Leland.*

Figure 3.34.
A side view of a ***Sentinel Butte***, Billings, Montana saddle shows the full seat covering with no opening in the center. Sentinel Butte made quality goods which were highly sought after in the trade. *Courtesy of T. Leland.*

Figure 3.35.
The "EDL" initials on the back of the cantle clearly show this was a custom-order saddle, which probably also included the unique full-covered seat (figure 3.34). *Courtesy of T. Leland.*

Figure 3.36.
The spring-clip holster and the single-action holster with the characteristic Montana single wide loop were both made by the ***Sentinel Butte Saddlery*** in Billings. The spur straps were marked "Sentinel Butte" but are silent as to the city of manufacture. This is a nice grouping of rare saddlery items in very good condition. *Courtesy of T. Leland.*

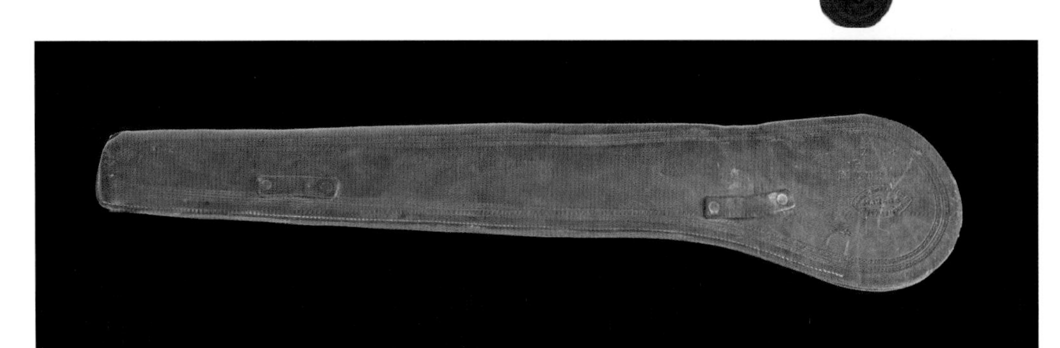

Figure 3.37.
Sentinel Butte Saddlery Company marked this rifle scabbard in their Billings, Montana shop. It is fairly plain in appearance and was clearly for use. Any items with this mark are considered rare.

Figure 3.38.
The tenure of the ***Sentinel Butte Saddlery Company*** is unclear (see text), but they started a satellite shop in Billings in c. 1918. Although the shop was short-lived, they made some interesting items during that period. They used this football-shape mark on everything that we have seen made in Billings. At one point they employed W. E. Ten Eyck in their saddlery, after his business firm had terminated (figure 3.37).

Figure 3.39.
Tooled bags are rare in any size and from any saddler. This large bag was made by ***Sentinel Butte Saddlery Co***. in North Dakota and is so well done as to be considered an art form. *Courtesy of T. Leland.*

The Connolly brothers (Jack, Andrew, and Pat) were rather peripatetic in the saddlery business and have an interesting history. Their father, John, was a maker of horse collars in Ireland and immigrated to the United States in the 1870s, where he settled in Minneapolis. His three sons moved to Butte, Montana, in approximately 1907 and started Connolly Bros. Harness Shop. In 1912 Jack and Pat moved to Billings, where Pat continued with harness production and Jack expanded the business to include saddles. After another move in 1919, and the building of new quarters in Billings, the Connolly Bros. Saddlery continued to produce saddles and leather goods, did repair work, and began to sell clothing, as the harness business declined with the adoption of modern farming and transportation. In the year of the stock market crash that led to the Great Depression (1929), the partnership was terminated, and Jack moved to Livingston (Jack Connolly Saddlery, see table 8.1) while Pat continued the business in Billings as the Pat Connolly Saddlery. Pat's son John entered into the business in 1937 and was later joined by other family members, who advanced the Connolly Saddlery Co. into the 1990s when it finally left family hands after eighty-three years of continuous operation (Grosskopf, 1995). A photograph of Connolly Bros. Saddles in Billings appears in figure 3.40.

Figure 3.40.
Early photograph of "***Connolly Bros. Saddles***," Billings, Mont. The brothers, Pat and Jack, were in this business from 1912–1929.

A varied selection of items produced by the Connolly Bros. is shown in the figures. An impressive pair of orange woolly chaps showing real "cowboy wear" was personalized by its owner (John) with his name and address (figures 3.41 through 3.43). A heavy, impressive pair of chaps bears the same mark (figures 3.44 and 3.45), as do the pommel bags (figures 3.46 and 3.47). A different, lozenge-shaped mark was imprinted on the shoulder holster and wide belts shown in figures 3.48 through 3.52.

The work of Pat Connolly bore his own mark and was distinctive. A saddlery order form, completed by Frances Joyce of White Sulphur Springs, Montana, indicates the options available at that time for a custom saddle (figure 3.53), which in 1947 cost $170.00. One of the most exacting and beautiful creations of Pat Connolly appears in figures 3.54 through 3.57, a "his and hers" matching pair of saddles made for an unidentified but clearly wealthy couple, who were presumably ranchers in the area. A saddle made for David Fratt of Billings (Musselshell Cattle Co., see figures 3.20 and 3.21) is shown in figures 3.58 and 3.59. Produced c. 1930, the saddle bears the brand of the cattle company and Pat Connolly's mark is clear. Another saddle, shown in figures 3.60 and 3.61, is of later manufacture, c. 1940s, and bears the same mark. The flap holster (figures 3.62 and 3.63) of the 1950s design shows a different mark and was made after the Connolly brothers reunited in 1951.

This chapter closes with two advertisements from saddle makers located at a distance from Billings—J. S. Solberg, established in 1889, in Big Timber, and W. A. Talmage, of Red Lodge (figure 3.64 and figures 3.65 and 3.66, respectively). Both of these firms advertised in the Van Dersal and Conner–compiled Directory of Montana Businesses published in 1900. Unfortunately, there are no known examples of the work of either of these saddle makers.

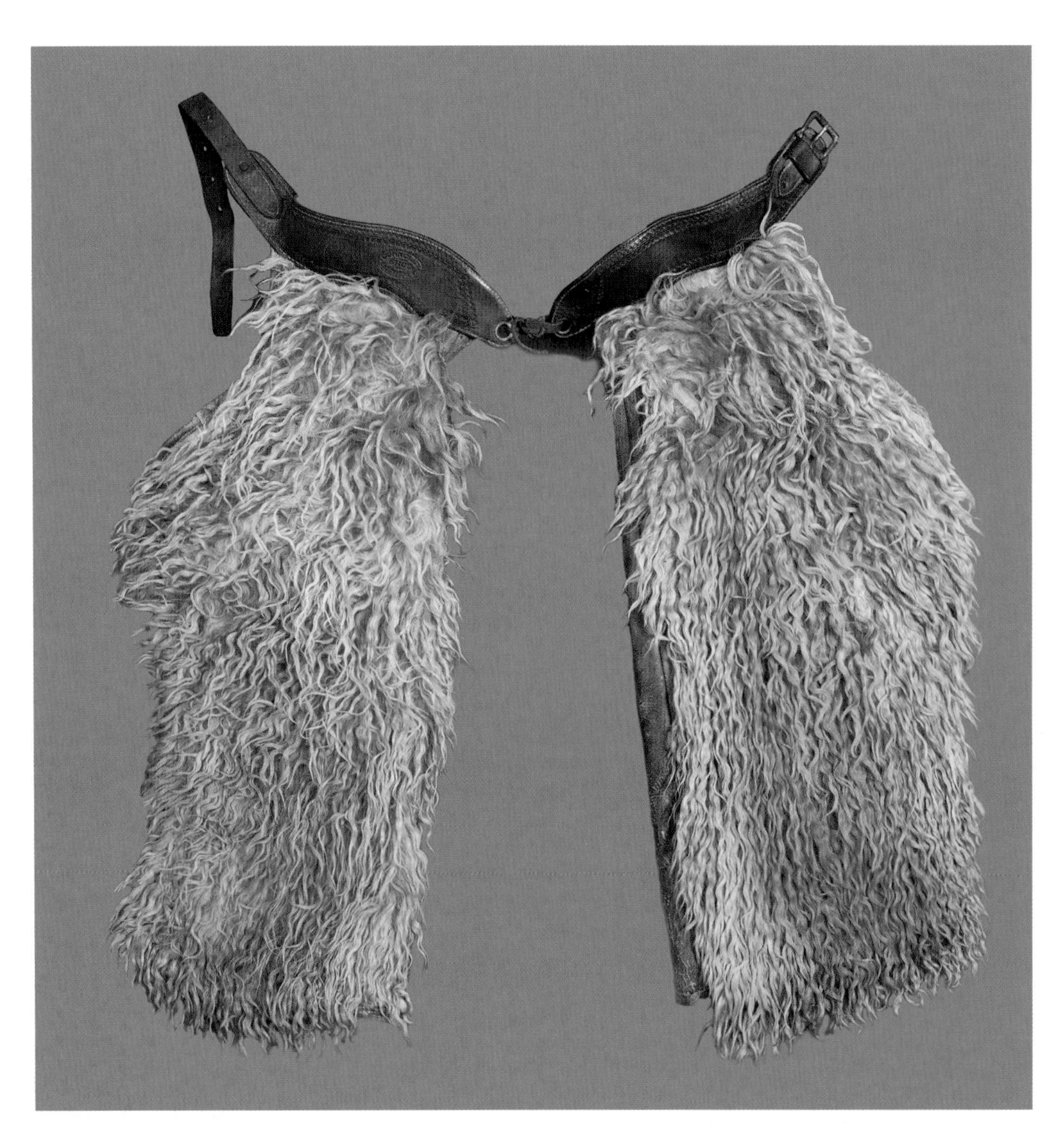

Figure 3.41.
Connolly made these chaps to be used, and the cowboy used them devotedly. This pair that has just the "right" look was owned and used less than 10 miles from Billings.

Figure 3.42.
Many cowboys chose to personalize their chaps. Fancy cowboy duds were expensive and no one wanted to have them stolen (figure 3.41).

Figure 3.43.
The standard mark used by the ***Connolly Brothers Saddlery*** (figure 3.41). The brothers, Pat and Jack, had moved to Butte with their father, where they had established their first shop. They moved to Billings c. 1912 where the cattle trade was still thriving, because mules and thus harness ceased to be used in the operation of the underground mine in Butte.

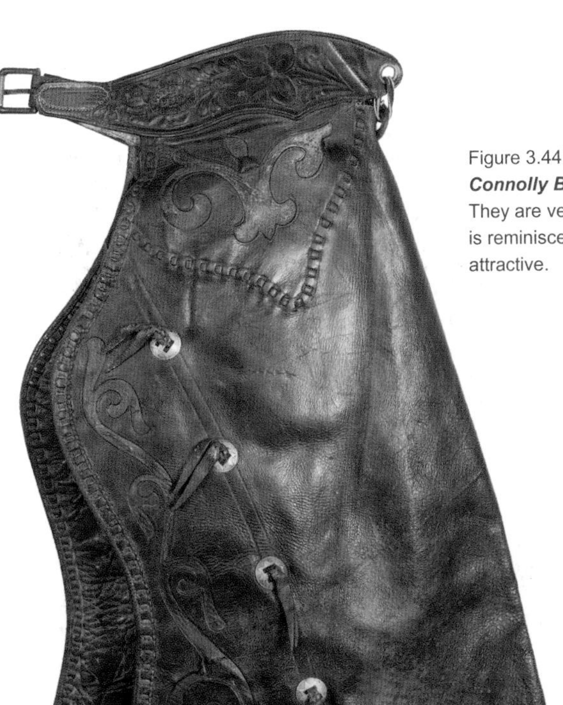

Figure 3.44.
Connolly Bros. made quality cowboy gear and this pair of chaps is a good example. They are very heavy, almost to the point of being difficult to lift. The design on the batwing is reminiscent of chaps made by Hamley of Pendleton, Oregon, but is more ornate and attractive.

Figure 3.45.
An example of the earliest of the ***Connolly Bros***. marks in Billings. This mark predates the division of the company and was in use during the period from 1912 to their separation in 1929 (figure 3.44).

Figure 3.46.
A set of saddle bags made by ***Connolly Bros.*** These well-designed bags have seen hard use and were modified (holes) to fit several different saddles during their lifetime. The holes accommodated strings, or latigos, that secured the bags to the rear skirts of the saddle.

Figure 3.47.
Connolly Bros. mark (BILLINGS, MONT.) on saddle bags shown in figure 3.46.

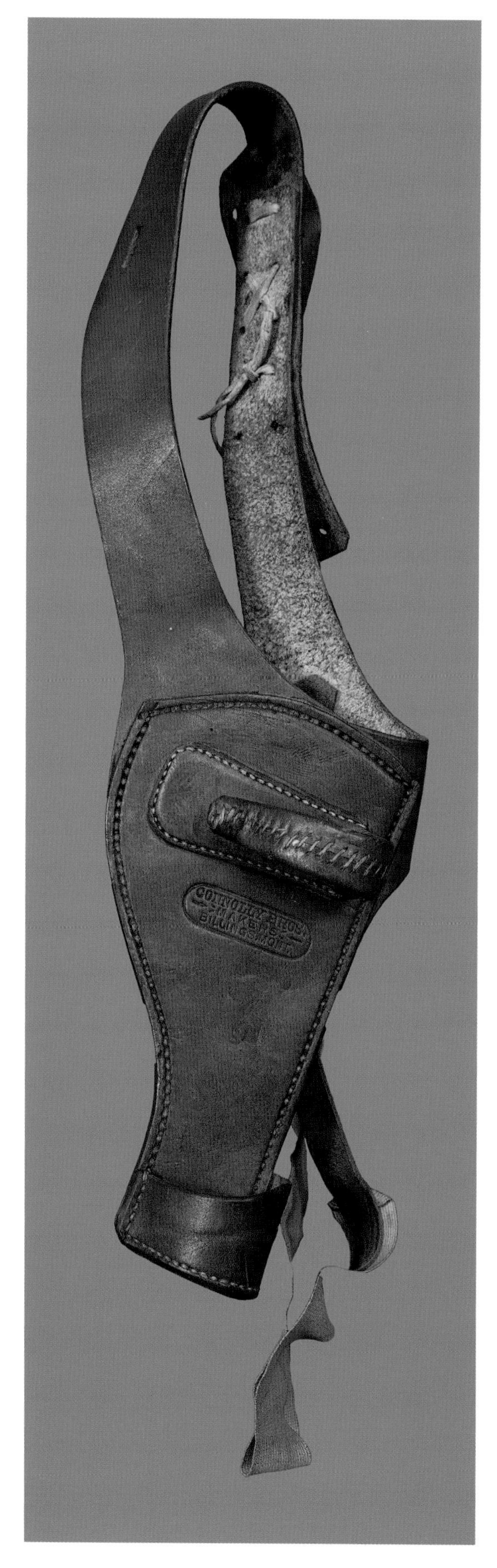

Figure 3.48.
Spring clip shoulder holsters were produced by many saddlers in Montana. This one was made by ***Connolly Brothers*** for a short-barreled, single-action pistol. It is in nice condition and is an excellent example of what many of the lawmen in the area were ordering. Although George Robbins apparently obtained the original patent for this design, upon his quitting the saddlery business many others started making these holsters; it can be assumed that Robbins did not defend his patent.

Figure 3.49.
Shown is a clear image of the prominent ***Connolly Brothers***, Billings, Montana, mark (see figure 3.48) that was stamped on all the items they made.

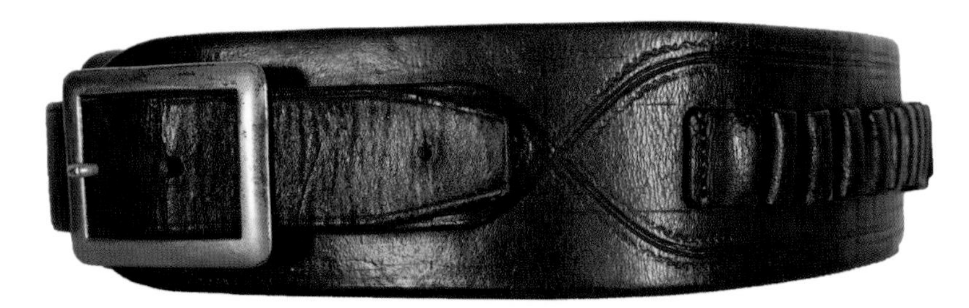

Figure 3.50.
The ***Connolly*** family of saddlers produced quality goods. This well-made money belt is an example of their work. It has sturdy loops highlighted by a distinctive tooling pattern.

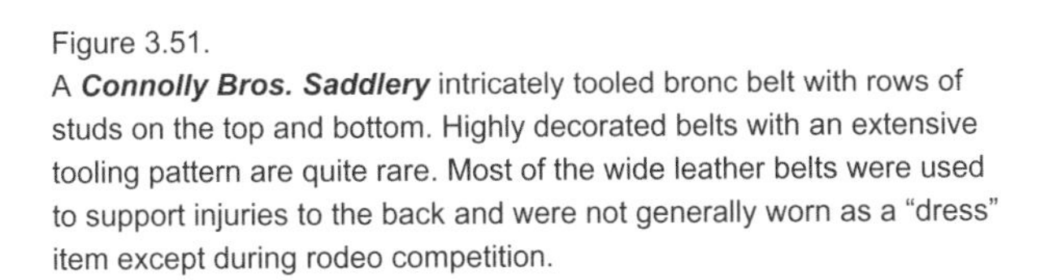

Figure 3.51.
A ***Connolly Bros. Saddlery*** intricately tooled bronc belt with rows of studs on the top and bottom. Highly decorated belts with an extensive tooling pattern are quite rare. Most of the wide leather belts were used to support injuries to the back and were not generally worn as a "dress" item except during rodeo competition.

Figure 3.52.
A detailed view of the ornate bronc belt shown in figure 3.51.

Order Blank

PAT CONNOLLY SADDLERY
MANUFACTURERS OF
SADDLES, RIDING GOODS AND HARNESS
The Leather Goods Store
Luggage
BILLINGS, MONTANA

write when finished About 1 month.

Saddle 170.00
deposit 50.00
Bal 120.00

Date Aug. 25 1947

Write name plainly Frances Joyce
P. O. at which you get your mail White Sulpher Springs
Nearest R. R. Station or Express office
Price of Saddle $ 170.00 Amount sent with this order $ 50.00
Saddle Number All around Skirts, round or square Round
Name of tree Size 13 1/2 Width of swell
Rig: Spanish—three-quarter—center fire or double 3/4 Flate Plate Double
Horn: leather covered—wrapped—braided lea Cover
Stirrups: visalia or oxbow 2 1/2 Visalia with foot piece
Cinch: angora—cotton—fishcord mohair
Seat: high, medium or low Reg Wide or narrow Reg
Do you want your saddle oiled? (no extra charge) Yes
Please give height 5-10 Leg measure Weight
How do you want it stamped? Plain
Brands or initials, free of charge 2 pc tail piece
Remarks: 3" Cantle

Flate plate 150
Double Rig 7.50
1 Piece fender 7.50
5.00
170.00

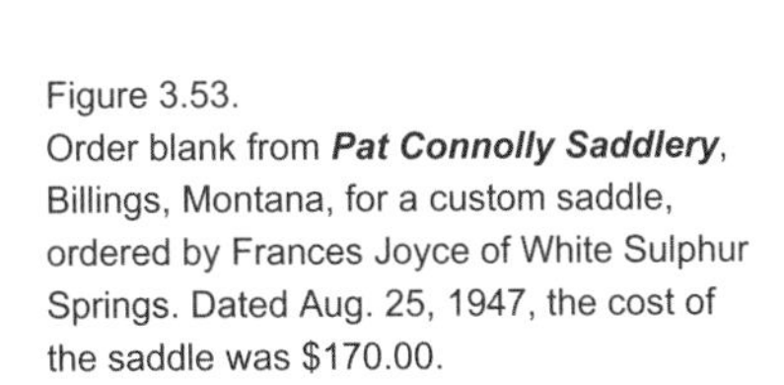

Figure 3.53.
Order blank from ***Pat Connolly Saddlery***, Billings, Montana, for a custom saddle, ordered by Frances Joyce of White Sulphur Springs. Dated Aug. 25, 1947, the cost of the saddle was $170.00.

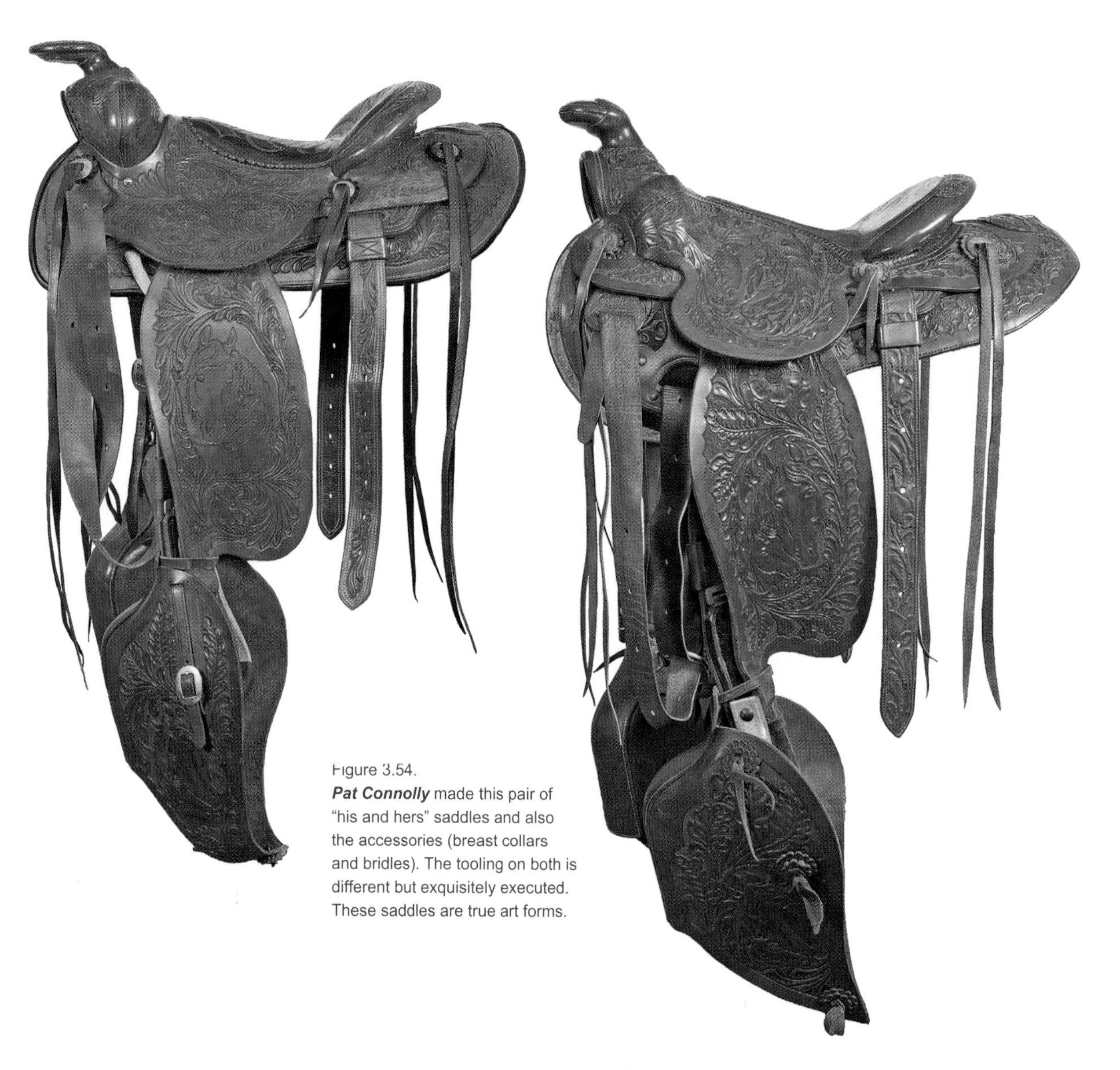

Figure 3.54.
Pat Connolly made this pair of "his and hers" saddles and also the accessories (breast collars and bridles). The tooling on both is different but exquisitely executed. These saddles are true art forms.

Figure 3.55.
The incorporation of the owner's initials into the horn cover is a technique that is not often employed. The tooling on the rest of the front of the saddle is also visible and is equally impressive (figure 3.54).

Figure 3.56.
When Jack Connolly and ***Pat Connolly*** divided the family business and Jack moved to Livingston, Pat acquired a new saddle stamp. This clear view of the mark located just behind the cantle of a custom saddle shows his artistry. The stamp is raised in *bas*-relief from the leaf tooling around the elliptical mark. This work requires a level of skill not often attained by saddle makers, no matter how experienced they were (figure 3.54).

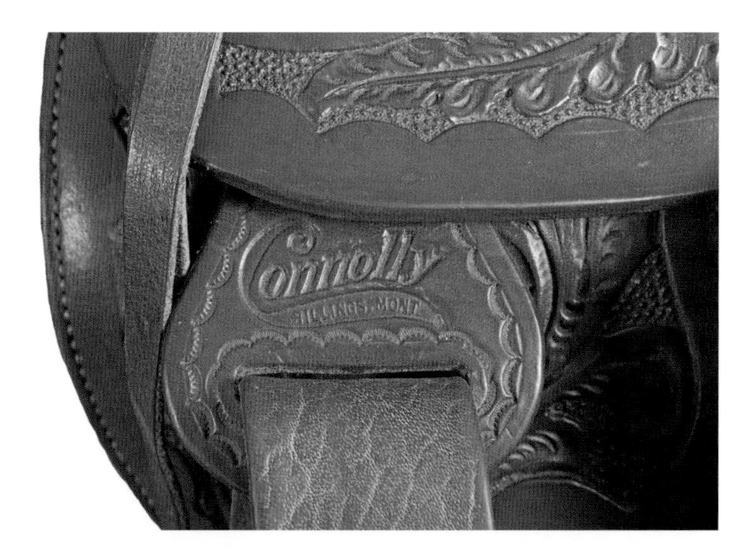

Figure 3.57.
This is one of the Connolly saddle marks used in this case on the latigo keeper of a very ornate custom-made saddle made by ***Pat Connolly*** (figure 3.54).

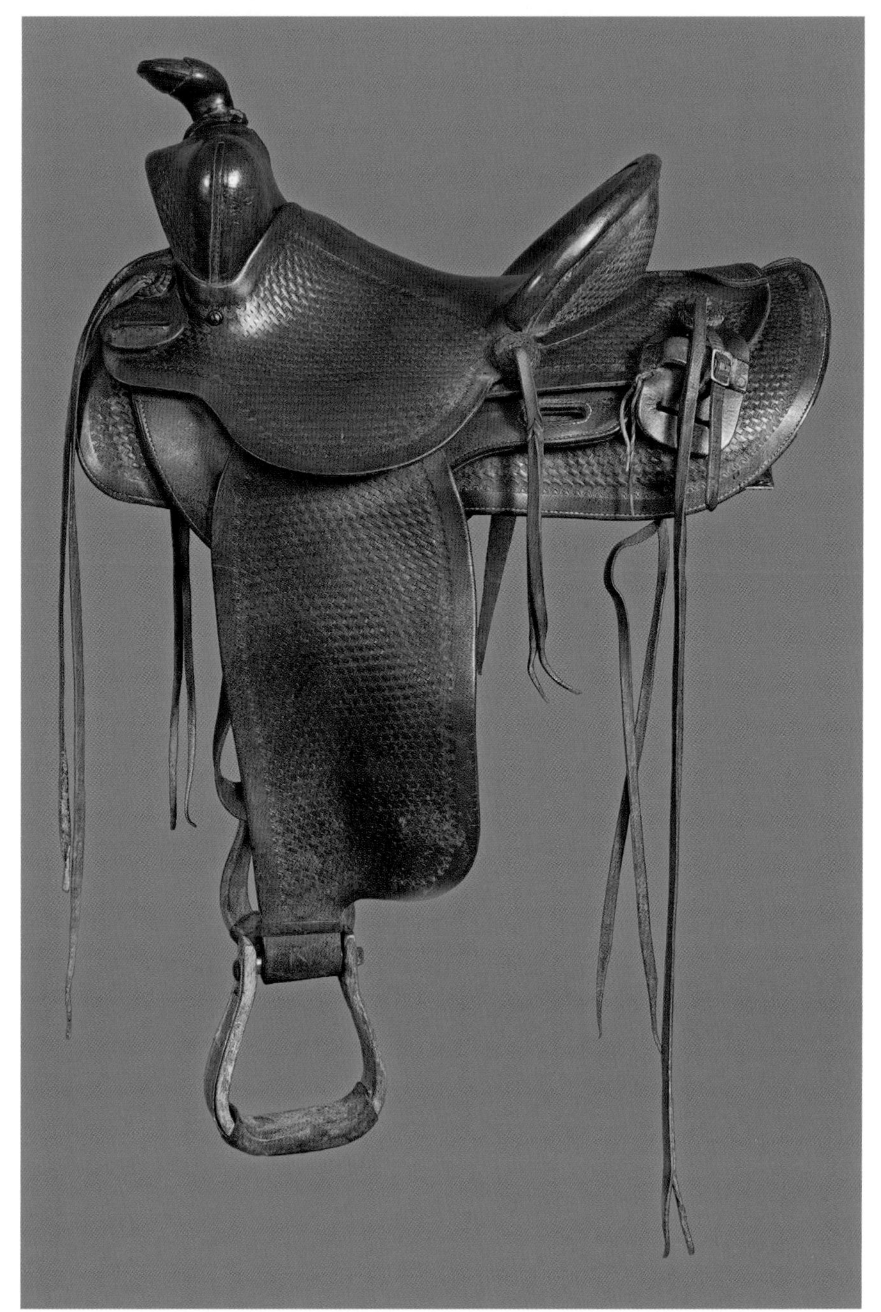

Figure 3.58.
Pat Connolly made this saddle for David Fratt of Billings. The pear was Fratt's recorded brand, tooled into the top skirt just behind the center of the cantle. Fratt came to Billings when it was first established in 1882 (or slightly earlier) and raised cattle north of Billings in the Musselshell area; eventually he moved to Billings where he became a banker and businessman. It appears from the mark and the style that the saddle was made c. 1930.

Figure 3.59.
The seat mark of the ***Pat Connolly*** saddle made for David Fratt (figure 3.58). It is the authors' opinion that Pat Connolly used this mark twice: when the brothers first came to Billings after leaving Butte, and after his brother Jack left and started his own saddlery in Livingston.

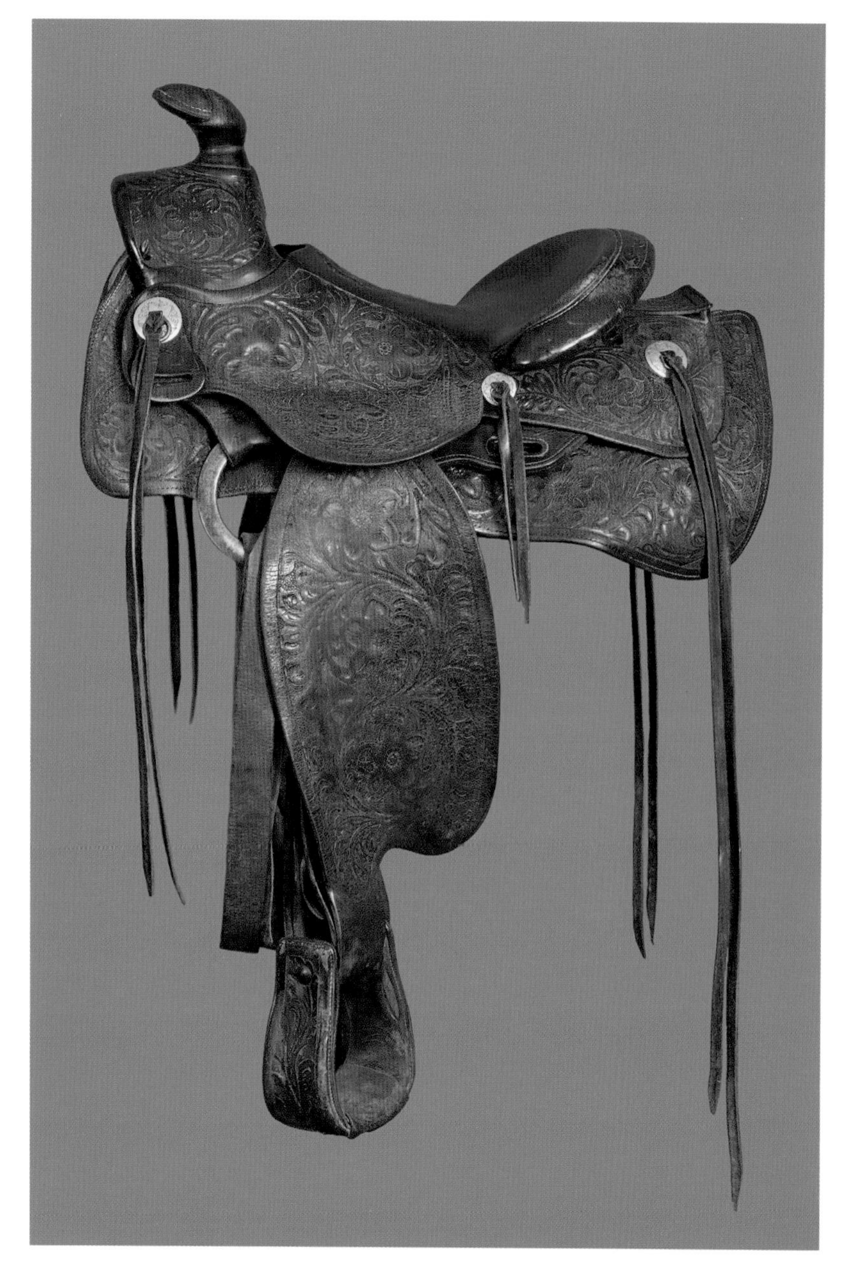

Figure 3.60.
This saddle was a work of art when it was made by ***Pat Connolly*** in the 1940s or '50s. The style was popular during that time period, and a great many of them were made by all of the saddleries. It is exactly what one would expect to see hanging in a ranch barn in 1950.

Figure 3.62.
This flap holster was made after the ***Connolly*** brothers reunited in the early 1950s, and it has the later design of holster construction.

Figure 3.61.
An early example of the ***Pat Connolly***–embossed saddle mark used for a long period of time when the brothers operated saddleries (figure 3.60).

Figure 3.63.
Connolly Saddlery Company was formed in 1951 several years after the brothers Pat and Jack reunited and Pat's children became involved (figure 3.62).

Established 1889. The Pioneer Harness Shop.

J. S. SOLBERG,

BIG TIMBER, MONTANA

SADDLES, HARNESS

Collars, Bridles, Whips, Robes, Horse Blankets, Fly Nets, Etc.

OUR SPECIALTIES:

Heavy Stock Saddles, Hand-made Farm Harness and Repairing. Write for Prices

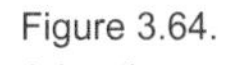

Figure 3.64.
Advertisement for ***J. S. Solberg***, Big Timber, Montana. Also known as the Pioneer Saddle Shop, this saddlery was established in 1889. From Van Dersal and Conner (1900).

W. A. TALMAGE

RED LODGE, MONTANA.

Hardware and ...Implements

Manufacturer of

HARNESS AND SADDLES

STOCK SADDLES A SPECIALTY.

Figure 3.65.
Advertisement for ***W. A. Talmage***, Red Lodge, Montana. From Van Dersal and Conner (1900).

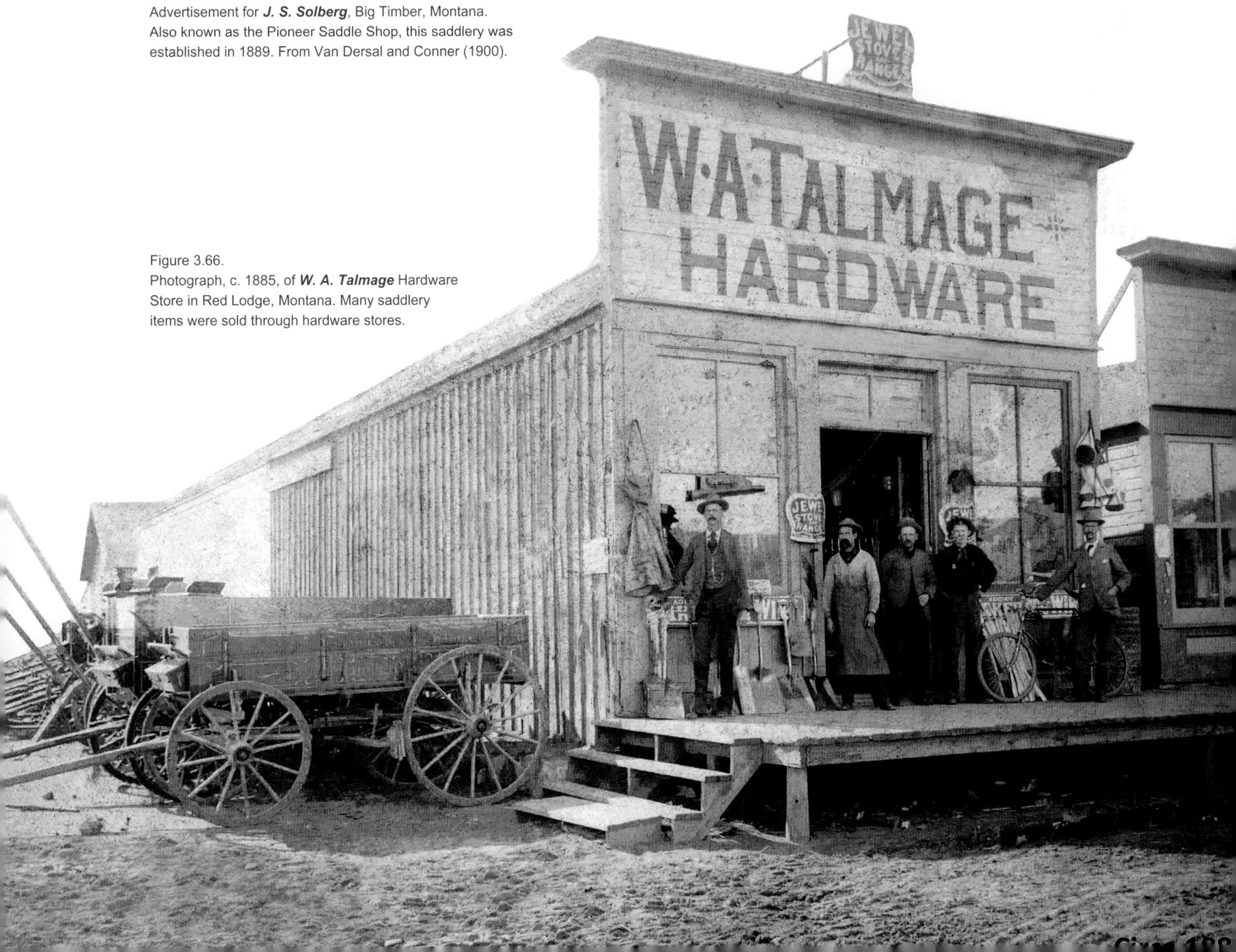

Figure 3.66.
Photograph, c. 1885, of ***W. A. Talmage*** Hardware Store in Red Lodge, Montana. Many saddlery items were sold through hardware stores.

Lincoln
Libby
Flathead
Kalispell
Glacier
Cut Bank
Toole
Shelby
Liberty
Chester
Hill
Havre
Chinook
Blaine
Malta
Phillips
Valley
Glasgow
Scobey
Daniels
Plentywood
Sheridan
Roosevelt
Wolf Point
Pondera
Conrad
Sanders
Thompson Falls
Lake
Polson
9
Teton
Choteau
5
Chouteau
Fort Benton
4
McCone
Circle
Richland
Sidney
Superior
Mineral
Missoula
Missoula
7
6
Lewis and Clark
Cascade
Great Falls
Stanford
Judith Basin
Fergus
Lewistown
Petroleum
Winnett
Garfield
Jordan
Dawson
Glendive
Wibaux
Prairie
Terry
Wibaux
Granite
Philipsburg
Powell
Deer Lodge
Helena
Meagher
White Sulphur Springs
Wheatland
Harlowton
Golden Valley
Ryegate
Musselshell
Roundup
Hysham
Treasure
Rosebud
Forsyth
2
Miles C'ty
Custer
Fallon
Baker
Hamilton
Ravalli
Anaconda
Deer Lodge
Silver Bow
Butte
Boulder
Jefferson
Townsend
Broad-water
Gallatin
Bozeman
Park
Livingston
Sweet Grass
Big Timber
Stillwater
Columbus
Yellowstone
Billings
3
Hardin
Big Horn
Carbon
Red Lodge
Ekalaka
Powder River
Broadus
Carter
Beaverhead
Dillon
Madison
Ennis
8

4

North-Central Montana

Lewistown

Malta

Chinook

Harlem

Lewistown is situated very near to the center of the state of Montana and was established in 1882, as the result of a gold rush spanning that decade. Fort Lewis was built there in 1874 by the 7th US Infantry (Company "F") to defend immigrants on the Carroll Trail (Carroll to Helena) from Native Americans who were hostile to their settling and usurpation of land. After the gold rush in the neighboring Judith Mountains had diminished, miners and those associated with that industry moved to Lewistown, which was also the eastern terminus of the Montana Railroad. The seat of Fergus County, Lewistown benefited from the extensive cattle ranching operations on the open range begun in 1879 by Granville Stuart, Samuel Hauser, and Andrew J. Davis. These ranching activities provided a market for the several influential saddleries in this area. In addition, the Homestead Act of 1862 attracted settlers from the eastern, southern, and midwestern United States to central M.T.

Table 4.1 lists saddleries from Area 4. Most of the saddleries in Area 4 were located in Lewistown, in Fergus County, readily accessible to the ranchers and cowboys working on the large spreads nearby. The area is also represented by smaller towns such as Chinook, Shelly Junction, Two Dot, and Harlowton. The last-mentioned begins this chapter with a photograph of the A. Webster Harness and Saddlery shop (figure 4.1). A collar, harness, and two saddles can be seen in the foreground, but further information on this saddler remains obscure.

Figures 4.2 through 4.7 show an invoice, letter, and advertisements from the Judith Hardware Co., Matt Regan, C. C. Jeffrey, and Geo. M. Stafford, respectively. Although Stafford's pieces are extremely rare, several examples of his work, all marked M.T., are shown in figures 4.8 through 4.13. The rifle scabbard, cuffs, and saddle pockets all bear the lazy diamond cartouche and show "cowboy use," understandable because Stafford was one of the earliest saddle makers in central Montana. The example shown from the Lewistown Saddlery (see figures 4.14 and 4.15), a well-made cartridge belt with a finely-stamped and unusual mark, appears to be of later manufacture, post-1900, but so few pieces from this saddlery exist that further conclusions become difficult.

Table 4.1. Saddleries of Montana1

MAKER	LOCATION	DATES[2]
Art Benjamine & Co.	Lewistown	(1909)
DeKalb Harness Co.	Lewistown	(1911)
Duke, A. B.	Chinook	1890–early 1900s
Ettinger, Harry	Chinook	c. 1900–1918
Fernald, W. H.	Lewistown	1904†
Grisette, Arthur	Lewistown	(1902)
Guth, H. F.	Shelby Junction	1901
Harlem Saddlery (Cowan, W. S.)	Harlem	c. 1920–1937
Harlem Saddlery (W. S. Cowan & R. Corbett) (successor to Duke)	Harlem	Early 1900s
Jeffrey, G. L.	Lewistown	1920s
Jeffrey, Chris C.	Lewistown	1895–1913, (1909)
Judith Hardware Co.	Lewistown	(1906, 1924)
Koke, B. H.	Malta	1895–1920, (1913)
Lewistown Saddlery	Lewistown	
Regan, Matt	Lewistown	(1902)
Richardson, W. H.	Malta	
Spicker Harness Co.	Lewistown	1910§
Spratte & Thomann	Lewistown	M.T.
Stafford, G. M.*	Lewistown	1883, (1902)
Stephens & Jeffrey	Lewistown	1908–1909‡, (1909)
Two Dot Hardware Co.	Two Dot	(c. 1913)
Webster, A.	Harlowton	(c. 1919)
Young, Andrew	Lewistown	1904†, 1908‡, 1909‡

1. Products made or sold by these saddleries included harness, saddles, bits, spurs, whips, boots, bridles, accessories (horse blankets, grooming tools, trunks, bags, and/or robes), vehicles (sleighs, buggies, wagons, carts), and Indian-made goods (e.g., saddle blankets).

2. Dates in parentheses are specified on the company letterhead or in a newspaper/journal advertisement. Inclusive dates for the tenure of the company have been provided where data are available and reliable.

† Polk Directory (R. L. Polk & Co.'s Directory for Fergus County area), 1904.

‡ Polk Directory, 1908–1909

§ Polk Directory, 1910

* Chris Jeffrey bought the G. M. Stafford store in Lewistown (*Fergus County Democrat*, December 21, 1909); William Gordon bought the G. M. Stafford store in nearby Moore (*Fergus County Argus*, December 14, 1906).

Figure 4.1.
Photograph of ***A. Webster's*** "Harness and Saddles/Tents and Awnings" shop, in Harlowton, Montana.

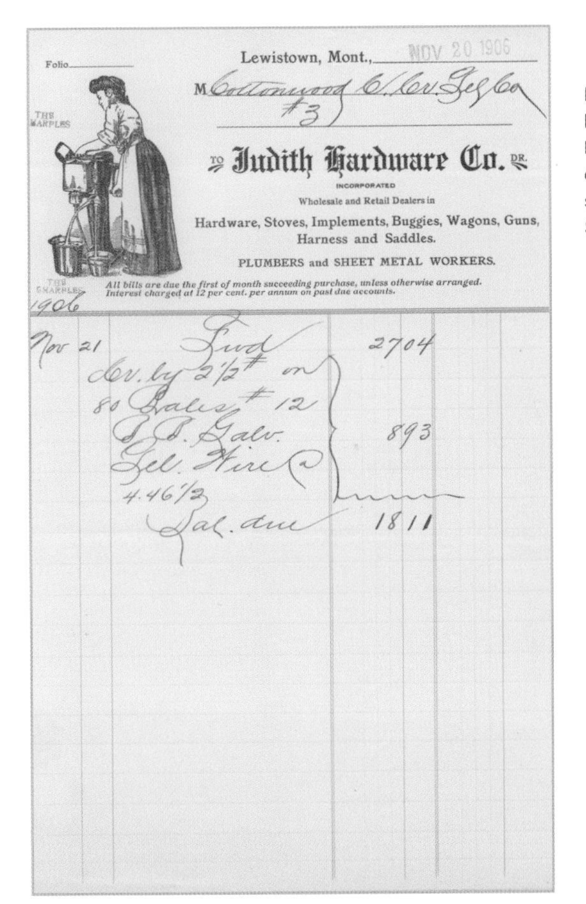
Folio
Lewistown, Mont., NOV 20 1906
M Cottonwood C. Cv. Tel. Co #3
TO **Judith Hardware Co.** DR.
INCORPORATED
Wholesale and Retail Dealers in
Hardware, Stoves, Implements, Buggies, Wagons, Guns, Harness and Saddles.
PLUMBERS and SHEET METAL WORKERS.
All bills are due the first of month succeeding purchase, unless otherwise arranged. Interest charged at 12 per cent. per annum on past due accounts.
1906

Nov 21 | | 27 04
| | 8 93
| | 18 11

Figure 4.2.
Letterhead/invoice from ***Judith Hardware Co.***, Lewistown, Mont., dated Nov. 20, 1906. Note the diversity of the offerings, including stoves, saddles, and plumbing services. By 1924, it was advertised as "The Winchester Store" and still sold saddlery.

MATT REGAN

Fine Carriage
Harness and
Saddlery

A Full Line of Turf Goods---Horse Clothing

STOCK SADDLES, FANCY BITS,
SPURS, BRIDLES AND QUIRTS.

LEWISTOWN, - - MONTANA.

Figure 4.3.
Advertisement for ***Matt Regan***, Lewistown, Montana. *From Van Dersal and Conner, 1900.*

Figure 4.4.
Photograph of ***Matthew E. Regan***, contemporaneous with figure 4.3. *Courtesy of the Lewistown Public Library.*

Figure 4.5.
Advertisement for the ***C. C. Jeffrey Saddlery***, Lewistown, Mont., from the Lewistown Directory, 1912. Jeffrey opened this business in 1895 and became an influential member of Lewistown society. He died in 1913.

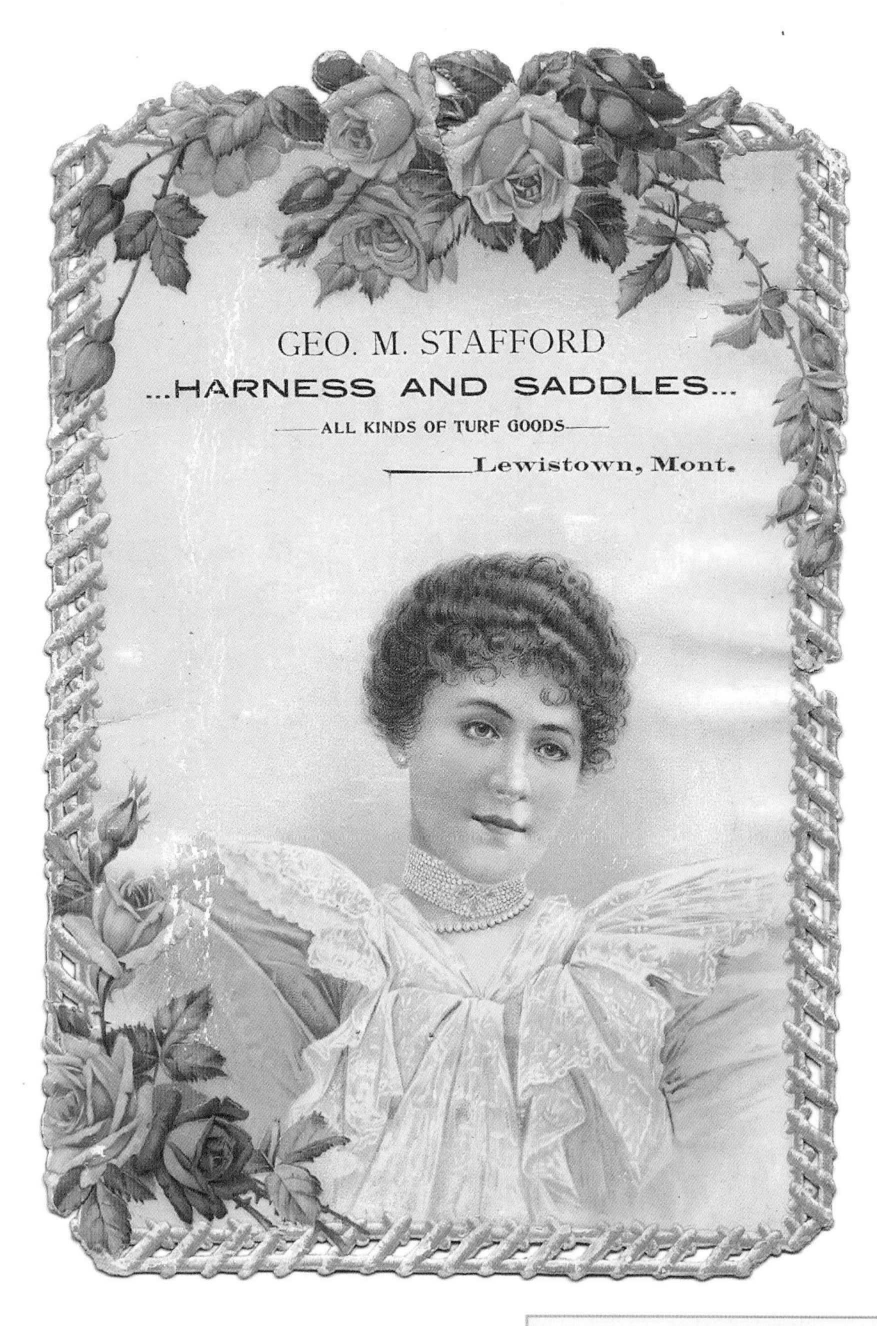

Figure 4.6.
Advertising card for ***Geo. M. Stafford***, Lewistown, Mont. Stafford was a Territorial saddle maker whose use of this attractive Victorian image to advertise his business was unusual for someone in his trade. *Courtesy of Brian Lebel.*

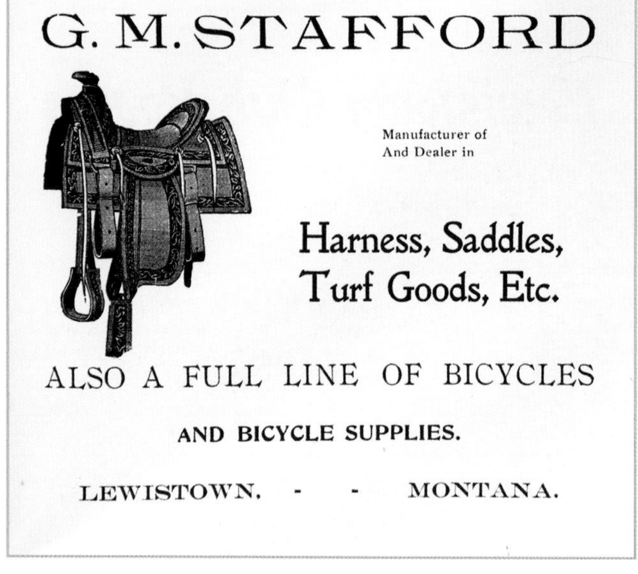

Figure 4.7.
Advertisement for ***G. M. Stafford***, Lewistown, Montana. From Van Dersal & Conner, 1900.

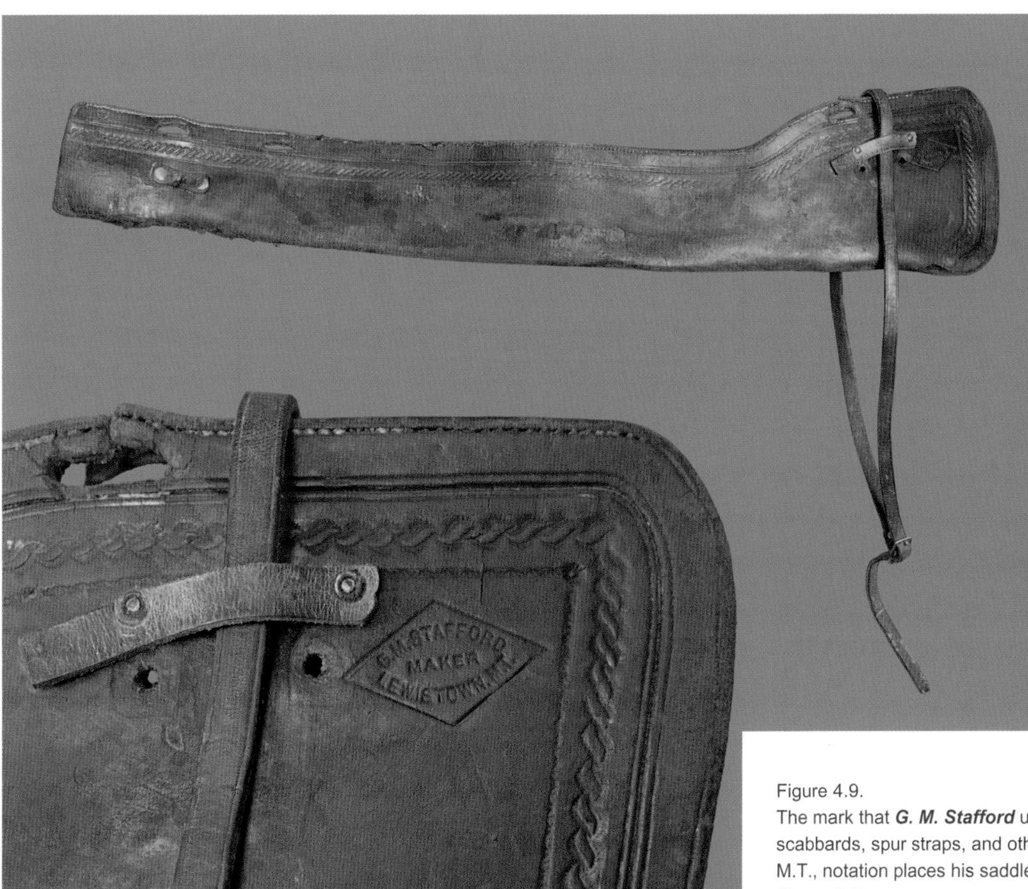

Figure 4.8.
A unique rifle scabbard made by ***G. M. Stafford***, Lewistown, M.T. Despite its rough condition, it is the only one known. It was made for a large single-shot rifle (probably a Sharps) and was cut off so that the rifle could be pointed and shot while still in the scabbard. This scabbard could probably tell a very interesting story.

Figure 4.9.
The mark that ***G. M. Stafford*** used on all of his production (rifle scabbards, spur straps, and other small items). The Lewistown, M.T., notation places his saddlery's establishment prior to 1889 (figure 4.8).

Figure 4.10.
G. M. Stafford was likely the first saddler in Lewistown (M.T.). Stafford's distinctive mark is a lazy diamond, rather resembling a brand. These cuffs are in nice condition, and Stafford's work is quite rare.

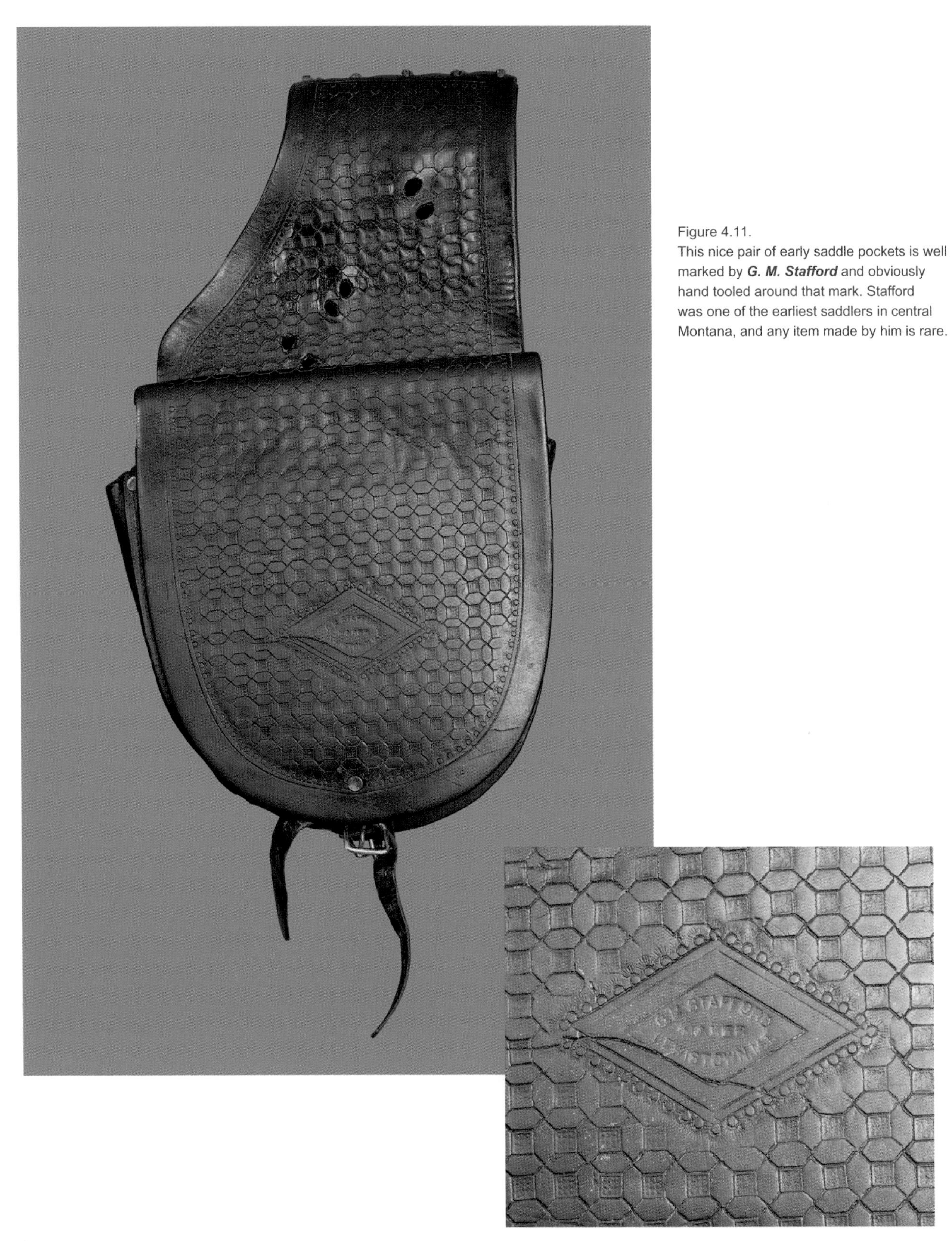

Figure 4.11.
This nice pair of early saddle pockets is well marked by ***G. M. Stafford*** and obviously hand tooled around that mark. Stafford was one of the earliest saddlers in central Montana, and any item made by him is rare.

Figure 4.12.
One of the more interesting and unique saddlery marks is that of ***G. M. Stafford***, Lewistown, M.T. (figure 4.11).

Figure 4.13.
G. M. Stafford of Lewistown made this large single-action holster before 1889. It has a rare configuration for Montana holsters and may be the only one in existence.

Figure 4.14.
Lewistown Saddlery Company made this cartridge belt, which is in extraordinary condition. It does not appear to be early but is attractive with the different colored leather for the cartridge loops and billet. It is difficult to make comparisons among this company's output to determine the age of the item, because no other examples of their work are known.

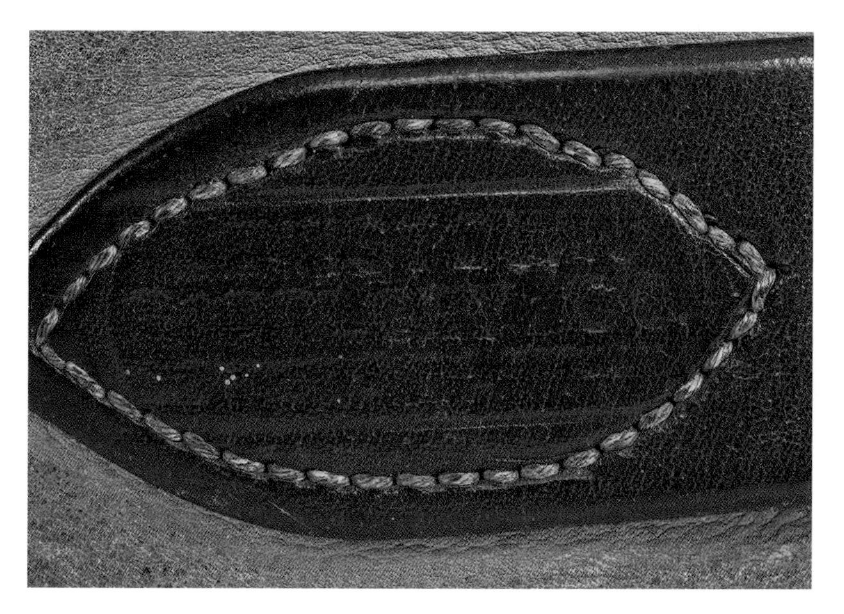

Figure 4.15.
The ***Lewistown Saddlery Company*** used this rare and interesting mark embossed into the cartridge belt shown. The authors have never seen another example. In this case the mark is applied very lightly and is difficult to see (figure 4.14).

The town of Malta lies to the far north of Lewistown, in Phillips County. Bernard H. Koke, a post-Territorial saddle maker, was located there (figure 4.16). A saddle from B. H. Koke, marked "MALTA, MONT.," is shown in figures 4.17 and 4.18. Koke's business dated from 1893 to 1920, and again, his output is highly desired by collectors, due in part to its limited availability. He used at least two slightly different marks, as can be seen on a binocular case and a holster (figures 4.19 through 4.21).

W. H. Richardson produced different items from shops in both Malta and Dillon. A mark for each site can be seen on each gun rig shown in figures 4.22 (Dillon, no border) and 4.23 (Malta, with hand-stamped border); the rigs are shown in figure 4.24.

The town of Chinook is represented here by two nearly contemporaneous saddlers, A. B. Duke and Harry Ettinger (table 4.1). A working cowboy's saddle with the owner's initials tooled on the cantle was marked by Harry Ettinger (figures 4.25 and 4.26). Ettinger produced leatherwork from several other Montana towns, including Dillon and Livingston.

This chapter closes with a photograph of the Two Dot Hardware Co. in Two Dot (near Harlowtown), c. 1913. Note the blanketed horses and the snow, typical for this northern part of the state, located between the Big Snow and Little Belt mountains (figure 4.27).

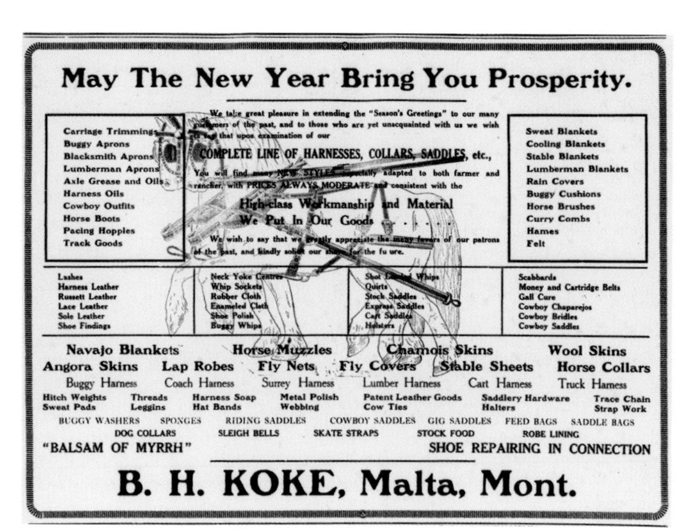

Figure 4.16.
Advertisement for ***B. H. Koke***, Malta, Mont. showing a remarkable inventory. From *The Enterprise* (Harlem, Montana), December 11, 1913.

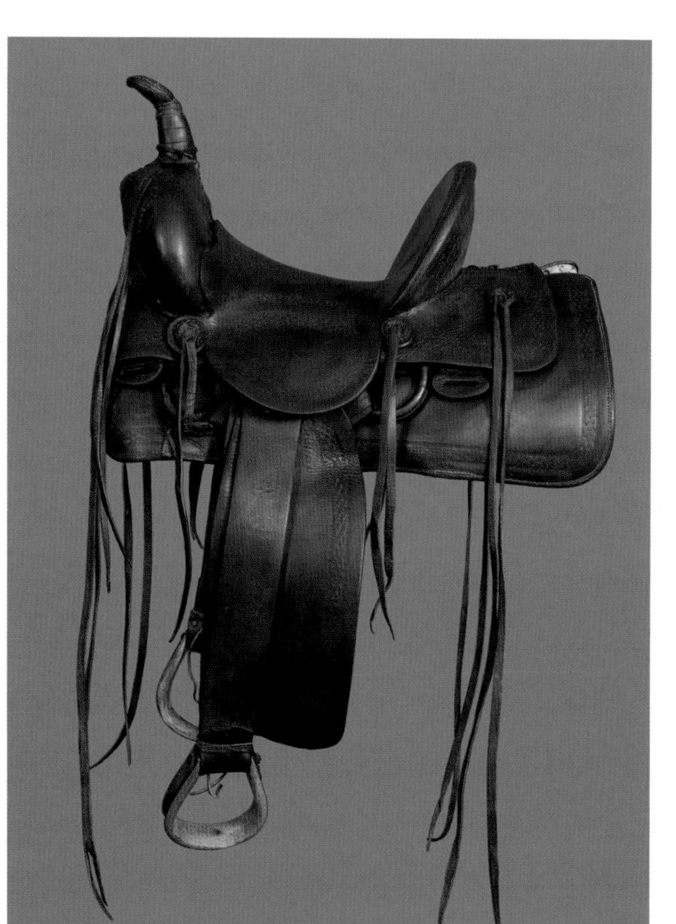

Figure 4.17.
This ***Koke***-marked saddle is a good double-rigged working cowboy's saddle. It shows some minor repair, e.g., replaced stirrup leathers, which one would expect to see on a well-used saddle.

Figure 4.18.
The saddlery of ***B. H. Koke*** in Malta, Montana used an elliptical mark like many of the saddlers of the time. Any production from this saddlery is quite rare (figure 4.17).

Figure 4.19.
B. H. Koke produced the several items shown with his mark, placed here on the top of a binocular case. This type of item is rare and is only the second marked binocular case that the authors have observed. The large single-action holster is nicely tooled and is also marked ***B. H. Koke***.

Figure 4.20.
B. H. Koke's maker's mark stamped on the lid of the binocular case shown in figure 4.19.

Figure 4.21.
This is the second of the ***B. H. Koke*** marks we have identified, on the holster in figure 4.19. The difference from the first mark shown (figure 4.20) is the addition of the three little lines at each end of the word "MAKER."

Figure 4.22.
W. H. Richardson of Dillon, Montana marked this cartridge belt with this interesting oval mark lacking a border.

Figure 4.23.
W. H. Richardson of Malta, Montana marked this holster with almost the same oval mark he had used in Dillon, this time with a hand-tooled border.

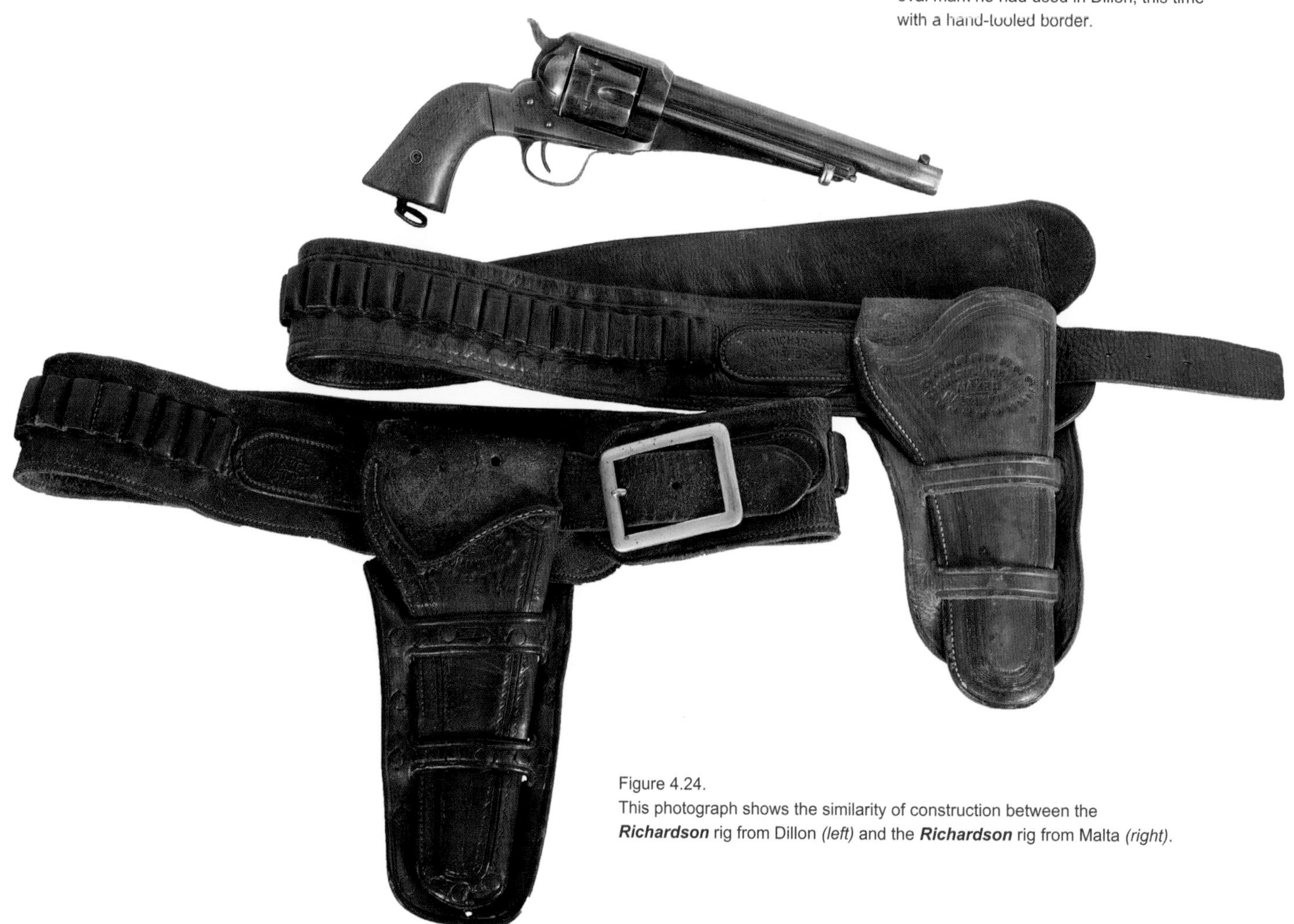

Figure 4.24.
This photograph shows the similarity of construction between the ***Richardson*** rig from Dillon *(left)* and the ***Richardson*** rig from Malta *(right)*.

Figure 4.25.
A loop-seat working cowboy saddle with large square skirts made by ***Harry Ettinger***, Chinook, Mont. Ettinger was located variously in several Montana towns, including Dillon and Livingston. The initials "W.S.L." are tooled on the back of the cantle.

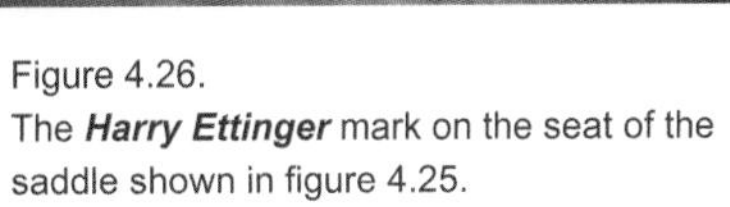

Figure 4.26.
The ***Harry Ettinger*** mark on the seat of the saddle shown in figure 4.25.

Figure 4.27.
Photograph of the ***Two Dot Hardware Co.***, Two Dot, Montana, c. 1913.

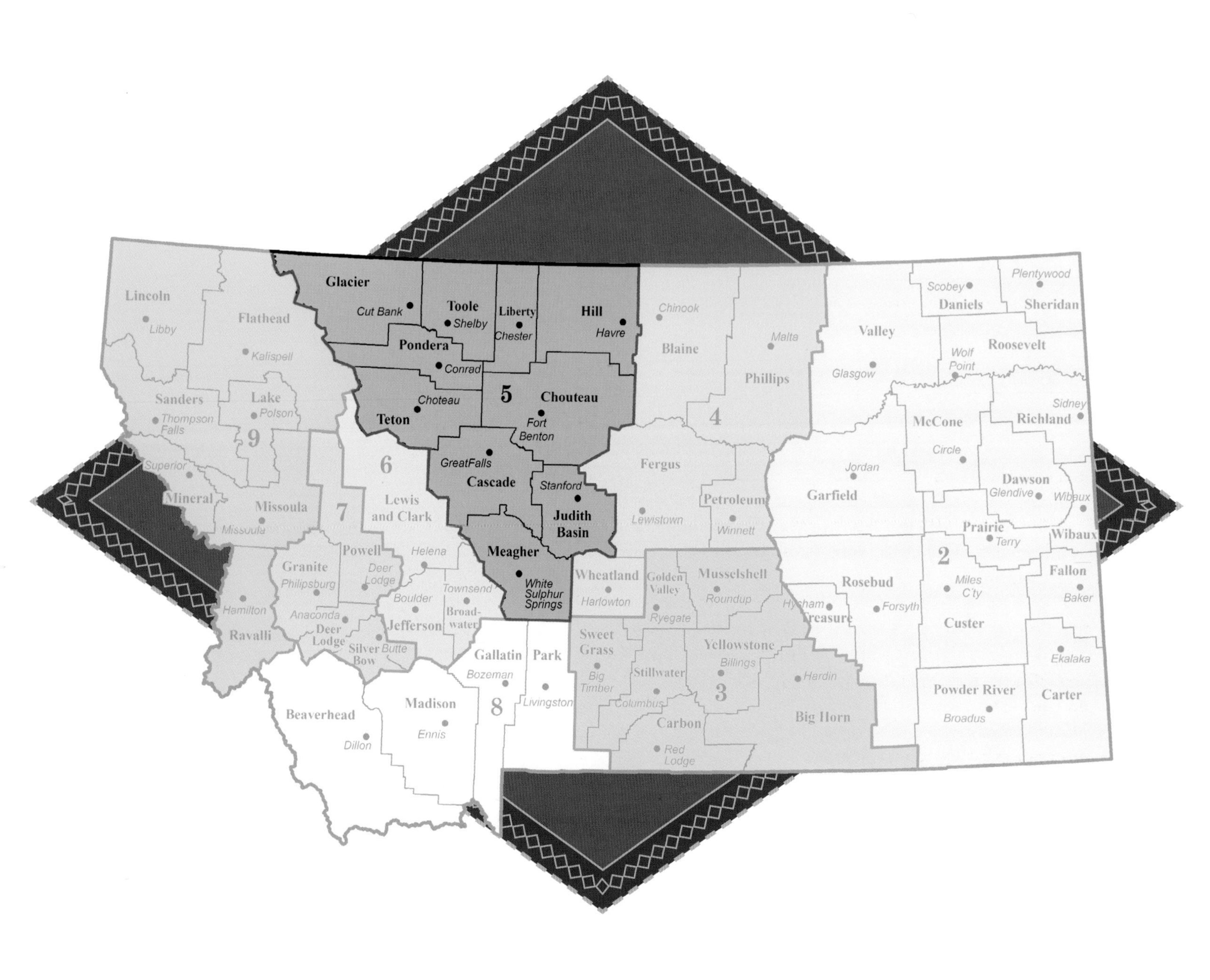

Glacier
Cut Bank
Toole
Shelby
Liberty
Chester
Hill
Havre
Pondera
Conrad
5
Chouteau
Fort Benton
Teton
Choteau
GreatFalls
Cascade
Stanford
Judith Basin
Meagher
White Sulphur Springs
Lincoln
Libby
Flathead
Kalispell
Sanders
Thompson Falls
Lake
Polson
9
Superior
Mineral
Missoula
Missoula
6
7
Lewis and Clark
Helena
Powell
Deer Lodge
Granite
Philipsburg
Hamilton
Ravalli
Anaconda
Deer Lodge
Silver Bow
Butte
Boulder
Jefferson
Townsend
Broad-water
Gallatin
Bozeman
Park
Livingston
8
Beaverhead
Dillon
Madison
Ennis
Chinook
Blaine
Malta
Phillips
4
Fergus
Lewistown
Petroleum
Winnett
Wheatland
Harlowton
Golden Valley
Ryegate
Musselshell
Roundup
Sweet Grass
Big Timber
Stillwater
Columbus
Yellowstone
Billings
3
Carbon
Red Lodge
Hardin
Big Horn
Hysham
Treasure
Valley
Glasgow
Scobey
Daniels
Plentywood
Sheridan
Roosevelt
Wolf Point
McCone
Circle
Sidney
Richland
Jordan
Garfield
Dawson
Glendive
Wibaux
Prairie
Terry
Wibaux
Rosebud
Forsyth
2
Miles City
Custer
Fallon
Baker
Ekalaka
Powder River
Broadus
Carter

5

Northwestern Montana

Great Falls

Fort Benton

Sun River

White Sulphur Springs

One of the largest and most beautiful sections of Montana and encompassing ten counties, Area 5 includes the cities and towns of Great Falls, Fort Benton, Sun River, and White Sulphur Springs. Most of the saddleries for which records have been found existed in the southern half of this Area, with the majority in Great Falls and Fort Benton.

The seat of Cascade County, Great Falls is famous for the five waterfalls along the upper Missouri River basin that occasioned a ten-mile portage by the Lewis and Clark expedition on their western journey to the Oregon coast in 1805–1806. It is also famous as the home and studio of the artist Charles M. Russell (see chapters 2 and 8), whose inspiration for his paintings was derived from the local Native Americans, cowboys, townsfolk, and Glacier National Park. Subsequent to the portage by Lewis and Clark, the trapper and guide Jim Bridger, with Andrew Henry, established a fur-trading camp in 1823 on the site that became the city of Great Falls. This camp was in effect the first commercial enterprise by Euro-American explorers, yet it was only in 1859 that the first steamboat arrived at the townsite, which became permanent in 1883 and was incorporated in 1888, shortly after the arrival of the Great Northern Railroad. Hence, the construction of several dams, the presence of the Anaconda Copper Mining Company, and the influx of municipal and commercial services created a thriving community in which saddle and harness makers could do business.

Figure 5.1.
Early photograph of a saddler's workshop in "Old Town," Great Falls, Montana. The older gentleman is working close to his stove and is surrounded by a wide variety of harness and other tack items, including sleigh bells and a whip holder at the top of the ceiling. Note the two side saddles in the foreground—the one on the floor has a leaping head (second horn) and both are of an English design. The saddler is Joseph Sullivan, and his workshop in Fort Benton was reconstructed in Great Falls's "Old Town" by State Senator Charles Bovey in 1941.

Table 5.1 lists these makers, their locations, and dates (where known) of operation. Note that most of the Great Falls makers are post-Territorial, whereas the earliest shops were in Fort Benton, Sun River, and White Sulphur Springs (see below). Figures 5.1 through 5.3 show a saddler's shop (possibly Sullivan's, see below) and letterheads from J. B. Steffen and W. W. Waters, respectively. It is likely that the latter formed a partnership with Wales, in Great Falls—figures 5.4 and 5.5 show the Waters & Wales elliptical stamp on a wide belt, a rare item.

Table 5.1. Saddleries of Montana[1]

MAKER	LOCATION	DATES[2]
Ario, Victor	Great Falls	1903–1953
Beckman, August	Fort Benton	1878–1888
Browning Saddlery Co.	Browning; Shelby	1920; 1921
Collins, J. S.	Great Falls	
Cut Bank Saddlery Co.	Cut Bank	(1912)
Davidson, A. J. & Moffit, John; A. J. Davidson & Co.	Fort Benton	1881–1883, (1881, 1882); (1884)
Fisher, Theodore	Sun River	M.T. (1884)
Gibbons & Maher	Great Falls	(1889)
Gibbons, J. J.*	Great Falls	(1886), (1887)
Glassman, William	Fort Benton	1883–1885
Goettlich, Charles	Fort Benton	d. 1914
Great Falls Saddlery	Great Falls	(1908)
Kline (or Cline), Sam J.	Fort Benton	1880s
MacDonald, James	White Sulphur Springs	1882/4 –1906/7, (1883)
Moreland & Ario	Great Falls	1897–1903
Potter, R.	Belt	(1897)
Power, T. C. & Bro.	Fort Benton	(1903)
Ritschel, G. J.	White Sulphur Springs	
Roberts, B. R. & Best, William	Sun River	(1884)
Rosecrans, L. (Lucius) H. (Pioneer Harness Shop)	Fort Benton	1877–1883 (1877)
Rosecrans, Lucian H.	Fort Benton	1876, (1882)
Steffen, J. B.	Great Falls	1893–1897, (1895)
Sullivan, Jos.	Great Falls	(1888)
Sullivan, Joseph	Fort Benton	1882–1926
Sullivan, Joseph & Goss, V. K.	Fort Benton	1881–1882, (1882)
Waters, W. W.	Great Falls	(1896)
Waters & Wales	Great Falls	
Wellman, William	White Sulphur Springs	1888–1936
Westfall, Arnold	Fort Benton	1904–1931

1. Products made or sold by these saddleries included harness, saddles, bits, spurs, whips, boots, bridles, accessories (horse blankets, grooming tools, trunks, bags, and/or robes), vehicles (sleighs, buggies, wagons, carts), and Indian-made goods (e.g., saddle blankets).

2. Dates in parentheses are specified on the company letterhead or in a newspaper/journal advertisement. Inclusive dates for the tenure of the company have been provided where data are available and reliable.

* In 1888 Gibbons used the name Great Falls Harness Store (*Great Falls Tribune*, July 7, 1888).

«Office of»

J. B. Steffen

HARNESS, . SADDLES . AND . SADDLERY . HARDWARE.

Great Falls, Mont. June 1 1893

A. M. Holter Hardware Co

Helena Mont.

Gentlemen:

Enclosed please find 35¢ cents in stamps for bill of May 29th

Yours truly
J. B. Steffen

Dr Sir—
There was only 25¢ enclosed, 12.2¢ & 1.1¢ stamps.

A. M. HOLTER HARDWARE CO.

Here is the other 10 cents which you claim was missing
J. B. Steffen

A.M./13/93.

Figure 5.2.
Letterhead from ***J. B. Steffen***, Great Falls, Mont., dated June 1, 1893, concerning some postal stamps.

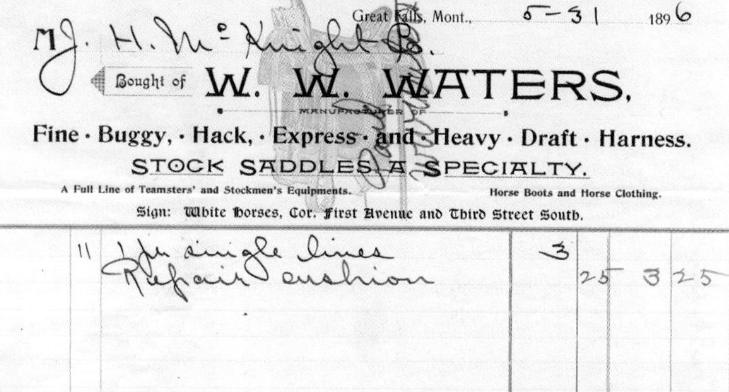

Great Falls, Mont., 5-31 1896

M J. H. McKnight Co.

Bought of W. W. WATERS,

MANUFACTURER OF

Fine · Buggy, · Hack, · Express · and · Heavy · Draft · Harness.

STOCK SADDLES A SPECIALTY.

A Full Line of Teamsters' and Stockmen's Equipments. Horse Boots and Horse Clothing.

Sign: White Horses, Cor. First Avenue and Third Street South.

11	1 pr single lines	3		
	Repair cushion		25	3 25

Figure 5.3.
Letterhead/invoice from ***W. W. Waters***, Great Falls, Mont., dated 5-31, 1896. Note: "Stock Saddles a Specialty."

Figure 5.4.
Waters and Wales of Great Falls, Montana made this large border-tooled bronc or riding belt and embossed the initials HCP on the back. Items from this saddlery are extremely rare, and this belt is the only example of which we are aware.

Figure 5.5.
Unknown to us until recently, the maker ***Waters and Wales*** of Great Falls used this elliptical stamp.

Austrian-born Victor Ario became a prominent saddle maker and distributor in the early twentieth century, but was first seen in partnership with Moreland (figure 5.6) during the last decade of the nineteenth century. Subsequently, Victor Ario, and Victor Ario Saddlery Company (figures 5.7 through 5.9) more or less dominated the saddlery and harness scene in Great Falls. A page from his catalog No. 41 shows a selection of chaps (figure 5.10), and number 5 (Wyoming eight-inch batwings) is shown in figures 5.11 and 5.12. Additional chaps (Ario was known for his showy creations) can be seen in figures 5.13 and 5.14 (chrome leather) and figures 5.15 and 5.16 (possibly a cowgirl's pair). Ario also produced excellent saddles with intricate tooling and, in some cases, personalized features (for example, the customer's initials or brand). Figures 5.17 through 5.23 are examples of three such saddles with their characteristic marks.

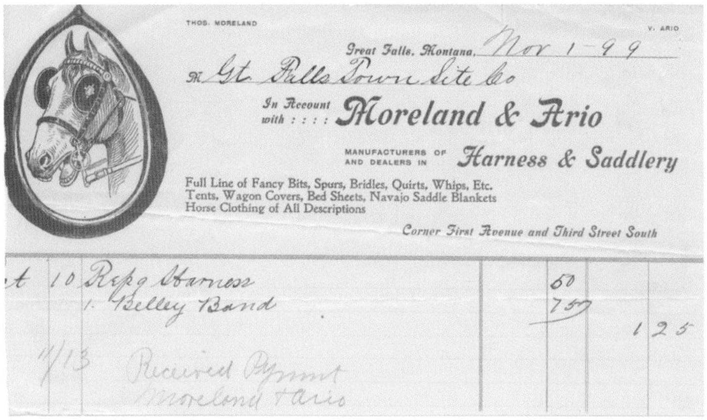

Figure 5.6.
Letterhead/invoice from ***Moreland & Ario***, Great Falls, Montana, dated "Nov. 1-99," for harness repair, to the "Gt. Falls Town Site Co."

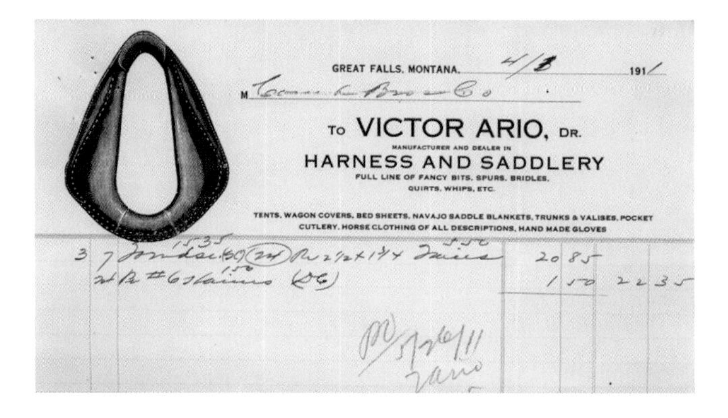

GREAT FALLS, MONTANA, 4/3 1911

TO VICTOR ARIO, DR.

MANUFACTURER AND DEALER IN

HARNESS AND SADDLERY

FULL LINE OF FANCY BITS, SPURS, BRIDLES, QUIRTS, WHIPS, ETC.

TENTS, WAGON COVERS, BED SHEETS, NAVAJO SADDLE BLANKETS, TRUNKS & VALISES, POCKET CUTLERY, HORSE CLOTHING OF ALL DESCRIPTIONS, HAND MADE GLOVES

Figure 5.7.
Letterhead/invoice from ***Victor Ario***, Great Falls, Montana, dated "4/3, 1911." This early stationery was decorated with a handsome horse collar.

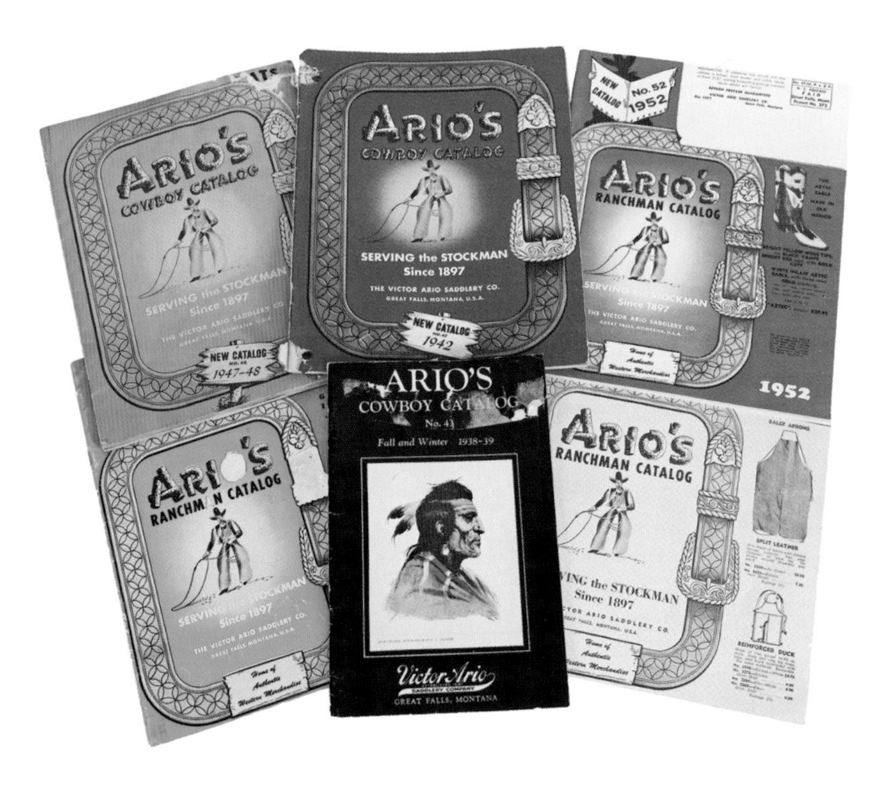

Figure 5.8.
The covers of ***Victor Ario's*** catalogs were colorful and decorative. These dated archival publications contain a wealth of information and are a necessity for collectors of Western antiquaria.

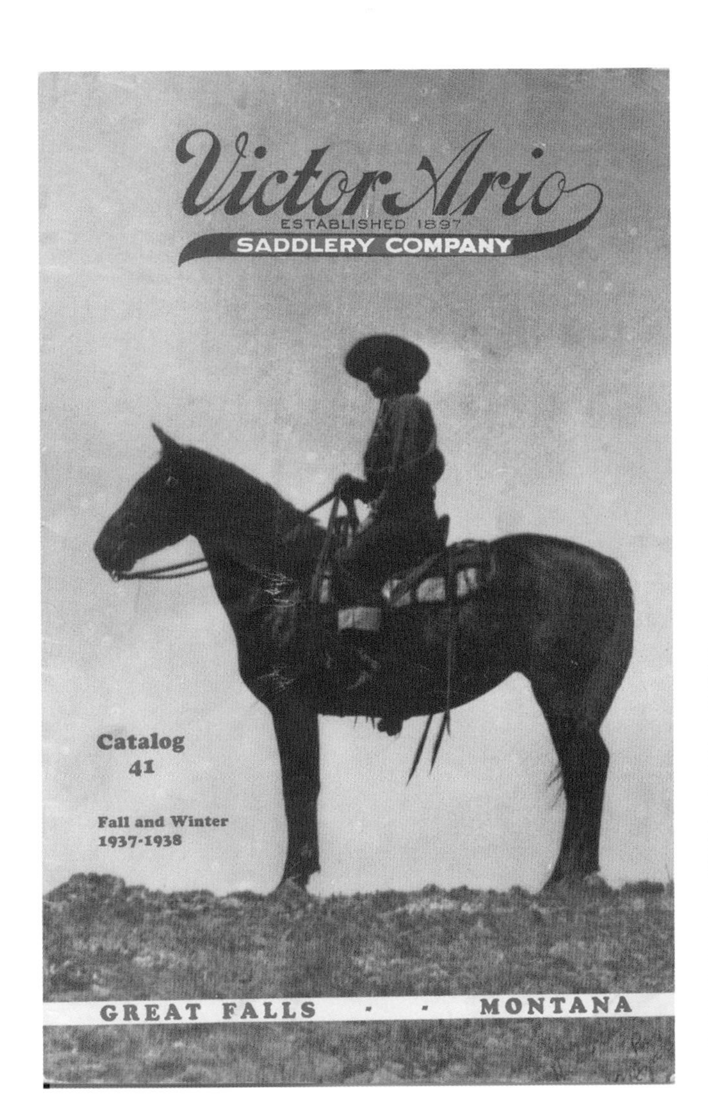

Figure 5.9.
Cover of ***Victor Ario Saddlery Company***, Great Falls, Montana, catalog, No. 41 (Fall and Winter, 1937–1938). Emphasis has shifted to cowboy gear and Western outfits.

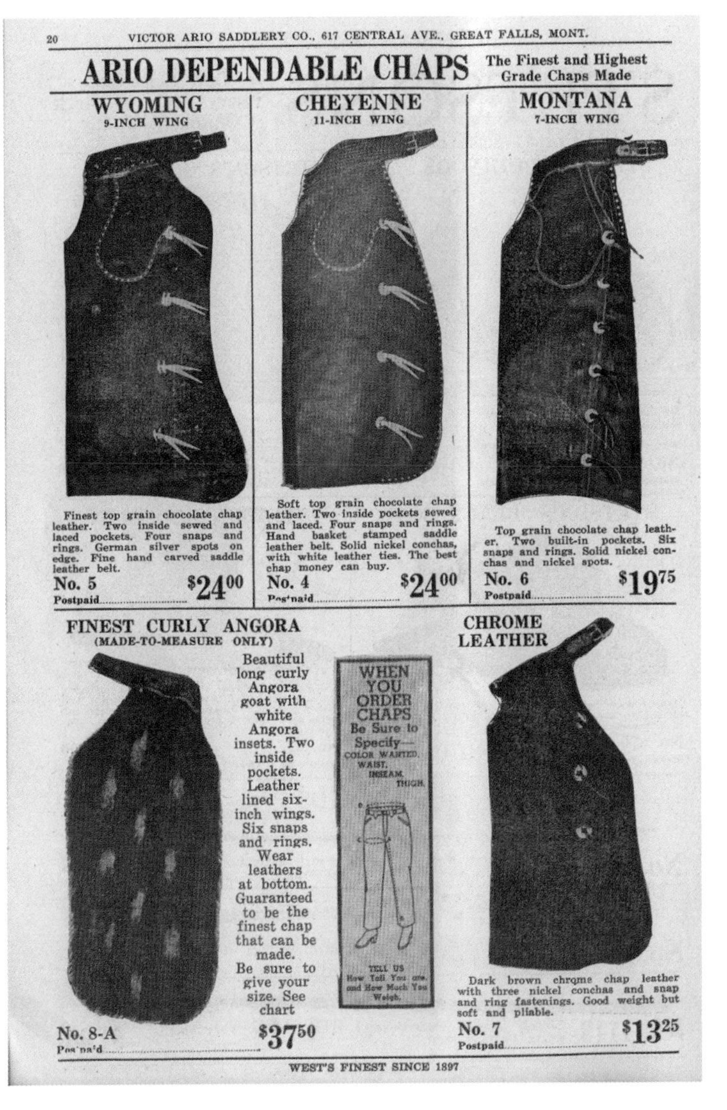

20 VICTOR ARIO SADDLERY CO., 617 CENTRAL AVE., GREAT FALLS, MONT.

ARIO DEPENDABLE CHAPS The Finest and Highest Grade Chaps Made

WYOMING
9-INCH WING

Finest top grain chocolate chap leather. Two inside sewed and laced pockets. Four snaps and rings. German silver spots on edge. Fine hand carved saddle leather belt.

No. 5 Postpaid $24.00

CHEYENNE
11-INCH WING

Soft top grain chocolate chap leather. Two inside pockets sewed and laced. Four snaps and rings. Hand basket stamped saddle leather belt. Solid nickel conchas, with white leather ties. The best chap money can buy.

No. 4 Postpaid $24.00

MONTANA
7-INCH WING

Top grain chocolate chap leather. Two built-in pockets. Six snaps and rings. Solid nickel conchas and nickel spots.

No. 6 Postpaid $19.75

FINEST CURLY ANGORA
(MADE-TO-MEASURE ONLY)

Beautiful long curly Angora goat with white Angora insets. Two inside pockets. Leather lined six-inch wings. Six snaps and rings. Wear leathers at bottom. Guaranteed to be the finest chap that can be made. Be sure to give your size. See chart

No. 8-A Postpaid $37.50

WHEN YOU ORDER CHAPS Be Sure to Specify—
COLOR WANTED.
WAIST.
INSEAM.
THIGH.

TELL US How Tall You are, and How Much You Weigh.

CHROME LEATHER

Dark brown chrome chap leather with three nickel conchas and snap and ring fastenings. Good weight but soft and pliable.

No. 7 Postpaid $13.25

WEST'S FINEST SINCE 1897

Figure 5.10.
Page from ***Victor Ario Saddlery Company*** (see figure 5.9) showing five different styles of batwing chaps. Note the fancy angora (goat skin) chaps with contrasting angora insets on the *lower left* of the page.

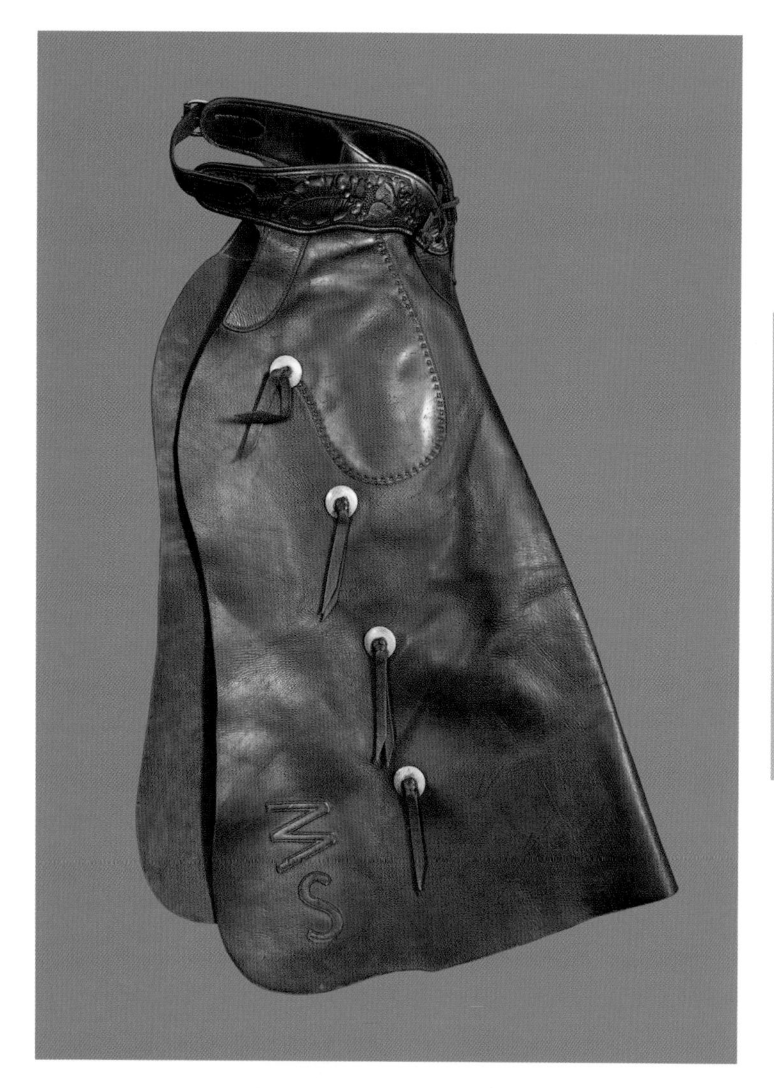

Figure 5.11.
A nice pair of working cowboy chaps with a brand in the corner of the batwing. They have a very attractive floral-carved belt and are in great collectible condition.

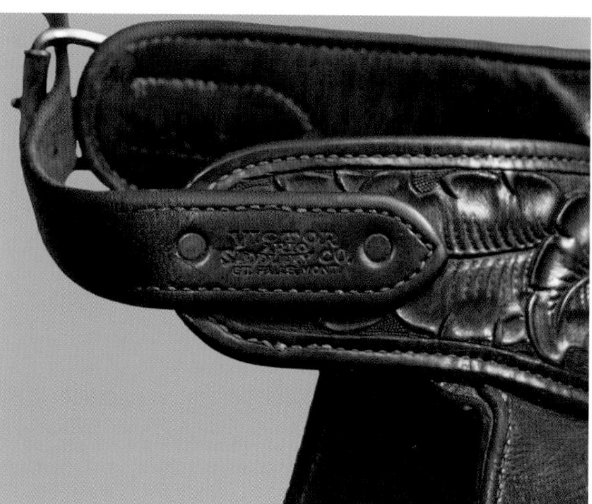

Figure 5.12.
Victor Ario Saddlery Company located in Great Falls, Montana had one of the most stylized and interesting of all the Montana saddlery stamps. The letters vary in size and the Ario last name is sandwiched between the first and third lines in a distinctive and attractive manner. This particular mark appears on many of the chaps and saddle bags that were made in the 1930s, 1940s, and early 1950s (figure 5.11).

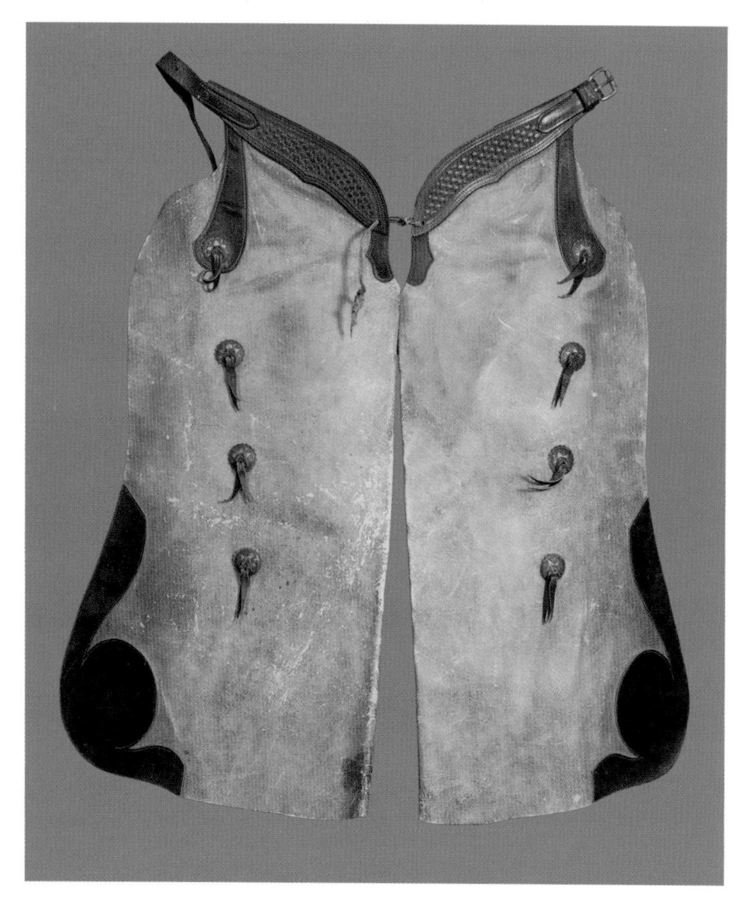

Figure 5.13.
A nice example of the work of the ***Victor Ario Saddlery***. These chaps were shown in the catalog and are what the working cowboy wore daily.

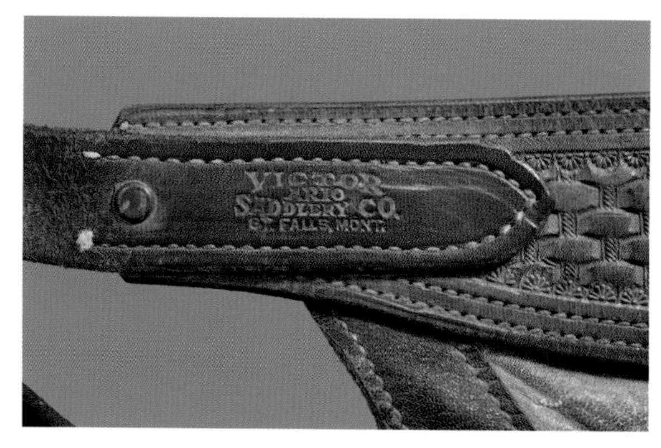

Figure 5.14.
An example of the ***Victor Ario Saddlery*** mark used in the 1940s and throughout the remainder of the saddlery's existence (figure 5.13).

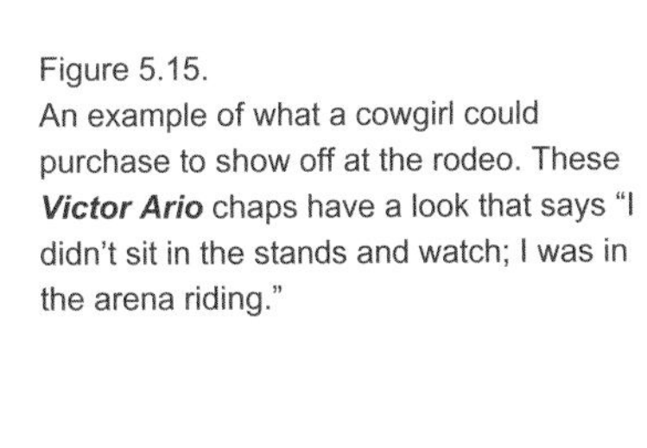

Figure 5.15.
An example of what a cowgirl could purchase to show off at the rodeo. These ***Victor Ario*** chaps have a look that says "I didn't sit in the stands and watch; I was in the arena riding."

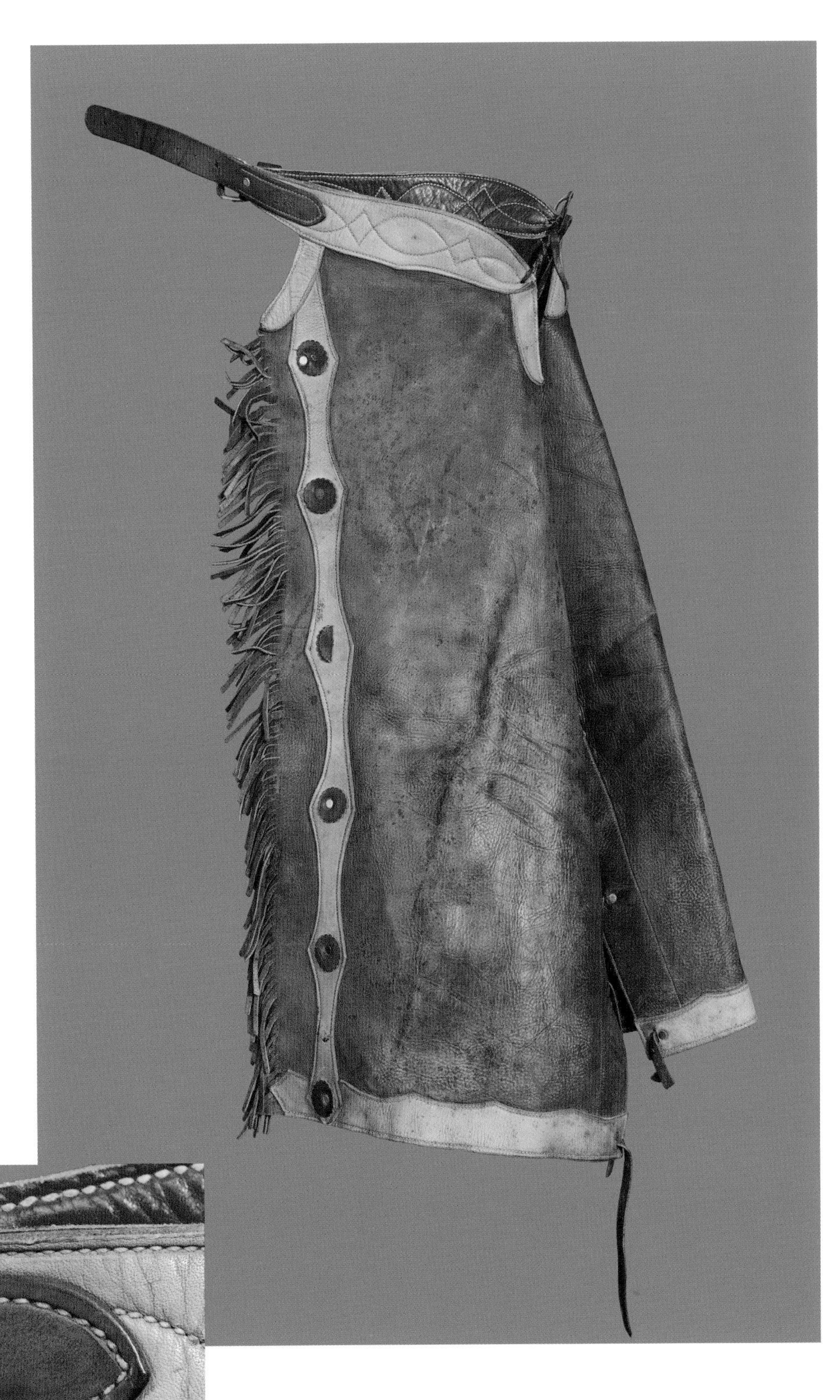

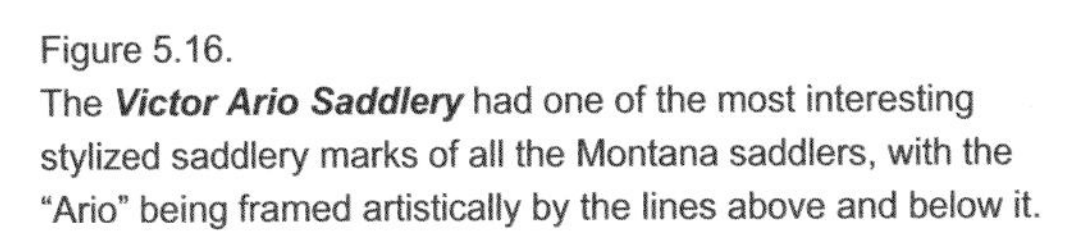

Figure 5.16.
The ***Victor Ario Saddlery*** had one of the most interesting stylized saddlery marks of all the Montana saddlers, with the "Ario" being framed artistically by the lines above and below it.

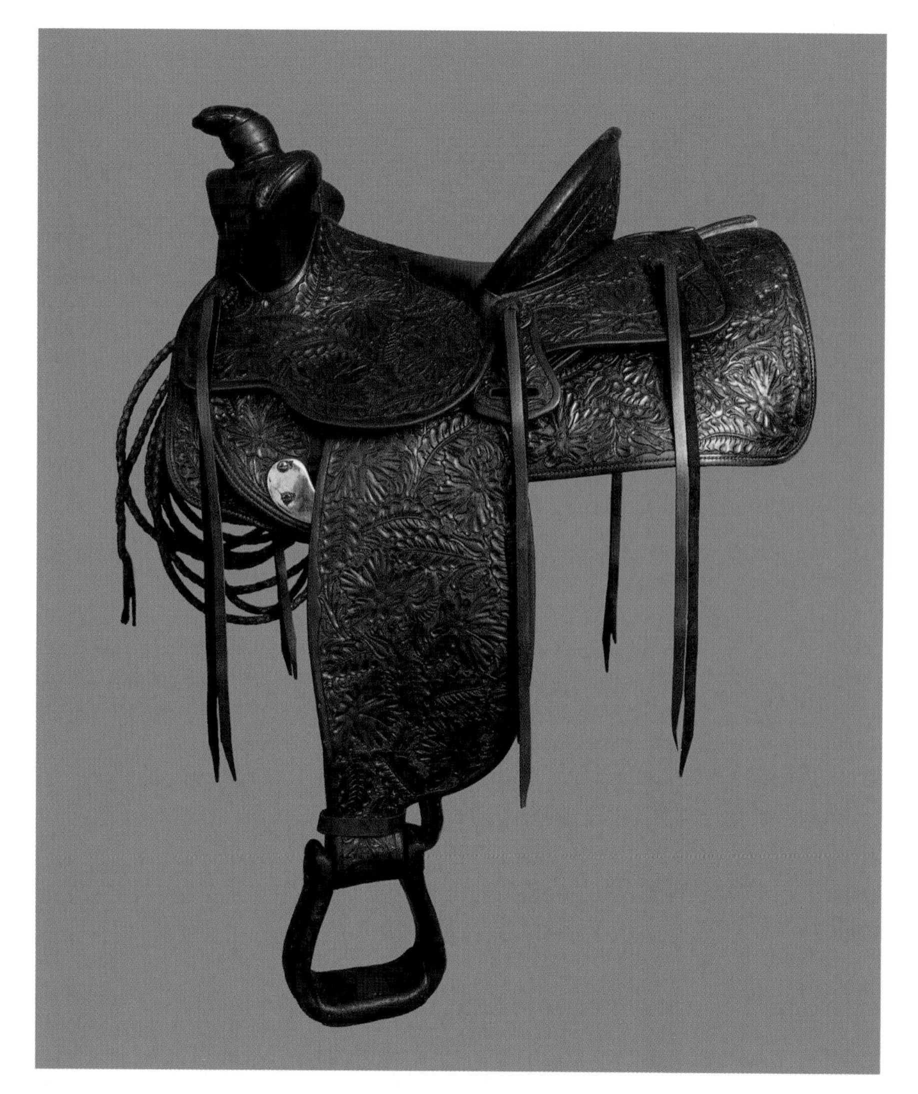

Figure 5.17.
Victor Ario of Great Falls, Montana made this saddle with an interesting combination of features. It is exquisitely carved and resembles something one would want for a parade. It also has "bear trap" swells which were designed for riding bad broncs, similar to some of the Hamley saddles (Pendleton, Oregon) made for breaking horses. Apparently the owner's parade stallion wasn't that gentle.

Figure 5.18.
The back of the cantle of the ***Victor Ario*** saddle shown in figure 5.17. It is stamped "8889" and "4259" at the bottom.

Figure 5.19.
The saddlery blended its mark into the tooling concept of the entire saddle, a focal point that is not in the least distracting. One of the stamps used by ***Victor Ario*** for most of the early years of the saddlery.

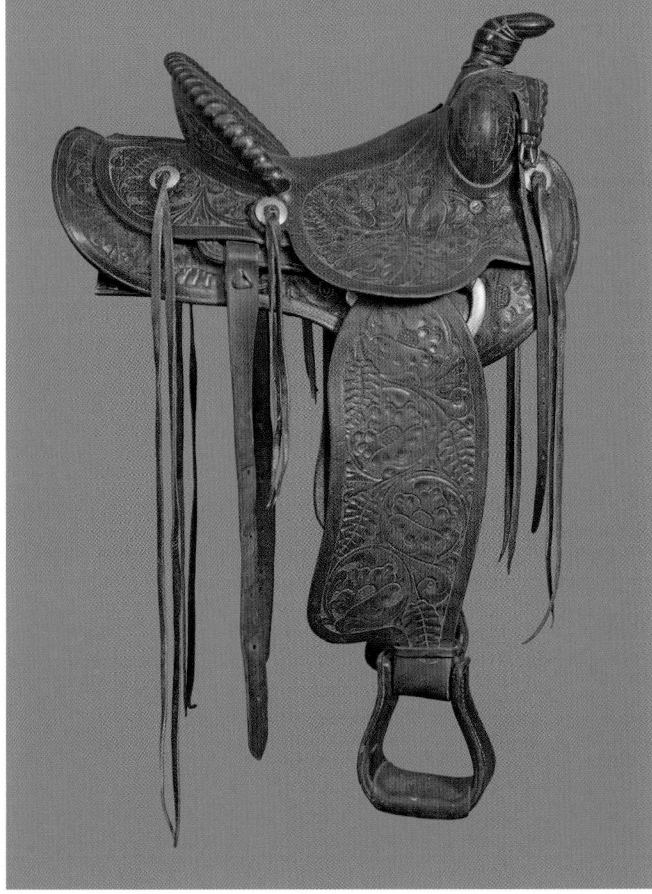

Figure 5.20.
A great ***Victor Ario*** saddle with an attractive tooling pattern and a unique rope edge at the top of the cantle.

Figure 5.21.
The seat mark that the ***Victor Ario Saddlery*** used after the earliest mark that was spelled out in horizontal lines. The sunburst makes it one of the most attractive seat marks of this era.

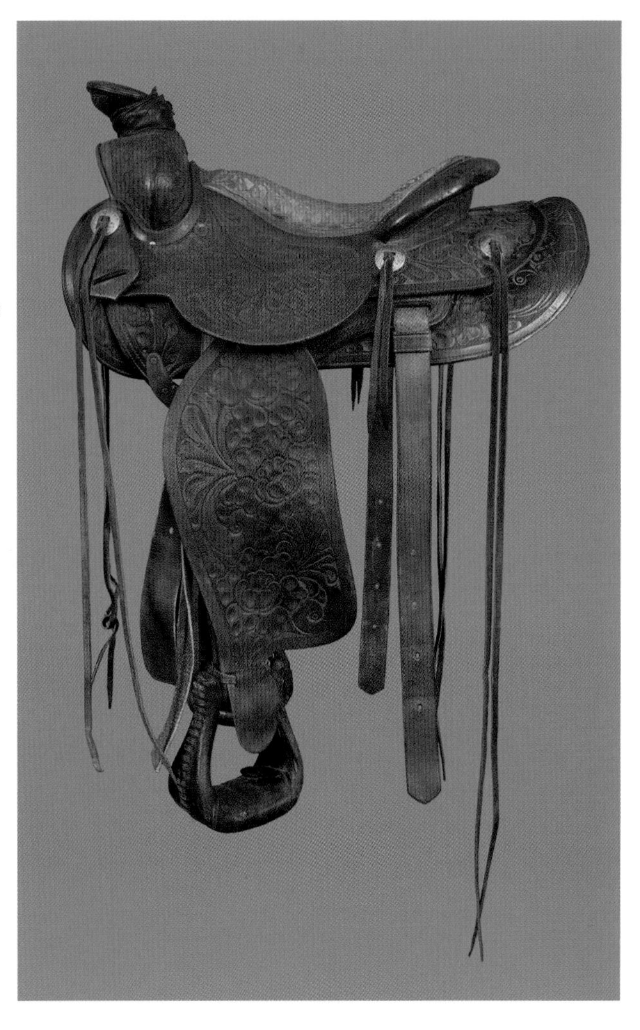

Figure 5.22.
For a time padded seats on saddles were in vogue. ***Victor Ario*** made custom saddles, and it appears that this customer wanted a ladies-size saddle with a green padded seat. It is an interesting combination that one does not often see in the saddlery world.

Figure 5.23.
Victor Ario used this stamp on many of the items produced by the saddlery. The circular center mark was applied and often accented with custom tooling to match the item.

Joseph Sullivan (c. 1860–1940), born in Port Chester, New York, traveled westward and initially formed a partnership with V. K. Goss in Deer Lodge (see chapter 7). The Jos. Sullivan Saddlery was located in Fort Benton, after dissolution of the partnership in 1882 (figures 5.24 and 5.25). There is a suggestion that Sullivan moved his shop to Great Falls in 1888, but we have not found data to confirm this new location. Rather, it seems that Sullivan remained in Fort Benton for the rest of his life. The postcard shown in figure 5.1, captioned as "Old Town / Great Falls," portrays a reconstruction in Great Falls of the early Fort Benton shop by State Senator Charles Bovey in 1941.

Figure 5.24.
Early photograph of ***Jos. Sullivan's*** store in Fort Benton, Montana. His inventory was apparently large and varied.

Fort Benton was an early settlement, established in 1847 by Auguste and Pierre Chouteau of St. Louis as a fur-trading post and fort on the upper Missouri River. Consequently a large number of settlers, miners, and merchants, as well as their supplies, arrived by steamboat at this ultimate terminus. The US Army completed the Mullan Road (642 miles) in 1860, allowing Fort Benton to become an important trading post between the Missouri River and the Columbia River, at Fort Walla Walla, Washington Territory. When the fur industry ceased to be profitable, due to the dwindling populations of the valuable fur-bearing animals, the post was sold by the American Fur Company to the US Army in 1865, at which point the name was changed to Fort Benton (for Senator Thomas Hart Benton). The importance of the town as a major inland port on the Missouri-Mississippi River system declined with the arrival of the railroads. As one of the oldest settlements in the West, and presently the seat of Chouteau County, Fort Benton was home to several early saddleries. Paper ephemera relating to the firm of Jos. Sullivan, including records of his purchases from other parts of the United States, are shown in figures 5.26 through 5.31.

Figure 5.25.
Early photograph of ***Jos. Sullivan,*** standing in his shop in Fort Benton, Montana. Note the huge inventory. *Courtesy of R. Bachman.*

JOS. SULLIVAN,
MANUFACTURER OF AND WHOLESALE AND RETAIL
DEALER IN
HARNESS AND SADDLERY.
ALSO DEALER IN
FISH BROS. WAGON CO.'S
RACINE, WIS.
FARM AND SPRING WAGONS.
Fort Benton, Mont., 189

Figure 5.26.
Letterhead from ***Jos. Sullivan***, Fort Benton, Mont., with date 189_. The firm also dealt in Fish Bros. wagons.

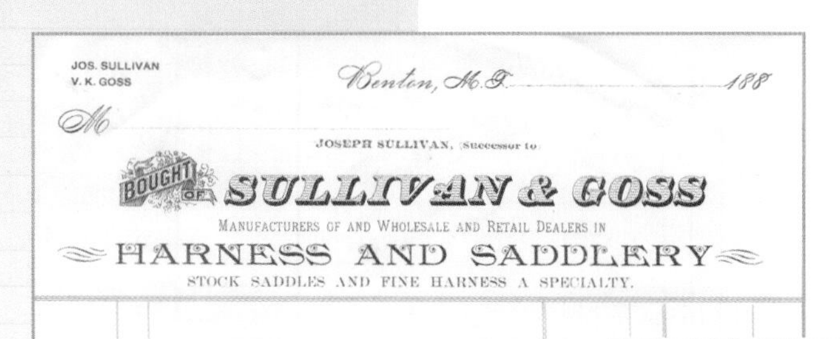
JOS. SULLIVAN
V. K. GOSS
Benton, M.T. 188
M
JOSEPH SULLIVAN, Successor to
BOUGHT OF SULLIVAN & GOSS
MANUFACTURERS OF AND WHOLESALE AND RETAIL DEALERS IN
HARNESS AND SADDLERY
STOCK SADDLES AND FINE HARNESS A SPECIALTY.

Figure 5.27.
Letterhead of ***Sullivan & Goss***, Benton, M.T., dated 1888. Note above the firm's name, in red ink, "JOSEPH SULLIVAN, (successor to)." Sullivan's business was in Fort Benton from 1882–1926. *Courtesy of R. Bachman.*

JOS. SULLIVAN,
Harness and Saddle Manufacturer.
FINE HARNESS AND STOCK SADDLES A SPECIALTY.
Mitchell Wagons, McCormick Reapers, Mowers
McCormick Mountain Rakes. Binding Twine.
FORT BENTON, - - MONTANA.

Figure 5.28.
Business card for ***Jos. Sullivan***, Fort Benton, Montana. *Courtesy of R. Bachman.*

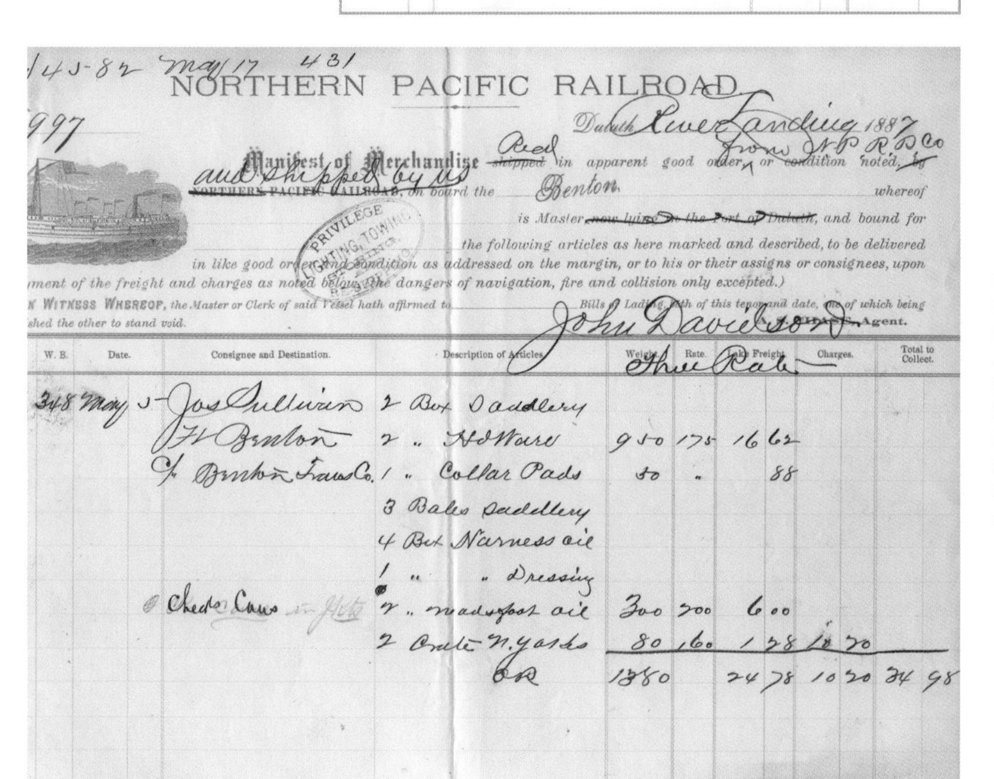
NORTHERN PACIFIC RAILROAD
Duluth River Landing 1887
Manifest of Merchandise Rec'd in apparent good order, or condition noted, from N.P. R.R. Co and shipped by us on board the Benton whereof is Master, and bound for the following articles as here marked and described, to be delivered in like good order and condition as addressed on the margin, or to his or their assigns or consignees, upon payment of the freight and charges as noted below, the dangers of navigation, fire and collision only excepted.)
In Witness Whereof, the Master or Clerk of said Vessel hath affirmed to Bills of Lading, both of this tenor and date, one of which being accomplished the other to stand void.
John Davidson, Agent.

W. B.	Date.	Consignee and Destination.	Description of Articles.	Weight.	Rate.	Freight.	Charges.	Total to Collect.
348	May 5	Jos Sullivan Ft Benton C/o Benton Trans Co.	2 Box Saddlery					
			2 " Hdware	950	175	16 62		
			1 " Collar Pads	50	"	88		
			3 Bales Saddlery					
			4 Box Harness oil					
			1 " " Dressing					
		Charges	2 " neatsfoot oil	300	200	6 00		
			2 Crate M. yards	80	160	1 28	10 70	
				1380		24 78	10 20	34 98

Figure 5.29.
Invoice from the Northern Pacific Railroad (River Landing, 1887) to ***Jos. Sullivan*** (Fort Benton). This bill of lading indicates that Sullivan had moved from Great Falls to Fort Benton and was purchasing saddlery, harness dressing and neatsfoot oil, and hardware from outside sources.

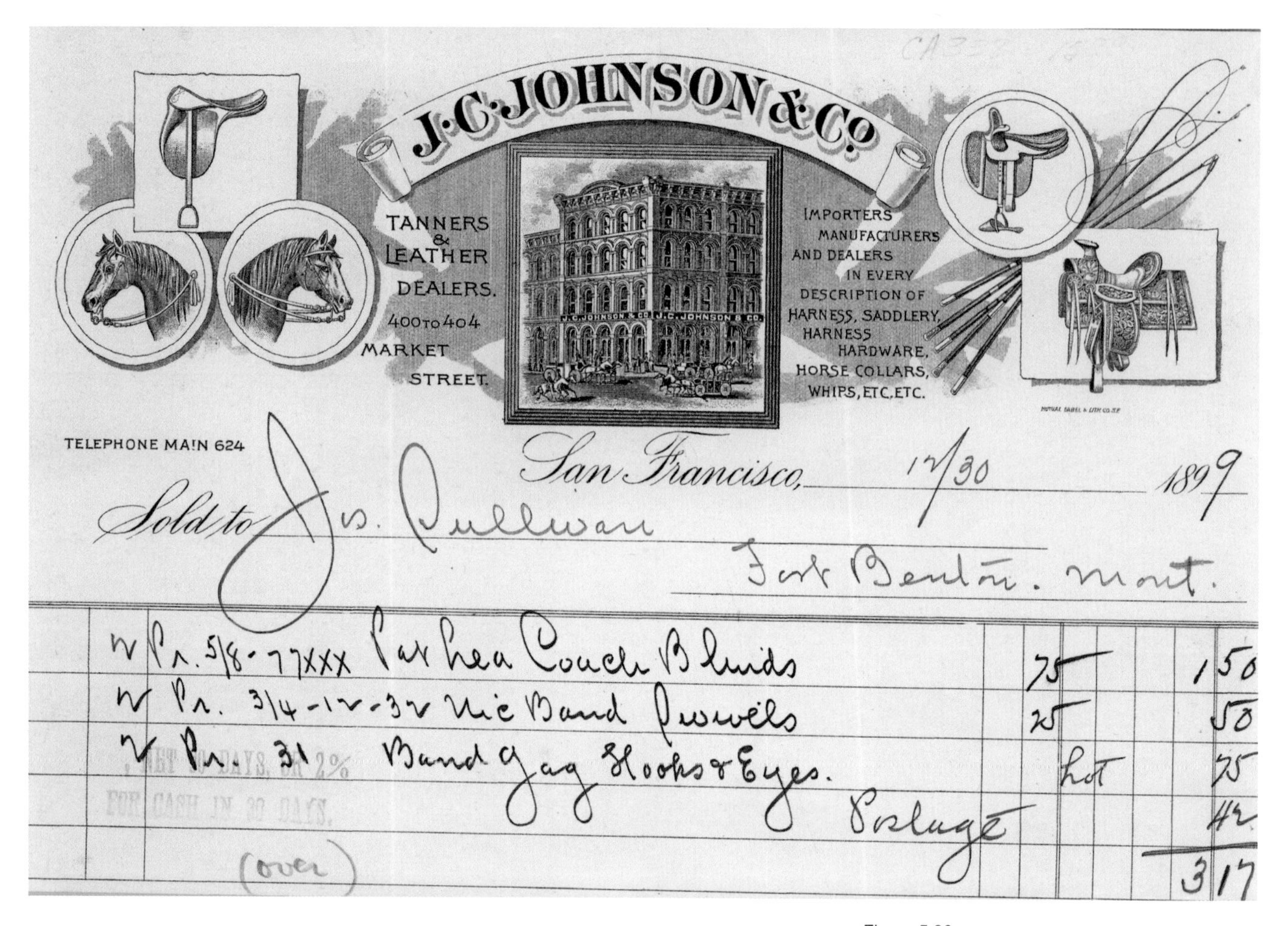

J.C. JOHNSON & CO.

TANNERS & LEATHER DEALERS. 400 TO 404 MARKET STREET.

IMPORTERS MANUFACTURERS AND DEALERS IN EVERY DESCRIPTION OF HARNESS, SADDLERY, HARNESS HARDWARE, HORSE COLLARS, WHIPS, ETC. ETC.

TELEPHONE MAIN 624

San Francisco, 12/30 1899

Sold to Jos. Sullivan
Fort Benton. Mont.

NET 30 DAYS, OR 2% FOR CASH IN 10 DAYS.

Item	Price	Amount
2 Pr. 5/8-77XXX Pat lea Coach Blinds	75	1 50
2 Pr. 3/4-12-32 Nic Band Swivels	25	50
1 Pr. 31 Band Gag Hooks & Eyes.	Lot	75
Postage		42
		3 17

(over)

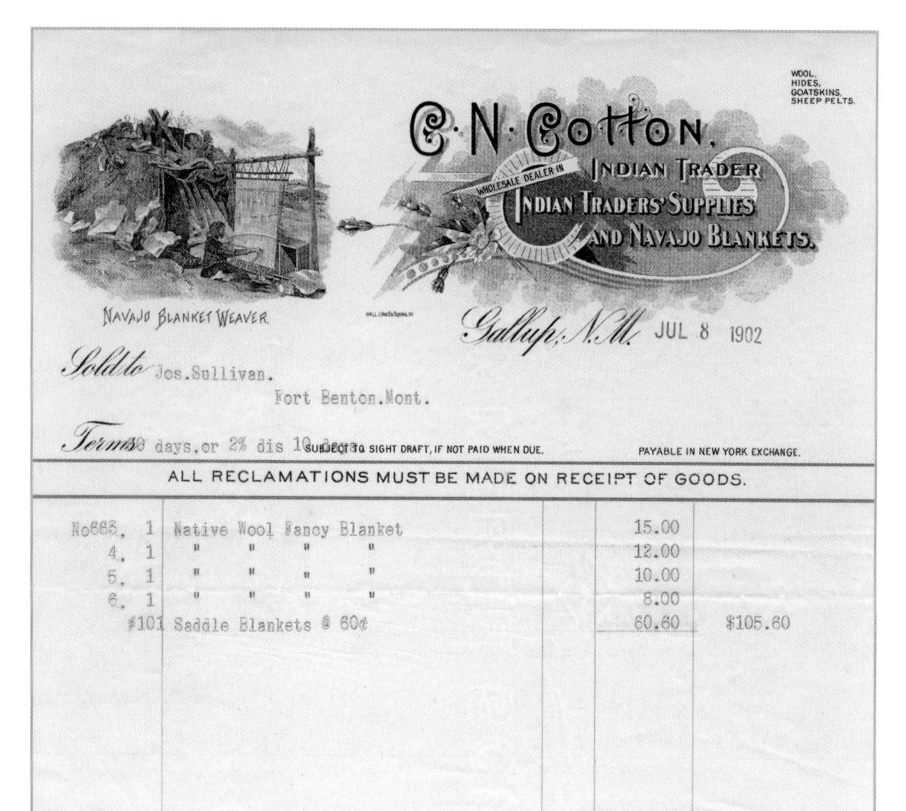

C. N. Cotton,
WHOLESALE DEALER IN
INDIAN TRADER
INDIAN TRADERS' SUPPLIES AND NAVAJO BLANKETS.

WOOL, HIDES, GOATSKINS, SHEEP PELTS.

NAVAJO BLANKET WEAVER

Gallup, N.M. JUL 8 1902

Sold to Jos. Sullivan.
Fort Benton. Mont.

Terms 30 days, or 2% dis 10 days. SUBJECT TO SIGHT DRAFT, IF NOT PAID WHEN DUE. PAYABLE IN NEW YORK EXCHANGE.

ALL RECLAMATIONS MUST BE MADE ON RECEIPT OF GOODS.

No.	Qty	Description	Amount	Total
No663.	1	Native Wool Fancy Blanket	15.00	
4.	1	" " " "	12.00	
5.	1	" " " "	10.00	
6.	1	" " " "	8.00	
	#101	Saddle Blankets @ 60¢	60.60	$105.60

Figure 5.30.
Invoice from ***J. C. Johnson & Co.***, San Francisco, dated "12/30/1899," to Jos. Sullivan, Fort Benton. Although the purchased items appeared to be largely hardware, the Johnson Co. dealt in English and Western tack (note English flat saddle on the *left* and side saddle with slipper stirrup on the *right*, and Mexican-style ornate Western saddle on the *upper right*).

Figure 5.31.
Invoice from C. N. Cotton, Indian Trader from Gallup, New Mexico (then a Territory), dated "Jul. 8, 1902," to ***Jos. Sullivan***, Fort Benton, Mont. Clearly Sullivan purchased Navajo saddle blankets from this trader (note Navajo weaver on stationery).

"Sullivan & Co." might have been Sullivan's first mark, accompanied by "BENTON" (rather than FT. BENTON); an example of this rare and early mark can be seen on a holster (figures 5.32 and 5.33). An early Sullivan A-fork, loop-seat saddle, dated "July 11, 1882" (figures 5.34 through 5.36) has been termed the "Texas" saddle due to the Texas star and the Texas longhorn tooled on the back and front of the cantle, respectively, likely the choice of a Texas cattleman visiting Fort Benton.

An unusual (probably made through a contract with the US Army) set of saddlebags or dispatch bags with the Sullivan territorial mark is shown in figures 5.37 and 5.38. Other items made by this prominent saddler include a wide cartridge belt with a slightly later mark (see captions, figures 5.39 and 5.40). A holster, a pair of cuffs, and a binocular case (figures 5.41 through 5.46) all display the early (pre-1900) "FT. BENTON" mark. A well-marked, left-handed holster is shown in figures 5.47 and 5.48. Another early (Fort) Benton saddler that should be mentioned here is L. (Lucius) H. Rosencrans, who established his business, the Pioneer Harness Shop, in 1877 (*Benton Record*, January 12, 1877). His firm was purchased by William Glassman in 1883. Formerly of Helena (in partnership with Roberts), Glassman earned a substantial reputation as a first-class maker of saddles for the working cowboy. The editors of the *River Press* (Fort Benton), March 12, 1884, stated:

> On the Judith round-up four fifths of the saddles are Mr. Glassman's work; on the Sun River, Chestnut and Smith river ranges "Glassman" saddles outnumber any others three to one; and the cowboys of the Teton, Shonkin and Musselshell are loud in their praises of the same saddle.

Quite a tribute to this saddler, whose Fort Benton advertisement is shown in figure 5.49.

Figure 5.33.
This early holster made by ***Sullivan and Company***, Benton, M.T., is interesting for a few reasons: it has a short skirt reminiscent of the holsters made by many of the Texas saddlers of the same period; it looks as if it was made originally for a short-barreled Colt single action and later altered to fit another revolver; the mark is one of the earliest Sullivan marks and is certainly pre-1889.

Figure 5.32.
Joseph Sullivan was one of the first saddlers in Montana. He arrived in Deer Lodge in the 1870s and started a saddlery with ***V. K. Goss***. When it was suggested that he relocate to Fort Benton, he immediately saw the opportunities afforded by its important location. He went to Fort Benton with Goss (who soon left) and began his own company supplying saddlery goods to almost everyone that was passing through on the way to the gold fields. This saddlery stamp for ***Sullivan and Company*** might have been his first stamp. The authors have never seen another in years of collecting, and the Benton identification, rather than Fort Benton, indicates that it was used early in the 1880s (figure 5.33).

It is always exciting to find a rare M.T. maker–marked item from a small town (figure 5.50), such as the holster shown in figures 5.51 and 5.52. Theo. Fisher opened his shop in 1884 in Sun River, M.T., located near Great Falls (*Sun River Sun*, November 27, 1884). Virtually nothing is known about him aside from his being "the absconding harness maker of Augusta" whose accounts were garnished by Spencer and Nye of Helena (*Helena Weekly Herald*, June 16, 1887); the wide-loop construction of the holster is unique. Sun River was a market both for ranchers (the Sun River Ranch, which raised cattle and horses, was started by J. C. Adams in 1874) and the military personnel at nearby Fort Shaw, which closed in 1890. Other firms, Roberts of Helena and Fort Benton (see chapter 6) and Roberts & Best, were also doing business in Sun River in 1884 (*Sun River Sun*, April 3, 1884), but no items marked by them have been found.

Figure 5.34.
A profile view of this ***Sullivan*** saddle shows the A-fork loop-seat construction and the fact that it saw hard use. Not all collector items are in mint condition and this saddle is exactly as it was collected 20 years ago.

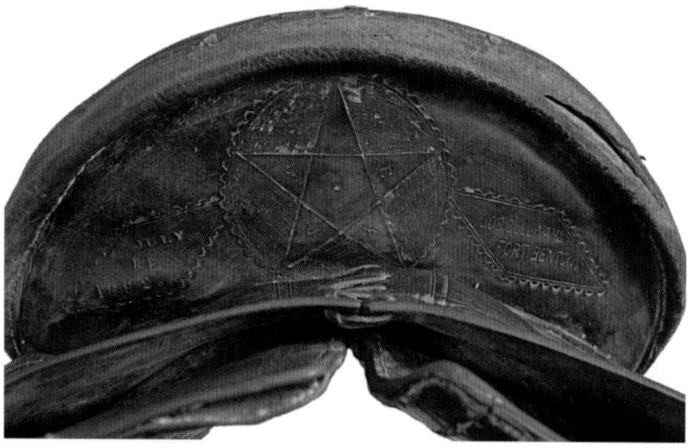

Figure 5.35.
The back of the cantle of the ***Joseph Sullivan***, Fort Benton saddle that was obviously custom made for a Texas buyer. It shows the Texas star in the center of the seat with a circle around it and "TEXAS" in the center of each of the points of the star. It also shows the Sullivan identification and the date "July 11, 1892" (figure 5.34).

Figure 5.36.
A Texas longhorn adorns the inside of the seat of the Sullivan "Texas" saddle. This engraving and that on the back of the cantle make it likely that the purchaser came to Montana during the Texas cattle drives and ordered this one-of-a-kind saddle (figure 5.35).

Figure 5.37.
Joseph Sullivan had contracts with the military during his time in Fort Benton. These oversized saddlebags are more correctly called dispatch bags and were probably used to transport military documents from post to post during the latter part of the Indian War period. The authors have never seen another large pair of these bags made and marked by a saddlery. There is a small brand on the cover of the bags that was likely added by a later owner after their military use.

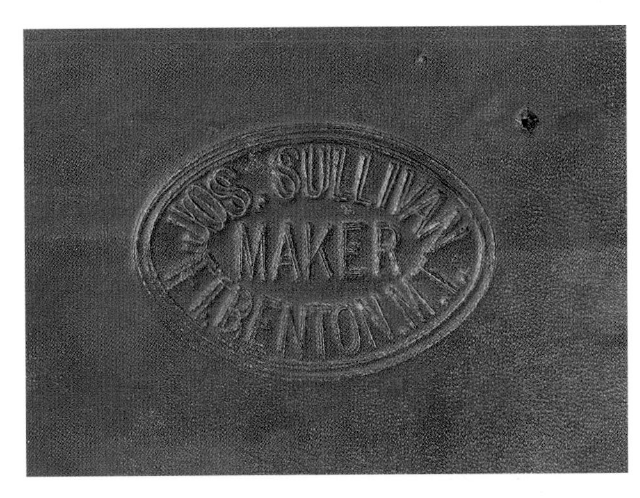

Figure 5.38.
Joseph Sullivan used his territorial mark on this pair of oversized saddlebags (figure 5.37). The mark is obviously double-struck; saddlery marks can be double marked or double struck and still be absolutely correct.

Figure 5.39.
Joseph Sullivan in Fort Benton made this cartridge belt in the 1880s or, possibly, slightly later. The light, attractive tooling pattern appears to be early, as does the lightweight japanned buckle. The cartridge loops are small enough to accommodate only the 44 rimfire flat cartridges from a Henry rifle. The "Henry" was a tremendous improvement in technology when it was first manufactured, but it was replaced by an even greater improvement when the 1866 and 1873 Winchesters were introduced.

Figure 5.40.
Joseph Sullivan arrived early to the saddle-making business in Montana and stayed late. Another Joseph Sullivan mark on an early cartridge belt tells its own story. The belt is tooled lightly and looks as if it were converted from a man's belt to a cartridge belt. With the early japanned buckle, this single mark with letters only appears to have been used in the 1880s after the early circular mark (see figure 5.39).

Figure 5.41.
This holster has been cut down, trimmed off, and the entire back removed, "cowboy" alterations that make it minimally collectible. Nonetheless, it was made by ***Joseph Sullivan*** in Fort Benton and bears his saddlery imprint on the front. Normally reserved for saddles, this large stamp is unusual on smaller items like holsters. It is nicely tooled and would be a great collectible had it not been altered so substantially.

Figure 5.42.
Joseph Sullivan of Fort Benton, M.T., made this nicely tooled holster prior to 1889. The image is a good representation of the saddle mark that was normally reserved for larger items and is rare when found on something as small as this holster (figure 5.41).

Figure 5.43.
Joseph Sullivan of Fort Benton was one of the first saddlers in eastern Montana. He saw the advantage of founding a saddlery in Fort Benton at the terminus of the steamboats arriving from the Missouri and the upper Mississippi rivers that were carrying supplies needed for the gold miners in southwestern Montana. The arriving miners needed saddles and horses, and the freighting companies needed new harness as well as repairs to their existing equipment used for the 200-mile trip to the gold fields. He was in the perfect location to provide those services and did so for almost 60 years. These cuffs bear his mark.

Figure 5.44.
A clear example of the mark that ***Joseph Sullivan*** used in his saddlery in Fort Benton. Sullivan did not actually make this pair of cuffs, as they have a George Lawrence (Oregon) snap button. We have examples of several dozen invoices (see figures 5.29 through 5.31) indicating that Sullivan was buying items from many of the large saddleries along the Missouri, from the George Lawrence saddlery, and from Clark on the West Coast.

Figure 5.45.
Custom-made saddlery items are always rare and even more so when the mark is territorial (pre-1889), for example, this binocular case made by ***Joseph Sullivan*** in Fort Benton. In early Montana, Fort Benton was the terminus of the northern steamboat route on the Missouri River and was a huge commercial hub. Most of the gold seekers in Montana Territory came up the Missouri on steamboats, and most of the gold was shipped back downriver to the commercial banks in the Northeast. The gold rode along with millions of buffalo hides also going downriver. The ***Joseph Sullivan*** saddlery prospered for over fifty years as a result of his location.

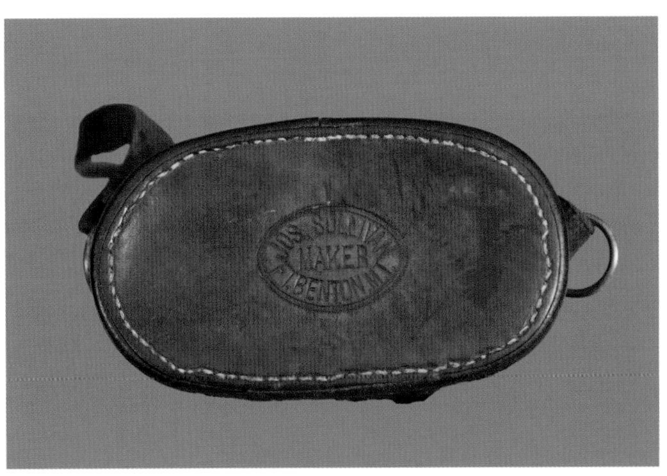

Figure 5.46.
The side view of the ***Sullivan*** binocular case (see figure 5.45) shows the saddlery mark on the front and the top, and the binoculars that it was made to protect. Items like this one are extremely rare and collectible.

Figure 5.47.
Left-handed holsters are quite rare and this one is a beauty. It is almost certain that ***Sullivan*** made this holster himself before 1889, and it shows the simple tooling and construction of the time. *Courtesy of R. Bachman.*

Figure 5.48.
A clearly marked and very good example of the ***Sullivan*** saddle stamp. Clear marks like this are necessary to ensure that one is buying authentic pieces (figure 5.47). *Courtesy of R. Bachman.*

STOCKMEN LOOK HERE

WM. GLASSMAN

Fort Benton, M. T.

Manufacturers of and Dealers in

HARNESS, SADDLES

BRIDLES,

Chaps, Spurs, Bits, Etc.

Mr. Glassman is the original owner of the patent Trade Mark, which consists of a horse or cow engraved on the saddle, with a fac simile of the purchaser's brand. This patent trade mark was all the rage while Mr. Glassman was of the firm of Roberts & Glassman, of the Cheyenne Saddle Shop, at Helena.

STOCK SADDLES a SPECIALTY

Give us a call; we will put up as good saddles as can be found in Montana. Orders by mail will receive prompt attention.

Figure 5.49.
Advertisement for ***Wm. Glassman***, Fort Benton, M. T. From the *River Press* (Fort Benton), August 18, 1883.

THEODORE FISHER,

MANUFACTURER OF AND DEALER IN

HARNESS, SADDLES, CHAPS,

Bridles, Fancy Bits, Spurs, Lariets, Whips,

And in fact everything usually found in a First-Class Harness Shop.

SATISFACTION GUARANTEED.

New Work Solicited.

CHARGES VERY REASONABLE.

Repairing of all kinds promptly attended to.

Sun River, - - - - Montana Ter.

Figure 5.50.
Advertisement for ***Theodore Fisher***, Sun River, Montana Ter. From the *Sun River Sun*, Dec. 26, 1884.

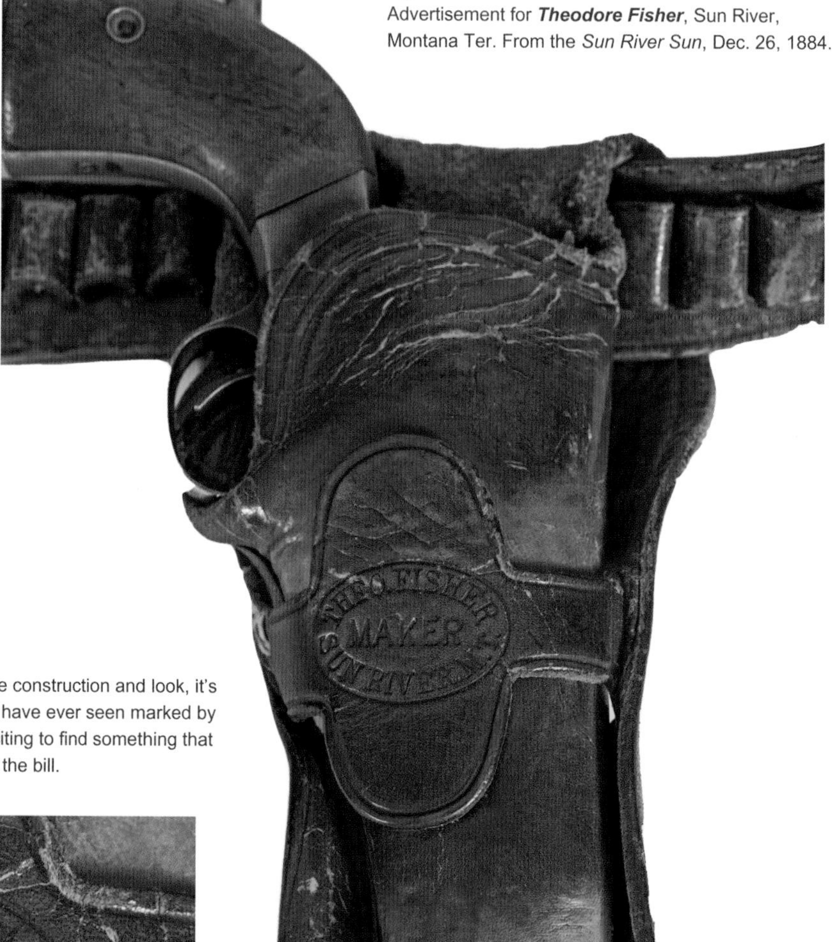

Figure 5.51.
This holster has to be one-of-a-kind. It has a unique construction and look, it's from a rare town, and it's the only item the authors have ever seen marked by ***Theo. Fisher*** from Sun River, M.T. It is always exciting to find something that one has not seen before and this item certainly fits the bill.

Figure 5.52.
Hard use by a cowboy either gives an item character or makes it look terrible. This holster and cartridge belt ensemble by ***Theo. Fisher*** has character and one of the most unique wide loop and cartouches of all the Montana saddlers. It is marked on the only holster loop made in this fashion and is a unique item from a rare town in Montana Territory—a town that was somewhat of a crossroads on the freight roads from Fort Benton to Helena and the southern Montana gold fields (figure 5.51).

The town of White Sulphur Springs was originally called Brewer Springs, after its discoverer, in 1886. The town was a trading center, famous for its hot springs and the surrounding Smith River Valley. Both cattle ranching and silver mining established this town, now the seat of Meagher County. It was also the business location of at least three saddleries: Jas. MacDonald (figures 5.53 and 5.54), William Wellman (figures 5.55 and 5.56), and G. J. Ritschel. James MacDonald first established a saddlery and harness shop in the growing town of White Sulphur Springs in 1882 (*Rocky Mountain Husbandman*, July 13, 1882), and William Wellman purchased the building in 1907 to continue the leather trade that he had started in 1888. He became a respected and influential member of the community. Figures 5.57 and 5.58 show a rarely-seen product, a child's saddle with a unique Wellman stamp; an adult loop-seat saddle with essentially the same mark can be seen in figures 5.59 and 5.60. An attractive money/cartridge belt, with an unmarked holster, is shown in figure 5.61, and a set of saddlebags with his effaced but readable mark in figure 5.62.

G. J. Ritschel's work has remained elusive. The single example known, shown in figures 5.63 and 5.64, is a Montana-style single wide-loop holster. More information on this maker from White Sulphur Springs would be highly desirable.

This chapter concludes with stationery (dated 1897) from R. Potter, a harness and saddlery dealer in Belt, Montana (figure 5.65). This town is located slightly east of Great Falls, but items produced by this maker have not surfaced in the collectors' world.

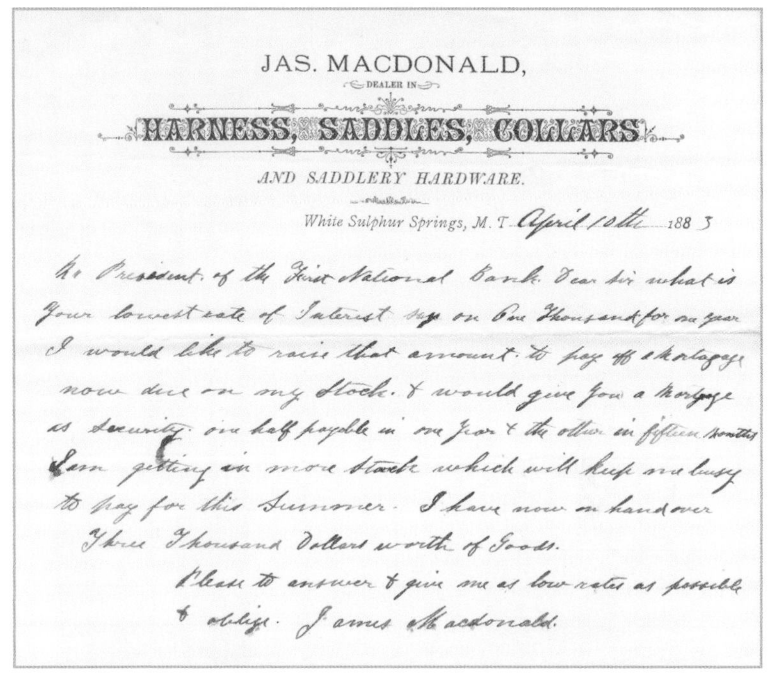

JAS. MACDONALD,
DEALER IN
HARNESS, SADDLES, COLLARS
AND SADDLERY HARDWARE.
White Sulphur Springs, M.T. April 10th 1883

To President of the First National Bank. Dear Sir what is your lowest rate of Interest say on One Thousand for one year I would like to raise that amount to pay off a mortgage now due on my Stock. I would give you a mortgage as security one half payable in one year & the other in fifteen months I am getting in more Stock which will keep me busy to pay for this Summer. I have now on hand over Three Thousand Dollars worth of Goods.

Please to answer & give me as low rates as possible & oblige. James Macdonald

Figure 5.53.
Stationery from ***Jas. MacDonald***, White Sulphur Springs, M.T., dated April 10, 1883. This letter was directed to the President of the First National Bank, requesting a quote for the "lowest rate of interest on One Thousand for one year." MacDonald further states that he has "on hand over Three Thousand Dollars worth of Goods."

JAMES MACDONALD

MANUFACTURER AND DEALER IN

Harness and Saddles,

Saddlery Hardware,

Montana, Texas, Cheyenne and California Saddles,

TEAM, COACH, STAGE AND BUGGY HARNESS

Always on Hand.

Whip-sticks, Stage lashes, Spanish bits, Buggy whips, Saddle cloths, Horse blankets, Cartridge belts, Stirrups, Horse and Mule collars, Fancy bridles, Cinches, Quirts, Race, Driving, Stock, California and Mexican Bits, Chaps, Curry Combs, Brushes, &c., &c., &c.

ALL WORK GUARANTEED TO GIVE SATISFACTION.

(*Old Post Office Building*) *WHITE SULPHUR SPRINGS, M. T.*

Figure 5.54.
Advertisement for ***James MacDonald***, White Sulphur Springs, M.T., from the *Rocky Mountain Husbandman* (Diamond City, M.T.), June 21, 1883.

Saddle Shop built by Wm. Wellman after selling his Main Street building. Located one block south on Second Street (now First Avenue SE) and known as Nelson Electric. This building housed the White Sulphur Springs Post Office for at least 12 years up until 1938. 1938-1960 post office was located in Main Street Wellman building, now owned by Taylor Gordon.

Figure 5.55.
William Wellman's saddle shop, on Second Street in White Sulphur Springs. From the Meagher County Historical Society.

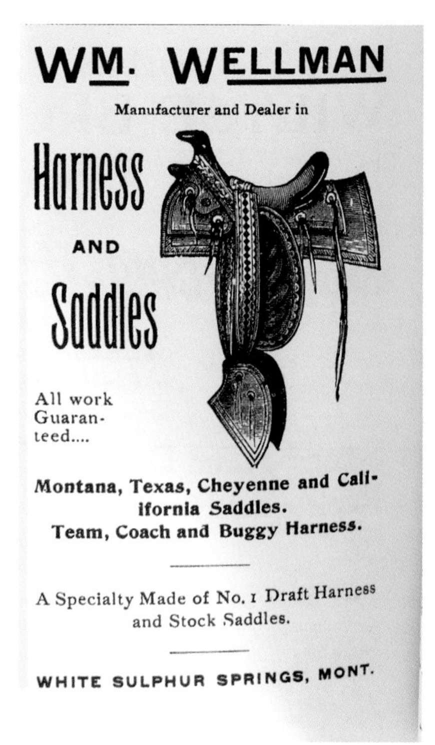

Figure 5.56.
Advertisement for ***Wm. Wellman***, White Sulphur Springs, Mont. *From Van Dersal & Conner, 1900.*

Figure 5.57.
An A-fork, Sam Stagg–rigged, half-seat child's saddle by ***Wm. Wellman***. It is exceedingly rare and is the only one the author has seen in over thirty years.

Figure 5.58.
The ***Wellman*** stamp is unique in placing "Montana" in the space usually used for the term "maker" and curving "White Sulphur Springs" across the bottom. Although caused by the length of the WSS combination, it seems to be the only stamp constructed in this way (figure 5.57).

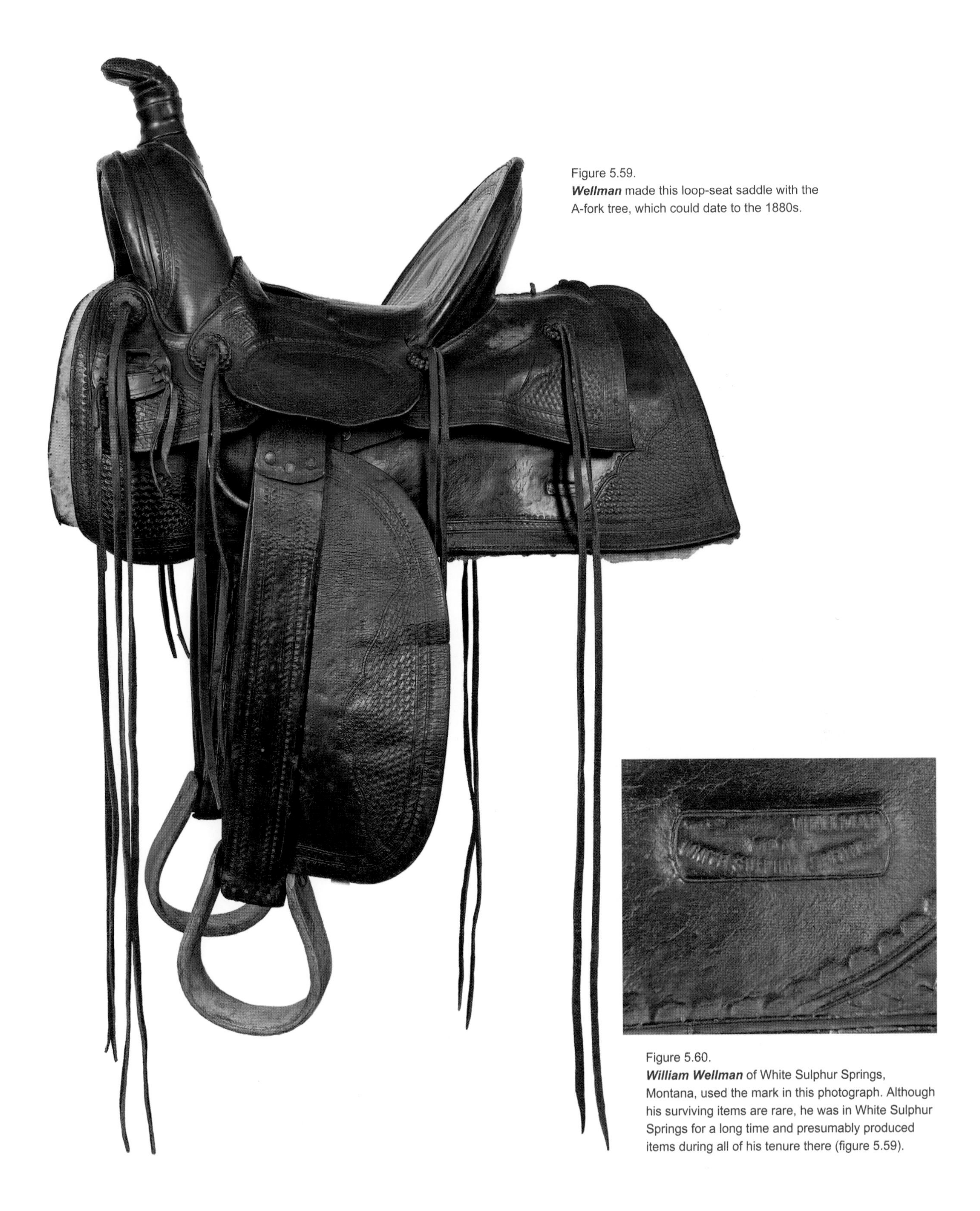

Figure 5.59.
Wellman made this loop-seat saddle with the A-fork tree, which could date to the 1880s.

Figure 5.60.
William Wellman of White Sulphur Springs, Montana, used the mark in this photograph. Although his surviving items are rare, he was in White Sulphur Springs for a long time and presumably produced items during all of his tenure there (figure 5.59).

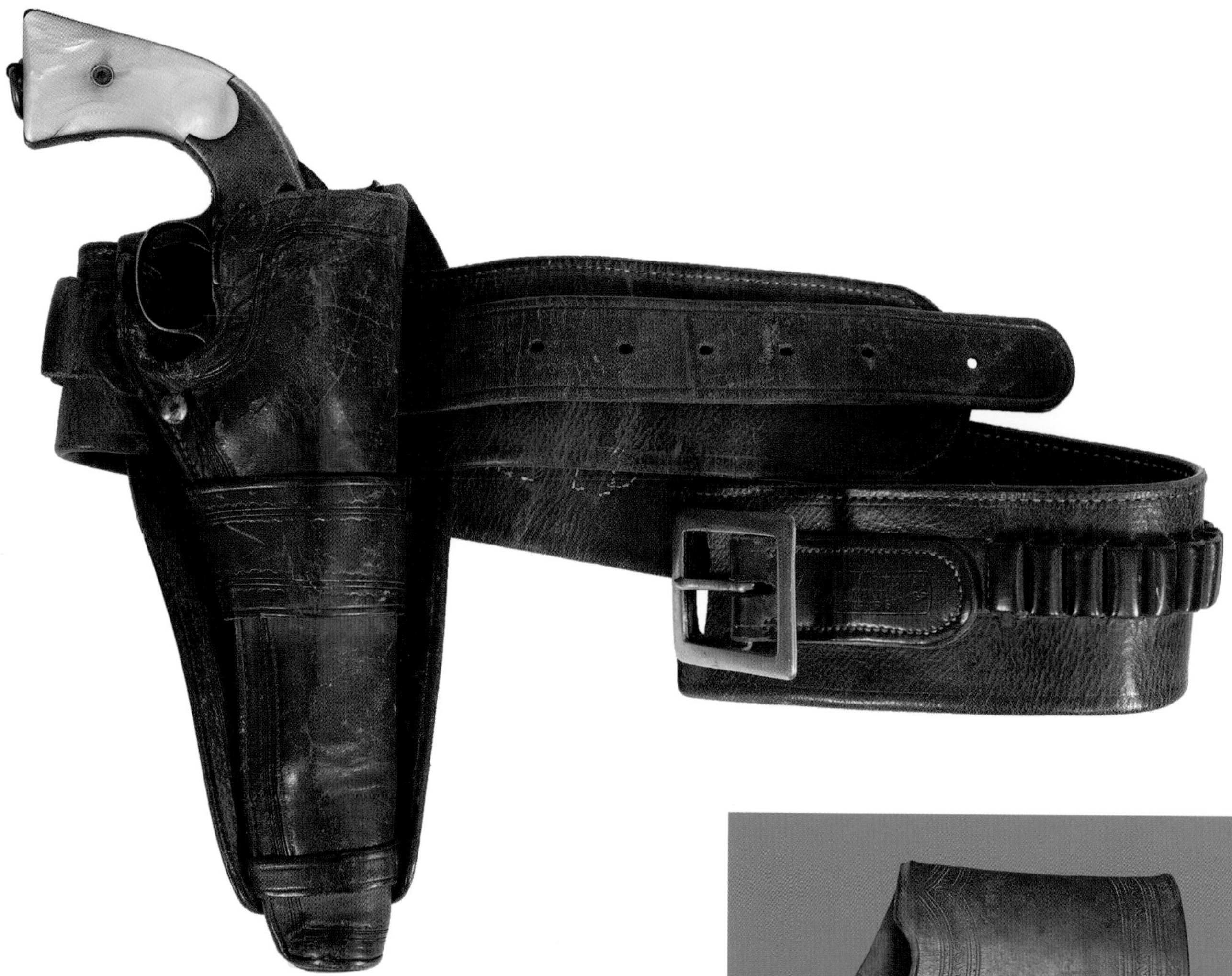

Figure 5.61.
William Wellman made this single wide-loop money belt in White Sulphur Springs, Montana. He has one of the most interesting of the Montana marks and made high-quality items. This rig is extremely collectible and, although the holster is unmarked, it is made in the single wide-loop "Montana style" with the lower loop added for stability. It may have been made by Wellman as well.

Figure 5.62.
This pair of saddlebags was made by ***William Wellman***, White Sulphur Springs, Montana. They show the normal amount of wear and bunkhouse repairs that collectors normally see on this sort of item. They are a typical example of what a cowboy wanted for carrying those belongings on his saddle that he could not put in his pockets.

Figure 5.63.
G. J. Ritschel marked this early single-action holster. It is a Montana-style single wide-loop holster with an additional small loop at the toe to hold the gun barrel in place. It also appears to have had a hole at the toe where a leather lanyard would have been used to tie the holster to a cowboy's leg. Production from this maker is so rare that this is the only example of which the authors are aware.

Figure 5.64.
The ***G. J. Ritschel*** mark on the holster shown in figure 5.63.

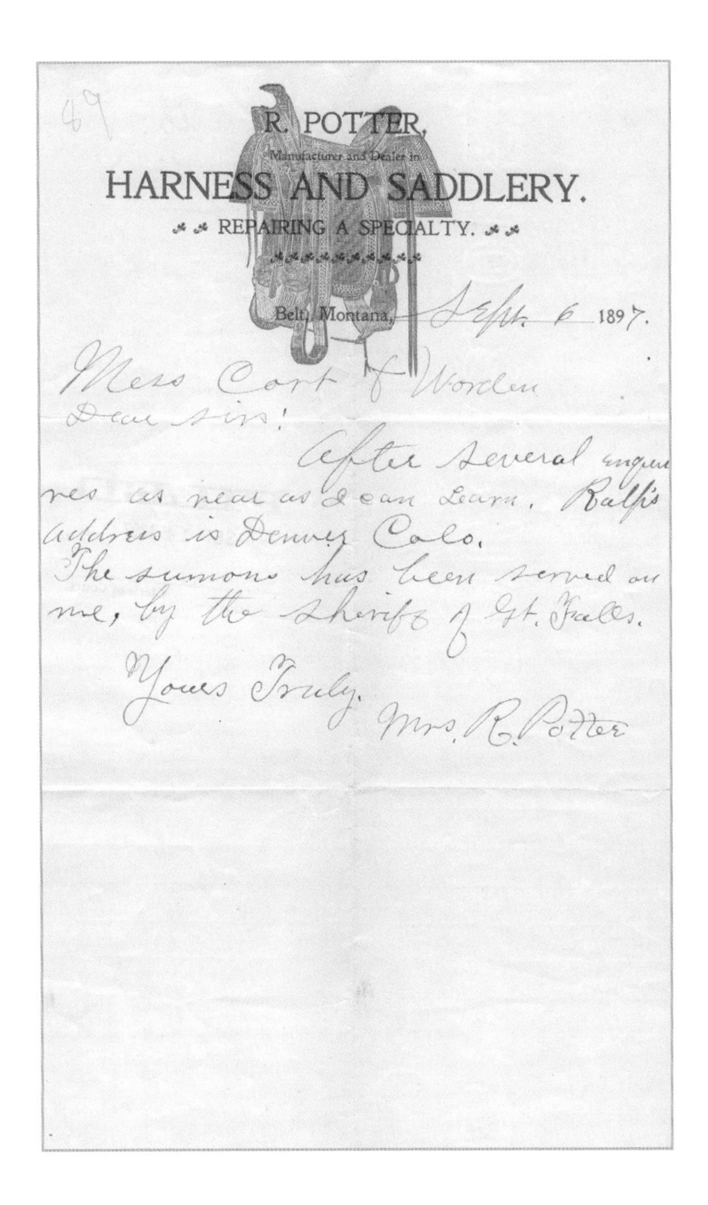

R. POTTER,
Manufacturer and Dealer in
HARNESS AND SADDLERY.
REPAIRING A SPECIALTY.

Belt, Montana, Sept. 6 1897.

Mess Cort & Worden
Dear sirs!
After several enquires as near as I can Learn. Ralfs address is Denver Colo.
The sumons has been served on me, by the sheriff of Gt. Falls.
Yours Truly
Mrs. R. Potter

Figure 5.65.
Stationery and letter from ***R. Potter***, Belt, Montana, dated Sept. 6, 1897. The letter was written by Mrs. R. Potter, stating that a summons has been served on her by the sheriff of Great Falls. *Courtesy of the Lewistown Public Library.*

Lincoln
Libby
Flathead
Kalispell
Glacier
Cut Bank
Toole
Shelby
Liberty
Chester
Hill
Havre
Chinook
Blaine
Malta
Phillips
Valley
Glasgow
Scobey
Daniels
Plentywood
Sheridan
Roosevelt
Wolf Point
Pondera
Conrad
Sanders
Thompson Falls
Lake
Polson
9
Teton
Choteau
5
Chouteau
Fort Benton
4
McCone
Circle
Sidney
Richland
Superior
Mineral
Missoula
Missoula
7
6
Lewis and Clark
GreatFalls
Cascade
Stanford
Judith Basin
Fergus
Lewistown
Petroleum
Winnett
Jordan
Garfield
Dawson
Glendive
Wibaux
Wibaux
Prairie
Terry
Helena
Powell
Deer Lodge
Granite
Philipsburg
Hamilton
Ravalli
Meagher
White Sulphur Springs
Wheatland
Harlowton
Golden Valley
Ryegate
Musselshell
Roundup
Hysham
Treasure
Rosebud
Forsyth
2
Miles City
Fallon
Baker
Custer
Townsend
Boulder
Jefferson
Broad-water
Anaconda
Deer Lodge
Silver Bow
Butte
Gallatin
Bozeman
Park
Livingston
8
Sweet Grass
Big Timber
Stillwater
Columbus
Yellowstone
Billings
3
Hardin
Big Horn
Carbon
Red Lodge
Ekalaka
Powder River
Broadus
Carter
Beaverhead
Dillon
Madison
Ennis

6

Central-Western Montana

Helena

Townsend

Founded in 1864, Helena was named the third capital of Montana Territory (after Bannock and Virginia City) in 1875, and today retains that distinction, while also serving as the seat of Lewis and Clark County. Mining ventures drove the development of Helena and surrounding areas; the first gold discovery in M.T. occurred at Gold Creek (near present-day Garrison [Area 7, slightly north of Deer Lodge]) in 1852. Within a decade thousands of miners populated the central western Territory, and many rich strikes were made in gold and silver, as well as copper, lead, and coal. Last Chance Gulch was a particularly lucrative placer, its gold the essential founder of Helena, with its rumored fifty millionaires by 1888, a record at that time for per capita wealth in any known city. Clearly this wealth supported mansions, fine architecture, and many businesses, including several excellent saddleries.

Table 6.1 lists an impressive number of saddleries, most of which pre-date statehood. Creative letterheads and invoices from several of them are shown in figures 6.1 through 6.9. One of the earliest saddlers, Roberts & Glassman, started its firm in Helena in 1882 and specialized in Cheyenne (Wyoming) stock saddles (*River Press*, May 24, 1882) (figure 6.10). In 1884, after dissolution of the partnership in 1883, Glassman purchased the shop of L. H. Rosencrans, of Fort Benton (see chapter 5) (*The Benton Weekly*, February 9, 1884). He later became mayor of Ogden, Utah, and subsequently ran for US senator (Utah) in 1904.

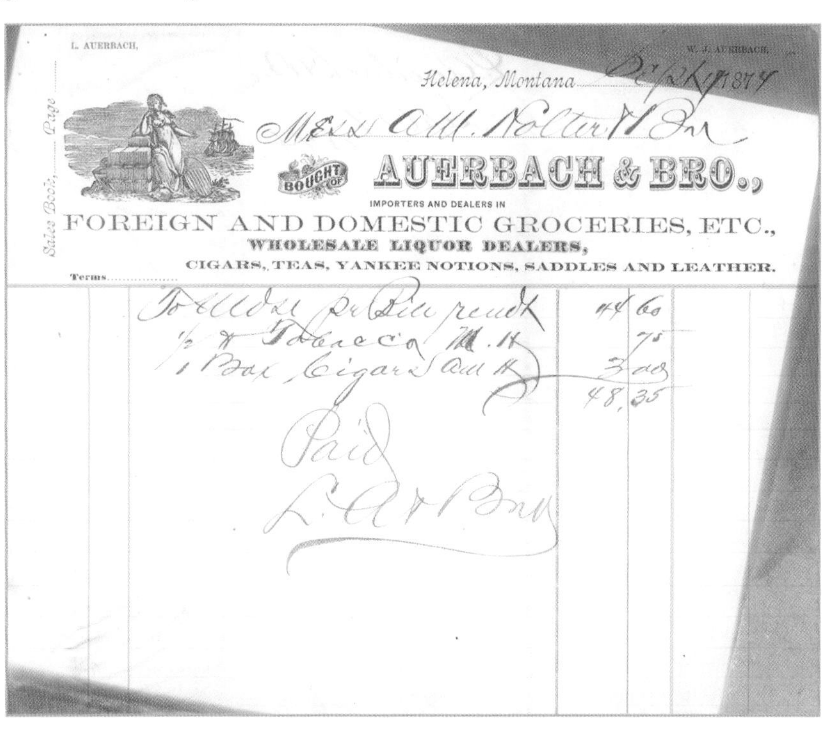
L. AUERBACH, W. J. AUERBACH.
Helena, Montana
BOUGHT OF
AUERBACH & BRO.,
IMPORTERS AND DEALERS IN
FOREIGN AND DOMESTIC GROCERIES, ETC.,
WHOLESALE LIQUOR DEALERS,
CIGARS, TEAS, YANKEE NOTIONS, SADDLES AND LEATHER.
Sales Book, Page
Terms

	44 60
	75
	3 00
	48 35

Paid

Figure 6.1.
Letterhead/invoice from ***Auerbach & Bro.***, Helena, Montana, dated Sept. 1874.

Table 6.1. Saddleries of Montana[1]

MAKER	LOCATION	DATES[2]
A. J. Davidson & Co.; A. J. Davidson	Helena; Helena	(1884), 1888–1897; (1875, 1876), (1884)
Auerbach & Brothers	Helena	(1874)
Carson, Alex C.	Townsend	(1893), (1895)
Cheyenne Saddle Shop (Roberts, B. R. & Glassman, William)	Helena	1880–1883, (1882)
Cheyenne Saddle Shop (Roberts, B. R.)	Helena	(1883)
Davidson, A. J.	Helena	1876–1888
DeVore's Saddlery	Helena	1937–present
Franklin, Peter	Helena	
Goettlich, Charles	Helena	1900 Directory
Goettlich, E. L.	Helena	1885–1937
Heavener, F.	Helena	(1890)
Helena Saddlery & Tent Co.—Ernest Goetlich	Helena	1885–1937
Knapp & Buck	Helena	(1941)
Lobenstein, W. C.	Helena	(1874, 1875, 1876)
Mann, W. M.	Helena	(1881–189?)
Markham, Charles	Helena	1867, (1876)
Neill, R. W.	Helena	(1889), (1890)
Nye, Frank J.	Helena	(1891, 1892)
Rosencrans, Lucian H.	Helena	1866, (1876), (1879)
Secord, George & Jacobs, Edward C.	Helena	1867–Directory
Spencer, Loyal W. & Nye, Frank J.	Helena	1883–1890

1. Products made or sold by these saddleries included harness, saddles, bits, spurs, whips, boots, bridles, accessories (horse blankets, grooming tools, trunks, bags, and/or robes), vehicles (sleighs, buggies, wagons, carts), and Indian-made goods (e.g., saddle blankets).

2. Dates in parentheses are specified on the company letterhead or in a newspaper/journal advertisement. Inclusive dates for the tenure of the company have been provided where data are available and reliable.

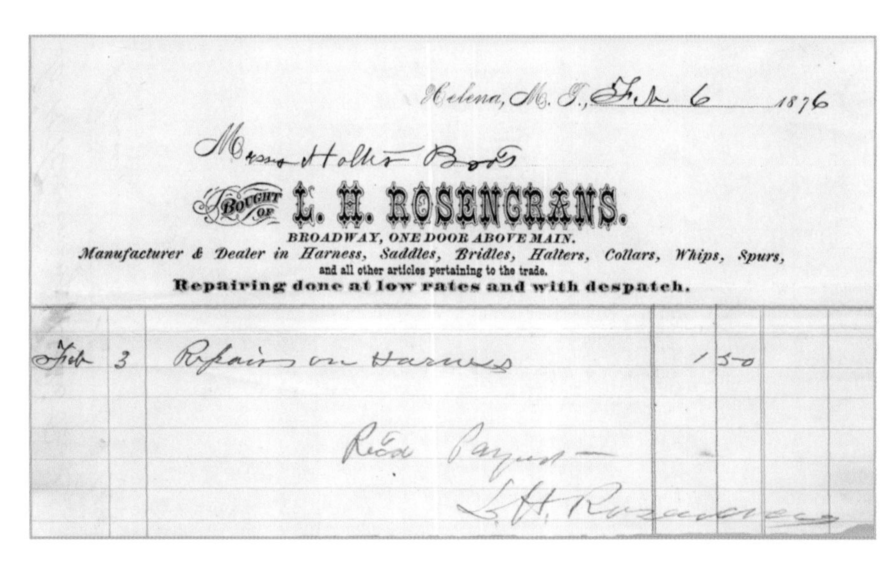

Helena, M. T., Feb 6 1876

Messrs Holter Bros

Bought of L. H. ROSENCRANS.

BROADWAY, ONE DOOR ABOVE MAIN.

Manufacturer & Dealer in Harness, Saddles, Bridles, Halters, Collars, Whips, Spurs,
and all other articles pertaining to the trade.

Repairing done at low rates and with despatch.

Feb	3	Repairs on Harness	1 50

Rec'd Payment —
L. H. Rosencrans

Figure 6.2.
Letterhead/invoice from ***L. H. Rosencrans***, Helena, M.T., dated Feb. 6, 1876.

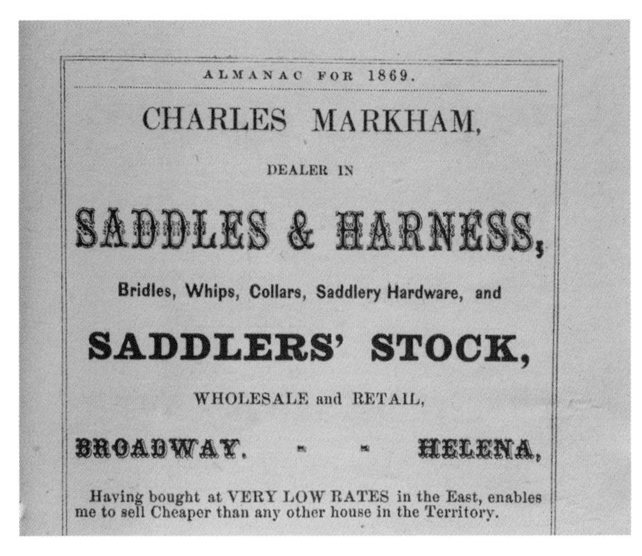

Figure 6.3.
Advertisement for ***Charles Markham***, Helena, Montana. *From Montana Publishing Co., Statistical Almanac for 1869.*

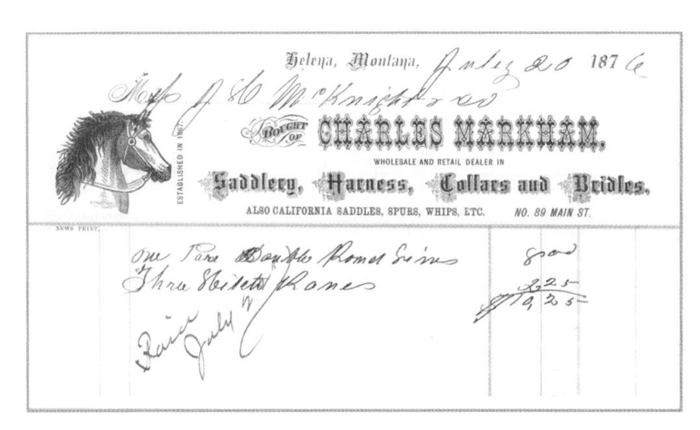
Helena, Montana, July 20 1876

Mess J & C McKnight & Co

Bought of CHARLES MARKHAM,
ESTABLISHED IN 1867
WHOLESALE AND RETAIL DEALER IN
Saddlery, Harness, Collars and Bridles,
ALSO CALIFORNIA SADDLES, SPURS, WHIPS, ETC. NO. 89 MAIN ST.

Figure 6.4.
Letterhead/invoice from ***Charles Markham***, Helena, Montana, dated July 20, 1876. Note the use of "Montana" despite the Territorial date.

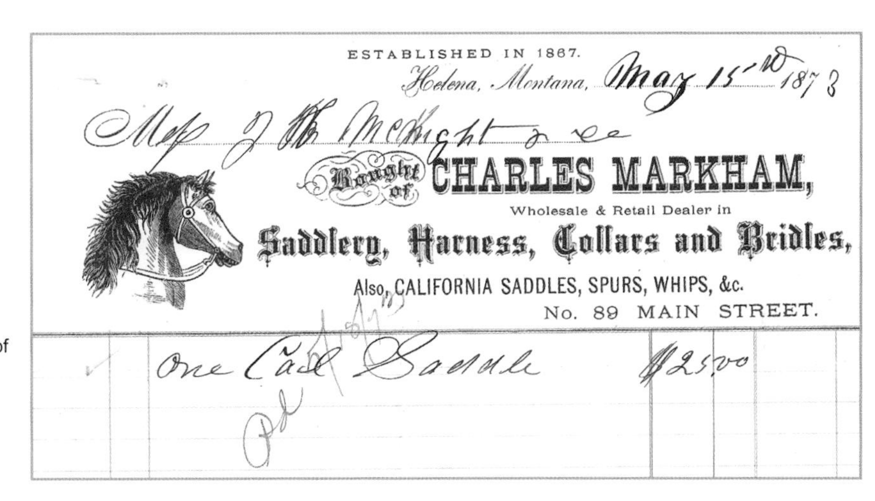
ESTABLISHED IN 1867.
Helena, Montana, May 15th 1873

Mess J & C McKnight & Co

Bought of CHARLES MARKHAM,
Wholesale & Retail Dealer in
Saddlery, Harness, Collars and Bridles,
Also, CALIFORNIA SADDLES, SPURS, WHIPS, &c.
No. 89 MAIN STREET.

One Cask Saddle $25.00

Figure 6.5.
Fancy letterhead/invoice from ***Charles Markham***, Helena, Montana, dated May 1, 1873. Note date of establishment as 1867.

Helena, M. T., Oct 3rd 1876

Bought of W. C. LOBENSTEIN,
DEALER IN
Harness, Saddles, Saddlery-Hardware, Leather, Shoe Findings, Hides, Furs & Wool,
TERMS CASH. Bentley's Block, Main Street.

Aug 4	1 Bell Collar	1 00		
Sept 2	1 Sett Concord Light Hack Harness	80 00		81 00

Paid Oct 3rd
W. C. Lobenstein

Figure 6.6.
Invoice from ***W. C. Lobenstein***, Helena, M.T., dated Oct. 3, 1876.

R. W. NEILL,

MANUFACTURER AND DEALER IN

Stock Saddles, Side Saddles,

Light and Heavy Harness,

Bits, Spurs, Quirts, Whips, Lashes, Blankets, Sheets, Dusters, Slickers, Nose Bags, Sweat Collars, Horse Boots and all other goods usually kept in a first-class harness store. Hand made driving harness a specialty.

Opposite Grand Central Hotel, Main St., Helena, M. T.

Figure 6.7.
Advertisement for ***R. W. Neill***, Helena, M.T. Note inclusion of Stock and Side Saddles, among light and heavy harness and horse-related accessories. *From the* Helena Independent, *Oct., 1, 1889.*

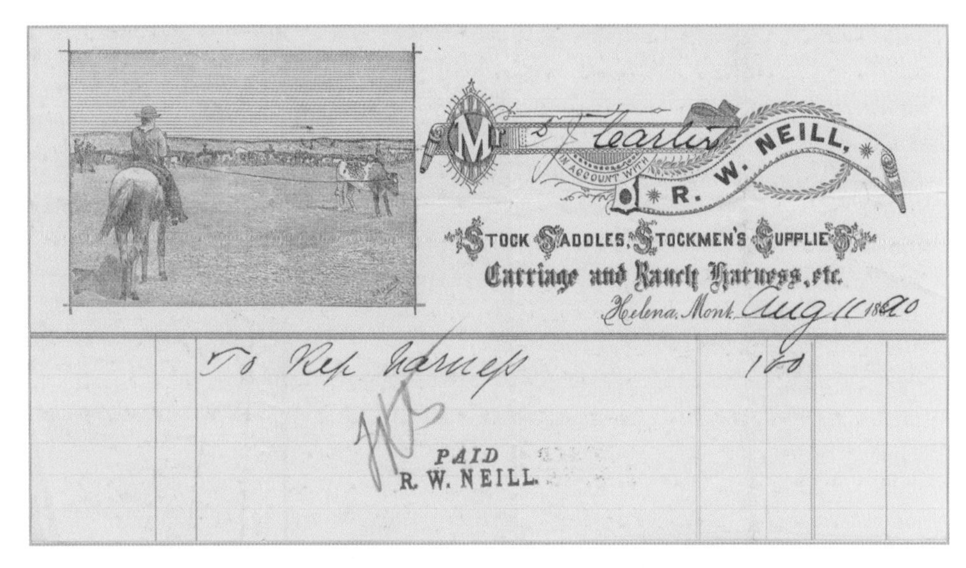

M
In account with R. W. NEILL,
STOCK SADDLES, STOCKMEN'S SUPPLIES
Carriage and Ranch Harness, etc.
Helena, Mont. Aug 11 1890

To Rep harness	1 00

PAID
R. W. NEILL

Figure 6.8.
A beautiful letterhead/invoice from ***R. W. Neill***, Helena, Mont., dated Aug. 11, 1890.

Helena, Mont. Feb 1 1890

M A M Holter Hardware Co.
Thomas Moreland

Bought of F. Heavener

DEALER IN

Harness and Saddlery, Fancy Bits, Spurs,

BRIDLES AND QUIRTS. FULL LINE OF HORSE CLOTHING

310 N. MAIN STREET

T. MORELAND, Manager

Jan	11	To 1 Brush	50
"	26	" Handle in wright	1 50

O.K. Jake

Paid Thos Moreland

Figure 6.9.
Letterhead/invoice from ***F. Heavener***, Helena, Mont., dated Feb. 1, 1890.

Figure 6.10.
Advertisement for the ***Cheyenne Saddle Shop, Roberts & Glassman***, Helena, Montana. *From the* Helena Weekly Herald, *May 3, 1883.*

One of the most elusive (and therefore desirable) Helena, M.T., makers is A. J. Davidson, who produced extremely high-quality leather goods. One of his invoices, dated 1880, shown in figure 6.11, states that this firm is a successor to W. C. Lobenstein (purchased in 1876, *Rocky Mountain Husbandman*, October 12, 1876) (see table 6.1). A second invoice, dated Dec. 12, 1887 (figure 6.12), does not include the statement of successorship but uses "A. J. Davidson" as the name of the firm, which sold saddles, harness, wagons, and acted as a brokerage for "hides, furs, and wool." A letter written on the A. J. Davidson stationery, dated November 27, 1884, reveals two additional branch stores: A. J. Davidson, Fort Benton, and A. J. Davidson & Co., Deer Lodge. In December 1888, the firm incorporated as A. J. Davidson & Co. opened a branch store in Butte. The saddle shown in figure 6.13 is a fine example of Davidson's output—a loop-seat saddle with double rigging and an interesting, but not showy, Greek key border design; a similar saddle is shown in figure 6.14. A pair of rare pommel bags marked "MANUFACTURED BY A. J. DAVIDSON/HELENA M.T." is shown in figures 6.15 and 6.16. Of interest is the use of the word "manufactured" rather than the almost universally used "maker" or "made by." As Territorial pieces, both the saddle and bags are highly collectible.

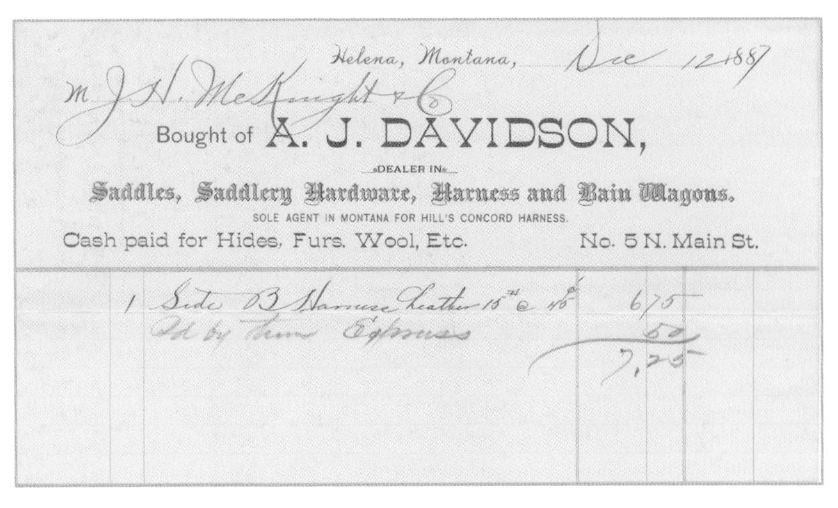
Helena, Montana, Dec 12 1887
Bought of A. J. DAVIDSON,
DEALER IN
Saddles, Saddlery Hardware, Harness and Bain Wagons.
SOLE AGENT IN MONTANA FOR HILL'S CONCORD HARNESS.
Cash paid for Hides, Furs. Wool, Etc. No. 5 N. Main St.

1 Side B Harness Leather 15 @ 45 6 75
50
7.25

Figure 6.12.
Letterhead/invoice from ***A. J. Davidson***, Helena, Montana, dated Dec. 12, 1887.

Charles Goettlich worked briefly in Helena (figure 6.17), but his brother Ernest Goettlich arrived in Helena in 1877 and was employed by A. J. Davidson. After working briefly for Frank Esler (Bozeman), he set up his shop in Miles City in 1881, which was later sold in 1894 to Al Furstnow. This peripatetic saddle maker returned to Helena, subsequently purchased William Mann's business (see below), and named it The Helena Saddlery and Tent Co. This enterprise was successful until 1937 when, shortly before his death, Goettlich sold the concern to L. G. DeVore (today known as DeVore's Saddlery). Figures 6.18 and 6.19 are a rare example of Goettlich's marked leather: a pair of cuffs with the small "Helena Mont." mark.

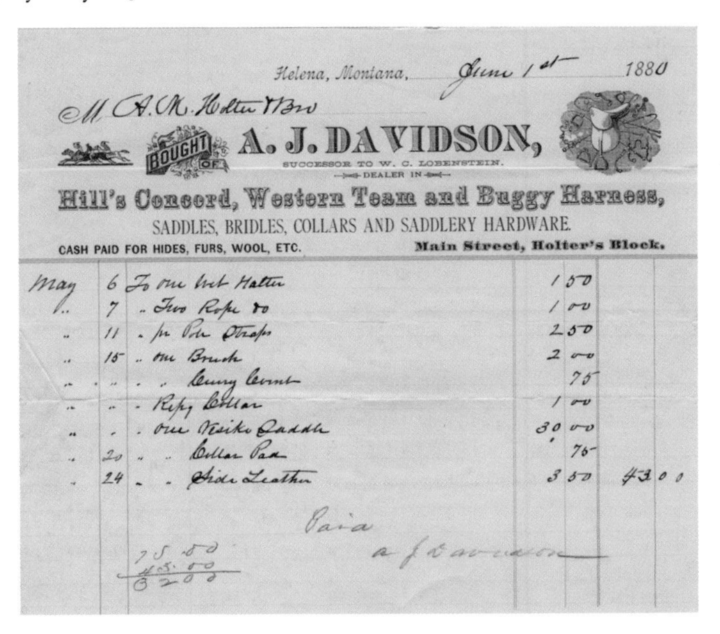
Helena, Montana, June 1st 1880
M A. M. Holter & Bro
BOUGHT OF A. J. DAVIDSON,
SUCCESSOR TO W. C. LOBENSTEIN.
DEALER IN
Hill's Concord, Western Team and Buggy Harness,
SADDLES, BRIDLES, COLLARS AND SADDLERY HARDWARE.
CASH PAID FOR HIDES, FURS, WOOL, ETC. Main Street, Holter's Block.

May	6	To one Web Halter	1 50	
..	7	.. Two Rope do	1 00	
..	11	.. pr Pole Straps	2 50	
..	15	.. one Brush	2 00	
..	..	.. .. Curry Comb	75	
..	..	.. Rope Collar	1 00	
..	..	.. one Saddle	30 00	
..	20	.. .. Collar Pad	75	
..	24	.. .. Side Leather	3 50	43 00

Paid
A J Davidson

Figure 6.11.
Letterhead/invoice from ***A. J. Davidson***, Helena, Montana, dated June 1, 1880. Note "Successor to W. C. Lobenstein." *Courtesy of Ken Hamlin.*

Figure 6.14.
This well-used ***Davidson*** saddle with the classic Sam Stagg rigging, a half-seat, A-fork, and double-rigged design was popular with pre-1889 cowboys.

Figure 6.13.
A. J. Davidson (Helena, M.T.). This Territorial loop-seat saddle has a double rigging for two cinches, large square skirts, Sam Stagg rigging, and full side jockeys. There is a "Greek key" border design around the edges of the leather. It is a true classic and bears the stamp "A. J. Davidson/Helena, M.T." Davidson was in business between 1876 and 1888, after which the firm was incorporated as A. J. Davidson & Co., with a branch in Butte.

Figure 6.16.
Shown in this image is a unique saddlery stamp from ***A. J. Davidson***, Helena, M.T. It shows Davidson as a manufacturer and not a maker, unique in all of the saddlery world. The stamp is bold and easy to read (figure 6.15).

Figure 6.15.
Pommel bags are rare as they are generally very prior to 1890—and did not survive well. This marked set of bags from ***A. J. Davidson***, Helena, M.T., are in good condition given their age and use. That and their rarity make these bags highly collectible.

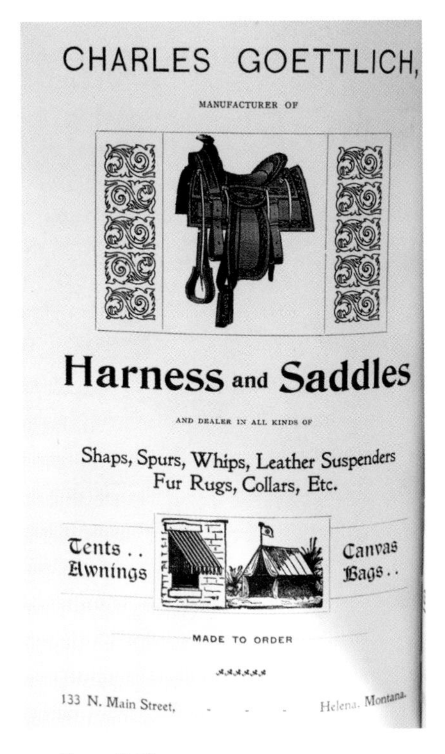

Figure 6.17.
Advertisement for ***Charles Goettlich***, Helena, Montana. *From Van Dersal & Conner, 1900.*

Figure 6.18.
Ernest Goettlich was one of the first saddlers in Miles City in the early 1880s, but had a serious run of bad luck and eventually established himself in Helena. This pair of cuffs is marked by him and was made when he was operating the Helena saddlery. All of his output is rare, and this is a nice example his work.

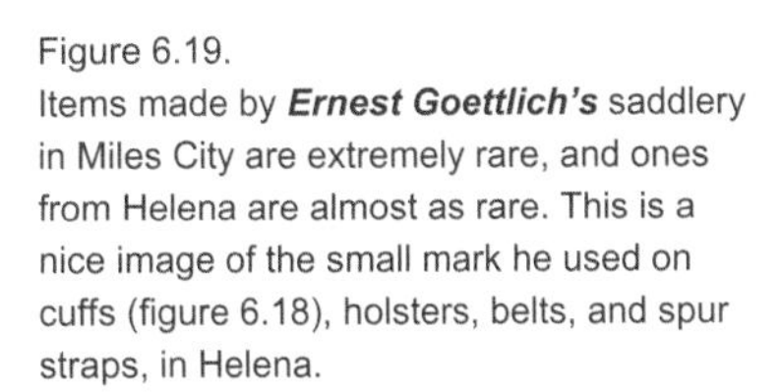

Figure 6.19.
Items made by ***Ernest Goettlich's*** saddlery in Miles City are extremely rare, and ones from Helena are almost as rare. This is a nice image of the small mark he used on cuffs (figure 6.18), holsters, belts, and spur straps, in Helena.

W. M. Mann was another saddle maker who worked for several saddleries in different states but spent at least nine years in Helena (see letterheads, figures 6.20 through 6.22. Items marked by him, especially pre-1889, are rare. A pair of his cuffs is shown in figures 6.23 and 6.24; unfortunately the mark was partially obliterated by the cowboy's later addition of brass studs.

An interesting Texas-style holster bearing Mann's mark (figures 6.25 and 6.26) reflects his Texas origins and makes a treasured collectible antique.

Figure 6.20.
Letterhead/invoice from ***W. M. Mann***, Helena, Montana, dated Oct. 3, 1881.

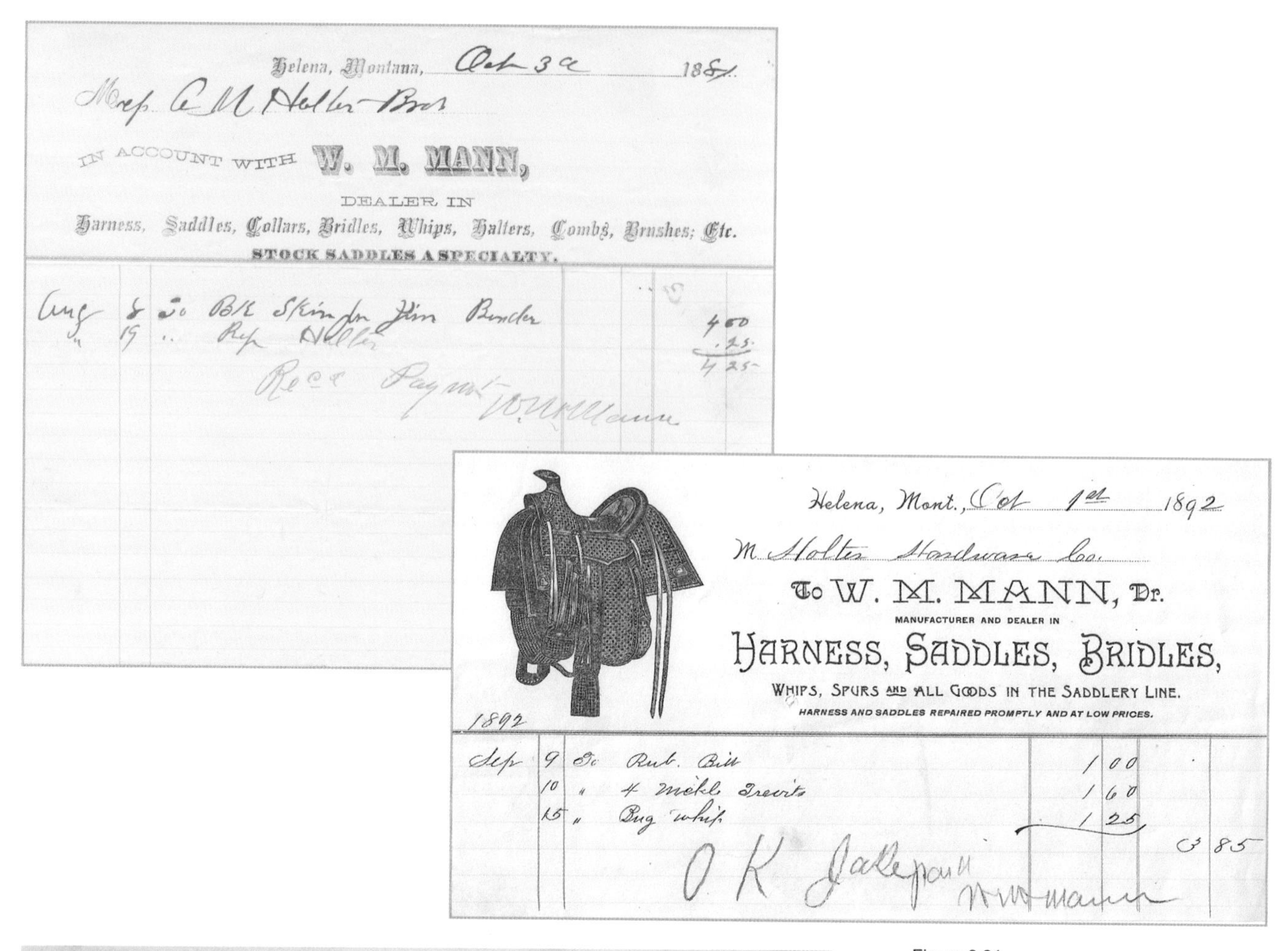

Helena, Montana, Oct 3d 1881

Mess. C M Holter Bros

IN ACCOUNT WITH W. M. MANN,

DEALER IN

Harness, Saddles, Collars, Bridles, Whips, Halters, Combs, Brushes; Etc.

STOCK SADDLES A SPECIALTY.

Aug	8	To Blk Skin for Jim Bender	4 00
"	19	.. Rep Holler	.25
			4 25

Rec'd Payment W M Mann

Helena, Mont., Oct 1st 1892

M Holter Hardware Co.

To W. M. MANN, Dr.

MANUFACTURER AND DEALER IN

HARNESS, SADDLES, BRIDLES,

WHIPS, SPURS AND ALL GOODS IN THE SADDLERY LINE.

HARNESS AND SADDLES REPAIRED PROMPTLY AND AT LOW PRICES.

1892

Sep	9	To Rub. Bitt	1 00	
	10	" 4 nickel Dees	1 60	
	15	" Bug whip	1 25	
				3 85

OK W M Mann

Figure 6.21.
Letterhead/invoice of ***W. M. Mann***, Helena, Mont., dated Oct 1st, 1892.

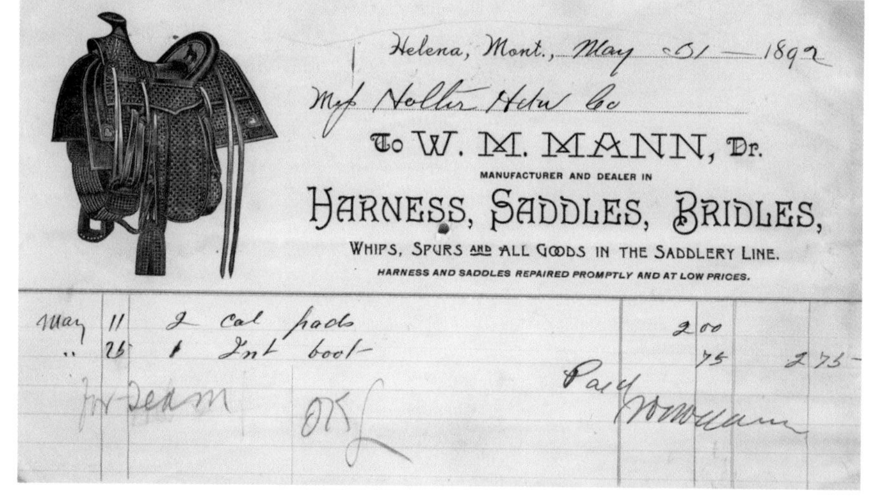

Helena, Mont., May 01 1892

Mess Holter Hdw Co

To W. M. MANN, Dr.

MANUFACTURER AND DEALER IN

HARNESS, SADDLES, BRIDLES,

WHIPS, SPURS AND ALL GOODS IN THE SADDLERY LINE.

HARNESS AND SADDLES REPAIRED PROMPTLY AND AT LOW PRICES.

May	11	2 Col pads	2 00	
..	26	1 Int boot	75	2 75

Paid W M Mann

OK

Figure 6.22.
Letterhead/invoice from ***W. M. Mann, Dr.***, Helena, Montana, dated May 189?.

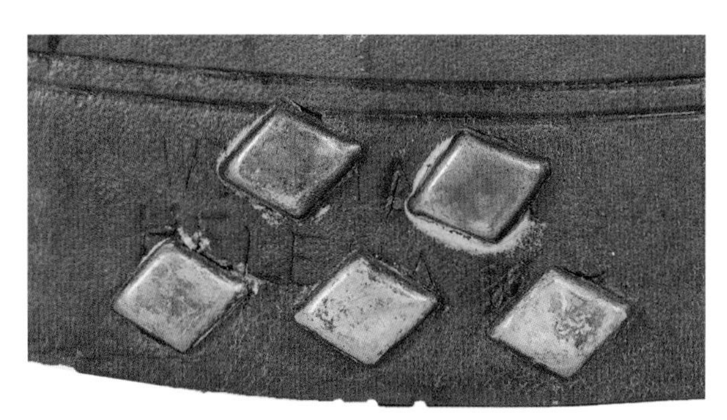

Figure 6.24.
Underneath the studs (figure 6.23), obviously added after the cuffs were made, one can see the name of the saddler that made the cuffs—***William Mann***.

Figure 6.23.
William Mann was an early saddler who arrived from Texas and worked in a couple of locations before he located in Helena. Studs were added to this pair of cuffs after the saddler stamped them with his maker's mark. Although difficult to discern, the mark is M.T., indicative of pre-1889 Montana Territory. Mann did not work in Montana for very long, and items bearing his Helena stamp are extremely rare.

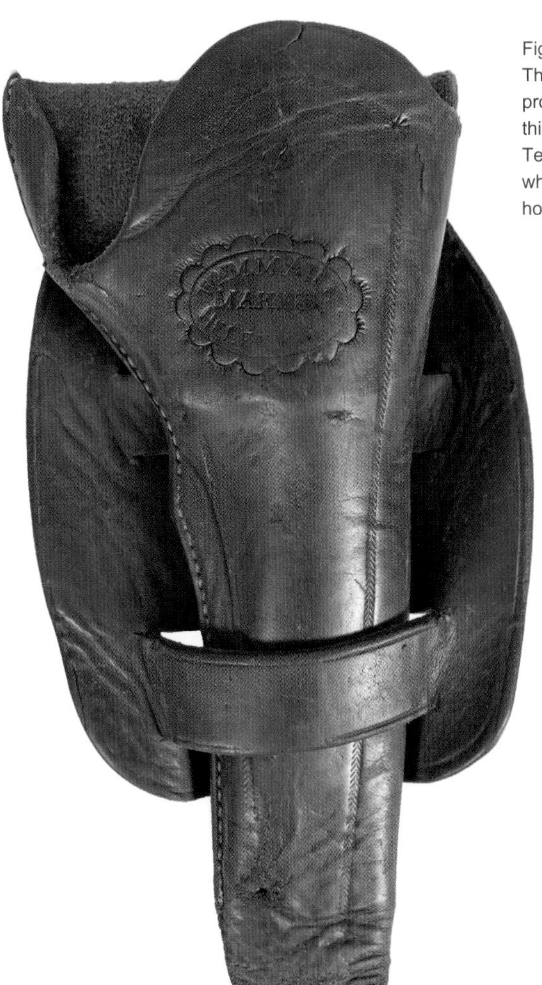

Figure 6.25.
That the style of this holster is atypical for the Montana saddlers was probably because ***Mann*** came to Montana from Texas. Therefore, this holster has the single loop and the short skirt normally made by Texas saddlers. It also has another loop cut above the one shown, where someone later tried to make it look like a Montana-style holster.

Figure 6.26.
For some reason (probably the discovery of gold) quite a few saddlers made their way to Helena before 1889. ***William Mann*** was one of them. His work is rare, possibly less than five surviving pieces (figure 6.25).

Another of the exceedingly rare Territorial saddlers was B. R. (Ben) Roberts & Co., successor to Roberts & Glassman (Cheyenne Saddle Shop) in 1883, also located in Helena (figure 6.27) (*Helena Weekly Herald*, October 4, 1883). An exciting loop-seat saddle made by him is shown in figures 6.28 through 6.30. The artwork on the saddle cantle depicts a horse resembling an English-style trotter or hunter/jumper, an unusual design, with its inspiration worthy of speculation. Roberts later became the father-in-law of the Montana cowboy artist C. M. Russell and published the first two books of Russell's drawing, *Studies of Western Life,* in 1890.

Cheyenne Saddle Shop

B. R. ROBERTS,

Sole Proprietor.

Manufacturer of and dealer in Saddles, Harness, etc. Not only the cheapest but the best and only one priced Saddlery House in Montana.

HOLTER'S BLOCK,

wly-ap3 Helena, M. T.

Figure 6.27.
Advertisement for the ***Cheyenne Saddle Shop, B. R. Roberts***, Sole Proprietor, Helena, M. T. *From the* Helena Weekly Herald, *October 4, 1883.*

A highly sought-after Territorial saddle maker is F. J. Nye of Helena. Originally a partner with L. W. Spencer (see table 6.1), he later established his own shop. A saddle card advertisement from a Directory listing (Van Dersal & Conner, 1900), his shop, his letterhead, and a second advertisement are shown in figures 6.31 through 6.34. Nye used no fewer than four different marks on his leather items. Figures 6.35 and 6.36 depict a "working" pair of plain wrist cuffs bearing a small oval mark. A pair of cuffs marked "MONT." (figures 6.37 and 6.38) and a single-action holster marked "MONTANA" (figures 6.39 and 6.40) are two more rare examples of his work.

The lone saddler found in nineteenth century Townsend (located about twenty-five miles southeast of Helena) is Alex C. Carson (figure 6.41); however, examples of his work have not surfaced.

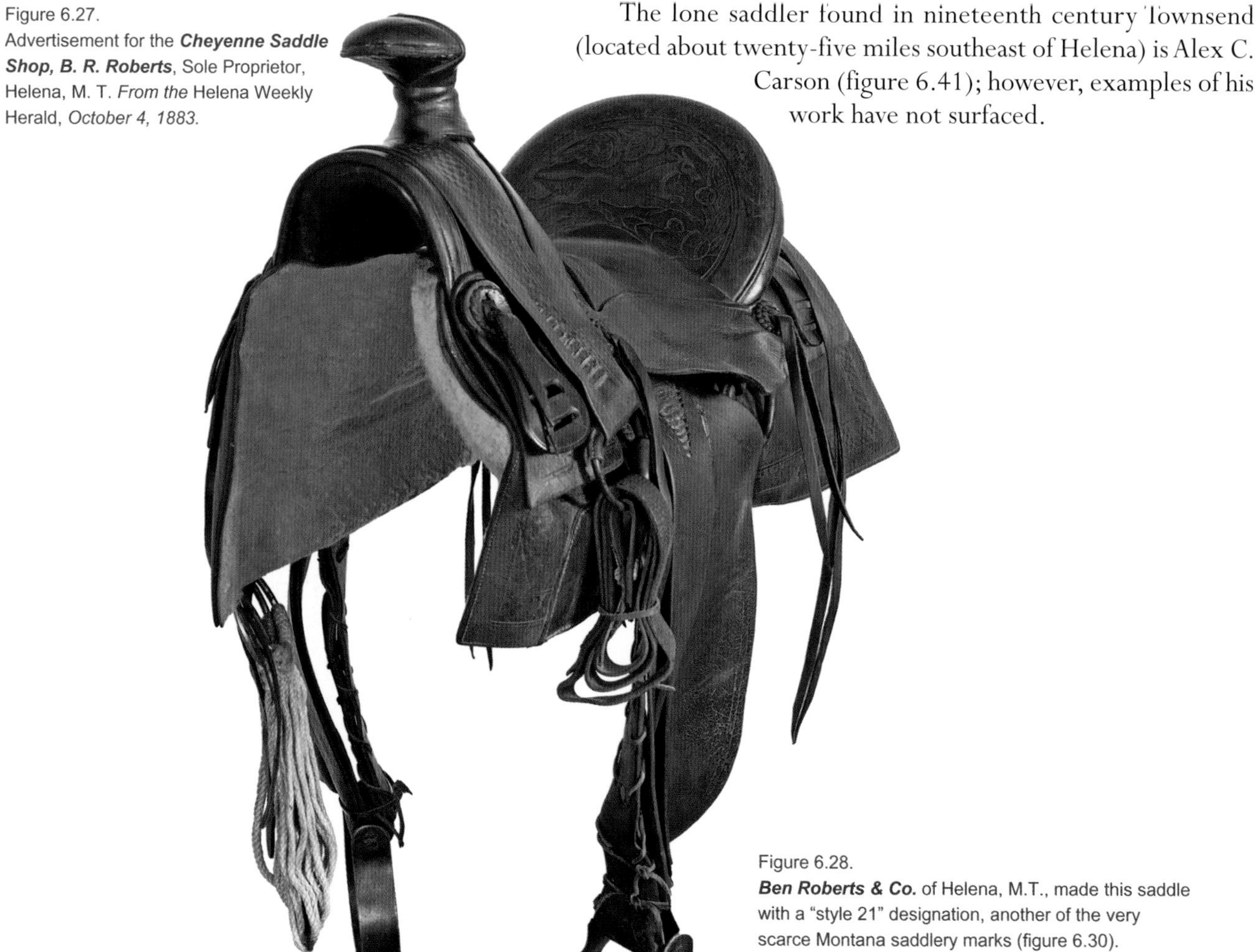

Figure 6.28.
Ben Roberts & Co. of Helena, M.T., made this saddle with a "style 21" designation, another of the very scarce Montana saddlery marks (figure 6.30).

Figure 6.29.
The tooled seat of the ***Roberts***, Helena, M.T., saddle is unusual for a couple of reasons. Early Territorial saddles with any tooling other than border work or basket weave patterns are very rare. The scene here depicts a stylized trotting horse or English hunter, neither of which had been in Montana for long (figure 6.30).

Figure 6.30.
B. R. (Ben) Roberts & Co. of Helena, M.T., made this rare A-fork, Sam Stagg–rigged, tooled saddle with a "style 21" designation. Roberts left Helena for Ulm, Montana (near Great Falls), soon after this saddle was made. He had adopted a daughter before moving to Ulm by the name of Nancy Cooper, who later attracted the attention of a wild young cowboy named Charlie Russell. After their marriage, Nancy started to civilize Charlie, and Ben Roberts published the first two books of Charlie's drawings, called *Studies of Western Life,* which are dated December 31, 1890. It is possible that Russell contributed to the art on the cantle of this saddle.

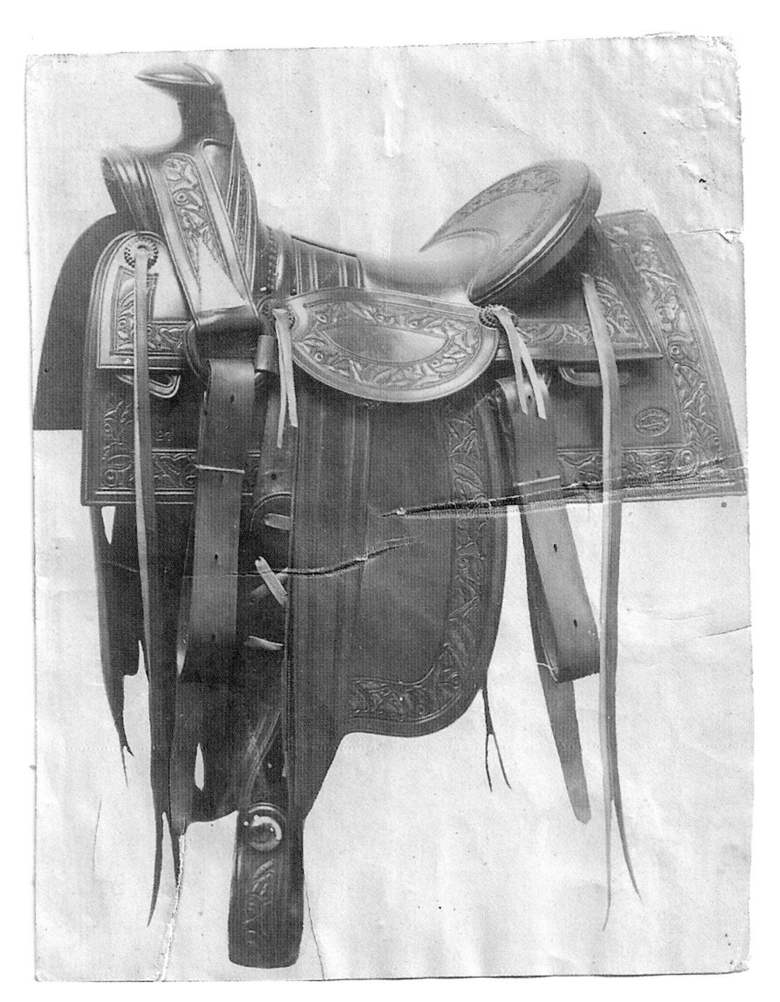

Figure 6.31.
Advertising card (on linen) for ***Spencer and Nye***, Helena, M.T., showing a fancy, loop-seat, square-skirted stock saddle with Sam Stagg rigging.

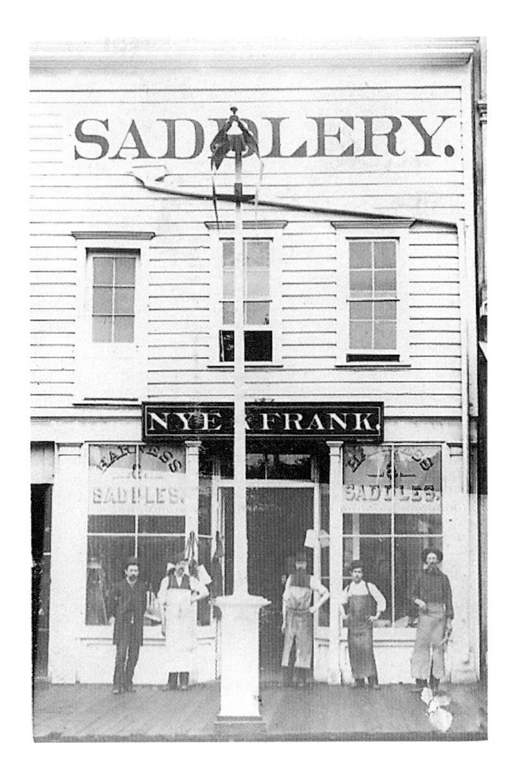

Figure 6.32.

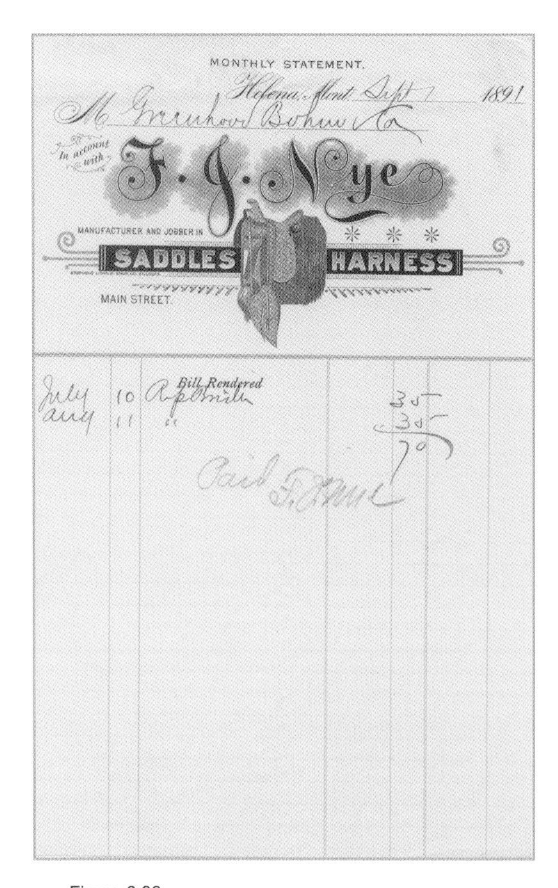

MONTHLY STATEMENT.

Helena, Mont. Sept 7 1891

In account with

F. J. Nye

MANUFACTURER AND JOBBER IN

SADDLES HARNESS

MAIN STREET.

Bill Rendered

Figure 6.33.
Letterhead/invoice from ***F. J. Nye***, Helena, Mont., dated Sept. 7, 1891.

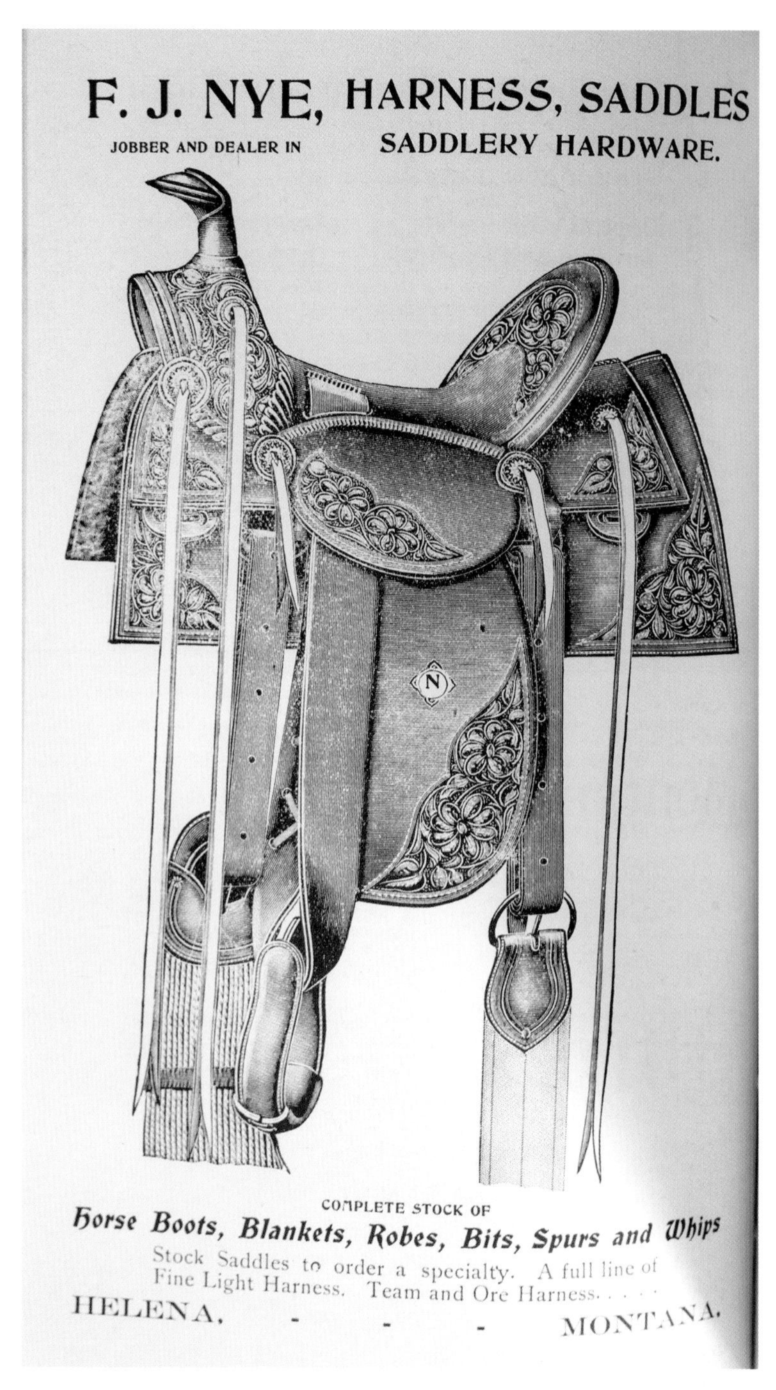

Figure 6.34.
Saddle card advertisement of ***F. J. Nye***, Helena, Montana. The loop-seat saddle is shown with a front cinch and back strap, and is nicely tooled. *From Van Dersal & Conner, 1900.*

Figure 6.35.
F. J. Nye of Helena made this plain pair of wrist cuffs for a customer that certainly planned to use them for work rather than church. He also had a larger saddle stamp, but one of his marks was a tiny oval that is hard to see and read. Although he was in Helena before 1889, his mark used the "Mont." abbreviation rather than the Territorial designation "M.T." *Courtesy of R. Bachman.*

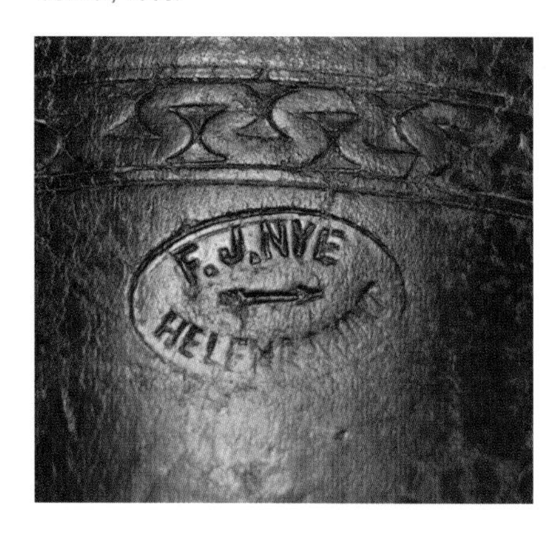

Figure 6.36.
F. J. Nye's mark, a tiny oval that is difficult to discern, is shown here (figure 6.35). *Courtesy of R. Bachman.*

Figure 6.37.
A nice pair of cowboy cuffs made and stamped by ***F. J. Nye*** of Helena, Montana. An early saddler in M.T., his work is rare and highly sought after by collectors.

Figure 6.38.
A view of the smaller mark ***F. J. Nye*** used on items too small for the large saddle stamp. The hand tooling used on the cuffs is markedly different from that of other saddlers because each individual used different tools and techniques (figure 6.37).

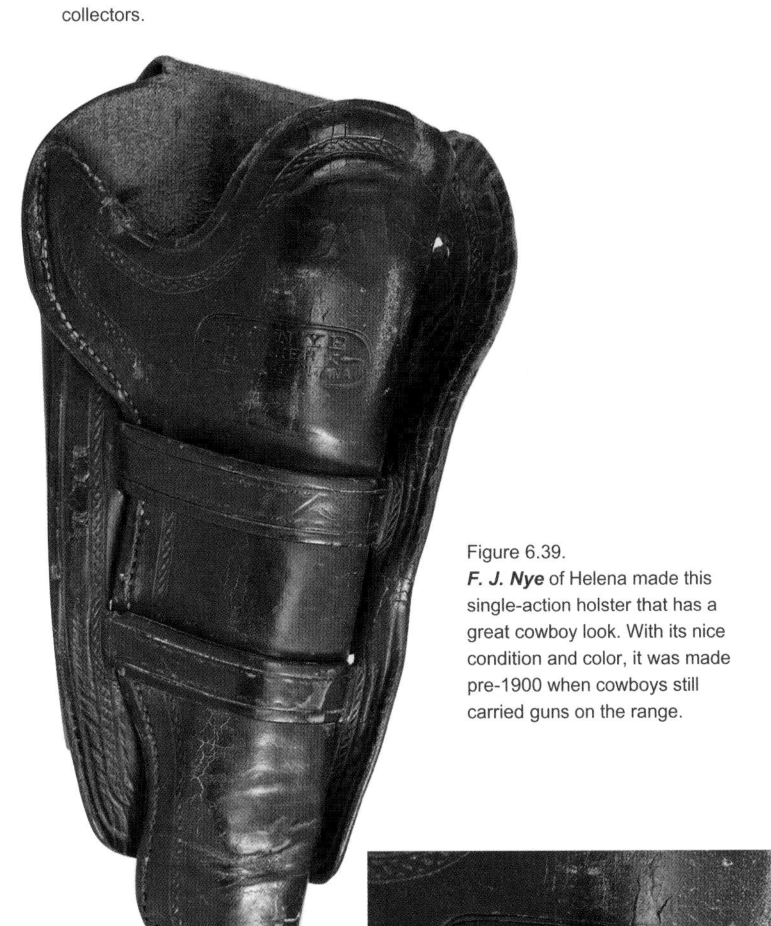

Figure 6.39.
F. J. Nye of Helena made this single-action holster that has a great cowboy look. With its nice condition and color, it was made pre-1900 when cowboys still carried guns on the range.

Figure 6.40.
F. J. Nye used at least four marks while he was operating in Helena, Montana. His territorial mark noted he was located in Helena, M.T., and he used a saddle stamp that also indicated the territorial status of Montana. This mark shows up on later production after Montana became a state. Nye items and thus examples of this mark are rare—this example can be distinguished from other marks used by competing saddleries in the Helena area (figure 6.39).

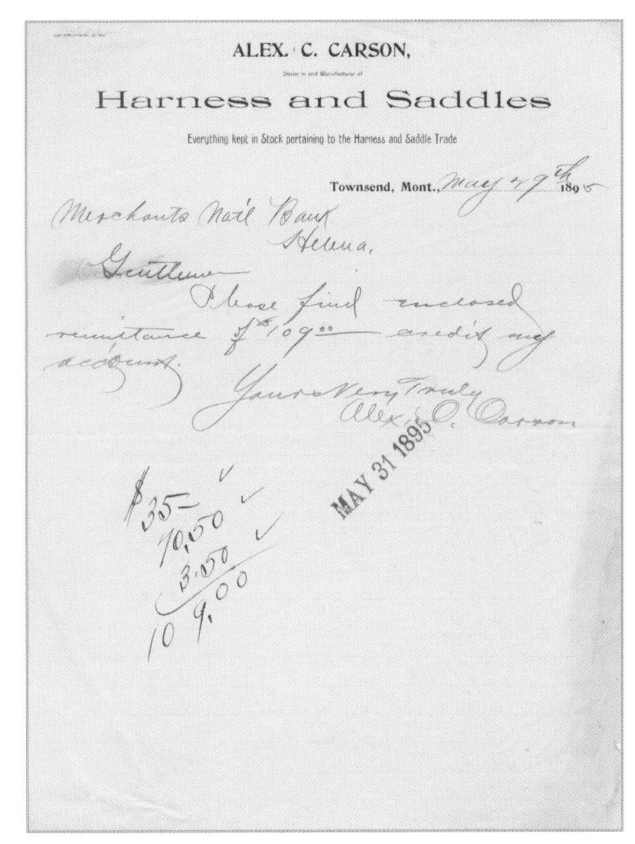

ALEX. C. CARSON,

Dealer in and Manufacturer of

Harness and Saddles

Everything kept in Stock pertaining to the Harness and Saddle Trade

Townsend, Mont., May 29th 1895

Merchants Nat'l Bank
Helena,

Gentlemen
Please find enclosed remittance $109.00 credit my account.

Yours Very Truly
Alex C. Carson

MAY 31 1895

$35.—
70.50
3.50
109.00

Figure 6.41.
Invoice from ***Alex C. Carson***, Townsend, Mont., dated May 29, 1895.

Lincoln
Libby
Flathead
Kalispell
Glacier
Cut Bank
Toole
Shelby
Liberty
Chester
Hill
Havre
Chinook
Blaine
Malta
Phillips
Valley
Glasgow
Scobey
Daniels
Plentywood
Sheridan
Roosevelt
Wolf Point
Pondera
Conrad
Sanders
Thompson Falls
Lake
Polson
9
Teton
Choteau
5
Chouteau
Fort Benton
4
McCone
Circle
Sidney
Richland
Superior
Mineral
Missoula
Missoula
7
6
Lewis and Clark
GreatFalls
Cascade
Stanford
Judith Basin
Fergus
Lewistown
Petroleum
Winnett
Jordan
Garfield
Dawson
Glendive
Wibaux
Prairie
Terry
Wibaux
Granite
Philipsburg
Powell
Deer Lodge
Helena
Meagher
White Sulphur Springs
Wheatland
Harlowton
Golden Valley
Ryegate
Musselshell
Roundup
Hysham
Treasure
Rosebud
Forsyth
2
Miles C'ty
Custer
Fallon
Baker
Hamilton
Ravalli
Anaconda
Deer Lodge
Silver Bow
Butte
Boulder
Jefferson
Townsend
Broad-water
Gallatin
Bozeman
Park
Livingston
8
Sweet Grass
Big Timber
Stillwater
Columbus
Yellowstone
Billings
3
Hardin
Big Horn
Carbon
Red Lodge
Ekalaka
Powder River
Broadus
Carter
Beaverhead
Dillon
Madison
Ennis

7

Central-Western Montana

Butte

Deer Lodge

Anaconda

Philipsburg

The city of Butte was the site of the largest mining operations in Montana. The adoption of the motto *Oro y Plata* ("Gold and Silver") for the Territory in 1865 reflected the major importance of mining to this immense geographical area. Mining's relative dominance was an identifier for much of western Montana. In the late 1800s and early 1900s, Butte was one of the largest cities in the Rocky Mountain area, but after about 1920 the population declined significantly, due in part to the post–World War I decrease in the price of copper. Yet the number of saddleries alone was an indication of the growing population and their affluence. Much of the population consisted of mine and farm workers recruited from many European countries, as well as from the Middle East and Asia. We speculate that some of these individuals also brought expertise in saddle- and harness-making to this thriving city.

Figure 7.1.
Early photograph of Montana Livery & Feed Stable, Butte.

Attesting to the size and growth of Butte and neighboring towns, including the fertile Deer Lodge Valley, table 7.1 provides a list of no less than twenty-seven saddleries, many of which were Territorial. Figures 7.1 and 7.2 show a typical livery stable and the D. J. Bricker "Harnesses and Saddles," on what was a pre-1900 dirt road. It is unfortunate that so few of the items manufactured and sold by these various saddleries are extant today. However, their letterheads (including envelopes and invoices) provide confirmation of their businesses, including mergers and changes in partnerships (figures 7.3 through 7.13). Figure 7.14 shows a McRae-Strasburger advertisement.

Table 7.1. Saddleries of Montana[1]

MAKER	LOCATION	DATES[2]
A. J. Davidson & Co.	Deer Lodge; Butte	(1884); 1888–1897
Barret & Jacky	Butte	(1882), (1886) 1885–1886 Directory
Barret & Jacky & Kramer	Anaconda	1885–1886 Directory, (1886)
Beardsley	Deer Lodge	M.T.
Bennett Brothers	Deer Lodge	1885–1886 Directory
Bricker, D. G.	Butte	
Butte Saddlery Co. (T. H. Wilson & E. Zimmerman)	Butte	(1929)
C. L. Metz Saddlery	Deer Lodge	(1869)
Cockrell Implement Co. (E. H. Irish & T. H. Wilson)	Deer Lodge	(1903)
Connolly Bros. (Andrew)	Butte	1912– c. 1914
Connolly Bros. (Jack, Patrick, Andrew)	Butte	1907–1912
Fitzhugh, Harley	Harrison	1923
Frakes, Geo. M.	Butte	(1893)
Goss, V. K.	Deer Lodge	1882– ?
Halvorson Harness & Saddlery	Deer Lodge	(1875)
Irish, E. H.	Butte	1896, (1916)
Jacky, Valentine	Philipsburg	1901 Directory
Jubinville, N.	Butte	(1907)
Jubinville & Irish	Butte	(1908), (1909)
Jubinville, Noel & Nance, John	Butte	1900 Directory
McDonald, J. D.	Philipsburg	(1913)
McRae-Strasburger Harness Co.	Butte	(1899)
Metz, C. L.	Deer Lodge	(1869)
Nevills, J. N. & Co.	Butte	(1899), 1900 Directory
New Harness Shop	Deer Lodge	(1882)
Richards, Frank E.	Butte	(1902)
Smith & Hodgman	Butte	M.T.
Sullivan & Goss	Deer Lodge	c. 1880–1881

1. Products made or sold by these saddleries included harness, saddles, bits, spurs, whips, boots, bridles, accessories (horse blankets, grooming tools, trunks, bags, and/or robes), vehicles (sleighs, buggies, wagons, carts), and Indian-made goods (e.g., saddle blankets).

2. Dates in parentheses are specified on the company letterhead or in a newspaper/journal advertisement. Inclusive dates for the tenure of the company have been provided where data are available and reliable.

Figure 7.2.
Expanded view of building to the left of the livery stable shown in figure 7.1. The saddlery was owned by ***D. G. Bricker***, Butte, Montana.

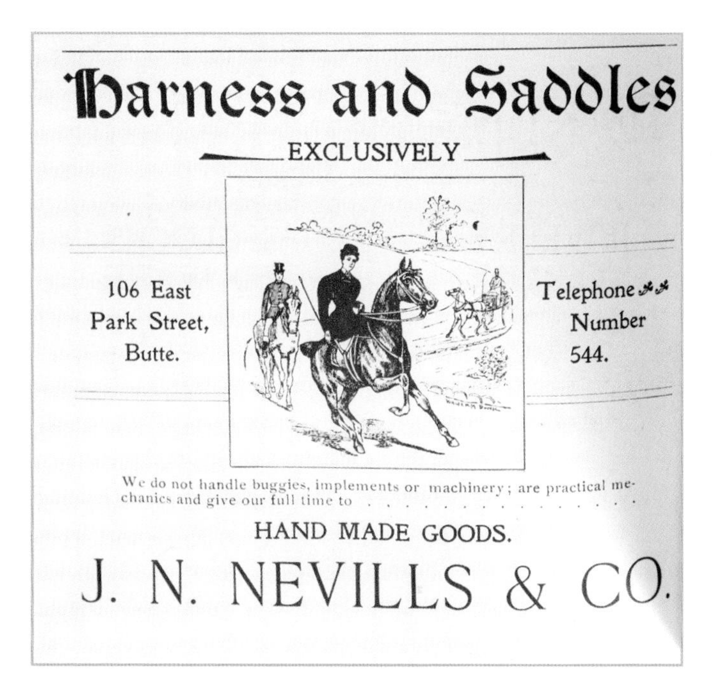

Figure 7.3.
Advertisement for ***J. N. Nevills & Co.,*** Butte, Montana. Note English side saddle rider and "we do not handle buggies . . . ." *From Van Dersal & Conner, 1900.*

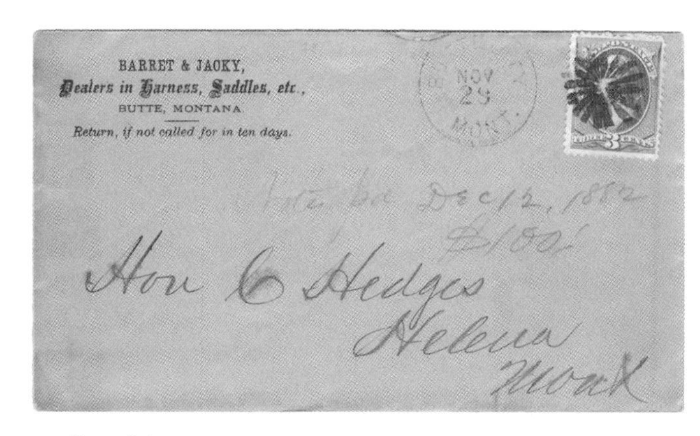

Figure 7.4.
Envelope from ***Barret and Jacky***, Butte, Montana (Dec. 12, 1882). *Courtesy of Ken Hamlin.*

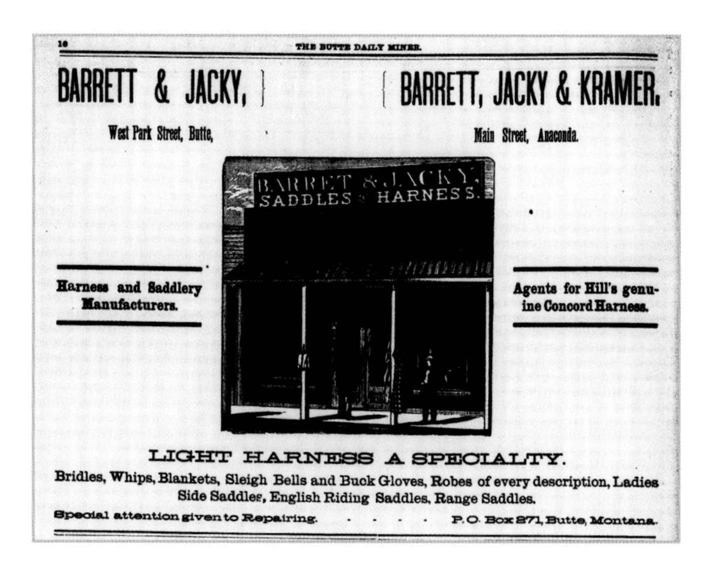

Figure 7.5.
Advertisement for ***Barrett & Jacky***, Butte, and ***Barrett, Jacky, & Kramer***, Anaconda, Montana. From the *Butte Daily Miner*, January 1, 1886.

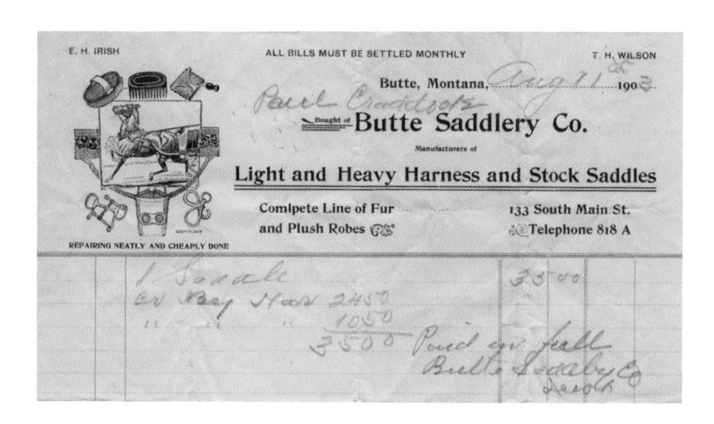

Figure 7.6.
Decorative letterhead and invoice from ***Butte Saddlery Co.***, Butte, Montana, dated Aug. 11, 1903. Note ownership by E. H Irish and T. H. Wilson. *Courtesy of Ken Hamlin.*

Figure 7.7.
Envelope from ***Frank E. Richards***, Butte, Montana (1902). Note the "Porter's Humane Bridle" as part of the harness. *Courtesy of Ken Hamlin.*

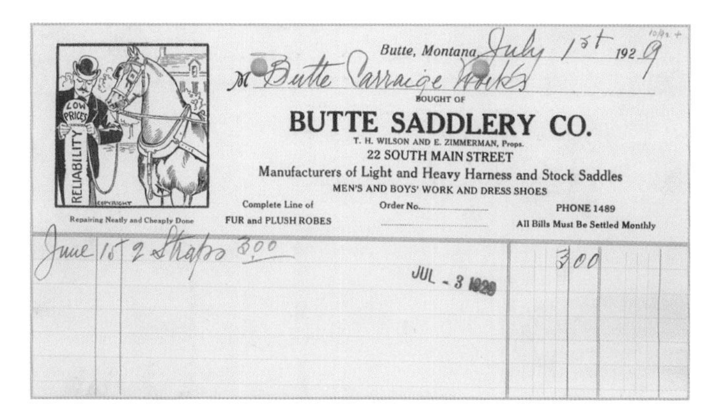

Figure 7.8.
Decorative letterhead and invoice from ***Butte Saddlery Co.***, Butte, Montana, dated July 1, 1929. Note ownership by T. H. Wilson and E. Zimmerman.

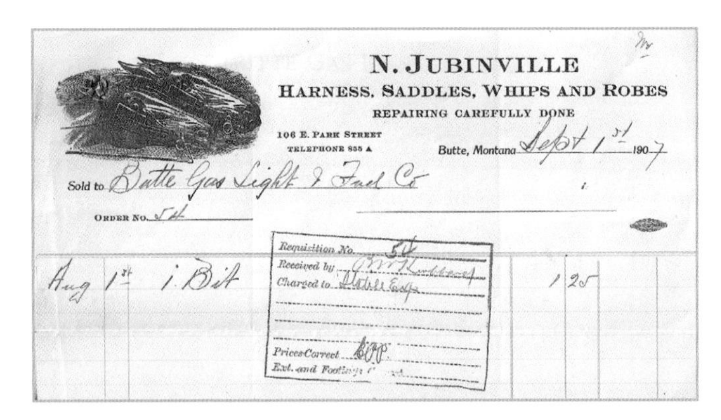
N. JUBINVILLE
HARNESS, SADDLES, WHIPS AND ROBES
REPAIRING CAREFULLY DONE
106 E. PARK STREET
TELEPHONE 855 A
Butte, Montana Sept 1st 1907
Sold to Butte Gas Light & Fuel Co
ORDER NO.
Requisition No. 50
Received by
Charged to
Prices Correct
Ext. and Footings
Aug 1st 1 Bit 1 25

Figure 7.9.
Letterhead/invoice from **N. Jubinville**, Butte, Montana, to the "Butte Gas, Light, & Fuel Co.," dated September 1, 1907. *Courtesy of R. Bachman.*

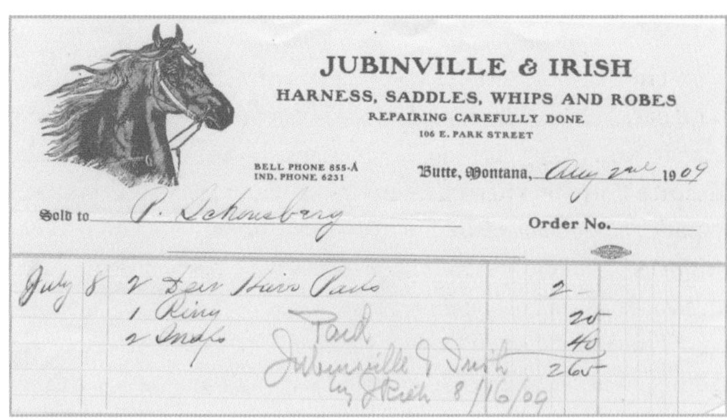
JUBINVILLE & IRISH
HARNESS, SADDLES, WHIPS AND ROBES
REPAIRING CAREFULLY DONE
106 E. PARK STREET
BELL PHONE 855-A
IND. PHONE 6231
Butte, Montana, Aug 2nd 1909
Sold to P. Schonsberg
Order No.
July 8 2 Deer Hair Pads 2 –
1 Ring 20
2 Snaps 40
2 60
Paid
Jubinville & Irish
by J Irish 8/16/09

Figure 7.10.
Letterhead/invoice from ***Jubinville & Irish***, Butte, Mont., dated Sept. 1, 1908. Note detailed image of fine harness horse with running martingale.

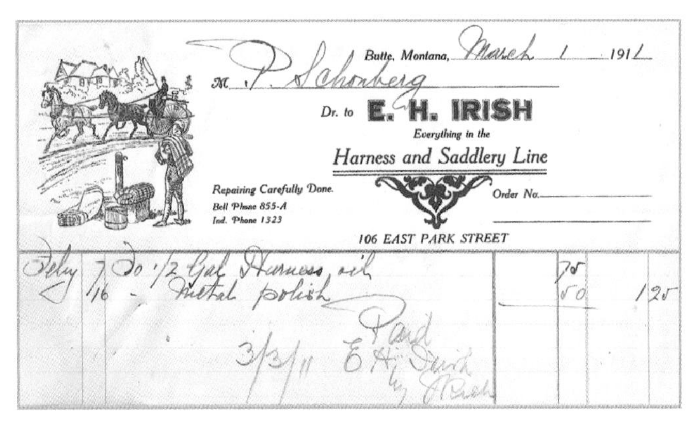
Butte, Montana, March 1 1911
M. P. Schonberg
Dr. to E. H. IRISH
Everything in the
Harness and Saddlery Line
Repairing Carefully Done.
Bell Phone 855-A
Ind. Phone 1323
Order No.
106 EAST PARK STREET
July 7 1/2 Gal Harness oil 75
16 Metal polish 50 1 25
Paid
3/3/11 E H Irish
by J Irish

Figure 7.11.
Letterhead/invoice from **E. H. Irish**, Butte, Montana, dated March 1, 1911. The successor to Jubinville & Irish (figure 7.10), Mr. Irish has retained the fine harness logo on his stationery. *Courtesy of R. Bachman.*

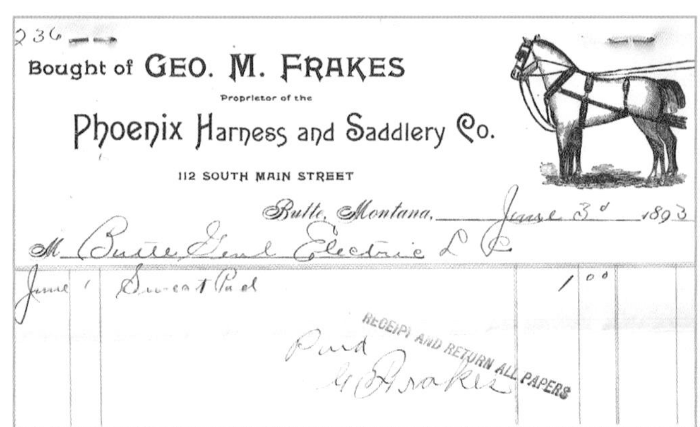
Bought of GEO. M. FRAKES
Proprietor of the
Phoenix Harness and Saddlery Co.
112 SOUTH MAIN STREET
Butte, Montana, June 3d 1893
M Butte Genl Electric L Co
June 1 Sweat Pad 1 00
RECEIPT AND RETURN ALL PAPERS
Paid
G Frakes

Figure 7.12.
Letterhead/invoice from **Geo. M. Frakes**, Butte, Montana, dated June 3, 1893. His establishment was named "The Phoenix Harness & Saddlery Co." *Courtesy of R. Bachman.*

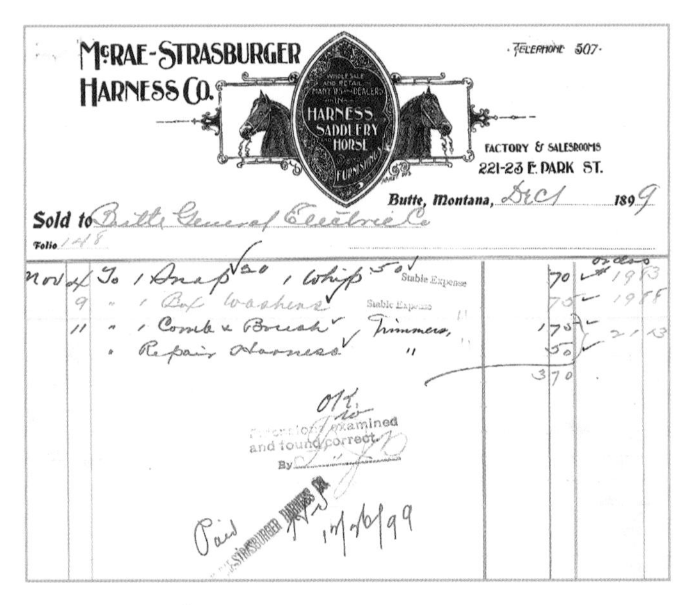
McRAE-STRASBURGER HARNESS CO.
TELEPHONE 507
WHOLESALE AND RETAIL MANUFACTURERS AND DEALERS IN HARNESS, SADDLERY, HORSE FURNISHINGS
FACTORY & SALESROOMS
221-23 E. PARK ST.
Butte, Montana, Dec 1 1899
Sold to Butte General Electric Co
Folio 148
Nov 4 To 1 Snap 20, 1 Whip 50 Stable Expense 70
9 " 1 Box washers Stable Expense 75
11 " 1 Comb & Brush Trimmers 1 75
" Repair Harness " 50
3 70
Invoice examined and found correct
By
Paid 12/26/99

Figure 7.13.
Letterhead/invoice from the ***McRae-Strasburger Harness Co.***, Butte, Montana, dated Dec. 1, 1899. *Courtesy of R. Bachman.*

Figure 7.14.
Advertisement for ***McRae-Strasburger Harness Co.***, Butte, Montana, claiming to be "The Largest and Leading Manufacturers and Dealers . . . . In the Entire Northwest." Western, side saddle, carriage and trap harness—it is all there. From the *Daily Inter Mountain*, Butte, Montana, June 3, 1899.

The firm of Barrett and Jacky is represented in figures 7.15 through 7.17. The early (M.T.) half-seat saddle was made with separate side jockeys and the classic Sam Stagg rigging. Their mark, however, used the abbreviation "MONT." despite their Territorial association. The rarity of this saddle is matched by the tapaderos produced by another M.T. firm, Smith and Hodgman, also of Butte (figures 7.18 and 7.19). These items are clearly stamped ("M.T.") and are highly desirable as collectors' pieces.

The Deer Lodge Valley was home to the first cattle-ranching effort in the 1850s, when Johnny Grant used the rich grasses of this area as a food source for his cows and horses during the winter months. The Grant-Kohrs Ranch was founded in 1862 in Deer Lodge, and remains today as a National Historic Site. Conrad Kohrs was one of the famous "cattle kings" of Montana whose outfit included parts of Alberta and Wyoming. Such an enterprise demanded equipment for the cattlemen and for the cowboys that managed the herds. Unfortunately, except for Deer Lodge Prison (see below), very little remains of the output from these saddleries (see table 7.1).

Figure 7.16.
Another view of the ***Barrett and Jacky*** (figure 7.15) saddle shows the classic Sam Stagg rigging that was the standard style of saddle made from the mid-1870s to the mid-1880s.

Figure 7.15.
Barrett and Jacky made this early half-seat saddle with separate side jockeys and a Sam Stagg rigging. It is a fine example of an early 1880s western cowboy saddle made in Butte, M.T. It has had some minor restoration, primarily the replaced stirrup leathers, and has been restrung. Only about three or four examples of Barrett and Jacky's work are known to exist.

Figure 7.17.
Although they were Territorial, the ***Barrett and Jacky*** saddle mark used the abbreviation "Mont." instead of the "M.T."

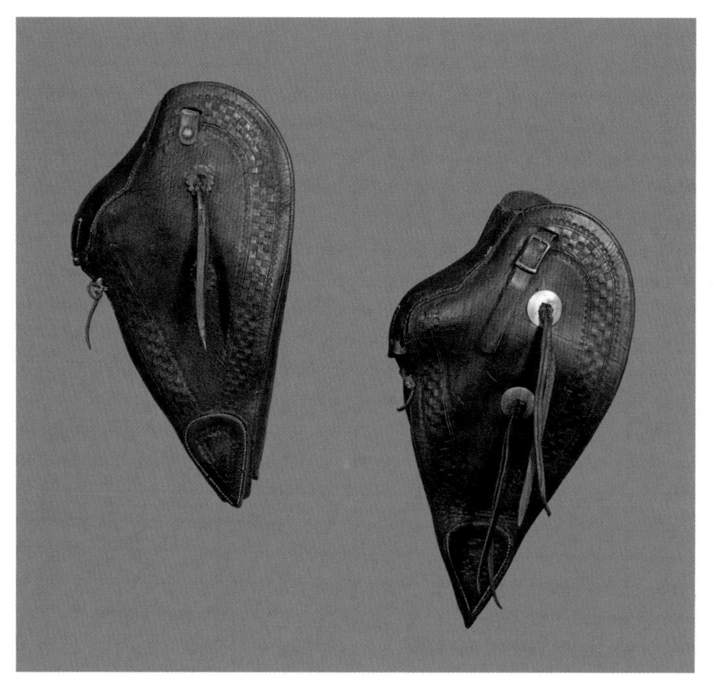

Figure 7.18.
This set of tapaderos was made by ***Smith and Hodgman*** of Butte M.T. (pre-1889) and is the only item by these rare saddlers the authors have encountered.

Figure 7.19.
Expanded views of rare M.T. saddlery marks give collectors a better frame of reference for evaluation of the authenticity of an item. This ***Smith and Hodgman*** saddle mark is the only one the authors have ever seen in over 30 years of Montana collecting.

The city of Deer Lodge is the location of the Montana State Prison, shown in figure 7.20 on its original site (now a museum) as Montana State Penitentiary. Despite the formidable walls and gates, and the violent criminals and executions that were part of prison life around the end of the nineteenth and beginning of the twentieth centuries, an amazing production of bridles, purses, hatbands, belts, and other related items, many of which were fashioned from horsehair, occurred within this fortress (Erickson, n.d.). The horsehair (natural or dyed) was collected from the prison's horse herds by "trusties," and the finished products were sold in the prison store. Upon the release of the convict, the proceeds from his work served as start-up funds for his new life beyond bars.

Figure 7.20.
Postcard c. 1900–1910 showing the ***Montana State Penitentiary, Deer Lodge, Mont***. This famous prison in central western Montana has a long history. In the early 1900s, several of its inmates became known for their production of exquisite hitched horse hair items, principally bridles, as shown in succeeding figures.

Deer Lodge Prison became well known for its beautiful leatherwork and horsehair pieces, especially the bridles, which were a combination of leather and hitched (woven) hair that assumed a myriad of designs. Figures 7.21 and 7.22 show a bridle made in 1933, allegedly for the prison warden; the natural colors and geometric designs complement the detailed starred leather rosettes, the reins with their white tassels, and the headstall itself. An equally elegant bridle, made from braided leather (calf or kangaroo skin) but without horsehair, is quite rare and exemplifies the skill of a true artisan (figures 7.23 and 7.24).

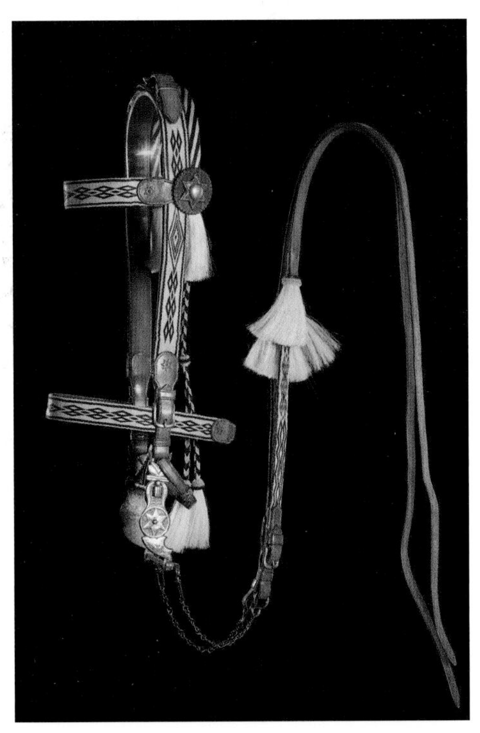

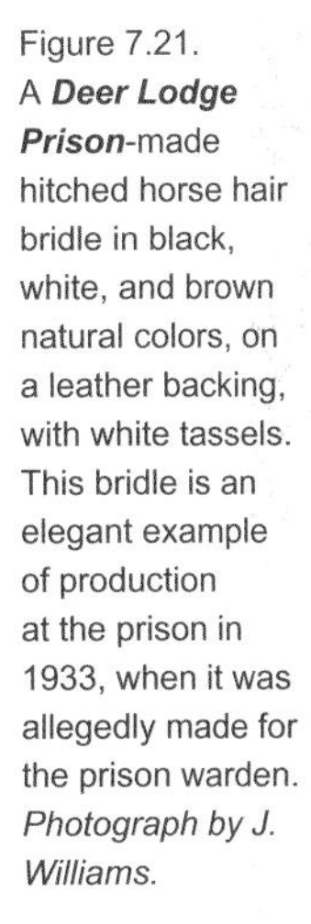

Figure 7.21.
A ***Deer Lodge Prison***-made hitched horse hair bridle in black, white, and brown natural colors, on a leather backing, with white tassels. This bridle is an elegant example of production at the prison in 1933, when it was allegedly made for the prison warden. *Photograph by J. Williams.*

Figure 7.22.
Details of horse hair bridle from ***Deer Lodge Prison*** shown in figure 7.21. Note the fine hitching with a nested diamond pattern in three colors, the stitched and embossed leather at the end of the browband, and the scalloped leather rosette with a 6-pointed star and center nickel stud. *Photograph by J. Williams.*

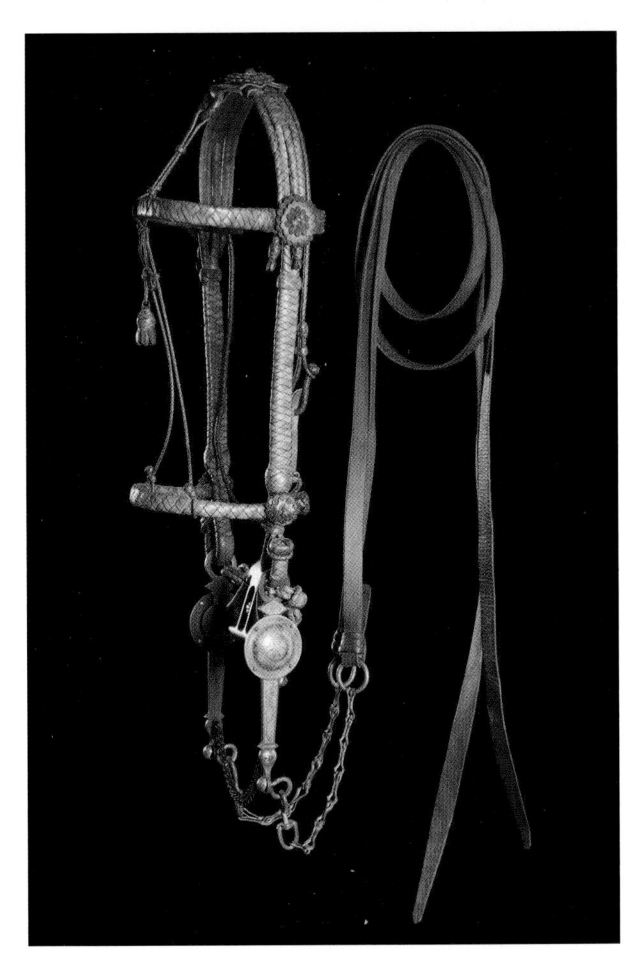

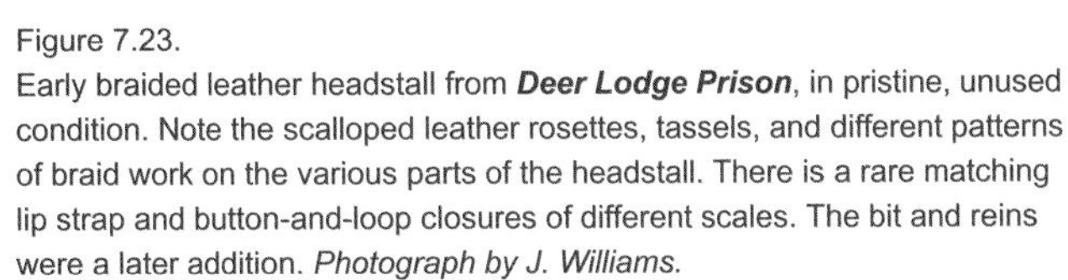

Figure 7.23.
Early braided leather headstall from ***Deer Lodge Prison***, in pristine, unused condition. Note the scalloped leather rosettes, tassels, and different patterns of braid work on the various parts of the headstall. There is a rare matching lip strap and button-and-loop closures of different scales. The bit and reins were a later addition. *Photograph by J. Williams.*

Figure 7.24.
Expanded view of the ***Deer Lodge Prison*** headstall shown in figure 7.23. One can readily appreciate the fine, light brown leather, the flat versus round braidwork, and the highly detailed 3-tiered rosette with its center knot. It is surely a one-of-a-kind, and possibly a custom-ordered, piece. The prison maintained a store that sold the inmates' work, including their bridles, and the proceeds were kept in reserve until the prisoner was released, with a nest-egg to begin a new life. *Photograph by J. Williams.*

Other than horsehair bridles, items produced by inmates at the Montana State Prison are scarce and, therefore, highly coveted. Figure 7.25 shows a pair of distinctly tooled chaps made by convicted horse thief Brian Thompson in 1936. Other prison-made items include a saddle rifle scabbard (figure 7.26) and a fancy set of holsters and belt, termed a "buscadero rig" (figure 7.27). Likely the latter item was made for sale in the prison shop, as the inmate, if released, would not have been allowed to own firearms.

Figure 7.26.
This saddle scabbard was also made at the ***Montana State Prison***. It is made rather crudely but shows the tooling of the style used by the inmates.

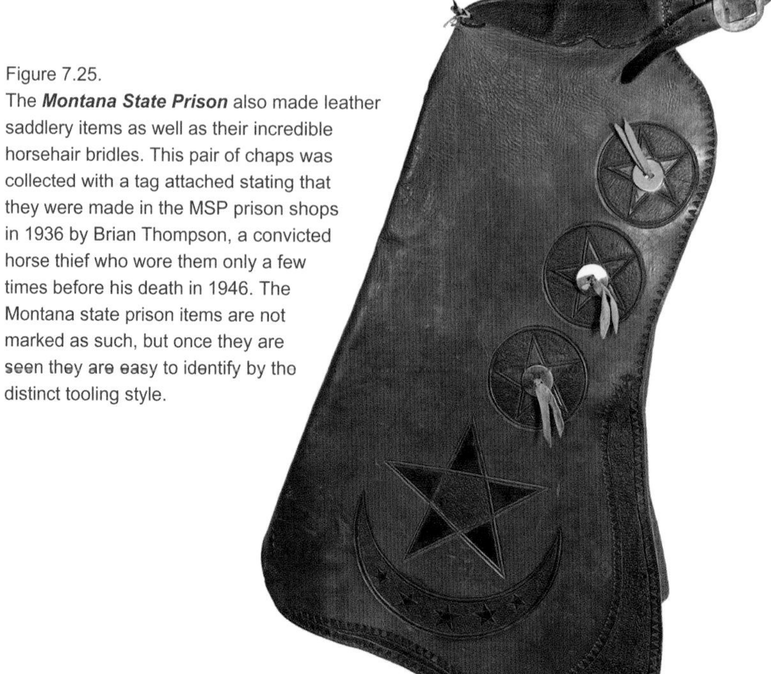

Figure 7.25.
The ***Montana State Prison*** also made leather saddlery items as well as their incredible horsehair bridles. This pair of chaps was collected with a tag attached stating that they were made in the MSP prison shops in 1936 by Brian Thompson, a convicted horse thief who wore them only a few times before his death in 1946. The Montana state prison items are not marked as such, but once they are seen they are easy to identify by tho distinct tooling style.

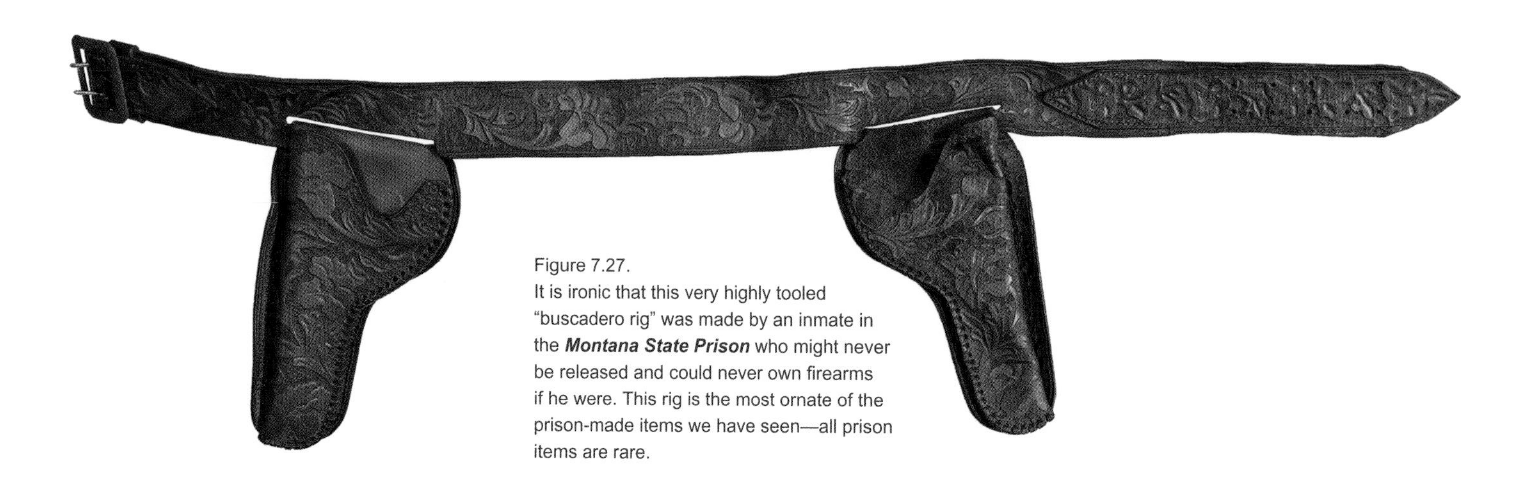

Figure 7.27.
It is ironic that this very highly tooled "buscadero rig" was made by an inmate in the ***Montana State Prison*** who might never be released and could never own firearms if he were. This rig is the most ornate of the prison-made items we have seen—all prison items are rare.

Paper ephemera from two other Deer Lodge saddleries are shown in figures 7.28 and 7.29, the latter (Sullivan and Goss) an M.T. firm. Beardsley's of Deer Lodge was a well-known saddlery around the end of the nineteenth century, but very few examples of his work are seen today. An interesting cartridge belt with a clipped-corner buckle and riveted cartridge loops is shown in figures 7.30 and 7.31. Figure 7.32 is an invoice from J. D. McDonald, of Philipsburg, dated 1913, for quite a few halters and "4 lbs. rope." Examples of his output remain undiscovered.

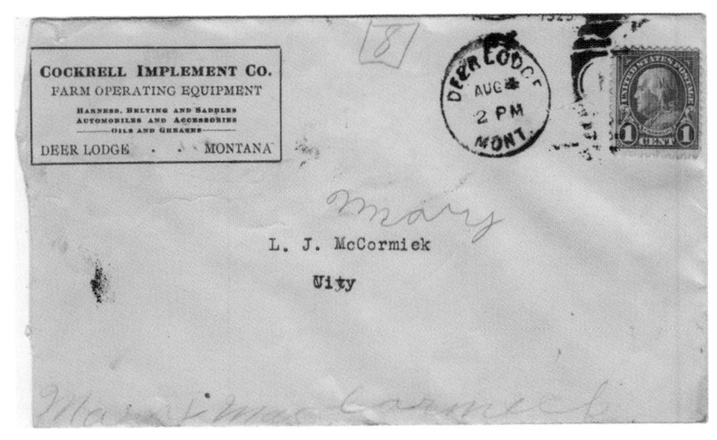

Figure 7.28.
Envelope from the ***Cockrell Implement Co.***, Deer Lodge, Montana. *Courtesy of Ken Hamlin.*

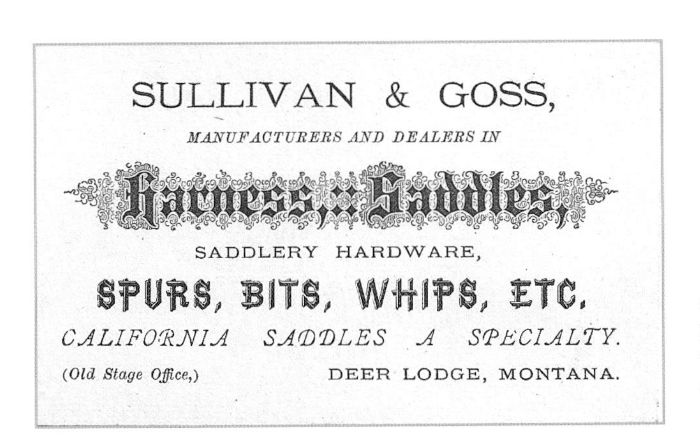
SULLIVAN & GOSS,
MANUFACTURERS AND DEALERS IN
Harness, :: Saddles,
SADDLERY HARDWARE,
SPURS, BITS, WHIPS, ETC.
CALIFORNIA SADDLES A SPECIALTY.
(Old Stage Office,) DEER LODGE, MONTANA.

Figure 7.29.
Business card from ***Sullivan & Goss***, Deer Lodge, Montana. Note "California Saddles a Specialty," indicative of a local demand for this style. *Courtesy of R. Bachman.*

Figure 7.30.
This cartridge belt made by ***Beardsley*** of Deer Lodge is unique in the way that rivets were used to fix the cartridge loops on the belt. Its tooling and clipped corner buckle date it to an earlier period. This rare saddler and saddlery are difficult to categorize thoroughly, as there is only one item to evaluate.

Figure 7.31.
Whenever one sees a mark from Deer Lodge, MT, it immediately generates interest because of the history of the prison, which made extraordinarily beautiful horsehair bridles that were sold through the prison stores and certain of the saddleries. The maker ***Beardsley*** is the first name that comes to mind when we think of Deer Lodge saddlers. The cartridge belt is well-made, yet more information about rare makers in this area is needed.

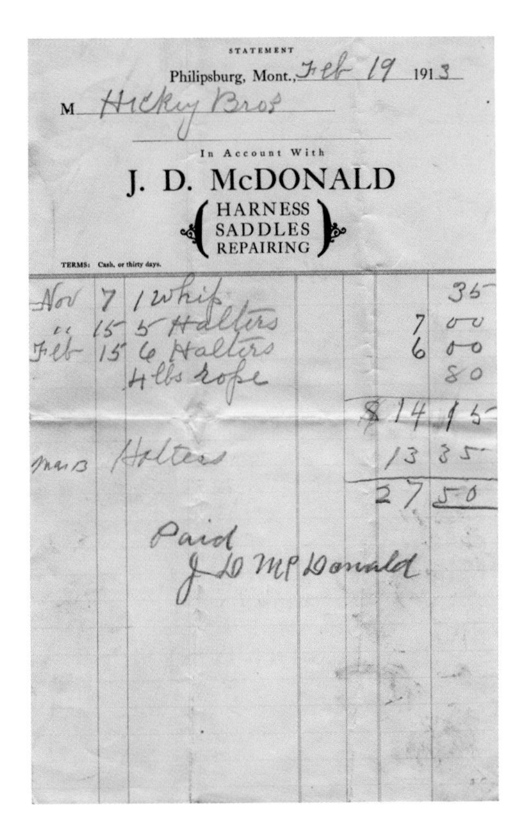
STATEMENT
Philipsburg, Mont., Feb 19 1913
M Hickey Bros
In Account With
J. D. McDONALD
HARNESS
SADDLES
REPAIRING
TERMS: Cash, or thirty days.

Nov	7	1 whip	35
"	15	5 Halters	7 00
Feb	15	6 Halters	6 00
		4 lbs rope	80
			$14 15
Mar 3		Halters	13 35
			27 50

Paid
J D McDonald

Figure 7.32.
Letterhead/invoice from ***J. D. McDonald***, Philipsburg, Mont., dated Feb. 19, 1913. *Courtesy of Ken Hamlin.*

Lincoln
Libby
Flathead
Kalispell
Glacier
Cut Bank
Toole
Shelby
Liberty
Chester
Hill
Havre
Chinook
Blaine
Malta
Phillips
Valley
Glasgow
Scobey
Daniels
Plentywood
Sheridan
Roosevelt
Wolf Point
Pondera
Conrad
Sanders
Thompson Falls
Lake
Polson
9
Teton
Choteau
5
Chouteau
Fort Benton
4
McCone
Circle
Richland
Sidney
Superior
Mineral
Missoula
Missoula
7
6
Lewis and Clark
GreatFalls
Cascade
Stanford
Judith Basin
Fergus
Lewistown
Petroleum
Winnett
Jordan
Garfield
Dawson
Glendive
Wibaux
Wibaux
Prairie
Terry
Granite
Philipsburg
Powell
Deer Lodge
Helena
Meagher
White Sulphur Springs
Wheatland
Harlowton
Golden Valley
Ryegate
Musselshell
Roundup
Hysham
Treasure
Rosebud
Forsyth
2
Miles City
Custer
Fallon
Baker
Hamilton
Ravalli
Anaconda
Deer Lodge
Silver Bow
Butte
Boulder
Jefferson
Townsend
Broad-water
Gallatin
Bozeman
Park
Livingston
8
Sweet Grass
Big Timber
Stillwater
Columbus
Yellowstone
Billings
3
Hardin
Big Horn
Carbon
Red Lodge
Ekalaka
Powder River
Broadus
Carter
Beaverhead
Dillon
Madison
Ennis

8

Southwestern Montana

Bozeman

Dillon

Virginia City

Livingston

Pony

Area 8, comprising the extreme southwestern counties of Montana (see figure 1.2), is geographically varied and was the location of no less than five cities or towns with thriving saddleries: Bozeman, Dillon, Virginia City, Livingston, and Pony. The area was settled relatively early, as rich gold deposits were discovered at Alder Gulch, which later became Virginia City, in 1863; at Grasshopper Creek (Dillon) in 1862; and on the eastern edge of the Tobacco Root Range in a creek bed that gave rise to a booming mining town called Pony, in 1866. In contrast to the mining activities, Livingston was once a trading post called Benson's Landing, and subsequently, Clark City, on the Yellowstone River. With the arrival of the Northern Pacific Railway in 1882, the town was given its present name and served as a gateway to Yellowstone National Park. In addition to clientele associated with the railroad and tourism, the nearby Paradise Valley was a ranching and, to a lesser extent, farming community with varied demands on harness and saddlery establishments.

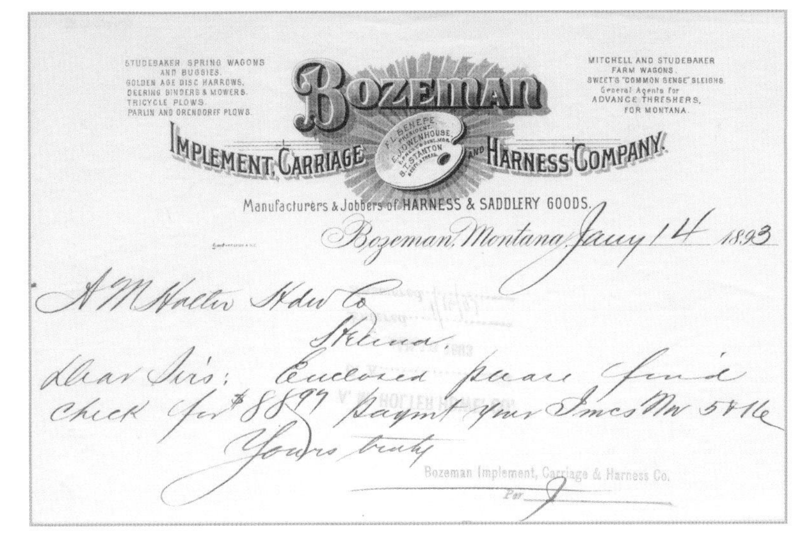
STUDEBAKER SPRING WAGONS AND BUGGIES.
GOLDEN AGE DISC HARROWS.
DEERING BINDERS & MOWERS.
TRICYCLE PLOWS.
PARLIN AND ORENDORFF PLOWS.

MITCHELL AND STUDEBAKER FARM WAGONS.
SWEET'S "COMMON SENSE" SLEIGHS.
General Agents for
ADVANCE THRESHERS,
FOR MONTANA.

BOZEMAN IMPLEMENT, CARRIAGE AND HARNESS COMPANY.

F. L. BENEPE, PRESIDENT.
E. J. OWENHOUSE
B. T. STANTON

Manufacturers & Jobbers of HARNESS & SADDLERY GOODS.

Bozeman, Montana, Jany 14 1893

A M Holter Hdw Co
Helena.
Dear Sirs: Enclosed please find
check for $88.97 paymt your Invs No 5816
Yours truly

Bozeman Implement, Carriage & Harness Co.
Per J

Figure 8.1.
Letter from the ***Bozeman Implement, Carriage, and Harness Company***, Bozeman, Montana, dated Jany 14, 1893.

Table 8.1 lists the numerous saddleries for these cities and towns. Beginning with Bozeman, letterheads and/or invoices from the establishments of the Bozeman Implement, Carriage, and Harness Company, Frank Esler, and E. J. Owenhouse are shown in figures 8.1 through 8.3. Several examples of Owenhouse's work can be seen in figures 8.4 (pommel bags), figures 8.5 and 8.6 (back belt), and figures 8.7 and 8.8 (saddle, probably imported from the California firm of Main and Winchester). The territorial mark (M.T.) used by Owenhouse is clearly seen on the loop-seat saddle pictured in figures 8.9 through 8.11. A notice printed in the *Livingston Enterprise* on July 30, 1887, states that Owenhouse had opened a branch Harness Shop in Livingston. He was bought out by his employee, W. H. Duke, in 1889 (*The Livingston Enterprise*, October 19, 1889.)

Table 8.1. Saddleries of Montana[1]

MAKER	LOCATION	DATES[2]
Bourret, Joseph & Co.	Dillon	(1893)
Bozeman Implement, Carriage & Harness Co.	Bozeman	(1893)
Crockett, Samuel H.	Virginia City	(1879)
Dillabaugh, John	Bozeman	(1871)
Dillon Implement Co.	Dillon	(1900), (1902)
Duke, W. H.	Livingston	1889–1890
Duke, W. H. & Work, John	Livingston	1890–1892
Engelfried & Esler	Bozeman	(1880)
Engelfried, Ferdinand	Bozeman	(1874)
Esler, Frank	Bozeman	(1882)
Gilroy, Edward	Dillon	(1882)
Goettlich, E. (Pioneer Harness Shop)	Livingston	(1883–1885)
Griffin, Frank	Bozeman	(1888)
Haines, S. J.	Dillon	(1907)
Hatfield, I. H.	Dillon	(1884), (1886), 1886–1910
Jack Connolly Saddlery	Livingston	1929–1937, 1940–1946†
Johnson, Edgar & Gary	Dillon	1914–1975‡
Ketcham, William S.	Virginia City	(1879)
Kraemer, Frederick	Virginia City	1886–1894
Leland, John	Pony	(1902)
Locke & Work, John	Livingston	(1892)
Long, J. F. (Pioneer Harness Shop)	Livingston	(1885), (1887)
Miles, Arthur W.	Livingston	(1897), (1900), (1904)
Nissen, John	Bozeman	(1885–1887)
Owenhouse, E. J.	Bozeman; Livingston	(1887), (1889), (1890); (1887)
Parks, Neil A.	Dillon	(1885–1886)
Richardson, W. H.	Dillon	
Secord, George	Virginia City	(1865)
Secord & Faucette	Virginia City	(1864)
S. J. Haines & Co.	Bozeman	(1903)
Three Forks Saddlery	Three Forks	????–1947

1. Products made or sold by these saddleries included harness, saddles, bits, spurs, whips, boots, bridles, accessories (horse blankets, grooming tools, trunks, bags, and/or robes), vehicles (sleighs, buggies, wagons, carts), and Indian-made goods (e.g., saddle blankets).

2. Dates in parentheses are specified on the company letterhead or in a newspaper/journal advertisement. Inclusive dates for the tenure of the company have been provided where data are available and reliable.

† Sold to Miles City Saddlery in 1946.

‡ Johnson's Trading Co. (1914), Johnson's Harness Shop, Johnson's Saddlery (1940s). http://dillontribune.com/node/18175.

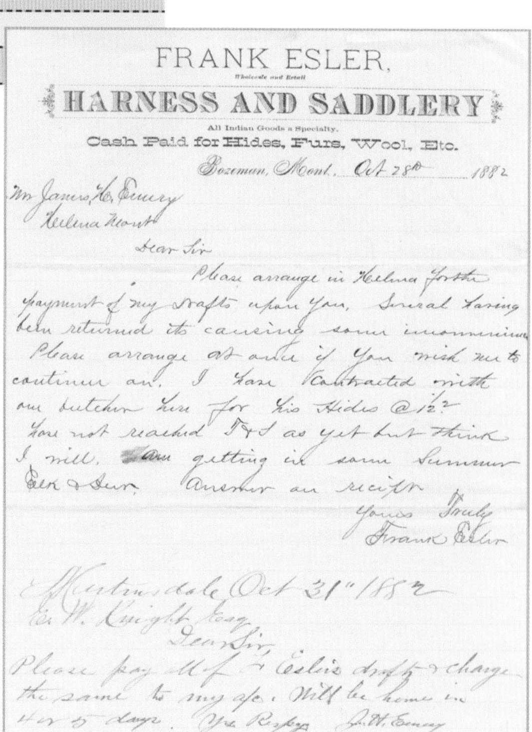

FRANK ESLER,
Wholesale and Retail
HARNESS AND SADDLERY
All Indian Goods a Specialty.
Cash Paid for Hides, Furs, Wool, Etc.
Bozeman, Mont., Oct 28th 1882

Mr James H. Emery
Helena Mont

Dear Sir

Please arrange in Helena for the payment of my drafts upon You, Several having been returned its causing some inconvenience. Please arrange at once if You wish me to continue on. I have Contracted with our butcher here for his Hides @ 12c. Have not reached T & S as yet but think I will. Am getting in some Summer Elk & Deer. Answer on receipt

Yours Truly
Frank Esler

Mistinsdale Oct 31" 1882
E. W. Knight Esq
Dear Sir,
Please pay M. F. Esler's draft & charge the same to my a/c. Will be home in 4 or 5 days. Yrs Resp J. H. Emery

Figure 8.2.
Letter from ***Frank Esler***, Harness and Saddlery, Bozeman, Mont., dated Oct. 28, 1882, concerning the payment of a customer's bank drafts. Note on letterhead, "All Indian Goods a Speciality."

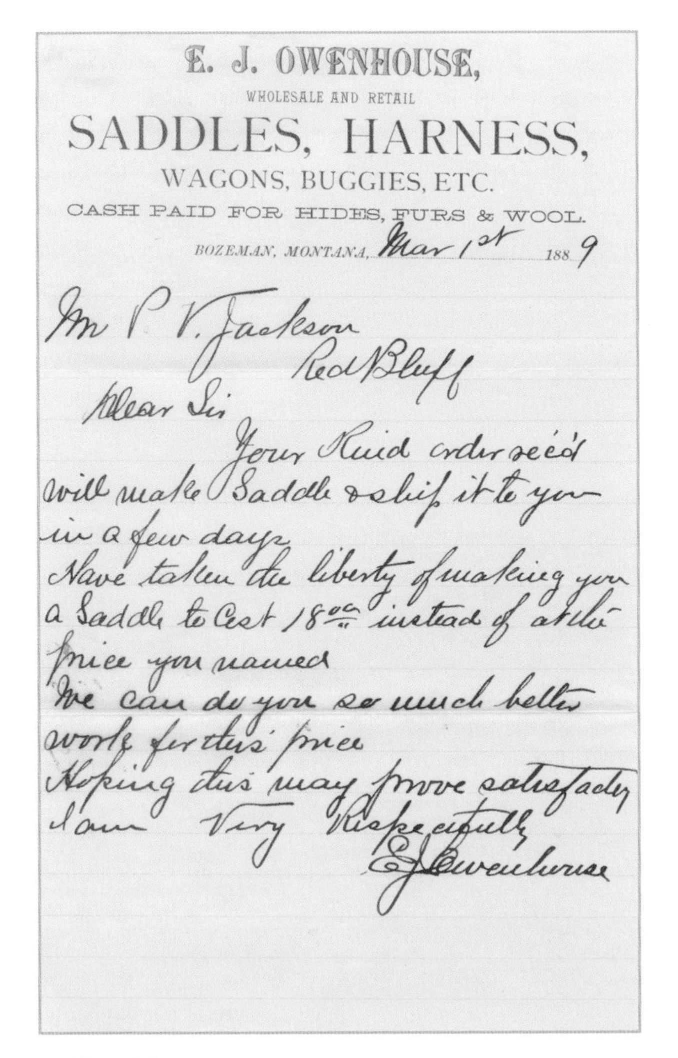

E. J. OWENHOUSE,
WHOLESALE AND RETAIL
SADDLES, HARNESS,
WAGONS, BUGGIES, ETC.
CASH PAID FOR HIDES, FURS & WOOL.
BOZEMAN, MONTANA, Mar 1st 1889

Mr P. V. Jackson
Red Bluff
Dear Sir
Your Reid order rec'd
will make Saddle & ship it to you
in a few days
Have taken the liberty of making you
a Saddle to Cost 18.00 instead of at the
price you named
We can do you so much better
work for this price
Hoping this may prove satisfactory
I am Very Respectfully
E J Owenhouse

Figure 8.3.
Letter from ***E. J. Owenhouse***, Bozeman, Montana, dated Mar. 1st, 1889, to a customer in Red Bluff concerning his custom saddle.

Figure 8.4.
E. J. Owenhouse of Bozeman, M.T., produced this early pair of pommel bags, which fit over the saddle horn of an A-fork saddle and contained an inside holster for a pistol. The later saddlebags generally were larger and were mounted behind the seat on the back skirt of the saddle.

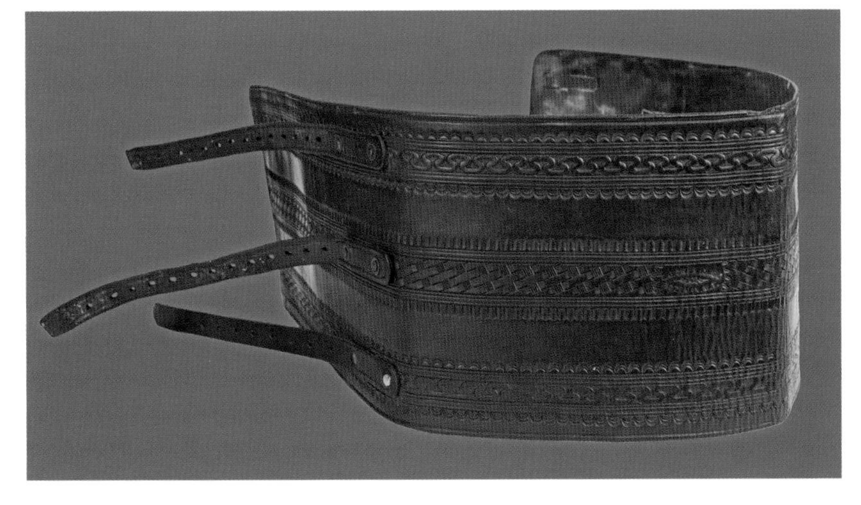

Figure 8.5.
E. J. Owenhouse of Bozeman, M.T., stamped this back belt, bronc belt, or freighter's belt (it actually could have been used by anyone). It is in extraordinarily good condition, has attractive tooling and stamping, and shows a highly collectible maker's mark that would be a welcome addition to most collections.

Figure 8.6.
E. J. Owenhouse of Bozeman, M.T., used this cartouche extensively on many of its production items, shown by this particularly good image (figure 8.5).

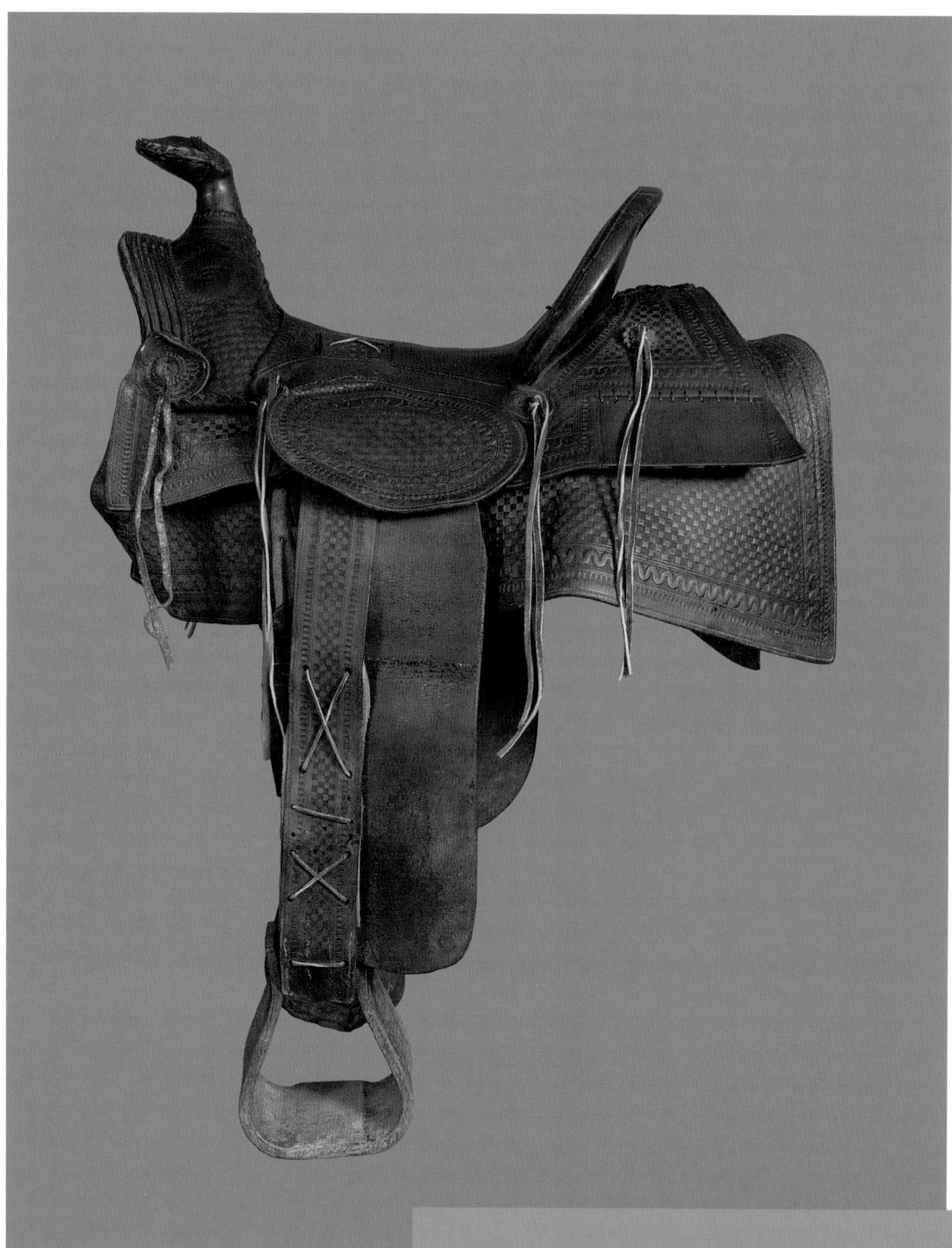

Figure 8.7.
E. J. Owenhouse sold this saddle marked M.T. in Bozeman before 1889. A reprinted catalog of Owenhouse goods shows a large line of saddles identified as "Main and Winchester." It is probable that Owenhouse ordered this saddle unmarked and applied his maker stamp before it was sold.

Figure 8.8.
The back of the seat of the ***E. J. Owenhouse*** saddle shown in figure 8.7.

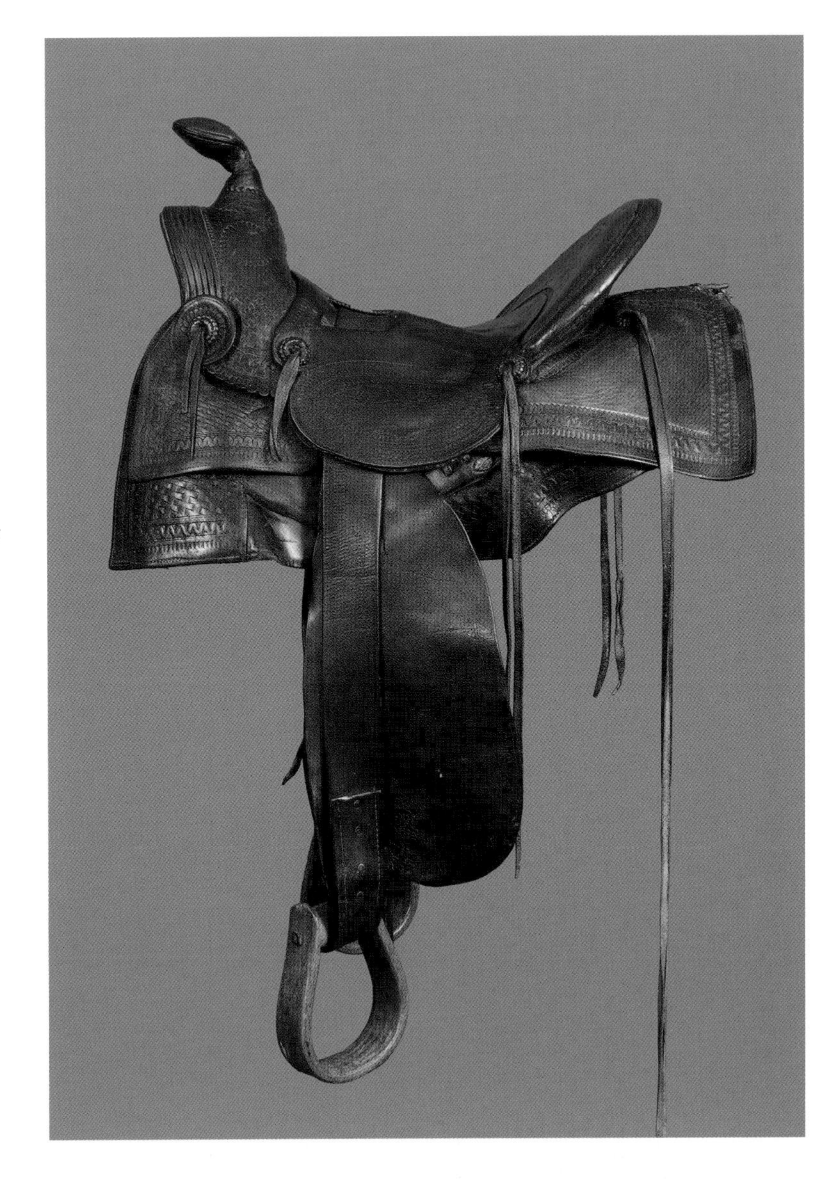

Figure 8.9.
An ***E. J. Owenhouse*** loop-seat saddle marked Bozeman, M.T. It shows an interesting rounded lower skirt and square upper skirt behind the cantle, a rare construction technique. The saddle has a significant amount of hand tooling and is quite attractive, considering its age and the fairly significant repairs to the stirrup leathers and fenders.

Figure 8.10.
Alternate view of the ***E. J. Owenhouse*** saddle shown in figure 8.9.

Figure 8.11.
The ***E. J. Owenhouse*** saddle mark is clearly shown in this photograph (figure 8.9).

A Territorial maker by the name of John Nissen is represented by the shotgun chaps in figures 8.12 and 8.13. These leather chaps with "spaghetti" strings are extremely rare, as scarce as information concerning this saddle maker. His advertisements appeared in the *Bozeman Weekly Chronicle*, September 16, 1885, and August 31, 1887, but his business closed in September 1887, and he relocated to Portland, Oregon.

The Bozeman Trail, established by John Bozeman and John Jacobs in 1863, opened the route leading from the Oregon Trail to Virginia City (Madison County) and through the Gallatin Valley to the settlement that became Bozeman (Gallatin County). It was over this trail that gold miner and cattleman Nelson Story drove approximately 1,000 longhorns into the Paradise Valley in 1866. Although the Bozeman Trail was closed in 1868 as a result of Sioux Chief Red Cloud's War, the Paradise Valley and Gallatin Valley ranches and their grazing areas grew into substantial holdings that attracted cowboys and farmers alike.

Dillon (now the seat of Beaverhead County) was founded in 1880 by Sydney Dillon, at that time president of the Union Pacific Railroad. The proximity of gold fields (such as the Grasshopper Creek discovery in 1862) and silver ore resulted in a large influx of miners and settlers, and the railroad served to connect Dillon with several other mining towns in the area. The town also served as a headquarters for cattle (1865) and sheep ranching, the latter becoming a dominant industry there.

Several saddleries stocking harness, horse-related equipment (blankets, brushes, halters, etc.), and farm implements and buggies served the Dillon area. Letterheads and invoices from Joseph Bourret & Co., the Dillon Implement Co., and I. H. Hatfield appear in figures 8.14 through 8.18. Particularly creative and entertaining art by Charles M. Russell was used by S. J. Haines (figures 8.19 through 8.21). The Russell postcard shown in figure 8.20 sets before us a potpourri of individuals likely populating Dillon in 1907: miners, cowboys, Indians, Chinese, farmers, drovers, buffalo hunters, and bankers/businessmen, all flanking the notorious artist in his characteristic red "cowboy" sash.

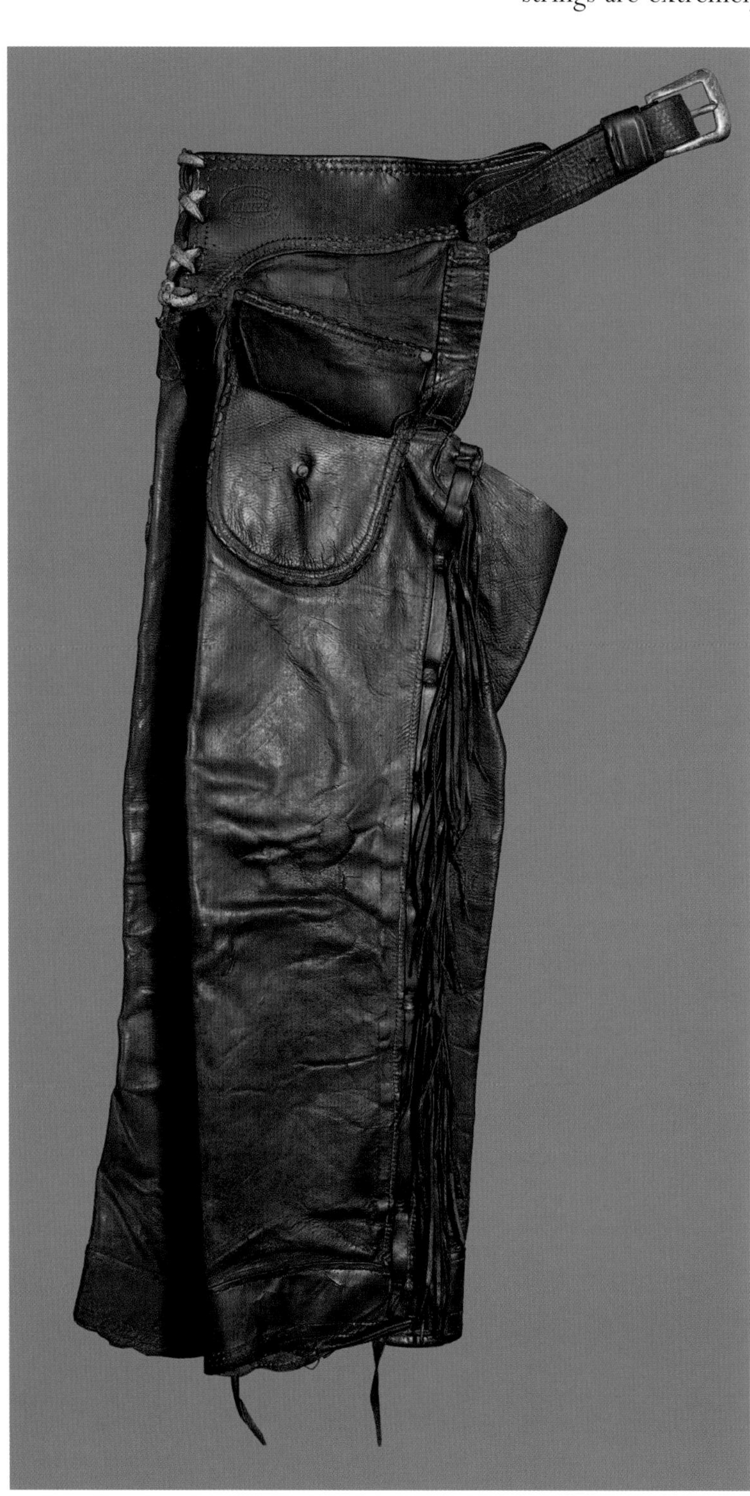

Figure 8.12.
The ***Nissen*** M.T.–marked chaps from Bozeman have the classic look of the early spaghetti-fringed shotgun cowboy gear. The chaps have some cowboy repairs and could use some restoration but are the true-life example of the gear available in Territorial Montana.

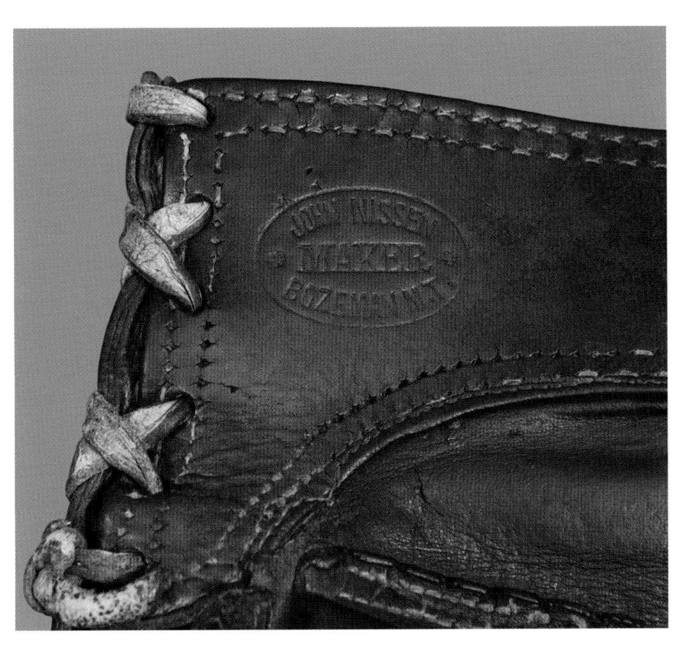

Figure 8.13.
Many of the early Territorial saddle makers (pre-1889) have little or no information available about their lives and businesses. ***John Nissen*** is one of them. The chaps have a clear and extremely rare mark (figure 8.12). This is the only example the authors have seen.

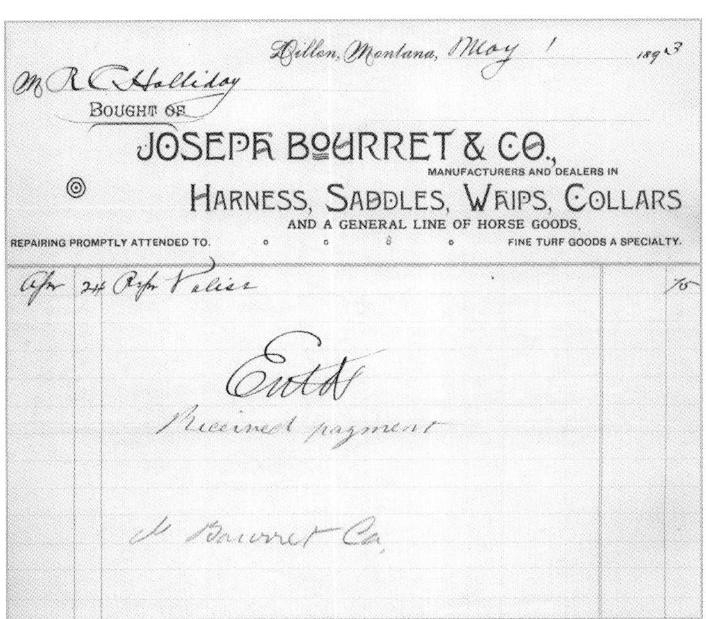

Dillon, Montana, May 1 1893

Mr R C Holliday

Bought of

JOSEPH BOURRET & CO.,

MANUFACTURERS AND DEALERS IN

HARNESS, SADDLES, WHIPS, COLLARS

AND A GENERAL LINE OF HORSE GOODS.

REPAIRING PROMPTLY ATTENDED TO. FINE TURF GOODS A SPECIALTY.

Apr 24 Repr Valise 75

Received payment

J Bourret Co.

Figure 8.14.
Letterhead/invoice from ***Joseph Bourret & Co.***, Dillon, Montana, dated May 1, 1893.

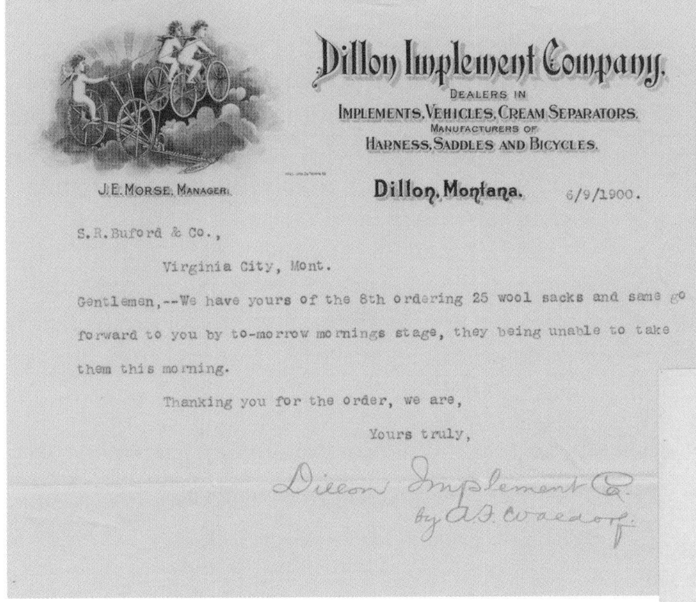

Dillon Implement Company,

DEALERS IN

IMPLEMENTS, VEHICLES, CREAM SEPARATORS.

MANUFACTURERS OF

HARNESS, SADDLES AND BICYCLES.

J.E. MORSE, MANAGER.

Dillon, Montana. 6/9/1900.

S.R.Buford & Co.,

Virginia City, Mont.

Gentlemen,--We have yours of the 8th ordering 25 wool sacks and same go forward to you by to-morrow mornings stage, they being unable to take them this morning.

Thanking you for the order, we are,

Yours truly,

Dillon Implement Co.
by A.F. Waldorf

Figure 8.15.
Letter from the ***Dillon Implement Co.***, Dillon, Montana, dated "6/9/1900," to S. R. Buford & Co., thanking them for their wool order that missed the morning's stage.

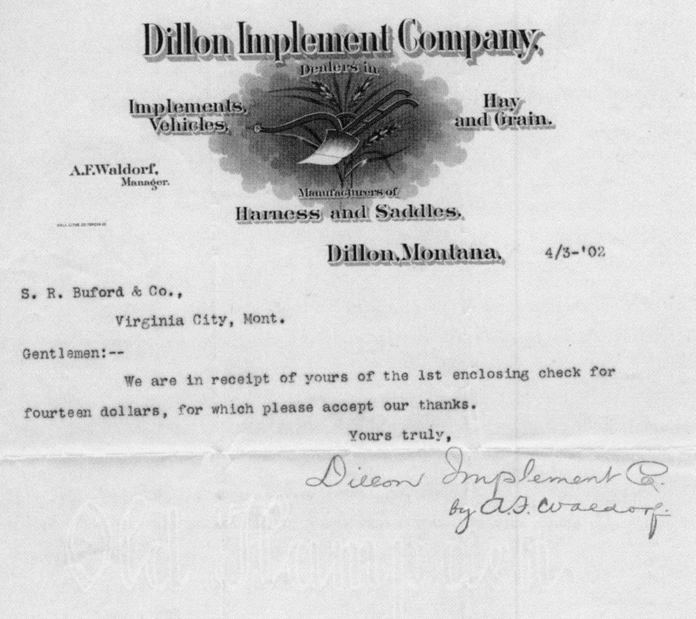

Dillon Implement Company,

Dealers in

Implements, Vehicles, Hay and Grain.

A.F.Waldorf, Manager.

Manufacturers of

Harness and Saddles.

Dillon, Montana, 4/3-'02

S. R. Buford & Co.,

Virginia City, Mont.

Gentlemen:--

We are in receipt of yours of the 1st enclosing check for fourteen dollars, for which please accept our thanks.

Yours truly,

Dillon Implement Co.
by A.F. Waldorf

Figure 8.16.
Letter from the ***Dillon Implement Co.***, Dillon, Montana, dated "4/3-'02," to S. R. Buford & Co., Virginia City, Mont. Note the fancy letterhead in colored ink. *Courtesy of Ken Hamlin.*

I. H. HATFIELD,

Has just opened the largest and most complete stock of

Harness, Saddles and Saddlery Goods

Ever brought to

DILLON.

ALL KINDS of GOODS MADE to ORDER

Repairing a Specialty

All goods of his own manufacture and warranted. Prices to suit quality. Satisfaction guaranteed. Give him a call before purchasing.

See Sign of the Big Sa... north of Postoffice.

Figure 8.17.
Advertisement for ***I. H. Hatfield***, Dillon, Montana. From *The Dillon Tribune*, Nov. 8, 1884.

Dillon Montana, Apr 1 188

Bought of I. H. HATFIELD,

WHOLESALE AND RETAIL DEALER IN, AND MANUFACTURER OF

HARNESS, SADDLES AND SADDLERY HARDWARE,

MONTANA STREET

Terms

Feb	26		1 25
March	2	lining robe	2 00
"	10	1 halter	2 25
"	"	single harness	7 50
			13.00
		total	$13 00

Rec Paymt
I H Hatfield

Figure 8.18.
Letterhead/invoice from ***I. H. Hatfield***, Dillon, Montana, dated Apr. 1, 1886.

Figure 8.19.
Advertising postcard from ***S. J. Haines***, Dillon, Montana, drawn by Charles M. Russell and dated with his buffalo skull logo 1907. A beautiful piece showing Russell's sense of humor regarding tourists and "tame" bears in Yellowstone (?) Park. *Courtesy of Ken Hamlin.*

Figure 8.20.
Advertising postcard from ***S. J. Haines***, Dillon, Montana, with illustration by Charles Russell, dated with his logo on 1907. "I savvy these folks." *Courtesy of Ken Hamlin.*

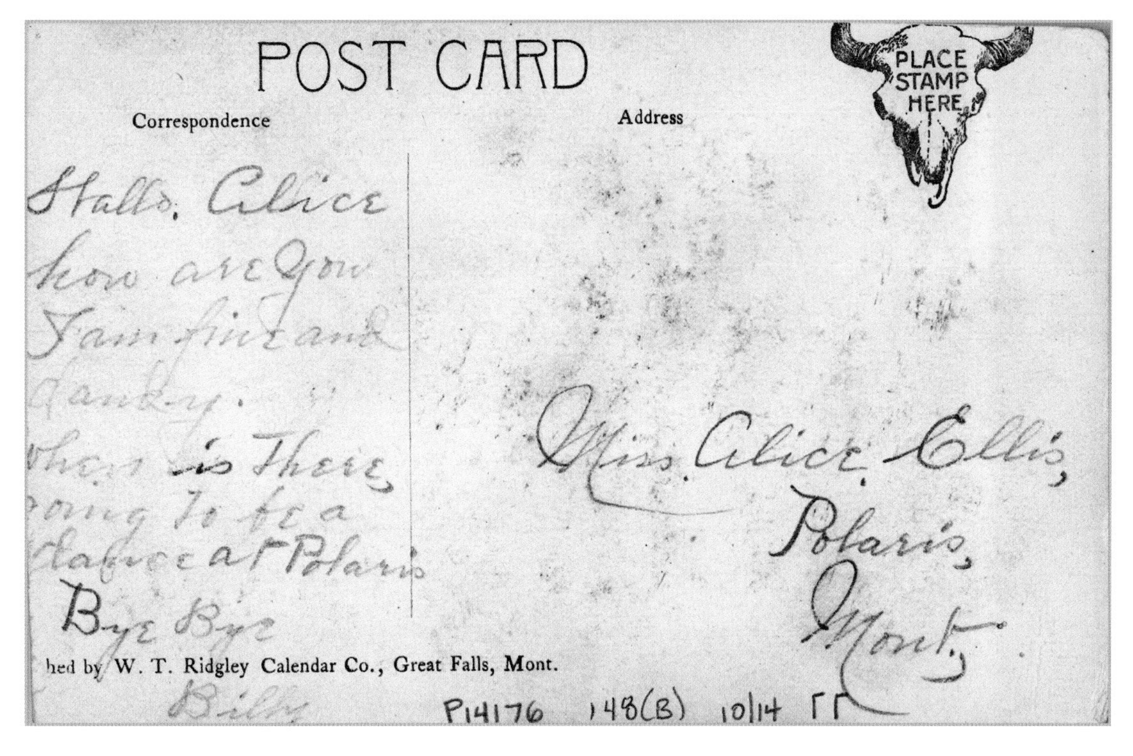

Figure 8.21.
Reverse side of postcard shown in figure 8.20. Note Russell's buffalo skull logo over which a stamp was placed. *Courtesy of Ken Hamlin.*

Virginia City, for a decade the second Territorial capital of Montana (1865–1875), was first organized as a township named Verina, close to the gold fields of Alder Gulch. A saddler, Secord & Faucette, was in business there in 1864, and Secord alone, in 1865. The uncontrolled influx of prospectors and gamblers amid a scene of great wealth gave rise to a serious criminal element that was dealt with by the famous Montana Vigilantes in the 1860s. As mining profits declined into the twentieth century, the city followed suit; the old town and township are now a National Historic Landmark District.

Saddleries, both territorial and turn-of-the-century, were numerous in Virginia City: Samuel H. Crockett, Wm. S. Ketcham, and Frederick Kraemer are represented in figures 8.22 through 8.25. Fred Kreamer's [*sic*] license, dated 1887 (M.T.), is shown in figure 8.16, and a rare example of his work, a hand-stamped back belt, appears in figures 8.27 and 8.28.

The seat of Park County, Livingston, is located on the Yellowstone River and serves as the northern access to Yellowstone National Park. A railroad town with proximity to extensive wildlife retreats, cattle grazing, and farming activities (for example, in the Paradise Valley), Livingston was the site of several saddleries. As recently as 1929–1937 and 1940–1946, Jack Connolly of the Connolly Brothers (see chapters 3 and 7) located his business in Livingston (figures 8.29 and 8.30 and 8.31). Earlier saddle makers included Arthur W. Miles (figures 8.32 through 8.35) and J. F. Long (figures 8.36 through 8.38). The former, a nephew of the famous General Nelson A. Miles, arrived in M.T. in 1880 as a paymaster's clerk in the Army at Fort Keogh. As a civilian Miles opened hardware stores in several Montana towns in the 1880s, as well as other business concerns that later included brick manufacture and a harness and saddlery shop in Livingston. He was a distinguished citizen of early Montana and contributed substantially to the development of Livingston and Park County (*The Livingston Enterprise*, January 1, 1900). In contrast, less information is available concerning J. F. Long, but an M.T. loop-seat saddle with a clear mark can be appreciated in figures 8.37 and 8.38. Long was manager of E. Goettlich's Pioneer Harness Shop, and then was able to purchase the business in 1885 after Goettlich's financial reverses (see chapter 2).

The town of Pony was home, around the turn of the nineteenth century, to a saddlery owned by one John Leland—a letterhead from this firm is shown in figure 8.39. An envelope from the Three Forks Saddlery (figure 8.40) was embellished with scenes from "Montana the Land of Shining Mountains." This saddlery was started shortly after World War II, in 1947, by Harley Fitzhugh, and was purchased from his widow by the Petersons of Malta in 1973.

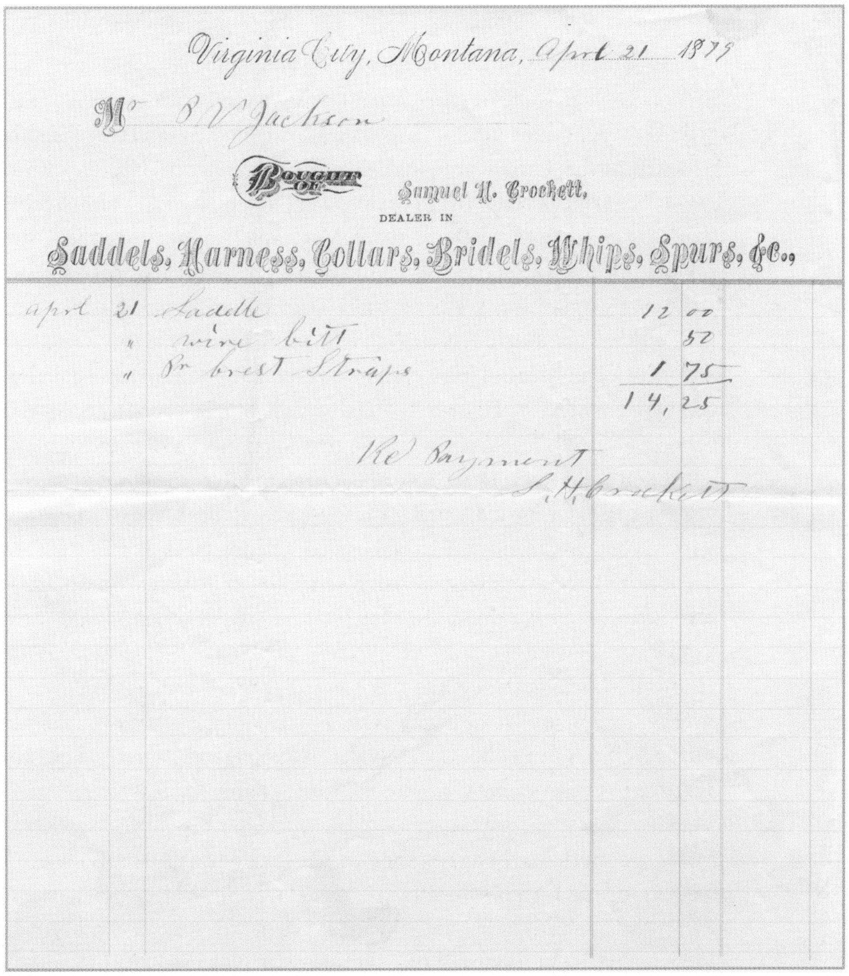

Virginia City, Montana, Aprl 21 1879

Mr S V Jackson

Bought of Samuel H. Crockett,
DEALER IN
Saddels, Harness, Collars, Bridels, Whips, Spurs, &c.,

aprl	21	Saddle	12	00
	"	wire bitt		50
	"	Pr brest Straps	1	75
			14,	25

Rcd Payment
S H Crockett

Figure 8.22.
Letterhead/invoice from ***Samuel H. Crockett***, Virginia City, Montana, dated April 21, 1879.

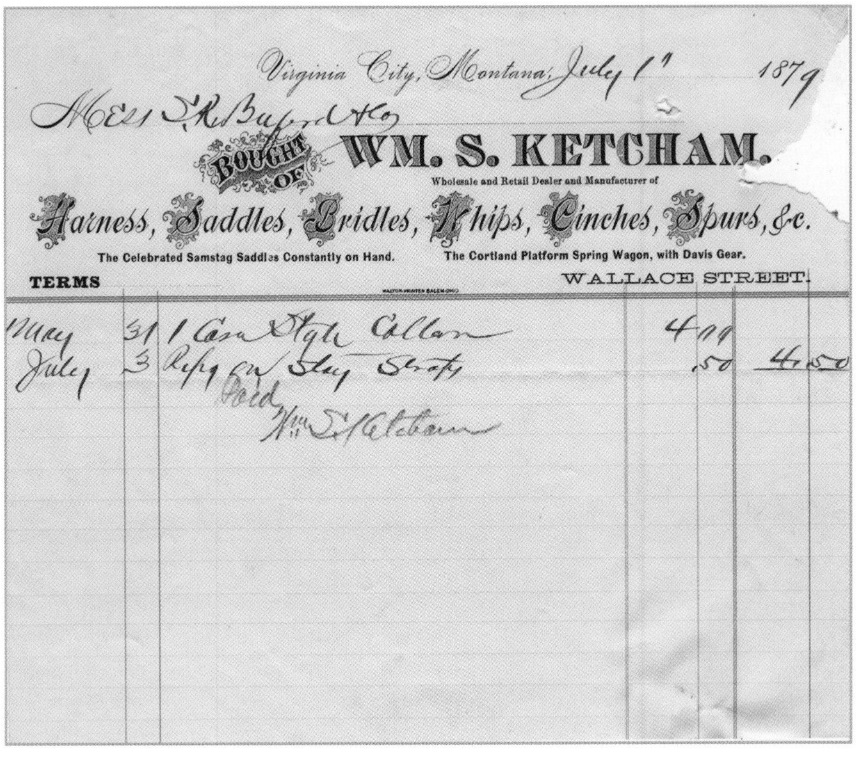

Virginia City, Montana, July 1st 1879

Messrs S. R. Buford & Co

Bought of WM. S. KETCHAM.
Wholesale and Retail Dealer and Manufacturer of
Harness, Saddles, Bridles, Whips, Cinches, Spurs, &c.
The Celebrated Samstag Saddles Constantly on Hand. The Cortland Platform Spring Wagon, with Davis Gear.
TERMS WALLACE STREET.

May	31	1 Con Style Collar	4 00	
July	3	Repg on Sleigh Straps	.50	4.50

Paid
Wm S Ketcham

Figure 8.23.
Letterhead/invoice from ***Wm. S. Ketcham***, Virginia City, Montana, dated July 1, 1879. *Courtesy of Ken Hamlin*.

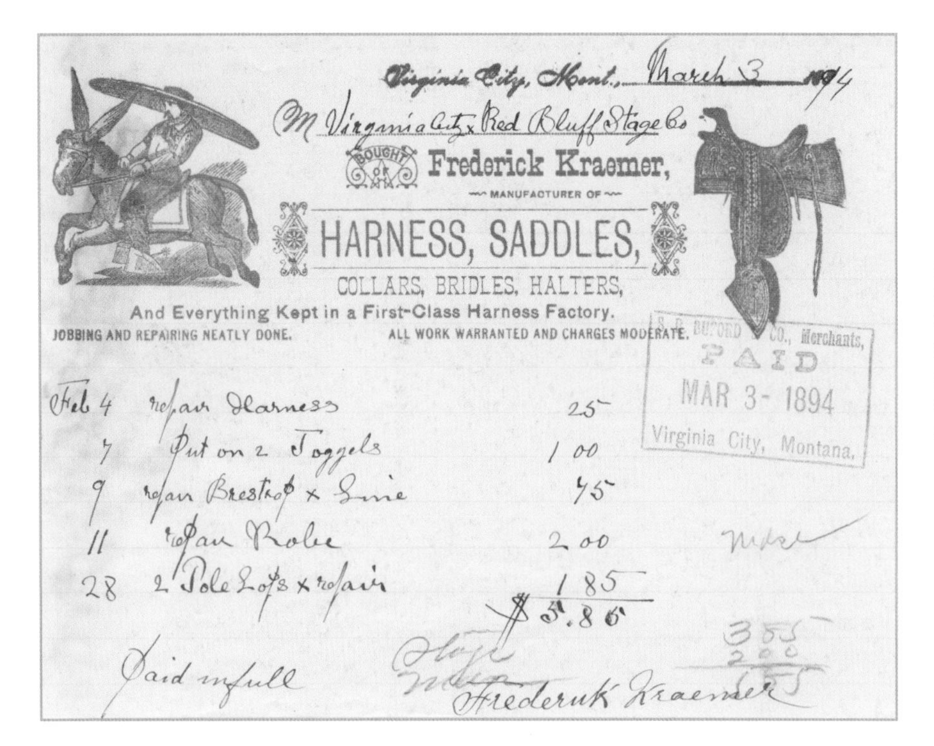

Virginia City, Mont., March 3 1894
M Virginia City & Red Bluff Stage Co
Bought of Frederick Kraemer,
MANUFACTURER OF
HARNESS, SADDLES,
COLLARS, BRIDLES, HALTERS,
And Everything Kept in a First-Class Harness Factory.
JOBBING AND REPAIRING NEATLY DONE. ALL WORK WARRANTED AND CHARGES MODERATE.

S. R. BUFORD & CO., Merchants,
PAID
MAR 3- 1894
Virginia City, Montana.

Feb 4	repair Harness	25
7	Put on 2 Toggels	1 00
9	repair Brestrop & Line	75
11	repair Robe	2 00
28	2 Pole Lops & repair	1 85
		$5.85

Paid in full
Frederick Kraemer

Figure 8.24.
Letterhead/invoice from ***Frederick Kraemer***, Virginia City, Mont., dated March 3, 1894. Note the detailed printing of an ornate loop-seat saddle on the *right* and a Mexican wearing a giant sombrero and riding a burro. The sale was made to the Virginia City & Red Bluff Stage Co.

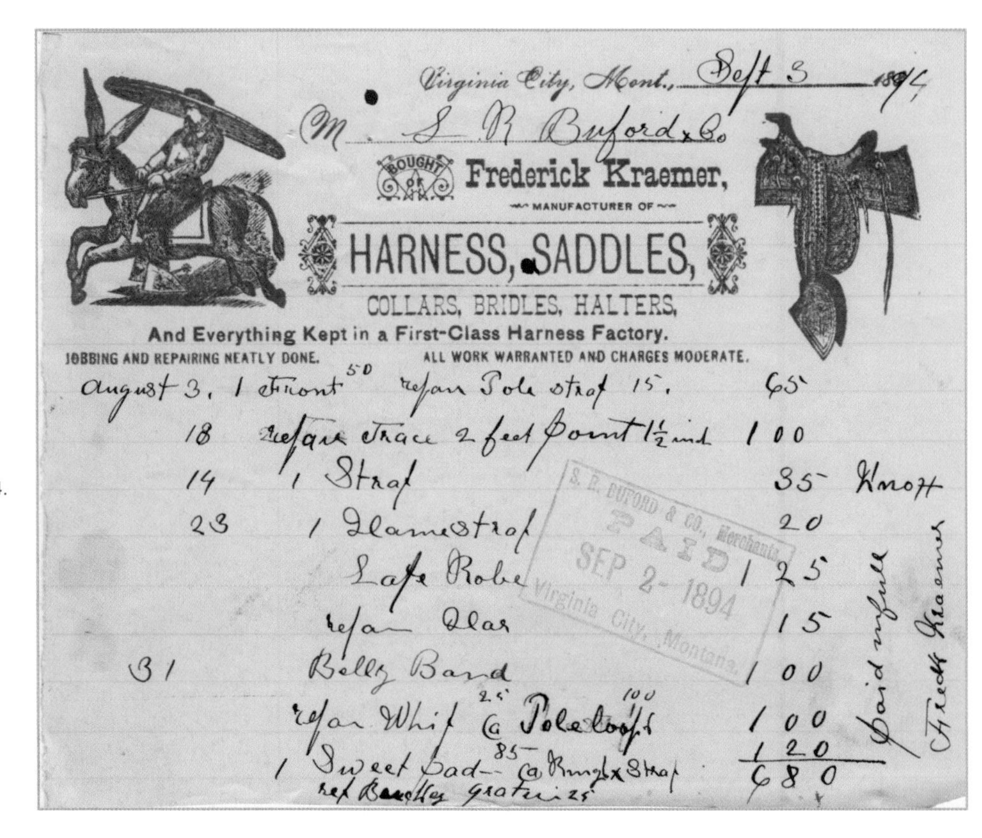

Virginia City, Mont., Sept 3 1894
M S R Buford & Co.
Bought of Frederick Kraemer,
MANUFACTURER OF
HARNESS, SADDLES,
COLLARS, BRIDLES, HALTERS,
And Everything Kept in a First-Class Harness Factory.
JOBBING AND REPAIRING NEATLY DONE. ALL WORK WARRANTED AND CHARGES MODERATE.

S. R. BUFORD & CO., Merchants,
PAID
SEP 2- 1894
Virginia City, Montana.

August 3.	1 Front 50 repair Pole strap 15.	65
18	repair Trace 2 feet Point 1½ inch	1 00
14	1 Strap	35
23	1 Hamestrap	20
	Lape Robe	1 25
	repair Har	15
31	Belly Band	1 00
	repair Whip 25 @ Pole loops 100	1 00
	1 Sweet pad 85 @ Rings & Strap	1 20
	rep Buckey gratis 25	
		6 80

Paid in full
Fredk Kraemer

Figure 8.25.
Letterhead/invoice from ***Frederick Kraemer***, Virginia City, Mont., dated Sep. 2, 1894. The buyer was S. R. Buford & Co. *Courtesy of Ken Hamlin.*

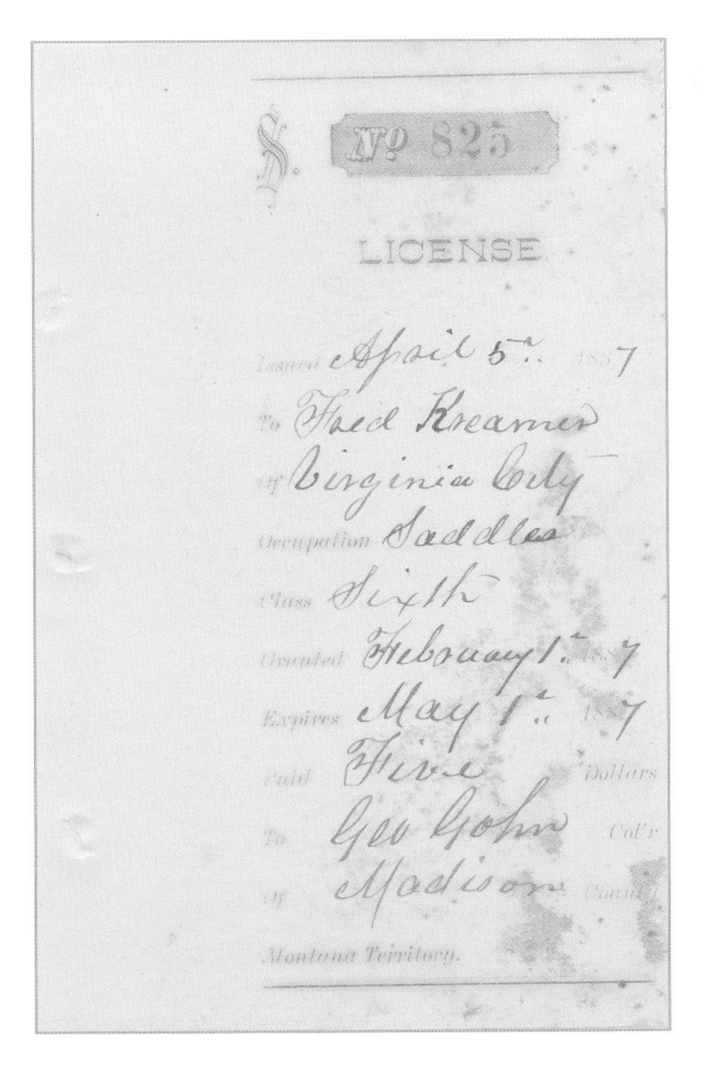
№ 825

LICENSE

Issued April 5th 1887

To Fred Kreamer

Of Virginia City

Occupation Saddles

Class Sixth

Granted February 1st 1887

Expires May 1st 1887

Paid Five Dollars

To Geo Gohn Coll'r

Of Madison County

Montana Territory.

Figure 8.26.
License, dated April 5, 1887, to "***Fred Kreamer***" [*sic*] "Occupation Saddles." The license was issued for Madison County and cost five dollars.

Figure 8.28.
F. Kraemer of Virginia City, M.T., is certainly one of the earliest, if not the earliest, saddlery marks in Montana's history. A substantial amount of the paper records from the F. A. Kraemer saddlery exist as a result of the extensive collection accumulated by the Bovey family in Virginia City. This unique early, obviously hand-stamped, saddle-maker's mark is the only one that the authors have encountered in 30 years of collecting and may very well be the only existing item that F. A. Kraemer made during his extended tenure (figure 8.27).

Figure 8.27.
Large wide belts that provided back support, termed bronc belts, back belts, or freighter's belts, were a necessity in the early West. This rare back belt was made by ***F. A. Kraemer*** of Virginia City, M.T. It has basic but attractive stamping, and the maker's cartouche was placed uniquely inside a pocket that was on the belt but is now missing. Some of these belts were also used to transport currency, and it is likely that whoever wore this belt used it to transfer gold dust, gold nuggets, or currency, given that Virginia City was primarily a gold mining town.

Figure 8.29.
Ornately-tooled saddle with rounded skirts and tapaderos, by ***Jack Connolly***, of Livingston, Montana. This saddle was termed the "Easy Rider," for which a patent was issued.

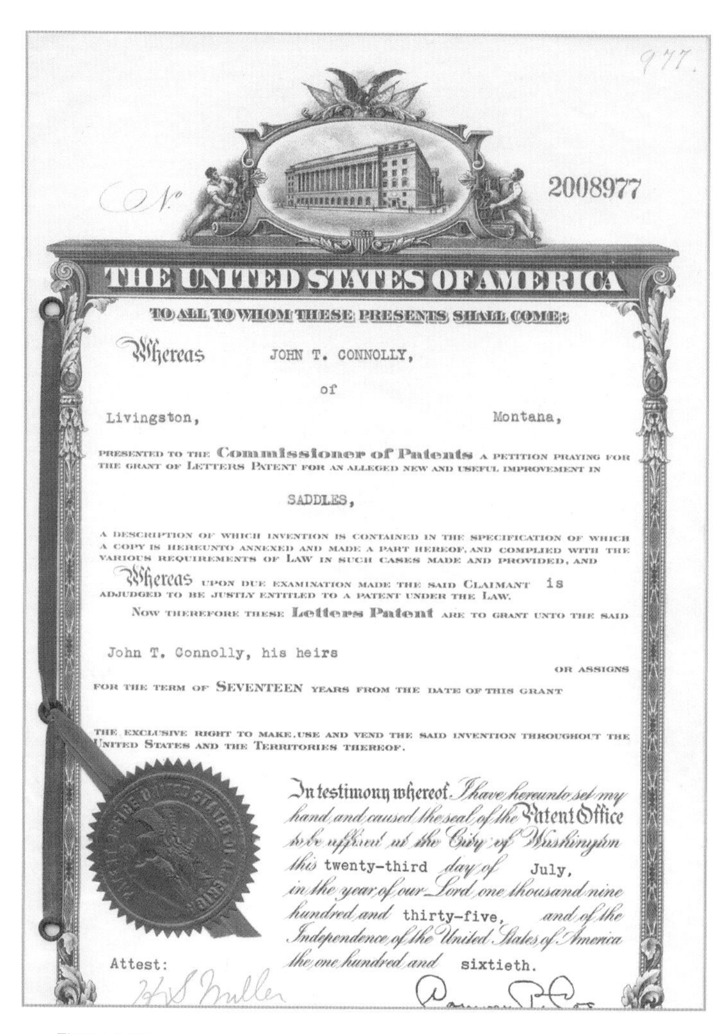

977.

No 2008977

THE UNITED STATES OF AMERICA

TO ALL TO WHOM THESE PRESENTS SHALL COME:

Whereas JOHN T. CONNOLLY, of Livingston, Montana,

PRESENTED TO THE Commissioner of Patents A PETITION PRAYING FOR THE GRANT OF LETTERS PATENT FOR AN ALLEGED NEW AND USEFUL IMPROVEMENT IN

SADDLES,

A DESCRIPTION OF WHICH INVENTION IS CONTAINED IN THE SPECIFICATION OF WHICH A COPY IS HEREUNTO ANNEXED AND MADE A PART HEREOF, AND COMPLIED WITH THE VARIOUS REQUIREMENTS OF LAW IN SUCH CASES MADE AND PROVIDED, AND

Whereas UPON DUE EXAMINATION MADE THE SAID CLAIMANT is ADJUDGED TO BE JUSTLY ENTITLED TO A PATENT UNDER THE LAW.

NOW THEREFORE THESE Letters Patent ARE TO GRANT UNTO THE SAID John T. Connolly, his heirs OR ASSIGNS FOR THE TERM OF SEVENTEEN YEARS FROM THE DATE OF THIS GRANT THE EXCLUSIVE RIGHT TO MAKE, USE AND VEND THE SAID INVENTION THROUGHOUT THE UNITED STATES AND THE TERRITORIES THEREOF.

In testimony whereof I have hereunto set my hand and caused the seal of the Patent Office to be affixed at the City of Washington this twenty-third day of July, in the year of our Lord one thousand nine hundred and thirty-five, and of the Independence of the United States of America the one hundred and sixtieth.

Attest:

Figure 8.30.
Patent for "an alleged new and useful improvement in saddles," to ***John T. Connolly*** (Jack, figure 8.29), dated July 23, 1935.

Figure 8.31.
Photograph of ***Jack Connolly***, Livingston, Montana, dated Aug. 21, 1942. Handwritten inscription: "Jack on the job. Sincerely, Jack & Mary."

FOLIO MONTHLY STATEMENT.

LIVINGSTON, MONT. Dec 23 1897

M J.H. Smith

In acct. with A. W. MILES,

Dealer in

....HARDWARE, IMPLEMENTS, MINING SUPPLIES....

Harness, Saddles, Etc.

Sporting Supplies a Specialty.

June 16	Bal o/c	14 96
" "	12# Nails 60 8# Nails 20	80
	Fork 85 Fork Hdl 20	1 05
	100# Coal	1 00
July 21	12½ Plow Steel	1 25
" 26	6 Crown Sections	60
Aug. 5	50# Twine	4 00
	Buggy Paint	1 00
	Babbitt	35
	½ Gal oil	40
	2# H Nails	40
" 13	1 Box 12 G Shells	50
	3# Shot	30
	1# Powder	50
	Box Caps	10
" 17	100# Coal	1 00
27	50# Twine	4 00
Sept 11	Rope 35 H Nails 40 90 Gal	1 65
		33 86

Figure 8.32.
Letterhead/invoice from ***A. W. Miles***, Livingston, Mont., dated Dec. 23, 1897.
Courtesy of Ken Hamlin.

Figure 8.33.
This ***A. W. Miles*** holster is one of only a few Miles items that have surfaced among collectors. Photographs of his business in Livingston show a large inventory of saddlery items in the back of a large store containing general merchandise. His advertising states that he is "the sole manufacturer of Miles' cowboy saddles," which would lead one to believe that he employed saddlers in the store. Because this holster is similar to other holsters, it could have been made by Miles or possibly purchased by him for resale. That it is rare and originated in early Montana adds to its desirability.

Figure 8.34.
This is one of the rare saddlery stamps in Montana. Miles was a merchant that had several stores in Montana, and they advertised saddlery made by their own saddler. It is therefore probable that they made some of the items they stamped and bought others for sale (figure 8.33).

Figure 8.35.
The whiskey jug in the center of this photograph is the only one of its kind known to exist. Whiskey was as highly sought after by the range cowboys as the best saddles and chaps. It was probably more important to many of the cowboys than their riding gear. The cuffs are also made by ***A. W. Miles*** of Livingston, Montana and, as noted before, are extremely rare. These cuffs bear a large collection of cattle brands neatly cut into the leather that gives them the great "cowboy look" that everyone wants to collect.
Courtesy of T. Leland.

Figure 8.36.
Advertisement for the ***Pioneer Harness Shop***, J. F. Long, Agt., in Livingston, Mont. *From the* Livingston Enterprise, *July 30, 1887.*

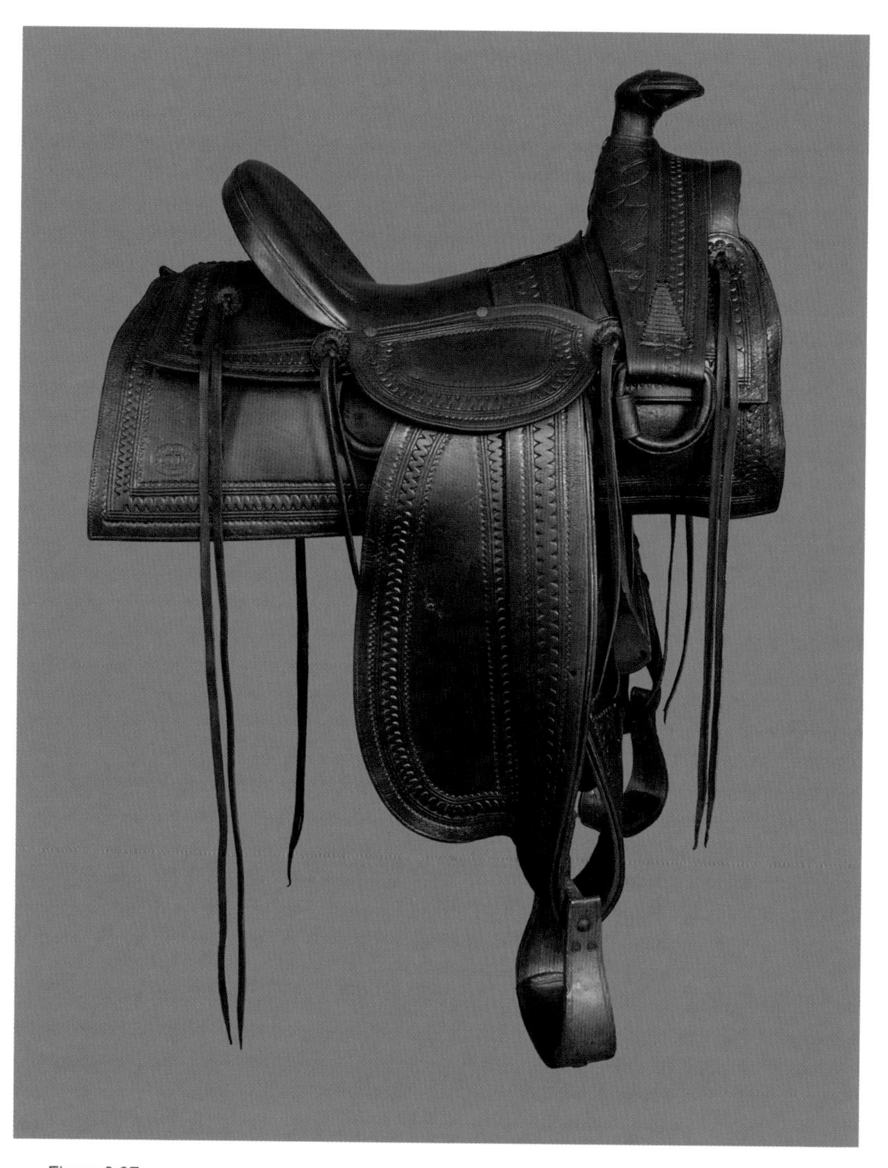

Figure 8.37.
An early half-seat saddle in very fine condition. It is Sam Stagg-rigged and looks like a Main and Winchester (California) saddle. Livingston is just 25 miles from Bozeman, where all of the die-cut examples of saddles in the E. J. Owenhouse catalog are clearly marked "Main and Winchester." It is possible, if not likely, that ***Long*** also purchased saddles and marked them himself. Because the saddle has a "Cheyenne roll," and if Long actually made it himself, the saddle was adapted to the Livingston/Bozeman style.

Figure 8.38.
Livingston, M.T., had few saddlers, one of whom was the maker whose stamp is shown here. ***J. F. Long*** was established early in Livingston, and his work is considered very rare (figure 8.37).

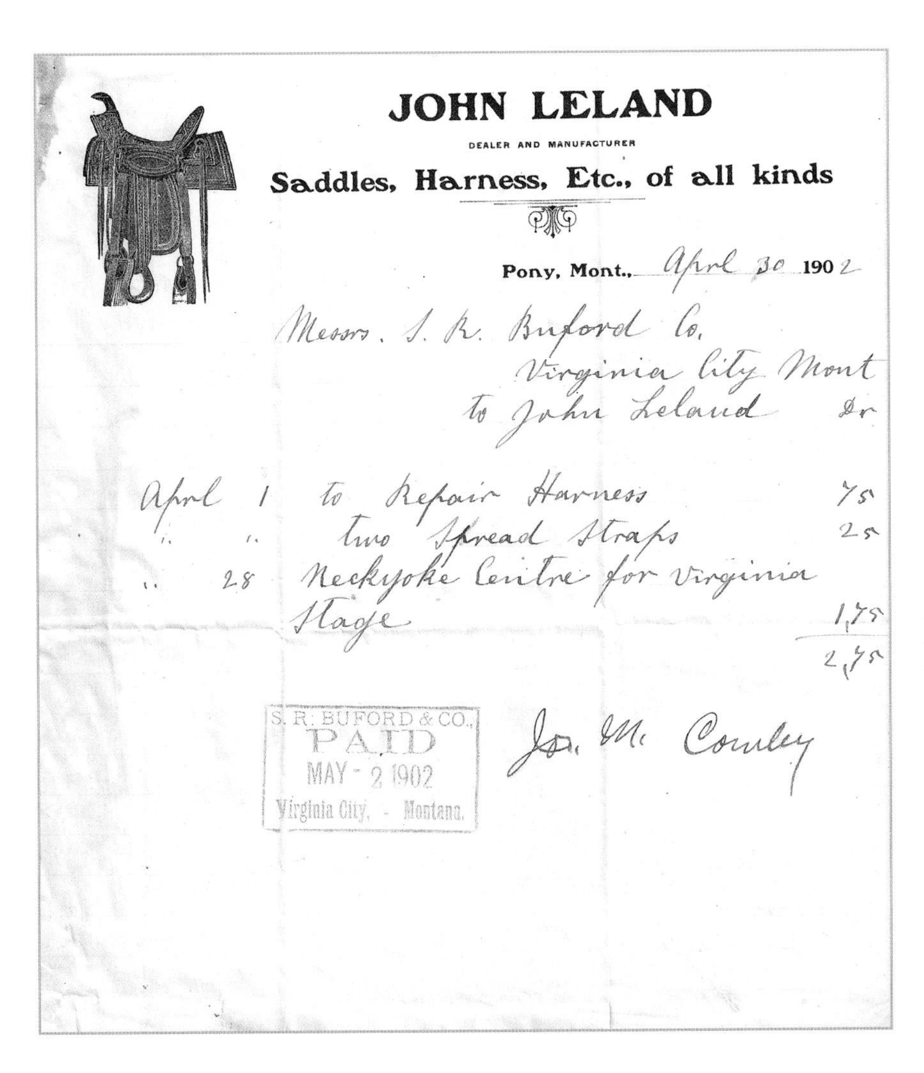

JOHN LELAND

DEALER AND MANUFACTURER

Saddles, Harness, Etc., of all kinds

Pony, Mont., April 30 1902

Messrs. S. R. Buford Co.
Virginia City Mont
to John Leland Dr

April	1	to Repair Harness	75
"	"	two Spread Straps	25
"	28	Neckyoke Centre for Virginia Stage	1,75
			2,75

S. R. BUFORD & CO.
PAID
MAY - 2 1902
Virginia City, - Montana.

Jos. McCowley

Figure 8.39.
Letterhead/invoice from ***John Leland***, Pony, Mont., dated April 30, 1902. The buyers were "Messrs. S. R. Buford Co.," for harness parts used "for Virginia Stage."

Figure 8.40.
Decorative envelope from ***Three Forks Saddlery***, Three Forks, Mont., Harley Fitzhugh, Prop. The date is obscured but was probably in the late 1950s or early 1960s. *Courtesy of Ken Hamlin.*

Lincoln
Libby
Flathead
Kalispell
Sanders
Thompson Falls
Lake
Polson
9
Superior
Mineral
Missoula
Missoula
Hamilton
Ravalli
Glacier
Cut Bank
Toole
Shelby
Liberty
Chester
Hill
Havre
Chinook
Blaine
Malta
Phillips
Pondera
Conrad
Teton
Choteau
5
Chouteau
Fort Benton
4
6
GreatFalls
Cascade
Lewis and Clark
7
Stanford
Judith Basin
Fergus
Lewistown
Petroleum
Winnett
Helena
Powell
Deer Lodge
Granite
Philipsburg
Meagher
White Sulphur Springs
Townsend
Broadwater
Boulder
Jefferson
Anaconda
Deer Lodge
Silver Bow
Butte
Wheatland
Harlowton
Golden Valley
Ryegate
Musselshell
Roundup
Gallatin
Bozeman
Park
Livingston
8
Sweet Grass
Big Timber
Stillwater
Columbus
Yellowstone
Billings
3
Carbon
Red Lodge
Big Horn
Hardin
Beaverhead
Dillon
Madison
Ennis
Valley
Glasgow
Scobey
Daniels
Plentywood
Sheridan
Roosevelt
Wolf Point
McCone
Circle
Sidney
Richland
Jordan
Garfield
Dawson
Glendive
Wibaux
Wibaux
Prairie
Terry
2
Rosebud
Forsyth
Hysham
Treasure
Miles City
Custer
Fallon
Baker
Ekalaka
Powder River
Broadus
Carter

Western Montana

Missoula

The first permanent European American settlement in Montana Territory was named St. Mary's and was founded in 1841, near present-day Stevensville, located directly south of Missoula. The importance of what became the city of Missoula was determined by the Missoula Valley (traversed by Lewis and Clark in 1804), the access to Lolo Pass leading across the Bitterroot Range into Idaho, the establishment of Fort Missoula by the US Army in 1877, and the arrival of the Northern Pacific Railroad in 1883. Consequently, Missoula became the major trade and distribution center positioned strategically in the extreme western part of the state.

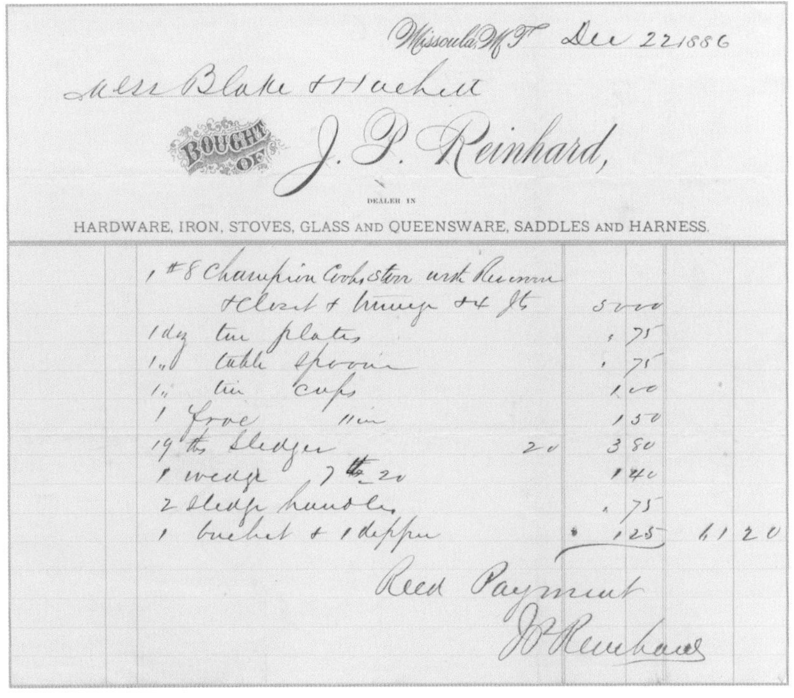
Missoula, M.T. Dec 22 1886

Blake & Hackett

BOUGHT OF J. P. Reinhard,

DEALER IN

HARDWARE, IRON, STOVES, GLASS AND QUEENSWARE, SADDLES AND HARNESS.

1 #8 Champion Cook Stove with Reservoir & Closet & furniture & 4 Jts — 50 00
1 doz tin plates — .75
1 " table spoons — .75
1 " tin cups — 1.00
1 Grove — 1.50
19 lbs Sledges 20 — 3.80
1 wedge 7 lb 20 — 1.40
2 sledge handles — .75
1 bucket & 1 dipper — 1.25 — 61.20

Recd Payment
J P Reinhard

Figure 9.1.
Invoice from ***J. P. Reinhard***, Missoula, M.T., dated Dec. 22, 1886.

As discussed in previous chapters, cattle, sheep, and horse ranches were not at all prevalent in Western Montana or M.T.; much of the output from this area resulted from the numerous farms in the Bitterroot Valley. It is for this reason that chapter 9 contains little information on the local saddleries of Missoula and outlying towns. Clearly more research is needed to uncover archival records for this large and significant area of Montana.

Table 9.1 provides a list of several saddleries that were established in Missoula at the end of the nineteenth century, the earliest of which belonged to J. P. Reinhard. The list of businesses in the city of Missoula in 1884 shows a "J. P. Reinhard, Hardware, Stoves, etc., Main St." Although two blacksmith shops and one livery stable also appear in that list, Reinhard is the only saddlery. An invoice dated 1886 from J. P. Reinhard is shown in figure 9.1.

An invoice from another saddlery, G. Marotz, dated 1897, is shown in figure 9.2. Marotz (unlike Reinhard) specialized in the manufacture and dealership of saddles and harness and also sold buggies, wagons, and sleighs. An image from the Missoula Fire Department, c. 1906, shows firemen posed on a horse-drawn fire wagon, with the G. Marotz Saddlery building in the background, next to the Boyd Bros. Livery Stable (figure 9.3).

Table 9.1. Saddleries of Montana[1]

MAKER	LOCATION	DATES[2]
Demers, Alexander L.	Missoula	1901–1907
Demers & Waters	Missoula	
Hay, C. H.	Missoula	
Jacky, Christian	Missoula	1901
Kohn, Herman	Missoula & Butte City	1880s
Marotz, G.	Missoula	(1897), (1906–07)
Reinhard, J. P.	Missoula	(1886), 1884 Directory
Ronan Harness & Saddlery Co. (Lawrence, F. H.)	Ronan	(1912)

1. Products made or sold by these saddleries included harness, saddles, bits, spurs, whips, boots, bridles, accessories (horse blankets, grooming tools, trunks, bags, and/or robes), vehicles (sleighs, buggies, wagons, carts), and Indian-made goods (e.g., saddle blankets).

2. Dates in parentheses are specified on the company letterhead or in a newspaper/journal advertisement. Inclusive dates for the tenure of the company have been provided where data are available and reliable.

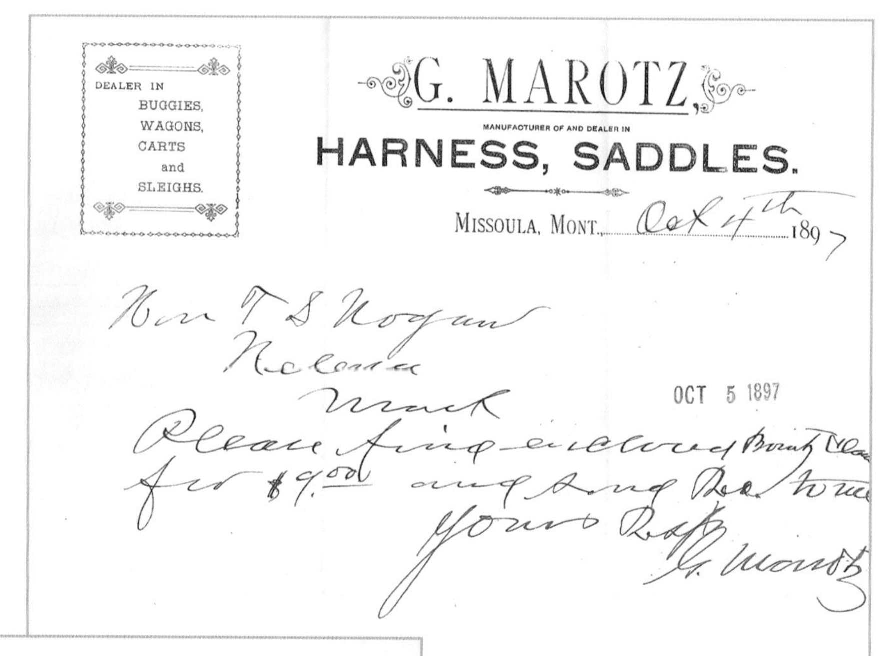
DEALER IN
BUGGIES,
WAGONS,
CARTS
and
SLEIGHS.

G. MAROTZ,
MANUFACTURER OF AND DEALER IN
HARNESS, SADDLES.

MISSOULA, MONT., Oct 4th 1897

OCT 5 1897

Figure 9.2.
Invoice from ***G. Marotz***, Missoula, Mont., dated Oct. 4, 1897. *Courtesy of Rick M. Bachman collection.*

Figure 9.3.
Photograph, c. 1906, showing the Missoula Fire Dept. firemen on a horse-drawn fire wagon, with the ***G. Marotz*** Saddlery building in the background. *Courtesy of the University of Montana, Archives and Special Collections, Mansfield Library, Missoula, Montana.*

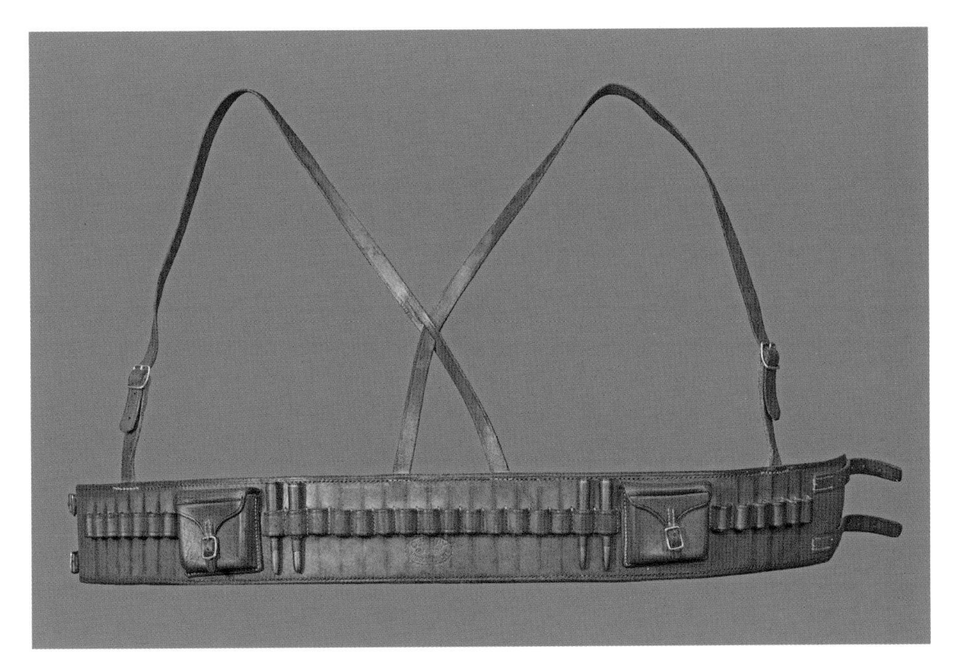

Figure 9.4.
Only a couple of examples of this type of cartridge belt, made by ***C. H. Hay*** for rifle cartridges and supported by shoulder straps, have surfaced. These belts are considered to have been made for buffalo hunters that were carrying very large and heavy cartridges for the long range Sharps buffalo rifles used in the West.

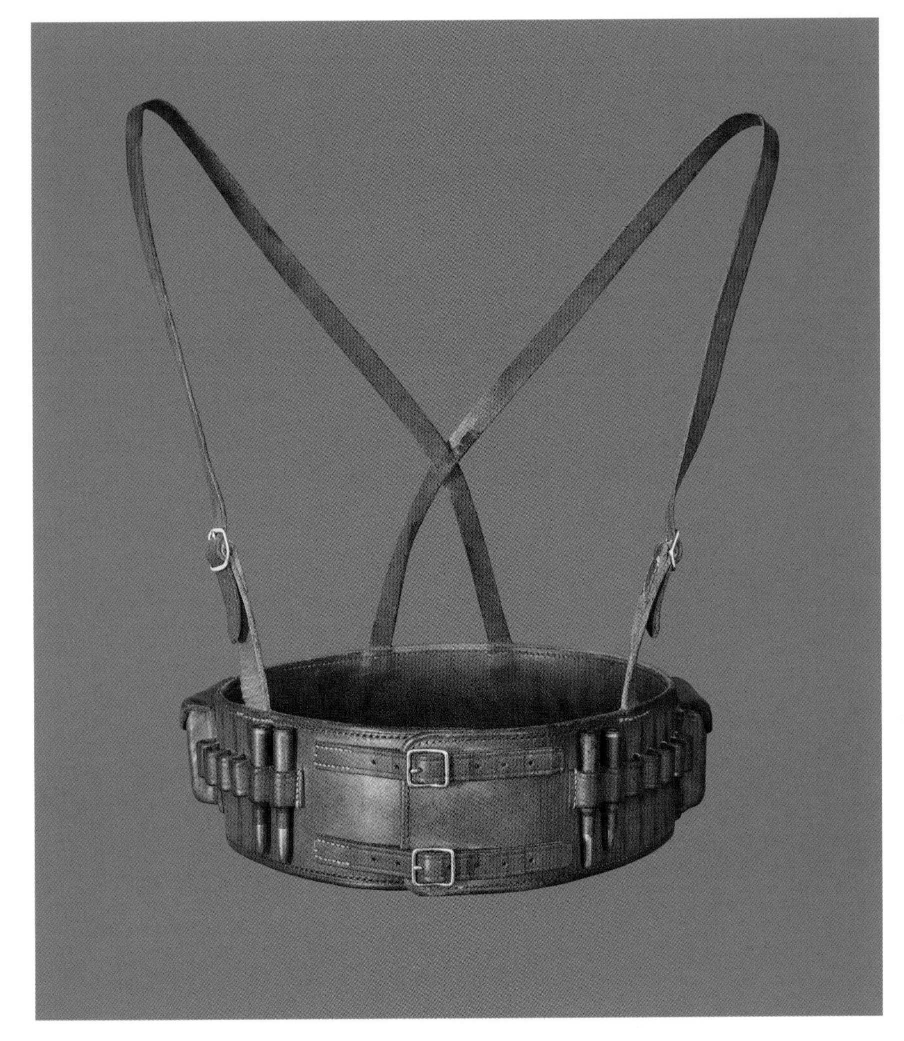

Figure 9.5.
A front view of the ***C. H. Hay*** belt (figure 9.4) shows the closures and how the belt was adjusted. Because the loops are made for cartridges smaller than the customary "buffalo calibers," this belt was likely made after the buffalo period by someone that knew how the early ones were designed.

Figure 9.6.
A unique border surrounds the maker's stamp for ***C. H. Hay*** of Missoula, Mont. (figure 9.4). This rare stamp is the only example of his work available for this book.

An outstanding cartridge belt marked by a rare stamp, that of C. H. Hay of Missoula, Montana, is shown in figures 9.4 through 9.6. The belt is supported by leather "suspenders," and the cartridge loops accommodate a smaller-caliber cartridge than earlier belts made for buffalo hunters using Sharps rifles. The product of another rare saddlery, that of Demers and Waters of Missoula, is a pair of spaghetti-fringed chaps (figures 9.7 and 9.8). Missoula, founded in 1887 at the northern steamboat terminus on Flathead Lake, was originally called Demersville. From the style of the chaps one could surmise that the firm originally was Territorial, perhaps as early as the 1880s. There was an Alexander Demers who owned a saddlery in Missoula, from 1901 to 1907 (table 9.1), possibly the same individual of Demers and Waters, or a relative.

Unfortunately, marked leather items from other establishments listed in table 9.1 have not been located, although an advertisement from Christian Jacky (1900) can be seen in figure 9.9, and one from the Ronan Harness and Saddlery Co. in figure 9.10.

Figure 9.7.
An early 1880s pair of spaghetti-fringed shotgun chaps with an interesting tie arrangement in the middle. They were made by ***Demers and Waters*** of Missoula, M.T., or Montana, estimated between 1880 and 1890 from the style and construction.

Figure 9.8.
Although difficult, it is possible to read the saddle stamp: it is the mark of ***Demers and Waters*** of Missoula, Montana. This partnership was one of the early saddleries in the western part of the state. The town located at the northern terminus of steamboating on Flathead Lake was named Demersville and was established in 1887. When the railroad bypassed the town, all of the buildings were moved a short distance to the new town of Kalispell.

CHRISTIAN JACKY,

Manufacturer of and Dealer in

Harness and Saddles

WHIPS, BLANKETS, ETC., ETC.

No. 310 Higgins Ave., MISSOULA, MONT.

Figure 9.9. Advertisement for the saddlery and harness firm of ***Christian Jacky***, Missoula, Mont. *From Van Dersal & Conner, 1900.*

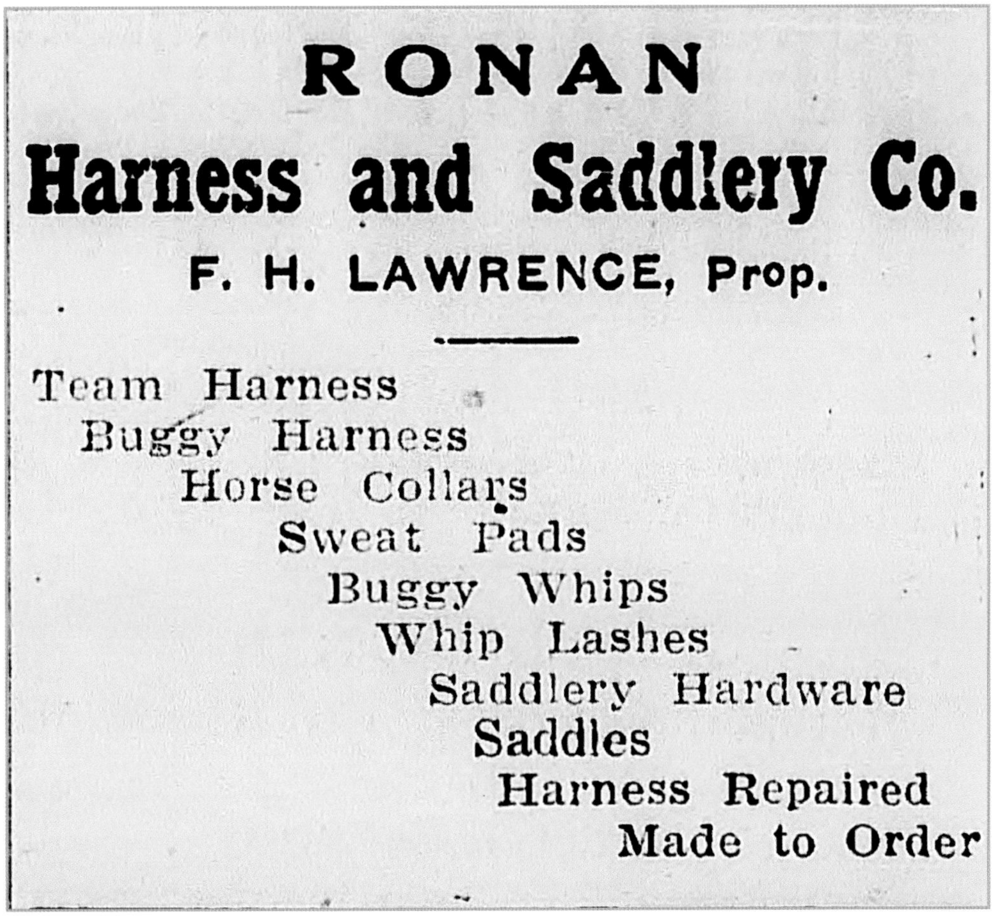

RONAN

Harness and Saddlery Co.

F. H. LAWRENCE, Prop.

Team Harness
Buggy Harness
Horse Collars
Sweat Pads
Buggy Whips
Whip Lashes
Saddlery Hardware
Saddles
Harness Repaired
Made to Order

Figure 9.10. Advertisement for the ***Ronan Harness and Saddlery Co.***, F. H. Lawrence, Prop. From *The Ronan Pioneer* (Ronan, MT), November 15, 1912.

Conclusion

In our research, several trends emerged that seem worthy of consideration as one attempts to embrace this rather large and diverse field of saddlery and harness manufacture in a Territory/State that was central to the development of the American West:

1. The number of saddleries in the period between the 1860s to approximately 1940 varied widely by district or area (see table 1 in each chapter and geographical map in figure 1.2). For example, 41 establishments were found for Eastern Montana (Miles City), whereas 8 were listed for Western Montana (Missoula). Other tallies include South- and North-Central Montana (Billings, 14, and Lewistown, 23), Northwestern Montana (Great Falls and Fort Benton, 29), Central Western Montana (Helena, 20, and Butte/Deer Lodge, 28), and Southwestern Montana (Bozeman/Dillon/Livingston, 31). These numbers are not absolute, as they reflect several different factors, such as the date the area was settled, the number of towns and cities in the area, the relative size of certain saddleries and the mergers or failures of named saddleries within the area, and the abundance or paucity of information relating to the area in question. These considerations aside, the most important factors for the establishment and success of the Montana saddleries were the geographical characteristics of the areas and the types of activities that were carried out there.

2. Eastern Montana, with its various towns and ranches, was the heart of cattle country and was therefore able to support the high number of saddleries that were established there, especially in Miles City. Two of the largest houses, Al Furstnow Saddlery and Miles City Saddlery, were located in Miles City and were influential in developing and manufacturing equipment suited to the cowboys and ranchers of eastern Montana.

3. Saddleries and saddle makers were established in Montana Territory (pre-1889) in all areas of what became the State of Montana. Some of the earliest makers (1870s) were found in Virginia City, Bozeman, Deer Lodge, Helena, and Fort Benton, with the greatest representation in the latter two towns. Two makers, Charles Markham and Secord & Jacobs, were doing business in Helena in 1867. It was in the two decades preceding 1900, however, that the numbers of saddleries and harness makers were at their zenith.

4. The proximity of Montana to Canada, Idaho, Wyoming, and the Dakotas influenced the output and, importantly, the styles of equestrian and ranch-related equipment produced by the Montana saddleries. A major influence from the southern states was exerted through the cattle drives that took place from Texas to the Northwest.

5. The so-called "Montana rig" evolved to accommodate the Montana cowboys' demands for a lighter construction of their saddles, with a single cinch in the three-quarter position and without tapaderos. Other styles were also made, however, including custom-designed saddles for famous persons and wealthy ranchers. Holsters also assumed a "Montana style" in their construction with a single wide loop.

6. The mark that the saddle maker impressed on his work, whether a saddle, belt, holster, chaps, binocular case, or dice cup, is a critical identifier and essential to the validation of the item. We have shown every mark that was distinctive for the maker and his work. These reference points are important to collectors of early Montana-made leather goods.

We have presented this compilation of Montana makers with the realization that existing data are not only limited, but also, in some cases, controversial and contradictory. In many instances it is preferable to allow the item, for example, a saddle or a pair of chaps, to speak for itself. The construction, the mark, and the decoration record the artistic accomplishment that is part of the settlement and development of the West.

Bibliography

Books

Ahlborn, R. E., ed. *Man Made Mobile—Early Saddles of Western North America.* Smithsonian Studies in History & Technology #39, Washington, DC: Smithsonian Institution Press, 1980.

Beatie, R. H. *Saddles.* Norman, OK: University of Oklahoma Press, 1990.

Eggen, J. E. *The West That Was.* Atglen, PA: Schiffer Publishing, 1991.

Friedman, M. *Cowboy Culture.* Atglen, PA: Schiffer Publishing, 1992.

Gorzalka, A. *The Saddlemakers of Sheridan, Wyoming.* Boulder, CO: Puett Publishing Co., 1984.

Hedges, W. A. *History of Fergus County, Montana*. Lewistown, MT: Lewistown Public Library, 1927.

Hutchins, D., and S. Hutchins. *Old Cowboy Saddles & Spurs*, sixth edition, Santa Fe, NM: Hutchins Publishing Co., 1996.

Laird, J. R. *The Cheyenne Saddle.* Cheyenne, WY: Cheyenne Corral, Westerners International, 1982.

Leeson, M. A. *History of Montana. 1739-1885: A History of Its Discovery and Settlement.* Chicago: Warner, Beers & Company, 1885.

Lindmier, T., and S. Mount. *I See by Your Outfit: Historic Cowboy Gear of the Northern Plains*. Glendo, WY: High Plains Press, 1996.

Manns, W., and E. C. Flood. *Cowboys and the Trappings of the Old West*. Santa Fe, NM: Zon Publishing Co., 1997.

Maulding, S. *Hitched Horsehair.* Kettle Falls, WA: River Publishing, 1997.

Morton-Keithley, L., ed. *Sitting Tall—Saddles and Saddlemaking in Idaho.* Idaho State Historical Soc., 2000.

Rattenbury, R. C. *Packing Iron—Gunleather of the Frontier West.* Millwood, NY: Zon International Publishing Co., 1993.

Reynolds, B. *The Art of the Western Saddle*. Guilford, CT: The Lyons Press, 2005.

Rice, L. M., and G. R. Vernam. *They Saddled the West*. Cambridge, MD: Cornell Maritime Press, 1975.

Rickey, D. *$10 Horse, $40 Saddle—Cowboy Clothing, Arms, Tools, and Horse Gear of the 1880s*. Fort Collins, CO: The Old Army Press, 1976.

Robison, K. *Cowboy Up! The Master Saddlers of Fort Benton*. Fort Benton, MT: Fort Benton River Press, 2007.

Sanders, H. F. *A History of Montana*, Vol. II. New York: The Lewis Publishing Co., 1913.

Sweetman, L. D. *Back Trailing on Open Range*. Caldwell, ID: The Caxton Printers, Ltd., 1951.

The Works of Hubert Howe Bancroft, Vol. XXXI. History of Washington, Idaho, and Montana, 1815–1889. San Francisco, CA: The History Company Publishers, 1890.

Periodicals/Catalogs

A. J. Davidson and Company Records, 1889–1897. http://archiveswest.orbiscascade.org/ark:/80444/xv54389.

Al. Furstnow Saddlery Catalog. Miles City, MT, c. 1913–1914.

A. L. Furstnow Saddlery Company, Catalog No. 31. Miles City, MT, c. 1930.

Al. Furstnow Saddlery Company, Catalog No. 35. Miles City, MT, c. 1935.

Erickson, M. "Vengeance Is Mine . . . ." Pamphlet. N.d.

Grosskopf, L. "Connolly Saddlery Got Its Start in Ireland." Billings, MT: *Agri-News*, August 25, 1995.

Knight, O. "Western Saddlemakers 1865–1920," *Montana—The Magazine of Western History*, Vol. XXXIII 2, Spring 1982. pp. 16–29.

Miles City Saddlery Co. Catalog, "Original Coggshall Saddles." Miles City, MT, 1951.

Miles City Saddlery Co., Catalog No. 26. Miles City, MT, 1925.

Miles City Saddlery Co., Catalog No. 29. Miles City, MT, c. 1929.

Montana Heritage, Series No. 13. Helena, MT, 1961.

Redmond, G. "Sentinel Butte Saddlery Company." Beach, SD: *Golden Valley County News*, April 30, 1992.

Reed, M. "Montana History 'Books.'" *The Western Horseman*, November 1994.

Terrett, C. "Miles City Saddles." *The Western Horseman*, September 1949.

Van Dersal & Conner's *Stockgrowers' Directory of Marks and Brands for the State of Montana 1872 to 1900*. Helena, MT, Van Dersal & Conner, 1900.

VerBeck, G., "Register of Saddlemakers, Miles City, MT, Dec. 1998. http://cdm15018.contentdm.oclc.org/cdm/landingpage/collection/p103401mcsad.

The Western Horseman, Vol. 23 (3), March 1958.

The Western Horseman, Vol. 46 (11), November 1981.

MILES CITY SADDLERY CO.
MILES CITY, MONT.
MAKERS
ORIGINAL COGGSHALL SADDLES